NATURE CONSERVATION LAW

Colin T. Reid

Senior lecturer in law
University of Dundee

W. GREEN/Sweet & Maxwell
Edinburgh
1994

First published 1994

© 1994

W. GREEN & SON LTD.

ISBN 0 414 00998 3

Computerset by P.B. Computer Typesetting
Pickering, North Yorkshire
Printed and bound in Great Britain by
Butler & Tanner Ltd, Frome and London

NATURE CONSERVATION LAW

Also by Colin T. Reid (ed.):
Green's Guide to Environmental Law in Scotland

PREFACE

Scope of this book

Although this book is entitled *Nature Conservation Law*, it must be recognised that no such sharply defined area of law exists. There are some statutory provisions which are clearly designed to further the interests of nature conservation, *e.g.* those parts of the Wildlife and Countryside Act 1981 giving protection to wild animals and plants and to areas of habitat. These provisions must form the core of any work claiming to deal with the law relating to nature conservation. However beyond this core there is a vast volume of law which does not have nature conservation as its main focus, but which is of great significance for man's impact on wild plants and animals.

Some of the legal measures outside the core may appear rather out of place in a book on nature conservation. The law on hunting and fishing may appear to oppose the conservation of nature. Yet by regulating the killing and taking of wild animals such measures affect the survival not only of the chosen prey but also of the habitat shared by the prey with many other species and of the other creatures which might be the incidental victims of unrestricted hunting. The guiding principle in selecting topics for this book has therefore been to deal with those legal provisions which directly affect the treatment of wild animals and plants or which expressly have concern for their habitat. In the final chapter attention is drawn to a number of other areas of law which also have significant, but less direct, consequences for wildlife.

The law discussed here is therefore linked more by its likely consequences than by any conceptual coherence. The law operates in several ways. There are direct criminal provisions rendering it an offence to kill wild birds and animals, there are regulatory schemes to control the ways in which land is used, there are provisions to support contractual arrangements determining the long-term management of land, and there are mechanisms for balancing nature conservation with conflicting social and economic interests. The law also derives from a range of sources. Some has developed from mediaeval controls on hunting and fishing, some is a response to public concern about the fate of certain creatures, whilst other provisions were adopted to implement measures agreed at an international or European level. In order to keep the book within a reasonable length it has not been possible to examine fully the background to the law, nor to embark on any thorough analysis of the various policy choices made and legal techniques adopted. Such a task would certainly be worthwhile, and now that the initial step of drawing together the various strands of relevant law has been made, may be more feasible. However, the primary objective in this book has been to explain the legal framework for nature conservation.

Two further issues affecting the scope of this work must also be addressed. The first is that this book is concerned with nature conservation law, not with nature conservation practice or policy. Much that is done to further nature conservation takes place without any detailed legal foundation or effects. There is the work of individuals, charities and private conservation bodies; there are many non-statutory designations of habitat, official and unofficial; and there are grant schemes and other financial incentives which are based on only the most general of provisions authorising the expenditure of public funds.

Quite rightly those concerned with nature conservation concentrate on what is happening in practice rather than on the legal background. Thus in practical terms the details of the licences actually granted to allow the occupiers of land to take action against birds which are pests are more important than the legal structure of the licensing scheme, and in practice it is more significant that English Nature chooses to refer to itself by that name than that its statutory title is the Nature Conservancy Council for England.

Yet it is the law which provides the only foundation for any interference with the rights of individuals to deal with their own property as they think fit, and it is the law which creates public authorities and lays down what they are and are not permitted to do in pursuit of the functions vested in them by law. It seemed that, even among some of those deeply involved in nature conservation, there was often a lack of knowledge about the law and consequently that there was a need for a book which set out to explain the legal structure within which the work of conservation must take place. The law sets the boundaries on what public authorities are permitted or required to do and on what individuals can be forced to do or abstain from doing. An awareness of these ultimate limits is essential to any proper study and understanding of nature conservation in practice.

Examining the law on nature conservation will give a very incomplete, indeed sometimes misleading, view of how nature conservation in Great Britain operates. In many circumstances the law provides only a general framework within which authorities and individuals have wide discretion as to how they are going to act, but it must always be remembered that the framework does set limits which cannot be passed. A full study of the administration and operation of nature conservation in practice would be very worthwhile (and almost certainly more interesting than the present work, which sadly at times has to become a catalogue of bald statutory powers and administrative arrangements), but it is hoped that this book will prove useful in providing an account of the essential legal basis on which conservation measures depend.

The second issue is the geographical one. This book deals with the law in Great Britain, *i.e.* in Scotland and in England and Wales. There are differences between the relevant administrative and legal backgrounds in the two jurisdictions, but much of the law is of recent origin, and in many cases the same or parallel legislation applies in both jurisdictions, utilising similar administrative arrangements. On other topics, although the statutory provisions are separate, the effects are so similar that they can usefully be discussed together, and only in a few instances is the law so different that wholly separate treatment has been necessary. Northern Ireland, however, has its own distinct legislation and administrative structure on every point, so that despite the many parallels to the position in Great Britain a quite separate discussion of almost every issue would have been necessary to do justice to the legal position there.

Structure of this book

The structure of this book can be regarded as falling into three parts. The first two chapters provide the legal and administrative background for the more detailed consideration of the law. In the first chapter, the development of nature conservation law in Great Britain is considered, followed by a description of the legal background against which it has to operate, a background offering few opportunities for concerned parties to make use of the general law to protect nature other than on their own land. The legal rules on standing, restricting those who can raise actions before the courts, are given particular attention as these pose a major obstacle to any legal intervention by conservation groups and individuals seeking to protect the interests of wildlife. The second chapter considers briefly the range of public authorities with responsibility for nature conservation, a few dedicated solely to this objective, but most having to balance a concern for nature conservation with a host of other responsibilities.

The core of the book is provided by Chapters 3–7, which deal with the main legal provisions directly affecting nature conservation. Chapter 3 considers the laws specifically designed to protect wild animals (including birds), and Chapter 4 deals with provisions which regulate the exploitation and destruction of wildlife (*e.g.* game and fishing laws and pest control measures), but in so doing have significance for nature conservation by preventing the indiscriminate destruction of wild creatures. The many designations and statutory regimes of importance to the conservation of habitat are considered in Chapter 5, whilst the legal position of wild plants, including the provisions on tree preservation contained in the planning legislation, is addressed in Chapter 6. That chapter also outlines the law relating to commercial forestry in Great Britain, as the regulation of forestry is rarely covered in legal works despite the major environmental consequences of this form of land use. Chapter 7 considers the international aspects of nature conservation, dealing with trade in wild plants and animals, the nature conservation measures adopted by the European Community (and therefore part of the British legal systems), and some examples of the international treaties designed to protect nature.

The final chapter of the book is intended simply to draw attention to some of the other areas of law which are not primarily directed at the conservation of nature, but which do have a considerable impact on wildlife and the countryside. These topics include town and country planning, aspects of the law regulating agriculture, pollution control and the law on water resources. The final topic to be considered is the extent to which a landowner encouraging wildlife on his land may run the risk of being held liable to neighbours who claim that their property is being harmed by plants or creatures spreading onto their land.

Statutory material

Writing on an area governed by statutory law brings its own difficulties. The frustration of chasing minor amendments from statute to statute and the annoyance when the long-wished-for consolidation takes place only after the fragments of the previous provisions have been laboriously rounded up are problems for the author, not the reader. But four points relating to the handling of statutory material are of significance to the reader and should be mentioned.

First, virtually none of the legislation mentioned here has escaped amendment. In particular, as legislation has given effect to alterations in the structure of local government, to changes in the water industry and other "public utilities" and to the restructuring of what was the Nature Conservancy Council, countless consequential amendments have been made to ensure that other legislation is adapted to refer to the appropriate titles of the restructured bodies and is adjusted to the new administrative arrangements. These amendments, which do not affect the substance of the law, have been referred to only generally in the notes, but I hope that all amendments of significance are recorded. Information on those which I have missed (or misunderstood) will be accepted with gratitude, not resentment.

The second point arises because this book deals with the law in two jurisdictions. Although the substance of the law may be the same in both, reference frequently has to be made to two sets of legislation. As it should be clear from the context or from the titles of the legislation which statute or Statutory Instrument refers to which jurisdiction, as a general rule I have not extended the notes by stating expressly that certain provisions apply only in Scotland or only in England and Wales.

Thirdly, for the sake of brevity the following abbreviations have been used in the footnotes to refer to the Acts which are most frequently mentioned:

CA	Countryside Act 1968
CSA	Countryside (Scotland) Act 1967
EPA	Environmental Protection Act 1990
NHSA	Natural Heritage (Scotland) Act 1991
NPACA	National Parks and Access to the Countryside Act 1949
TCPA	Town and Country Planning Act 1990
TCPSA	Town and Country Planning (Scotland) Act 1972
WCA	Wildlife and Countryside Act 1981.

Finally, items of European legislation are referred to in the text and notes merely by their number, but a fuller reference, including where they can be found in the *Official Journal*, is given in the Table of European Legislation.

I have endeavoured to state the law as in June 1993, but it has been possible to incorporate some later developments.

Acknowledgements

I must record my gratitude to those who have assisted me in preparing this book. Many colleagues at Dundee University have helped me by answering my stupid questions as I strayed into areas of law beyond my competence, and the staff at the Law Library have been of great assistance. As the idea for this book was initially developed while I was on the staff at Aberdeen University, my gratitude extends to those who helped me there, as it does to those in various government offices and public bodies who have also responded to my queries. Particular thanks go to Lesley Dron, Bob Elliot, Wyn Jones, Alan Page and Robin White who commented on draft versions of parts of the text. I must also express my gratitude to all of those at W. Green & Son for their work in producing this book and to Douglas Monaghan, Craig Young and especially Angus MacCulloch for their assistance with the Tables etc. Finally my thanks go to my wife Anne for her assistance on scientific matters and in so many other ways.

Colin T. Reid
Dundee
July, 1993

CONTENTS

TABLE OF CASES

TABLE OF STATUTES

TABLE OF STATUTORY INSTRUMENTS

TABLE OF EUROPEAN LEGISLATION

1. Introduction

HISTORY AND DEVELOPMENT

1.1.1 Although the law has concerned itself with the natural world from the earliest times, nature conservation law in its present form is a modern development. Inspired first by Victorian reactions against cruelty and blatantly destructive over-exploitation, the law has developed in keeping with changing perceptions of environmental issues and of the value of wild plants and creatures. The conservation of wild plants and animals is now widely recognised as a desirable policy objective. To some this conclusion is justified by moral or religious arguments, to others by aesthetic considerations. Justifications also exist from a utilitarian viewpoint, accepting the desirability of preserving resources for future generations and of maintaining genetic diversity in order to provide the basis for future developments of benefit to mankind. Whatever the justification, nature conservation is now accepted as a legitimate concern of the state and the law reflects this.

1.1.2 However, nature conservation is not the only concern of the state, nor is it necessarily high in the list of priorities. The claims of nature conservation will often have to compete against those of many other interests, such as economic development, agricultural production and the protection of individual rights. Much of the law in this area has accordingly been shaped by the need to balance a concern for nature conservation with the other demands on the state, an exercise which is frequently left to the wide discretion of public bodies to be exercised in individual cases. In many situations, therefore, nature conservation may be forced to take a back seat, but at least it now has official recognition and measures exist to ensure that those who are taking decisions do have to include the protection of habitats, plants and animals as one of the factors to be taken into account.

1.1.3 The policy in the early law was quite different. There were laws which addressed man's dealings with the natural world, but the sole aim was to serve immediate human interests. The law provided for the exploitation of plants and animals as valuable natural resources and for protection against the damage which uncontrolled nature could cause to man's interests. In both Scotland and England many laws were made and the legislation of the Scottish Parliament can serve to illustrate the sort of measures which were adopted. Although the frequent repetition of many provisions suggests that the law was not always rigidly observed or enforced — a situation not unknown today in many areas of environmental law — this legislation does reveal the attitudes and legal responses to issues involving wildlife. Several broad categories of laws can be identified.

1.1.4 One major category is provided by the laws aimed at the destruction of pests. Legislation was directed against rooks, crows, and other birds which destroyed corn,[1] and against birds of prey,[2] wolves[3] and foxes.[4] Landowners were instructed to destroy the nests of rooks on pain of forfeiting any tree wherein they were nesting,[5] to destroy the nests and eggs of "foulys of reif,"[6] and to destroy birds of prey by all means possible.[7] Organised wolf hunts were to be held[8] and there was a bounty on the head of foxes.[9] In relation to wolves at least, these measures proved successful. Local rules also existed to further these aims, *e.g.* for some years in Shetland all tenants, ministers, gentlemen and bailies had to produce at the annual head court the heads of weasels, crows, ravens or eagles, or their eggs, of else pay a fine, the number of items required (and the fine) increasing with status of the person (one for a tenant, six for a bailie),[10] while the slayers of eagles were entitled to a reward.[11] Measures also existed against farmers who allowed their crops to be infested with "guld," the corn marigold.[12]

---

[1] *e.g.* A.P.S. II 51 c.32 (1457).
[2] *Ibid.*
[3] See note 8, below.
[4] A.P.S. II 51 c.35 (1457).
[5] *Ibid.*, II 6 c.20 (1424).
[6] *Ibid.*, II 51 c.31 (1457).
[7] *Ibid.*, II 51 c.32 (1457).
[8] *Ibid.*, II 15 c.5 (1427), II 51 c.35 (1457).
[9] *Ibid.*, II 51 c.35 (1457).
[10] G. Donaldson (ed.), *Court Book of Shetland 1615–1629* (1992), pp. 160, 167.
[11] *Ibid.*, p. 165.
[12] Frag. Coll. 11–12 (A.P.S. I 750).

1.1.5 A second group of laws sought to protect animals which were a valuable resource to the community. Wild fowl were not to be slain at moulting time when they could not fly, and their eggs and nests were protected.[13] Hares were not to be killed "in time of snow,"[14] and for a period herons were given special protection, those who kept their nests and prevented others from killing them being entitled to the King's thanks.[15] Salmon, which were a major economic resource, were the subject of much legislation, regulating the size of cruives,[16] setting the close times and seasons,[17] prohibiting the taking of fish at mills,[18] and requiring the removal of obstructions and traps.[19] The law also protected[20] and encouraged[21] rabbit warrens and dovecotes, whose inhabitants were not treated as wild animals, and which were a valuable source of fresh meat to their owners, although presumably less welcome to those who were farming the surrounding land.

1.1.6 Such measures existed, of course, not for the benefit of the species concerned, but to ensure that there were adequate numbers for continuing exploitation, and particularly for hunting. Hunting played a very important part in the lives of the monarch, the nobility and their followers,[22] and produced a wealth of legislation. The special laws for the forests,[23] in essence hunting reserves, served to protect them and their game for their noble owners, and incidentally from being converted to agricultural use or denuded for timber. More general provisions prohibited hunting on other men's lands,[24] restricted the killing of particular game to particular classes of society,[25] while the shooting of deer, other beasts and wild fowl was prohibited.[26]

[13] A.P.S. II 51 c.31 (1457).
[14] *Ibid.*, I 576 (1400), II 52 c.36 (1457).
[15] *Ibid.*, II 235 c.19 (1493).
[16] *E.g. ibid.*, I 469 c.11 (1318), II 5 c.12 (1424), II 119 c.6 (1478).
[17] *E.g. ibid.*, II 7 c.12 (1424), VII 655 c.114 (1669).
[18] *E.g. ibid.*, II 96 c.13 (1469), II 221 c.15 (1489).
[19] *E.g. ibid.*, II 119 c.6 (1478).
[20] *E.g. ibid.*, II 7 c.10 (1424).
[21] *E.g. ibid.*, II 243 c.21 (1503).
[22] "... in time of peace in all time bygone the said pastimes of hunting and hawking were the only means and instruments to keep the whole lieges bodies from not becoming altogether effeminate" (A.P.S. IV 236 c.34 (1600)).
[23] For a detailed study of this topic and an edited version of the forest laws see J.M. Gilbert, *Hunting and Hunting Reserves in Medieval Scotland* (1979).
[24] A.P.S. II 107 c.15 (1474).
[25] *E.g. ibid.*, II 486 c.15 (1551), permitting only gentlemen and nobles using hawks to kill certain wild fowl.
[26] *E.g. ibid*, III 26 c.17 (1567).

1.1.7 A final category of legislation can be identified, often overlapping with the above, namely laws which recognise and try to limit the harm which man was doing to the bounty of the natural world. Several of the acts relating to hunting comment on the dearth of game compared to its past abundance and for this reason impose temporary restrictions,[27] while the harvesting of solan geese (gannets) on the Bass Rock was regulated because of over-exploitation, especially as those who were interested only in the feathers were destroying the value of the birds as meat.[28] Other laws were a response to the fact that "the wood of Scotland is utterly destroyed,"[29] requiring that woods, trees and broom be planted[30] and that all fencing be done by living hedges, not dry sticks.[31] In order to prevent erosion, especially in the wake of the disaster at Culbin where moving sandhills covered a village, the pulling of shrubs and vegetation on sand dunes was prohibited.[32]

1.1.8 This considerable legal heritage in both jurisdictions has had a significant influence on the law relating to game and fishing, and its spirit lives on in some pest control measures. However, as far as the modern law of nature conservation is concerned, a new start was made in relation to birds in Victorian times, and it is only within recent decades that legal protection has been extended to animals, especially reptiles, insects, other invertebrates, and non-commercial fish, and that broad protection has been given to wild plants.[33]

1.1.9 The modern legislation has its origin in two facets of nineteenth-century society. In the first place, there was the movement against cruelty to animals. The Society for the Prevention of Cruelty to Animals was founded in the 1820s (becoming the RSPCA in 1840) and in the following decades the concerns of its members and of those who shared their views expanded. The protection of wildlife, especially birds, was

---

[27] *E.g. ibid.*, II 486 c.15 (1551), II 96 c.13 (1469) (salmon).

[28] *Ibid.*, III 614 c.140 (1592).

[29] *Ibid.* II 242 c.15 (1503).

[30] *E.g. ibid.*, II 51 c.27 (1457), II 243 c.21 (1503).

[31] *Ibid.*, II 51 c.30 (1457).

[32] *Ibid.*, IX 452 c.54 (1695).

[33] On the development of the modern law see generally, J. Sheail, *Nature in Trust* (1976); D. Evans, *A History of Nature Conservation in Britain* (1992); D.E. Allen, *The Naturalist in Britain — A Social History* (1976); D. Stamp, *Nature Conservation in Britain* (1969).

added to the struggles against the ill-treatment of horses and other domesticated animals and against bear-baiting, cock-fighting, etc. In addition to the more general provisions, specific measures were promoted to prevent particular manifestations of cruelty to wildlife, *e.g.*, the banning of the use of pole-traps[34] and hooks[35] to catch birds.

1.1.10 The second factor which prompted legislation was an awareness of the gross overexploitation of wildlife which was taking place. The huge numbers of birds killed by shooting parties, the use of birds essentially as moving targets without any part of the carcase being collected or used, and the widespread use of feathers in the fashion trade[36] were all aspects of this mistreatment of a natural resource, aside from the cruelty involved in many cases.

1.1.11 More ironically, particular damage was done by the growing public interest in the natural world, as those with leisure to indulge their interest devoted their energies not simply to observing, but to amassing large collections of eggs and other specimens. Inevitably, the collectors were most interested in the rarest specimens and were prepared to pay for them, so that the damaging consequences of this hobby were concentrated on the species least able to bear the pressure. The greater accessibility of the countryside through the spread of railways and later the motor car allowed more people to become involved in collecting, and the efforts of collectors had a very damaging effect on some species of birds, insects and plants, many of which were already suffering as a result of changes in land use and agriculture.

1.1.12 A number of societies with concern for nature conservation were formed, *e.g.* the Selborne Society for the Protection of Birds, Plants and Pleasant Places, founded in 1885, and these and those who shared their views attempted to educate the public and to secure a measure of legal protection for birds, animals and plants. Slowly they made progress, and it

---

[34] Wild Birds Protection Act 1904.
[35] Wild Birds Protection Act 1908.
[36] This prompted particular attention, and the "Fur, Fin and Feather" movement was effective in persuading many women to refrain from wearing the feathers of birds not killed for food; generally the animal welfare and nature conservation movement was one where women became deeply involved in political activities.

is probably true to say that now it is only in a few cases (*e.g.*
orchids and some birds of prey) that animals and plants in
Britain are severely threatened by deliberate collecting or
hunting as opposed to the incidental results of man's other
activities.

1.1.13 It is birds which were the first recipients of protection
under the modern law, and which have been the subject of most
legislation.[37] Prompted particularly by the mass slaughter of sea-
birds at Flamborough Head, as sport and to provide plumage
for the fashion trade, the Sea Birds Preservation Act 1869 was
passed, imposing a close season during the breeding months for
over 30 kinds[38] of sea bird. A further 79 kinds of bird were
similarly protected by the Wild Birds Protection Act 1872, the
close season being extended by the Wild Fowl Preservation Act
1876. These early measures were replaced by the more general
Wild Birds Protection Act 1880. It is interesting to note that at
this stage the legislation already displayed many of the features
of the current law: a schedule to list species given additional
protection, offences based on the possession of dead birds with
the onus on the accused to show their lawful origin, ministerial
powers to vary the close seasons, powers to grant exemptions
for all or some birds in particular areas, and provisions to assist
in the enforcement of the law.

1.1.14 During the decades following the 1880 Act many
amendments, extensions and refinements of the law were made
before the law was again consolidated and reformed by the
Protection of Birds Act 1954. In the intervening period there
had been 14 statutes concerned with protecting birds, some
general, some relating to particular species: the Wild Birds
Protection Acts 1881, 1894, 1896, 1902, 1904 and 1908, the Sand
Grouse Protection Act 1888, the Wild Birds Protection (St.
Kilda) Act 1904, the Captive Birds Shooting (Prohibition) Act
1921, the Protection of Birds Acts 1925 and 1933, the Protection
of Lapwings Act 1928, the Quail Protection Act 1937, and the
Wild Birds (Ducks and Geese) Protection Act 1939. All of these
were repealed by the 1954 Act, following which two further

---

[37] Such special treatment for birds, with other forms of life being ignored, is
of long-standing; see Deuteronomy XXII: 6.
[38] The birds were identified by common names, which meant that there was
some uncertainty as to exactly which species were protected, with considerable
overlap in the list as names might apply to more than one species (*e.g.* gull),
and more than one name for a species was included (*e.g.* puffin and sea parrot).

statutes were enacted, the Protection of Birds Act 1954 (Amendment) Act 1964 and the Protection of Birds Act 1967.

1.1.15 The main statutory provisions are now to be found in the Wildlife and Countryside Act 1981, which has replaced the earlier legislation on the protection of wild birds, as well as that dealing with most other animals and plants and aspects of habitat conservation. Prompted by the need to implement the European Community's Directive on the conservation of wild birds[39] and by the United Kingdom's acceptance of the Bern Convention on the Conservation of European Wildlife and Natural Habitats,[40] as well as by more general pressure to do more for conservation, the 1981 Act recast the law on nature conservation in Britain. Its passage proved to be a battleground between conservationists and those with competing interests, with well over 2,000 amendments being proposed, and conservation and the environment firmly becoming issues of political importance.

1.1.16 While the protection of birds was dealt with by fairly far-reaching legislation as early as the 1880s, the protection of other animals has been more fragmented, and generally more recent. There had long been rules on game and fishing, which in regulating the exploitation of many species did contain an element of conservation, but the first statute primarily motivated by such concern was probably the Grey Seals (Protection) Act 1914.[41] This imposed a close season for the taking of such seals to coincide with the breeding period during which mothers and pups were on shore and particularly vulnerable to hunting parties. The 1914 Act was replaced by the Grey Seals (Protection) Act 1932, which in turn was replaced by the Conservation of Seals Act 1970, which extended protection to the common seal.[42]

1.1.17 As far as the conservation of other animals was concerned, it was only badgers that attracted specific protective legislation, through the Badgers Act 1973,[43] while deer were

---

[39] Directive 79/409; see paras. 7.4.3–7.4.11, below.
[40] See paras. 7.5.15–7.5.21, below.
[41] This was also the earliest to use the scientific name to assist in identifying the species concerned.
[42] See paras. 3.4.15–3.4.20, below.
[43] Replaced by the Protection of Badgers Act 1992; see paras. 3.4.6–3.4.14, below.

made the subject of comprehensive provisions dealing with both their conservation and exploitation, in the Deer (Scotland) Act 1959 and the Deer Act 1963.[44] It was with the Conservation of Wild Creatures and Wild Plants Act 1975 that protection was extended to other species, species less likely to have a place in the public's affections (two bats, a lizard, a snake, a toad and a butterfly). As in so many areas, the law here was transformed and greatly extended by the Wildlife and Countryside Act 1981, with subsequent amendments to its Schedules conferring protection on an increasing number of cold-blooded creatures and invertebrates.

1.1.18 The fate of birds and other animals overseas was also not wholly neglected. The Importation of Plumage (Prohibition) Act 1921 restricted the import of all feathers except those of the eider and ostrich. The Animals (Restriction of Importation) Act 1964 made similar provisions regarding some animals, alive or dead, but the law was wholly reshaped and greatly extended (covering plants as well as animals) by the Endangered Species (Import and Export) Act 1976, enacted largely to implement the Convention of International Trade in Endangered Species.[45]

1.1.19 Although the threat to wild plants from over-collecting[46] as well as changes in land use was well known from the middle of the nineteenth century, no general provisions were enacted until the 1970s. A major concern was the conflict between any conservation measures and the rights of landowners to do as they wish on their own land, and to their own property as unlike wild animals, plants, being an accretion to the ground, are owned by the owner of the land.[47] Although bye-laws prohibiting the picking or uprooting of plants were adopted by many counties, the Conservation of Wild Creatures and Wild Plants Act 1975 was the first national measure to prohibit (subject to a number of exceptions, particularly for landowners) the uprooting of plants, with 21 species being given further protection against being picked. Again, this is an area where the Wildlife and Countryside Act 1981 greatly changed the legal

[44] See now Deer Act 1991; see paras. 4.2.16–4.2.27, below.
[45] See paras. 7.3.6–7.3.27, below.
[46] Most notably, perhaps, the widespread devastation of ferns during the "fern fever" which raged from the 1840s to the 1870s; see D.E. Allen, *The Victorian Fern Craze — A History of Pteridomania* (1969), esp. pp. 54–55.
[47] See paras. 6.1.2–6.1.5, below.

position, with protection being extended to many more species. As with the provisions on animals, the amendments since 1981 have granted protection to many more species which are not so widely appreciated by the public, *e.g.* mosses.

1.1.20 While these measures designed to protect particular species from direct harm were being introduced, measures were also being taken to protect habitat. Individuals and local and national societies had been active for years in protecting nature at locations throughout the country, and in persuading public bodies and other landowners to manage their land with at least some regard for the wild animals and plants which it supported. After many years of work by interested groups and a number of influential reports,[48] legislation in 1949 finally created a number of official designations.

1.1.21 The National Parks and Access to the Countryside Act 1949 provided for the creation (in England and Wales only) of National Parks, where landscape and nature conservation were to be combined with the provision of access and facilities to allow public enjoyment of the countryside,[49] and of Areas of Outstanding Natural Beauty, areas where the planning system should have particular regard to natural beauty.[50] Nature reserves were given statutory recognition, at national and local level,[51] and the Act also created the system of Sites of Special Scientific Interest,[52] although in this first incarnation the designation served merely as a source of information for public bodies, without the owner or occupier of the site being even notified. Subsequent legislation provided for other designations, *e.g.* sanctuary orders under the Protection of Birds Act 1954. Again it was the Wildlife and Countryside Act 1981 that reformed this area of the law, with major changes to the system for SSSIs[53] and the creation of Nature Conservation Orders,[54] marine nature reserves[55] and protection for limestone pavement.[56]

---

[48] See generally J. Sheail, *op. cit.*, chaps. 6–7; D. Evans, *op. cit.*, chap. 4.
[49] See section 5.10, below.
[50] See paras. 5.11.1–5.11.3, below.
[51] See section 5.2, below.
[52] See section 5.4, below.
[53] See *ibid.*
[54] See section 5.5, below.
[55] See section 5.3, below.
[56] See section 5.6, below.

1.1.22 In relation to the role of official bodies in nature conservation, again the story is one of prolonged activity, with varying degrees of official involvement, by societies and interested individuals leading to several reports and committee investigations before formal action was taken.[57] The Nature Conservancy was established by royal charter in 1949. It derived its powers from the National Parks and Access to the Countryside Act 1949 and had as its main tasks the provision of scientific advice to the government, the establishment and maintenance of nature reserves, and the organisation of scientific research. Its links with the Natural Environment Research Council[58] were redrawn by the Science and Technology Act 1965, before it was given a full statutory basis and a new name, the Nature Conservancy Council, by the Nature Conservancy Council Act 1973. During the 1960s all public bodies were placed under a general duty to have regard to the desirability of conserving the natural beauty of the countryside, which includes its flora and fauna.[59]

1.1.23 The Environmental Protection Act 1990 and the Natural Heritage (Scotland) Act 1991 have radically changed the institutional structure, dividing the Nature Conservancy Council on a geographical basis and in Scotland and Wales merging its tasks with those of the Countryside Commissions.[60] The Countryside Commission for Scotland had been created by the Countryside (Scotland) Act 1967, with broadly defined functions (but little direct power) with regard to the provision, development and improvement of facilities for enjoying the countryside and to the conservation and enhancement of its natural beauty and amenity. For England and Wales, the starting point was the National Parks Commission established under the 1949 Act, and it was by the Countryside Act 1968 that this body's functions were extended, with broad functions similar to those of the Scottish Commission being added to its more specific role in the National Parks.

1.1.24 This brief account has recorded merely the stages in the development of the law, and is in no way a history of nature conservation in Britain. Any such history would emphasise the

---

[57] See J. Sheail, *op. cit.*, chap. 8.
[58] See para. 2.6.15, below.
[59] CSA, s.66; CA, s.11; see para. 2.2.2, below.
[60] See section 2.5, below.

massive contribution made by committed individuals and societies of various kinds, a commitment to practical conservation work, to the promotion of the ideas of nature conservation and to the development of appropriate structures and policies for public bodies. It is to these unofficial efforts, rather than to the law, that the main credit must go for the conservation of as much of our natural heritage as has survived to this day.[61]

NATURE CONSERVATION AND THE GENERAL LAW

1.2.1 The law on nature conservation is a statutory creation, operating against the background provided by the general civil and criminal law. An outline of this legal background is necessary so that the need for and form of the statutory intervention can be appreciated. In particular the law relating to the ownership of wild animals, of plants and of land must be considered, as a significant factor in shaping the law on nature conservation has been the potential conflict between the private property rights of individuals and the public interest in securing conservation.

Ownership

1.2.2 As far as plants are concerned, the law is simple; all plants growing in the ground belong to the owner of the land. This is the case regardless of whether the plant occurs naturally or has been deliberately planted. Subject to the rights of anyone else with an interest in the land, the landowner has the right to nurture or destroy the plant as he thinks fit, and statutory intervention has been necessary to restrict this freedom for a number of purposes, *e.g.* weed control, nature conservation and forestry. The legal position and its consequences are discussed more fully in Chapter 6.

1.2.3 The law relating to animals is more complicated. Apart from a handful of special rules relating to specific animals (such as the Crown's rights in swans[62], sturgeon and whales[63]), the starting point of the law, which essentially follows Roman Law on this topic, is a distinction between wild animals (animals

---

[61] See works cited at para. 1.1.8 (note 33), above.

[62] In England and Wales only; *Case of Swans* (1592) 7 Co.Rep. 15b.

[63] Stair, II. i. 5; Blackstone, *Commentaries* (1783) i, 223.

ferae naturae) and domestic ones (animals *mansuetae* or *domitae naturae*). The latter, such as dogs, horses, sheep and cattle are treated in the same way as all other moveable property, being fully owned throughout their lives and subject to the standard rules for lost or abandoned property. Wild animals are treated differently. While in the wild, they are deemed to be ownerless, *res nullius*, and become the subject of property only when seized and actually taken into possession.[64] The categorisation of an animal is a matter of law, and although generally straightforward may be uncertain in some cases, *e.g.* where domesticated animals become feral[65] or in relation to fish.[66]

1.2.4 In order for an animal *ferae naturae* to become the property of someone, it must be taken. This can be achieved by killing it or by taking it into captivity, *e.g.* putting it in a cage or restricting it within a park or enclosure.[67] A hunter who wounds an animal will be recognised as having rights over it so long as he continues to give chase, but once the chase is abandoned the animal is once again *res nullius* and free to become the property of the first person to seize it. In relation to some species, ownership is also recognised where the animal may be free to roam, but consistently returns to the owner's premises, displaying what is known as an *animus revertendi*. This applies, for example, to pigeons returning to a dovecote[68] and bees returning to a hive,[69] but is thought unlikely to extend to the habit of salmon returning to their spawning grounds.[70]

1.2.5 The principle that property is acquired by the person who takes such animals is subject to a qualification in England

---

[64] Stair, II. i. 33; Erskine, II. i. 10; Blackstone, *Commentaries* (1783) ii, 389–395.

[65] *Falkland Islands Co.* v. *R* (1863) 2 Moo. P.C. N.S. 266 (status of sheep and cattle found wild in the Falkland Islands after being introduced by earlier settlers).

[66] In *Valentine* v. *Kennedy*, 1985 S.C.C.R. 89 at p. 91 it was doubted that fish, even non-indigenous ones specially reared, could be properly regarded as "tamed" and therefore other than *ferae naturae*; see also, on the status of snails, A.P. Herbert's *Cowfat* v. *Wheedle*, reprinted in many collections including *Uncommon Law* (1982).

[67] Stair, II. i. 33; Blackstone, *Commentaries* (1783) ii, 389–392.

[68] *Hamps* v. *Darby* [1948] 2 K.B. 311.

[69] *Kearry* v. *Pattinson* [1939] 1 K.B. 471.

[70] This is an obstacle to the potential development of a "salmon ranching" industry, whereby salmon are reared to be released into the open sea then harvested by their "owner" on their return to fresh water to spawn; see W. Howarth, *The Law of Aquaculture* (1990), chap. 17.

and Wales. It is accepted that once killed and taken wild animals cease to be *res nullius* and become the subject of property, but as the courts have not been willing to recognise that a poacher could gain ownership by his unlawful acts, property has been held to vest in the owner of the land.[71] In Scotland, however, the courts have been willing to follow the logic of the basic principle, so that property is acquired even by a poacher taking animals unlawfully, contrary to the game rights of the owner of the land concerned.[72] In such circumstances the landowner may be entitled to claim compensation from the poacher, but has no right to restitution of the animals taken.

1.2.6 The English approach has perhaps been influenced by the tendency there to describe the owner of game rights over land as having a qualified property right in the game there, a right perfected on the taking of the game.[73-74] This is arguably a misleading way of expressing the position as although a landowner may have the power to control any hunting on his land, and have the exclusive right to take the game, he does not have any true property rights in the animals unless and until he physically takes them. Those who take game without any right to it may commit a wrong against the person who is entitled to take the game,[75] but it is not truly an interference with his property in the game. Similarly misleading are references to a form of property in young animals and fledglings not yet able to fly.

1.2.7 Ownership generally is lost once a wild animal ceases to be held in captivity (or to have an *animus revertendi*), but is retained so long as the owner is in pursuit.[76] In *Kearry* v. *Pattinson*,[77] a case involving bees swarming away from a hive, the English court considered the old statements that the owner retained his rights in animals escaping from captivity provided that he had the animals in sight and the power to pursue them. It was emphasised that the owner's rights lasted only as long as

[71] *Blades* v. *Higgs* (1865) H.L.C. 621.
[72] Erskine, II, i, 10; *Leith* v. *Leith* (1862) 24 D. 1059 (Lord Curriehill at 1077–1078); *Scott* v. *Everitt* (1853) 15 D. 288 (in the absence of a statutory entitlement police have no right to seize unlawfully taken game).
[73-74] See, *e.g. Case of Swans* (1592) 7 Co.Rep 15b at 17b.
[75] The right to take game may be separated from the ownership or occupation of the land; see paras. 4.2.6–8, below.
[76] Stair, II. i. 33; Blackstone, *Commentaries* (1783) ii, 393.
[77] [1939] 1 K.B. 471.

he had the lawful power to pursue the creatures, so that once the animals entered the land of another where their owner could not enter except as a trespasser, then they were no longer his property. In England and Wales, once an animal *ferae naturae* has ceased to be the property of someone, it reverts to its former status as *res nullius*, capable of being acquired by the first person to capture it again.[78] In Scotland the same rule, taken from Roman Law, applies and is a departure from the more general rule of feudal origin that property which has once been owned does not become *res nullius* once abandoned by its owner but reverts to the Crown, a rule which applies to animals not *ferae naturae*.[79]

1.2.8 The legal position on the ownership of wild animals has several consequences for the criminal and civil law. As far as the criminal law is concerned, the basic position that wild animals (unless in captivity) are not the property of anyone, means that they cannot be stolen at common law. In Scotland, therefore, it has been held that if a charge of theft is based on the taking of an animal *ferae naturae*, the charge must set out how the animal ceased to be *res nullius* and came to be somebody's property.[80] The same would apply to a charge of malicious mischief or vandalism.[81] It is also specifically provided by the Theft Act 1607[82] that a person who takes fish from a proper stank or bees is guilty of theft, and the taking of oysters and mussels from marked beds is also theft.[83] In *Valentine* v. *Kennedy*[84] four men were held guilty of stealing trout which had escaped from a reservoir into surrounding burns, but the fish in question were rainbow trout which are not indigenous and which the men knew must have come from the reservoir. The sheriff commented that if the fish in question had been native brown trout a charge of theft would have been unlikely to succeed as it was unlikely that it could have been proved that the trout came from the reservoir and were not simply wild.

[78] *Hamps* v. *Darby* [1948] 2 K.B. 311.

[79] Erskine, II. i. 10; D.L. Carey Miller, *Corporeal Moveables in Scots Law* (1991), para. 2.02; cf. *Valentine* v. *Kennedy*, 1985 S.C.C.R. 89 at p. 91.

[80] *Wilson* v. *Dykes* (1872) 10 M. 444.

[81] Criminal Justice (Scotland) Act 1980, s.78.

[82] As amended by Statute Law Revision (Scotland) Act 1964, Scheds. 1–2; see Lord Rodger of Earlsferry, "Stealing Fish" in R.F. Hunter (ed.) *Justice and Crime — Essays in Honour of the Rt. Hon. Lord Emslie* (1993).

[83] Oyster Fisheries (Scotland) Act 1840, s.1; Mussel Fisheries (Scotland) Act 1847, s.1.

[84] 1985 S.C.C.R. 89.

1.2.9 In England and Wales the position is governed by statute. Section 4(4) of the Theft Act 1968 states that wild animals, tamed or untamed, are to be regarded as property for the purposes of the Act. However, it continues to provide that although wild animals which are tamed or ordinarily kept in captivity may be stolen, a charge of theft of a wild animal or its carcase will otherwise be possible only where the animal has been reduced into possession by or on behalf of another person and the possession has not since been lost or abandoned, or where another person is in the course of reducing the animal into possession. A similar provision governs the position for criminal damage.[85] These provisions in essence repeat the common law rules on ownership, including recognition of the traditional rules of the chase.

1.2.10 The civil law is also affected. As wild animals do not form the property of anyone, and do not in themselves have any other recognition in the law, they fall outwith the law's protection. In the absence of statutory provisions, killing or destroying wild animals is not in itself a wrong against anyone, as no legally recognised personal or property rights are affected. The destructive conduct may involve a trespass or breach of other rights which the law will acknowledge, but any action must be based on the breach of those rights, and no legal value can be attached to the wild animals. This may affect the likelihood of obtaining a remedy, as the effect on wild animals of the unwanted conduct should be disregarded and wild animals, not being the property of anyone, have no legally recognised value.[86]

1.2.11 It follows that the standard civil law is of little use in securing the direct protection of wild animals. It can be invoked only when some legally recognised rights are also affected, *e.g.* a landowner may be able to take action if a trespass or nuisance is involved, or the holder of game or fishing rights may be able to intervene. However, conservation groups and individuals who have an interest in preserving wildlife, but no legal rights at stake, lack the standing to do anything.[87]

---

[85] Criminal Damage Act 1971, s.10(1); a news report in the *The Times* of August 19, 1993 notes that a man was convicted under this Act (and imprisoned) after injuring some swans, which, exceptionally, are the property of the Queen at all times (see note 62, above).

[86] A landowner might be able to create a value entitled to legal protection, *e.g.* by charging visitors to observe wild animals on his land.

[87] See section 1.3, below.

1.2.12 The law's failure to accord any value to wildlife may also have indirect consequences. Policies of land management and investment which protect and encourage wild plants and animals at the expense of maximising financial returns will be regarded as producing no legally recognised return. For someone dealing with his own property this is of no consequence, but much property is held by trustees who are under a duty to do their best for the beneficiaries. The duty of the trustees is to obtain the best return, regardless of moral, social and political considerations,[88] especially where property is expressly held for investment purposes, as is the case with considerable areas of land. Environmentally friendly management of land and recourse to "green investments" may well produce a satisfactory return. However, unless the power to be influenced by such matters is expressly included in the trust, trustees may be acting in breach of their duties if they allow a concern for nature conservation to stand in the way of obtaining any appropriate financial returns from the property which they hold, regardless of the value which they or others see in the conservation of nature.[89] On the other hand, the creation of a trust whose express purposes include the protection of wildlife on particular land will put the trustees in a stronger position to take action against anything which threatens this objective.

Land ownership

1.2.13 Under the general law it is the owner of a piece of land who enjoys the power to determine what happens on that land and therefore the extent to which plants and animals are conserved there. The owner of the land owns the plants growing on it, he controls who can enter the land, he decides the way in which the land is to be used. As far as nature conservation is concerned, this is a mixed blessing. If the owner is keen to protect wild plants and animals, he is in the position to ensure that this takes place by managing the land to preserve and enhance habitats, prohibiting activities which are likely to cause

---

[88] *Martin* v. *Edinburgh District Council*, 1988 S.L.T. 329; *Cowan* v. *Scargill* [1985] Ch. 270; *Harries* v. *Church Commissioners for England* [1992] 1 W.L.R. 1241.

[89] The same issue may arise in other circumstances, *e.g.* in *Williams* v. *Schellenberg*, 1988 G.W.D. 29–1254 one *pro indiviso* proprietor of land argued that her interest had been damaged by the proprietor in occupation encouraging the designation of the land as an SSSI, thereby restricting its management and reducing its value.

damage or disturbance, eliminating threats to the natural flora and fauna and excluding unwelcome visitors. On the other hand, if a landowner does not wish to conserve nature, any measures requiring him to do so will amount to an infringement of his right to do as he wishes with his own property, and any enduring restrictions may affect the value of property considerably.

1.2.14 It follows that if an individual or conservation body wishes to conserve nature in a particular area, the best approach is to acquire the land, or a sufficient interest in the land in order to ensure that appropriate steps are taken.[90] If an interest in the land cannot be acquired, it may be sufficient to enter an agreement with the landowner which obliges him to act, or refrain from acting, in particular ways. Difficulties arise, however, in trying to ensure the long-term protection of sites and in ensuring that the successors of the parties to the initial deal continue the conservation measures. The law on land-ownership and related matters in Scotland is very different from that in England and Wales, and in both jurisdictions is a subject of some complexity. What follows is merely a brief indication of some of the issues and possibilities which arise.

1.2.15 As far as ownership of the land is concerned, if one wishes to secure the land for more than the lifetime of one individual, or to protect against an individual owner's change of mind, the solution lies in the complexities of the law on trusts, charities and associations. Land may be acquired by a conservation body in its own right if it is an incorporated association and therefore enjoys its own legal personality. Otherwise, the land must be vested in trustees, either for an association, or subject to a trust the objectives of which include the conservation of nature. In the 1920s a trust to create a sanctuary for wild animals was held not to constitute a valid charitable trust as it had no benefit to the community,[91] but it must be doubtful whether the same result would occur today[92] and the obstacle is readily circumvented, *e.g.* by ensuring that the terms of the trust are drawn so as to include an educational element.

---

[90] Many National Nature Reserves are not owned by the conservancy councils but leased or simply subject to management agreements.

[91] *Re Grove-Grady* [1929] 1 Ch. 557.

[92] *Cf. Attorney General (New South Wales)* v. *Sawtell* [1978] 2 N.S.W.L.R. 200.

1.2.16 If outright ownership is not possible or desired, land may be taken on a lease, the terms of which allow the land to be managed in a way compatible with nature conservation. This is a common device as landowners may be reluctant to part with their land permanently, but be prepared to allow the land to be used for conservation purposes for a fixed term, at the end of which the owner will be free to reconsider how he wishes the land to be used.

1.2.17 A simple agreement between the owner of the land and some other party to the effect that the owner will do or not do certain things in order to conserve or enhance the nature conservation value of the land is also possible, and can be framed so as to be legally enforceable. However, such an agreement suffers from the severe drawback that it will be a personal agreement, which binds only the original parties. Therefore if the owner dies or sells the land to another, the agreement is at an end. In relation to such "management agreements" entered by many official bodies, this problem is solved by statutory provisions which ensure that such agreements, once registered, do run with the land, binding successors to the original contracting owner.[93]

1.2.18 Without statutory intervention, it is unlikely that similar management agreements between private parties can practically be prolonged and protected in such a way. In England and Wales agreements limiting the use of land, restrictive covenants, can run with the land, binding successors to the owner who initially agreed to the limitations, but this is possible only where the covenant is for the benefit of some land held by the other party to the agreement or his successors, and where the covenant has been registered. Moreover, it is only the holder of the benefitted land who can enforce the covenant.

1.2.19 An agreement not to use or develop a site in certain ways may in some circumstances be regarded as benefitting other land, but for this to be a useful conservation device, the conservation body or whoever made the initial agreement with the landowner must have done so in a capacity as owner of that benefitted land, and only if it continues to be the owner of the benefitted land (or the succeeding owner shares its views on this point) will the covenant be enforced. In practice, this requires a

---

[93] *E.g.* NPACA, s.16.

fairly unlikely combination of circumstances. Similar requirements that there be land which benefits from an obligation
before it can be recognised as running with the burdened land
prevent the development of "conservation easements," a
concept which has developed in many states of the USA.[94]

1.2.20 In Scotland the position is fundamentally different
because of the continuing effects of the feudal system. The
feudal superior retains the right to insert restrictions and
conditions in a feudal grant, so that a sale of land may be
subject to a number of restrictions on the use of that land. Once
recorded, these obligations can be enforced against the
proprietor of the land and his successors by the superior or in
some cases by others who hold neighbouring land granted by
the same superior with the power to enforce such (usually
mutually beneficial) restrictions. For sales where no feudal
superior is involved, conditions can be imposed but face the
same limitations as in England and Wales in that they will run
with the land only if imposed for the benefit of some adjoining
land and be enforceable only by those with an interest in such
land.

1.2.21 Feudal conditions have attracted some attention[95] as a
form of regulation of land because of their past use as an early
form of town planning, most notably in the New Town of
Edinburgh, but they are still an everyday part of conveyancing,
e.g. when housing estates are being developed. As the
conditions can cover a wide range of matters, not necessarily
conferring any benefit on other land, they may therefore be of
some use in securing the conservation of land for the benefit of
nature. However any attempt to use this mechanism depends on
there being a transfer of land by a superior prepared to impose
such conditions and the continued willingness of the superior
and his successors to enforce them.

1.2.22 Even if it does prove possible for an agreement to run
with the land as described above, in both jurisdictions a party
can apply to the relevant Lands Tribunal to be discharged from
his obligations under the agreement. The Tribunals have the
power to modify or discharge the obligations if in Scotland they
are found to be unreasonable or inappropriate, unduly

---

[94] See, *e.g.* J.A. Blackie, "Conservation Easements and the Doctrine of
Changed Conditions" (1989) 40 Hast. L. J. 1187.
[95] See (1984) 11 S.P.L.P. 1.

burdensome or impeding some reasonable use of the land,[96] or in England and Wales if they are found to be obsolete or to be impeding a reasonable use of land, or if the proposed modification or discharge causes no injury to the beneficiary of the covenant.[97] It is clear therefore that resort must be had to statutory provisions if effective steps are to be taken to control the way in which land is managed so as to further nature conservation.

Other rights

1.2.23 Certain rights relating to wild animals may be held by someone other than the owner of the land concerned. The rights to take fish and game are incidents of the ownership of land, but can be separated from the land and granted to others.[98] In Scotland the right to take salmon is exceptionally a separate tenement, belonging to the Crown as part of the *regalia minora* unless granted to others, but generally the extent of any separation will depend on the terms of the particular grant by the owner of the land. The issue is complicated as the nature of the grant will depend on its terms — it may be viewed as a form of lease or merely as a personal licence granted by the landowner — and is to some extent affected by statute, especially in relation to agricultural land.[99] The provisions relating to game or fishing may also form part of a broader agreement and be affected by its character, *e.g.* it is common for landowners to reserve game and fishing rights when leasing land.

1.2.24 From a nature conservation point of view the separation of game and fishing rights has significance in two ways. In the first place, if the wildlife of a site is to be protected, it may be necessary not only to ensure that suitable arrangements are made with the parties who own and occupy the land, but also to ascertain who holds the game and fishing rights and to make arrangements with them. Otherwise the measures undertaken to

[96] Conveyancing and Feudal Reform (Scotland) Act 1970, s.1.
[97] Law of Property Act 1925, s.84 (as amended by Law of Property Act 1969, s.28).
[98] See generally W.M. Gordon, *Scottish Land Law* (1989), chaps. 8 and 9; C. Parkes & J. Thornley, *Fair Game: The Law of Country Sports and the Protection of Wildlife* (rev. ed.) (1989), chaps. 3 and 12.
[99] *E.g.*, the rights of a tenant to kill ground game (Ground Game Act 1880, s.3); see paras. 4.2.6–4.2.8.

conserve nature may be undermined by the exercise of these separate rights over the land.

1.2.25 Secondly, game and fishing rights may be used as a means of furthering conservation. In order to protect the species concerned, such rights may be acquired by those with an interest in conservation and then not exercised, thereby producing a *de facto* ban on shooting and fishing on the land, subject to statutory rights and pest control measures.[1] Short of such a policy, the existence of separate rights ensures that there is some party other than the owner of the land with an interest in its management. As measures to encourage a large and sustainable harvest of game and fish may also be of benefit to other wildlife,[2] particularly in preserving land in a comparatively natural state, free from intensive agriculture, the protection and enhancement of game rights may in itself be beneficial for nature conservation. It must be recognised though, that the protection of game can also lead to measures highly detrimental to some wild species, *e.g.* the unlawful destruction of birds of prey.

LEGAL STANDING

1.3.1 The general position on the ownership of wild plants and animals has a further consequence of major significance for the law on nature conservation. This relates to the legal standing of those wishing to protect the interests of wild plants and animals, or rather to their general lack of standing. The courts will only entertain actions from parties with a legally recognised interest in the subject of the litigation, therefore the issue of standing is of crucial importance to the extent to which those concerned for nature conservation can invoke the courts' assistance to further their aims and prevent damaging activities taking place.

1.3.2 What qualifies a person as having legal standing depends on the nature of the action being raised, but generally the courts

---

[1] A similar policy has been adopted in relation to salmon in Scotland, with the acquisition and dismantling of coastal netting stations in order to increase the stocks entering the rivers to breed.

[2] But not always, *e.g.* the large numbers of deer in parts of Scotland, allegedly encouraged by shooting interests, can do a lot of damage by overgrazing and preventing natural regeneration of woodland.

insist on some direct connection with the matter in dispute. It is not enough that a person is interested in an issue, in the way that a person may be interested in sport or the arts as their leisure pursuit; the law requires the person to have some legal interest in the subject matter. In relation to judicial review a slightly more relaxed standard may be imposed, but the courts will still look for some real connection with the issue and will firmly shut their doors to anyone who appears to be interfering in something which is not properly his business.

1.3.3 Many of the provisions designed to protect wildlife do so by creating criminal offences. The extent to which nature conservation groups or concerned individuals can ensure that alleged offenders are brought to justice varies. In Scotland the position is that proceedings are instigated by the public prosecutors in all but the most exceptional circumstances. As any private prosecutor will have to show that he has been personally wronged by the alleged crime,[3] there appears no likelihood of private prosecution in the case of offences created to protect wild plants and animals or habitat.

1.3.4 In England and Wales the position is different,and although most prosecutions are handled by the public authorities, especially now the Crown Prosecution Service, prosecutions may be brought by private individuals, even where they have not themselves been the victim of the alleged crime. This means that action can be taken to invoke the criminal law, and prosecutions have been successfully brought by individuals, usually with the support of some organisation, *e.g.* cases relating to birds raised by officers of the Royal Society for the Protection of Birds. However, as it is only the police who enjoy the various statutory powers of search, etc., which may well be necessary in order to obtain the requisite evidence, cooperation with the public authorities is useful. Throughout Great Britian a number of police forces now have designated "wildlife" or "nature conservation" officers in an effort to make the work of the police in this field more effective.

1.3.5 In the civil law, the position in both jurisdictions is essentially the same. If there is an agreement of some sort with terms designed to promote nature conservation, in all but a handful of cases it is only the parties to that agreement who

---

[3] *McBain* v. *Crichton*, 1961 J.C. 25.

have the standing to enforce it.[4] Therefore, unless they are parties to the original agreement, there is no scope for conservation groups or the like to take action to ensure that a landowner keeps to the terms of a management agreement, or that the parties to a lease abide by terms designed to protect natural features.

1.3.6 For actions in delict or tort, the pursuer must be able to show that he has suffered some legal wrong. As animals in the wild are not owned by anyone, nobody suffers a wrong if they are harmed, so that no recourse can be had to the courts. Plants are the property of the owner of the land, so that he alone is in a position to respond to damage done to them. Actions may be possible if the damaging conduct can be shown to cause harm to the pursuer's domestic animals, or to an interest in the land concerned,[5] or in neighbouring land, but the class of potential pursuers is small and firmly excludes conservation bodies which may have a deep concern for, and interest in, the well-being of the species being affected, but no patrimonial interest which is being harmed.

1.3.7 Most nature conservation law at some stage involves public authorities, either the conservancy councils or central or local government in the exercise of their planning and other powers. As statutory bodies they must keep within the limits of their statutory powers, properly fulfil their responsibilities and follow the prescribed procedures for their action. In most cases considerable discretion is conferred on the authorities, but their conduct will usually be subject to judicial scrutiny,[6] and the courts will be prepared to intervene if they are found to be acting *ultra vires*, *i.e.* illegally, irrationally or in breach of procedural propriety.[7] In both Scotland and England and Wales special procedures exist for parties challenging the conduct of

---

[4] The general exceptions, such as the *jus quaesitum tertio* in Scots law are unlikely to be of relevance here; agreements which run with land, binding successors to the original parties, are discussed above (paras. 1.2.17–1.2.22).

[5] A news report in *The Times* of March 30, 1993, recorded that an angling club had obtained damages at Swindon County Court for damage to the fishings which they had leased when rainbow trout escaped and ruined the anglers' quest for brown trout (see (1993) 5 E.L.M. 79).

[6] Either under statutory procedures allowing reference to the court, *e.g.* in relation to Nature Conservation Orders (WCA, Sched. 11, para. 5), or by means of judicial review.

[7] *Council of Civil Service Unions* v. *Minister for the Civil Service* [1985] A.C. 374.

public authorities by means of judicial review,[8] and a fundamental element of both is that the court will only consider a case at the instance of someone with sufficient standing. A similar point arises under many statutory schemes where rights of appeal or challenge are restricted to "persons aggrieved."

1.3.8 The tests for standing differ to some extent in the two jurisdictions, and there are dangers in trying to draw lessons for one jurisdiction from the other, but the general approach in both is similar, namely that only a person with some direct connection with the issue will be recognised as having sufficient standing to invoke the court's powers of judicial review. As a general point, it seems that the courts in both jurisdictions agree that what should be looked at is the substance of the party's interest in the matter, and that the particular legal form of the party is not of crucial importance. Therefore if individuals would have title to sue in the particular circumstances, the fact that they have banded together to form an unincorporated association, or even an incorporated association which is in law a different person, is of no significance, and the association will enjoy standing to the extent that the individuals would personally.[9]

1.3.9 In Scotland the courts view the issue of title and interest to sue as a preliminary matter, to be determined before the substance of the case is considered,[10] and the two elements of the test may be treated separately, so that a party who is viewed as having title to sue, may fail on the basis that in the particular circumstances he has no sufficient interest.[11] No comprehensive definitions exist, but as far as title is concerned reference is frequently made to Lord Dunedin's comment in *D. & J. Nicol v. Dundee Harbour Trustees*[12] that to have title a person "must

[8] In Scotland, Rule of Court 260B (introduced by Act of Sederunt (Rules of Court Amendment No. 2) (Judicial Review) 1985, S.I. 1985 No. 500); in England and Wales, Supreme Court Act 1981, s.31 and R.S.C. Ord. 53.
[9] *Scottish Old People's Welfare Council, Petrs.*, 1987 S.L.T. 179 at p. 185; *R. v. Hammersmith and Fulham London Borough Council, ex p. People Before Profit Ltd.* (1982) 80 L.G.R. 322 at p. 333; *R. v. Secretary of State for the Environment, ex p. Rose Theatre Trust Co.* [1990] 1 Q.B. 504 at p. 521.
[10] *Scottish Old People's Welfare Council, Petrs.*, 1987 S.L.T. 179; in some cases, though, it is accepted that the issue of standing may not be separable from a consideration of the merits, *Gordon v. Kirkcaldy District Council*, 1989 S.L.T. 507.
[11] As in *Scottish Old People's Welfare Council, Petrs.*, note 10 above.
[12] 1915 SC (H.L.) 7 at pp. 12–13.

be a party (using the word in its widest sense) to some legal relation which gives him some right which the person against whom he raises the action either infringes or denies." This idea has been given a broad interpretation and in *Wilson* v. *Independent Broadcasting Authority*[13] it has been held that where a public body owes a duty to the public, individual members of the public may have title to sue. This may be significant in view of the general obligations placed on the conservancy councils and the like.

1.3.10 However, even if a person qualifies as having title to raise an issue, the court must also be satisfied that he has an interest to do so. This requires that the particular issue is of some real concern to the party, and not an academic issue or merely something which he is raising as a matter of general public spirited concern.[14] Such interest, though, need not be a formal legal or property interest, *e.g.* in *Kincardine and Deeside District Council* v. *Forestry Commissioners*[15] it was held that a local authority had interest on the basis of its "reasonable concern with a major project in their area which may affect the economy or amenity of the area generally." Given the legal background already discussed, members of a conservation group are unlikely to have a legally recognised interest in all matters which are of concern to them, but if they can show a lasting and genuine concern in a particular topic or site, particularly if they have invested time, effort and money to it, they may in some cases be able to use this to demonstrate an interest to accompany their title as members of the public.

1.3.11 In England and Wales the procedural reforms to the process of judicial review swept away a number of restrictive rules on *locus standi* and replaced them with the general test that the applicant must demonstrate "a sufficient interest in the matter to which the application relates."[16] This test has generally been given a fairly liberal interpretation, and been viewed as an issue which has to be considered as part of the broader consideration of the factual and legal circumstances of the case, not as a preliminary issue.[17] Some interest over and

---

[13] 1979 S.L.T. 279.

[14] *Scottish Old People's Welfare Council, Petitioners*, 1987 S.L.T. 179.

[15] 1992 S.L.T. 1180.

[16] Supreme Court Act 1981, s.31(3).

[17] *R.* v. *Inland Revenue Commissioners, ex p. National Federation of Self-employed and Small Businesses Ltd.* [1982] A.C. 617.

above that of the ordinary citizen has to be shown. If this is not possible, a party who does not have *locus standi* can attempt to persuade the Attorney General to instigate proceedings by way of a relator action, although the likelihood of success is small.[18]

1.3.12 In relation to planning decisions, actions have been permitted by groups representing local residents,[19] and the secretary of a local action group who was also proprietor of nearby premises was allowed to challenge an authority's response to a listed building falling into disrepair.[20] It was accepted, but without the point being fully argued, that the Child Poverty Action Group has standing to seek a declaration concerning delays in the handling of social security claims.[21]

1.3.13 Three decisions are of particular importance for the environmental field, and have lessons for Scotland as well as England and Wales. In *R.* v. *Secretary of State for the Environment, ex p. Rose Theatre Trust Co.*[22] it was held that the ordinary citizen (and hence any group of citizens, whatever their concern over the issue) did not have sufficient interest to challenge the scheduling of an ancient monument, *i.e.* its inclusion in the list of monuments granted legal protection. The same reasoning might well apply to prevent individuals or conservation groups challenging decisions relating to the many other forms of statutory designation or order provided for in the legislation on nature conservation. It is uncertain whether the same result would have occurred in Scotland or whether the broader approach taken in *Wilson* v. *Independent Broadcasting Authority*[23] might have enabled a challenge to be raised.

1.3.14 In *R.* v. *Poole Borough Council, ex p. Beebee*[24] a grant of planning permission affecting an SSSI on lowland heath which offered a habitat for lizards was challenged by representatives of the Worldwide Fund for Nature and the British

---

[18] H.W.R. Wade, *Administrative Law* (6th ed., 1988), pp. 603–612.

[19] *Covent Garden Community Association* v. *Greater London Council* [1981] J.P.L. 183; *R.* v. *Hammersmith and Fulham London Borough Council, ex p. People Before Profit Ltd.* (1982) 80 L.G.R. 322.

[20] *R.* v. *Stroud District Council, ex p. Goodenough* (1982) 43 P. & C.R. 59.

[21] *R.* v. *Secretary of State for Social Services, ex p. Child Poverty Action Group* [1990] 2 Q.B. 540; *cf. Scottish Old People's Welfare Council,Petrs*, 1987 S.L.T. 179.

[22] [1990] 1 Q.B. 504.

[23] 1979 S.L.T. 279.

[24] (1991) 3 J.E.L. 293.

Herpetological Society. It was held that the Society did have standing to challenge this decision because it had a long connection with the site through surveys and other research carried out there, because it had over the years made a significant financial input to the site, and because it was expressly connected with the permission granted as a condition therein stated that the Society should be given the opportunity to catch and relocate lizards found on the site before development commenced. On the other hand, the Worldwide Fund for Nature, which had only an indirect connection with the site and had not even made representations in response to the initial planning application had no standing. The importance of establishing a real and direct connection with the particular site involved is clearly demonstrated here. It may well be that just as a legally aided pursuer sometimes raises an action in order to allow a pressure group to take action which it could not otherwise afford,[25] a small local conservation group may provide a means through which a case can be brought to court, perhaps with financial assistance from larger bodies which would not themselves have standing.

1.3.15 The third case is *R. v. Swale Borough Council and Medway Ports Authority, ex p. Royal Society for the Protection of Birds*,[26] in which the delay in raising a challenge to certain planning decisions was held to have been too long for the court to entertain the case, but where the standing of the RSPB was acknowledged. This was based on the Society's legitimate expectation they they would be consulted before decisions were taken, an expectation based on undertakings given by the council. The courts will protect the legitimate expectations of parties that they will be consulted or otherwise involved in procedures, once such expectations have been created by either the consistent past practice of an authority or its express promise.[27] However, the courts are understandably reluctant to recognise expectations except in very clear cases. There is concern that if legally protected expectations are created too easily, public authorities, afraid that their future freedom of action will be hampered, will become too cautious in holding discussions and consultations with individuals and groups who

---

[25] *E.g. McColl v. Strathclyde Regional Council*, 1983 S.L.T. 616.

[26] (1991) 3 J.E.L. 135.

[27] *Council of Civil Service Unions v. Minister for the Civil Service* [1985] A.C. 374.

have expressed some interest in particular issues, a general practice which benefits all parties.

1.3.16 The *Swale* case offers one example of the ways in which conservation groups and the like can become involved in proceedings in a way which clearly establishes their standing. In relation to planning decisions, the simplest way to become involved is through making representations in reponse to the initial application or at a public inquiry or other appeal proceedings, as it is well established that objectors have a clear right to ensure that proceedings have been conducted lawfully. The same will be true of involvement in other forms of statutory consultation proceedings.

1.3.17 Such involvement can transform someone from a concerned bystander, but a bystander nonetheless, into a legally interested party. For example, in *Patmor Ltd.* v. *City of Edinburgh District Licensing Board*[28] it was held that the holders of a gaming licence had no title in that capacity to challenge the grant of a licence to another company for similar premises in the area, despite their obvious concern as rival traders to limit competition, but did have title in their capacity as objectors to the new application, having formally taken advantage of the opportunity to submit representations when the application was advertised. The importance of becoming formally involved in proceedings is thus clear, and such involvement need not be onerous, as a simple letter making representations in response to a planning application or the like will suffice in most cases. The restrictive nature of the law on standing in Britain does stand in the way of greater use of the courts in all areas of environmental law, but in many circumstances the position can be improved by interested parties acting early enough to establish some direct connection with the issue.

LEGAL APPROACHES

1.4.1 Since the general legal background does not offer many opportunities to ensure the protection of wild plants and

[28] 1987 S.L.T. 492 (affirmed 1988 S.L.T. 850).

animals, the development of nature conservation beyond the initiatives of private individuals dealing with their own property has depended on action by Parliament and government. The policies which have been adopted, the legislation enacted and the legal, economic and other tools used to give effect to policies aiming to further nature conservation display a range of approaches. A detailed analysis (legal, historical, social, economic, political) of the approaches and techniques adopted, and those which have been rejected, would be a fascinating and lengthy study, especially when comparisons are drawn with other areas of policy, *e.g.* agriculture and town and country planning, and with the situation in other countries. In the context of this book, however, it must suffice to identify three main ways in which legislation discussed in the following chapters has been used to confer some protection on wild creatures and plants.

1.4.2 Firstly, there have been direct prohibitions on certain forms of harmful conduct. Secondly, there have been measures to ensure that sites of special value are identified and their value taken into account when decisions affecting them are taken by public bodies. Thirdly, the "voluntary approach" has been adopted, providing incentives to encourage landowners to manage their land for the benefit of nature, rather than forcing them to do so. Each of these has its merits and weaknesses, and there is ample scope for argument as to the proper balance to adopt.[29] The attitudes expressed here are deliberately overstated in order to highlight the different views.

Criminal law

1.4.3 The criminal law is used to mark out forms of conduct which are considered to be unacceptable in society. As well as the direct penalties and deterrent, the use of the criminal courts and the stigma of conviction should bring home to offenders, and the public generally, the fact that such actions are regarded as unacceptable. The law has been used to create a number of offences prohibiting the killing, injuring or other harm to wild animals and plants.[30]

---

[29] See generally, L.M. Warren, "Conservation — A Secondary Environmental Consideration" (1991) 18 J. Law & Soc. 64; N. Hawke, *Nature Conservation: The Legal Framework and Sustainable Development* (1991).

[30] *E.g.* the intentional killing of most wild birds; see chap. 3.

1.4.4 There are good reasons for utilising laws which render harm to wild animals and plants criminal. In the first place the most obvious thing which man can do to protect wildlife is to refrain from killing, injuring or disturbing it, and making such conduct a crime is the most direct legal way of trying to prevent it. Secondly, from the legal point of view, such laws are comparatively simple. The undesirable conduct is defined, any necessary exceptions are stated, and then the operation of the law is left to the general system of law enforcement, with no need for special administrative arrangements. Thirdly, such laws are useful in terms of publicity and education, as they should be readily comprehensible, although public awareness of the law is not necessarily high, and there may be problems in relation to provisions designed to protect particular species which may not be widely recognised in the field.

1.4.5 However, there are factors which may reduce the effectiveness of this approach to conservation legislation. By requiring the express prohibition of the undesirable conduct, there is a risk that some forms of harm, or some species in need of protection, will be omitted. The presence of gaps and possible loopholes may undermine the law, and it may be difficult to persuade the legislators to make the effort to enact the necessary amendments promptly. In the second place, criminal offences are likely to be directed against obvious and direct harm, so that the gradual deterioration of habitats and the harmful consequences incidental to other legitimate activities are likely to escape sanction.

1.4.6 A third problem which affects the use of any criminal law in this area relates to enforcement. Even with the use of strict liability and the onus being put on the accused to establish that he falls within any exceptions to an offence, it may be hard to secure the evidence necessary for a conviction. There may be problems in identifying the species which are given special protection, and by their very nature many of the offences are going to be committed in remote places away from the eyes of witnesses. In Scotland some recognition is given to these difficulties by the relaxation in some instances of the rules on corroboration, allowing the evidence of one witness to suffice for conviction.[31] It may also prove difficult to persuade a busy

---

[31] *E.g.* Deer (Scotland) Act 1959, s.25(4); WCA, s.19A (added by Prisoners and Criminal Proceedings (Scotland) Act 1993, s.36).

police force and prosecutor's office that nature conservation cases should be given any priority over the mass of more standard crimes with which they have to cope. Likewise the effectiveness of the law can be undermined by the courts imposing only low penalties on offenders, penalties which are trivial in proportion to the economic gain which has been achieved by ignoring the law and the irreparable nature of the harm done. In recent years, though, a number of substantial fines have been imposed and occasionally judges have stated that in fact prison sentences, if available, would have been an appropriate sentence.

1.4.7 It should be noted that the criminal law is also used in another way, as the final sanction to secure compliance with a number of essentially administrative schemes, *e.g.* in relation to SSSIs.[32] In this context the use of the criminal law shares the features of its use in many other regulatory schemes, especially the general perception that the offences involved are not "real crimes." This means that the offences are given a low priority at all stages in the administration of justice, and that the consequences of conviction, in terms of penalty and stigma, are often minimal.[33]

Identification of sites

1.4.8 In relation to the protection of habitat, the effect of much of the law is not to lay down exact rules on how land should or should not be managed or requiring or prohibiting particular actions. Few formal and absolute obligations or restrictions are imposed. Instead sites which are identified as being of value are given official recognition by means of a formal designation and it is provided that through consultation and other procedures their conservation value is taken into account when decisions are taken as to their use. Thus the designation of a Site of Special Scientific Interest does not mean that the site will in fact be preserved, but both the occupier before making significant changes to its use or management and the planning authority before approving any development must inform the conservancy council so that discussions can be held

[32] See section 5.4, below.
[33] J. Rowan-Robinson, P.Q. Watchman, C.R. Barker, *Crime and Regulation: A Study of the Enforcement of Regulatory Codes* (1990).

and any final decision is taken with the consequences for nature
conservation being taken into account.[34]

1.4.9 This approach is in part an aspect of the more general
voluntary approach discussed below, and is a reflection of the
reluctance of the law to interfere with the rights of landowners
to use their property as they see fit. However it also a reflection
of the wider position of nature conservation in official thinking,
as merely one interest among many which must be balanced in
each particular set of circumstances. The state has many
concerns and there are many objectives to be satisfied in the
public interest. Nature conservation is granted recognition as
one of these concerns, but is not given absolute priority and
must find its place in competition with conflicting concerns in
the particular circumstances.

1.4.10 This flexible approach has advantages and disadvantages
for nature conservation. The very real disadvantage is that there
is no guarantee that even the most valuable sites will in fact be
protected. Landowners are not prevented from damaging
valuable sites. Planning authorites have the power to grant
permission for development which will destroy an SSSI from the
nature conservancy point of view, and although the conservancy
councils and the like must be listened to, there is no obligation
to heed their advice. Central government and local authorities,
driven by a variety of political pressures, may give priority to
other interests such as economic development, the provision of
roads or power stations, or even creating facilities for
recreation, which conflict with nature conservation and relegate
it to a low position on their list of priorities. Merely pointing
out the value of particular sites and the damage which may be
done may well achieve little in real terms. Nature conservation
is always likely to lose out when a conflict of interests arises.

1.4.11 The very weakness of the provisions may, however, be
presented as having some advantages in practical terms. Weak
provisions are more acceptable to the owners and occupiers of
land, and accordingly the designations cover a greater area than
would have been possible if stronger measures were adopted.
Even if absolute protection is not guaranteed, the designations
should exercise some influence over how the land is used and

---

[34] See section 5.4, below.

help to raise awareness of conservation issues. Those with little sympathy for nature conservation would regard stronger measures as "sterilising" the land, putting the interest of animals and plants above those of humans, and it is likely that such measures would be opposed vehemently; the level of opposition to existing measures which has been demonstrated by those with some political influence[35] suggests that there would be real political difficulties in establishing on a widespread basis any stronger form of protection. It can be argued that for nature conservation as a whole it is better to have many sites designated in some way, even if they are not strongly protected, than to have only a few sites protected, however secure their protection is. Against this, though, it could be said that, however well-intentioned, the designations are meaningless if they cannot in fact prevent a landowner from dealing with his land as he would have done regardless of any official intervention.

1.4.12 The current approach can also be presented as more proper in a democratic society, in that establishing the balance between nature conservation and other conflicting interests is frequently left to democratically accountable government bodies such as planning authorities. The involvement of the conservancy councils ensures that decisions are taken in the full awareness of the implications for nature conservation, but at the end of the day the choice between favouring nature conservation or other interests is essentially a political one, and should be left to the appropriate politically accountable bodies. To critics, giving the conservancy councils more power would be to create a form of tyranny, where unelected bodies, committed to a single issue, were able to pursue their narrow objectives regardless of the implications for the broader context.

1.4.13 The present approach should also help to spread an awareness of the value of nature conservation and the ways in which it can be promoted or harmed, educating decision-makers and inspiring good habits which might well apply in areas not covered by any explicit designation. Moreover, those responsible for the land are not merely ordered to do something, but are gently led to see the merits of supporting conservation

---

[35] See, *e.g.*, the debates in the House of Lords during the passage of the Natural Heritage (Scotland) Bill, especially on January 23, 1991; *Hansard*, H.L. Vol. 525, cols. 173–185.

and to giving it an appropriate place in their outlook. In this way it is hoped that conservation becomes an accepted part of everyday attitudes, not an external imposition which will at best be sullenly complied with.

The voluntary principle

1.4.14 The views expressed in the last paragraph lie at the heart of the voluntary approach which is evident in so much of the law on nature conservation. The objective is not to order people to do or refrain from doing certain things, but instead to offer encouragement in a range of ways to lead them to decide for themselves to act in the desirable way.[36] Thus most effective protection of habitat[37] depends on management agreements voluntarily entered by the owners and occupiers of land, payments are available to encourage farmers to continue with environmentally-friendly farming methods rather than maximising production,[38] and afforestation projects are brought under control through the availability of grants, not a formal regulatory scheme.[39]

1.4.15 The voluntary principle has critics and supporters.[40] A negative assessment of this approach is to say that it gives far too much weight to private interests at the expense of the public interest in nature conservation. The rights of landowners to do as they please with their property are given undue protection,[41] and landowners (often already of considerable wealth) receive large payments at the taxpayers' expense for doing nothing to their land. Moreover the system is open to abuse, as payments for maintaining the land as at present can be triggered by proposals which were at best speculative and which the landowner never really intended to carry through. This general

---

[36] "... we must create effective and appropriate management practices through information and advice, dialogue, negotiation, persuasion and coopera-tion, supported by a realistic system of funding." Report of the Cairngorms Working Party, *Common Sense and Sustainability: A Partnership for the Cairngorms* (1992), para. 4.3.1.1.

[37] *e.g.,* in SSSIs and many nature reserves; see chap. 5 below.

[38] In relation to Environmentally Sensitive Areas; see section 5.8, below.

[39] See section 6.3, below.

[40] For a brief example of the debate see the Report of the Cairngorms Working Party (above), paras 4.3.1.1–5.

[41] *Cf.* the restrictive approach to interpreting statutory provisions which interfere with property rights suggested in *North Uist Fisheries Ltd.* v. *Secretary of State for Scotland,* 1992 S.L.T. 333; see para. 5.5.6, below.

approach leaves unsympathetic landowners free to ruin even the most valuable of sites, and puts all habitat protection at the mercy of the willingness of landowners to cooperate and of the resources available to the conservancy councils and the like for compensation payments.

1.4.16 The voluntary approach to conservation issues can be contrasted with the town and country planning system. In both cases restrictions on the use of land are considered to be desirable in the public interest. However, apart from a few exceptional cases, the planning system offers no compensation to the landowner who finds that he cannot develop his land as he wishes, whereas in relation to nature conservation, it is only on the payment of compensation that meaningful restrictions can be imposed. In any event, the relentless history of habitat destruction over past decades suggests that the voluntary approach is not an effective way of achieving meaningful conservation.

1.4.17 The supporters of the voluntary approach can counter by arguing that the best guardians of the countryside and its valuable habitat are those who own it and live and work there. Successful conservation requires the continuing commitment of those on the ground, and this is best achieved by obtaining the willing cooperation of those involved. Any attempt to order them to manage their land in a particular way would in many cases be met with at best resentful compliance with the mere letter of the law, whereas proper conservation measures depend on a thorough acceptance of the objectives being pursued, so that the whole management of the land and of the activities on it takes account of the natural world. Even if it were possible to specify everything necessary to ensure appropriate management, the problems of monitoring and enforcement on a long-term basis would mean that laws imposed on unwilling landowners would not prove a success. The need for continuing management of the land in appropriate ways provides a valid distinction with the planning system. For this reason, nature conservation is better served by offering assistance and encouragement so that landowners become willing partners in the conservation enterprise, not reluctant servants.

1.4.18 The voluntary approach also emphasises the importance of education. The law cannot hope to deal with all of the matters of significance for nature conservation, therefore a general raising of awareness of the value and requirements of conservation is what is called for. Through the operation of the statutory designations and consultation requirements, and through the provision of advice and information, people can be made aware of how they can promote nature conservation, and, in many cases do so without prejudicing any of their other interests. In the long-term this gentle encouragement to a change in attitudes will provide a more secure basis for nature conservation than will any specific legal measures which are subject to repeal or amendment to suit the political exigencies of the day.

1.4.19 Moreover, supporters of the voluntary principle could also argue that in the past the principle has had to operate against a generally unsympathetic background, in which environmental concerns were a low priority for government and for individuals. Now that official and public attitudes are changing and there is an official commitment to sustainability, the opportunity is there for the voluntary principle really to come into its own, supported at last by adequate funding and by complementary policies in agriculture, forestry and other areas which have a major effect on the countryside. The past failures can be attributed to the fact that the principle was never given the opportunity to work properly.

1.4.20 The voluntary principle is likely to remain central to the government's approach to nature conservation. Despite the criticisms noted above, the overall structure of the law is unlikely to be altered, although some changes may be forthcoming in response to the requirements of European Community measures designed to provide stronger guarantees for vulnerable habitats and species than can be ensured under the voluntary principle.[42] Yet the absence of major reform does not necessarily mean that the status and effectiveness of nature conservation measures will remain the same.

1.4.21 Within the current framework, the law frequently allows wide discretion to official bodies of various sorts, and even where overt discretion is not created, the availability, or lack, of resources will inevitably affect considerably the way in which the law is administered. The legal framework may thus operate in

---

[42] Habitats and Species Directive (Directive 92/43); see paras. 7.4.12–7.4.35, below.

different ways according to the different priorities of different bodies at any given time. Moreover, there is increasing interest in the use of economic incentives to achieve environmental objectives, a policy which may bring about major changes in practice without necessarily involving any changes in the law. The crucial factor is whether there is the real political will to give priority to nature conservation, a priority which inevitably means that other interests must in some cases suffer. If the current rhetoric of sustainability is carried through into practice, and environmental considerations are truly integrated with other policies, then without any changes to the law, the impact of nature conservation measures may be considerably increased. Equally, a strong political commitment to nature conservation may lead to major changes in the law. It is politicians, not lawyers, who will determine the future of the law on nature conservation.

2. The Authorities Responsible for Nature Conservation

2.1.1 Responsibility for matters affecting nature conservation is spread among a range of official bodies. Various departments of central government are involved, as are both tiers of local government and to some extent the European Community. The most direct responsibility is borne by a group of public bodies which enjoy a degree of independence from government while in practical terms a major role is played by charitable organisations. The fragmentation of responsibility is exacerbated by the different structures which exist in the different jurisdictions in Great Britain.

2.1.2 In view of the many activities which can have an impact on the environment some division of responsibilities is perhaps inevitable. However, although it is sensible for there to be bodies dealing with all aspects of agriculture, of river quality, etc., such division can mean that the interests of nature conservation are pushed into the background. Because it is not the central concern of such bodies, conservation can be seen as a marginal issue, primarily the responsibility of others, and consequently not as something to be given any priority when policies are formulated or powers exercised. In this way, the approach to the countryside and the environment becomes fragmented and unnecessary conflicts and disputes can arise. What is required is an integrated approach, with cooperation between the various bodies so that complementary decisions are taken and conservation concerns are taken into consideration (whether or not they are fully accepted) from the earliest stage of formulating policy. Without such integration one can have the absurd situation of one official body offering grants to people to do things in the interests of agriculture or forestry while another official body offers payments in order to stop them in the interests of nature conservation.

2.1.3. Mechanisms for cooperation between the various authorities exist at different levels. The activities of the conservation bodies can to some extent be kept in line with other aspects of official policy by the power to issue ministerial directions and by requirements for ministerial consent before certain powers are exercised. The conservation authorities are also placed under a duty to have regard to more than just the interests of nature conservation in carrying out their functions. On the other hand, authorities whose main responsibilities lie elsewhere are bound to pay heed to the concerns of conservation both by similar "balancing obligations" and by more particular duties, especially by requirements that the conservancy councils be consulted either before particular powers are exercised or on the general management of certain issues. However the advice which is proffered need not be followed and in view of an authority's prime responsibilities it may be quite proper for it to place other interests before those of nature conservation.

2.1.4 Moves have been made toward greater integration in recent years. Most noticeably the institutional divide between the bodies responsible for landscape and natural beauty and those concerned with nature conservation has been ended in Scotland and Wales with the creation of Scottish Natural Heritage and the Countryside Council for Wales, although the divide continues in England.[1] Such mergers allow for a broader approach to be taken to issues affecting particular areas, but it must also be recognised that real conflicts remain to be resolved before an integrated policy can emerge, *e.g.* between the interests of public access and recreation and those of nature conservation. The creation of Natural Heritage Areas in Scotland is intended to provide a further means of ensuring cooperation between the many public bodies and private concerns whose activities affect land use and habitat in a particular area.[2]

2.1.5 More generally, one aspect of the government's commitment to environmental concerns, as set out in the 1990 White Paper *This Common Inheritance*,[3] is a recognition of the need to integrate environmental and other policies: "to ensure ... that

---

[1] See section 2.5, below.
[2] See section 5.9, below.
[3] *This Common Inheritance: Britain's Environmental Strategy*, Cm.1200 (1990).

we are not undoing in one area what we are trying to do in another."[4] This should mean that nature conservation and broader environmental considerations play a part in the formulation of policy in all areas, striving towards the officially embraced objective of sustainable development. The rhetoric of such an integrated approach is now becoming common, although the practical results may take longer to become obvious.

2.1.6 Whatever the formal policy and institutional structure, much depends on the attitudes and approaches of the people involved. A simple awareness of environmental concerns on the part of those responsible for branches of government and other activities will do much to prevent needless damage and conflict being caused. Constructive informal dialogue can achieve more in practice than the most carefully designed structure operating without goodwill or mutual understanding.[5]

BALANCING OBLIGATIONS

2.2.1 Before considering the authorities which have specific responsibilities for nature conservation, something should be said about the balancing obligations which require public authorities to have some regard to the environment in the exercise of their functions. Virtually all public authorities are the creatures of statute, and their powers and functions are defined by the legislation which creates them. It is only if legislation permits them to do so that they are allowed to shape their policy and conduct with regard to the concerns of nature conservation; without some such provision, the authorities might well be found to be acting *ultra vires* and unlawfully by allowing an irrelevant consideration to influence the exercise of their statutory functions.[6] The presence of such provisions is therefore important if nature conservation is not to be ignored and is to be integrated into the policies and actions of bodies across the public sector.

---

[4] *Ibid.*, para. 1.6.
[5] *Cf.* Alexander Pope, *An Essay on Man*, (1734) Epistle iii. 1.303:
  "For Forms of Government let fools contest;
  Whate'er is best administer'd is best."
[6] *Associated Provincial Picture Houses Ltd.* v. *Wednesbury Corporation* [1948] 1 K.B. 223.

2.2.2 One of the most general of these provisions is typical. In the exercise of their statutory functions relating to land, every minister, government department and public body is obliged to have regard to the desirability of conserving the natural heritage (in Scotland)[7] or the natural beauty and amenity of the countryside (in England and Wales).[8] As there is no obligation to act in the interests of conservation, merely to have regard to such matters, such a provision may not offer much by way of support for conservation. However, it does achieve something by ensuring that conservation is always a relevant consideration which cannot be wholly ignored when decisions are being taken and does open the remote possibility of a legal challenge to the validity of any action which is clearly damaging to the natural heritage and cannot be supported by any other considerations. Moreover, the fact that natural beauty and heritage must be borne in mind adds weight to the voices of conservation groups and others in pressing their arguments on the authorities in question, albeit that no legal standing is conferred. Other considerations may in practice override those of the countryside in individual instances, but authorities cannot completely shut their eyes to the impact of their activities on wildlife and natural habitats.

2.2.3 In addition to the very general terms of the provisions discussed above, some obligation with respect to the countryside or conservation is often imposed on specific bodies or in relation to specific tasks, although almost invariably such duties are expressed to be subject to the proper exercise of the primary statutory functions of the bodies involved. One formulation which is used is to require the authority in question to seek a balance between various interests, including those of conservation. The interests listed may be irreconcilable in many situations, but such an obligation does at least ensure that some thought is given to the matters specified.

2.2.4 Thus, "so far as may be consistent with the proper discharge of [their] functions" under the Forestry Acts 1967–1979, the Forestry Commissioners must "endeavour to achieve a reasonable balance between" the development and

---

[7] CSA, s.66 (amended by NHSA Sched. 10, para. 4(7)); for the meaning of "natural heritage" see para. 2.5.10, below.

[8] CA, s.11; conserving natural beauty includes conserving flora, fauna and geological and physiographical features (CA s.49(4)).

maintenance of forestry and timber production and the conservation and enhancement of natural beauty and the conservation of flora, fauna and geological or physiographical features of special interest.[9] The agriculture ministers[10] must seek a balance between the promotion and maintenance of a stable and efficient agricultural industry, the economic and social interests of rural areas, the conservation and enhancement of the natural beauty and amenity of the countryside[11] and its features of archaeological interest, and the promotion of the enjoyment of the countryside by the public.[12] Similarly, in discharging their functions under the Sea Fisheries Acts, ministers and local fisheries committees are obliged, so far as consistent with the proper and efficient exercise of those functions, to have regard to the conservation of marine flora and fauna and to endeavour to achieve a reasonable balance between conservation and their other concerns.[13]

2.2.5 In recent years the trend has been towards a fuller statement of the environmental responsibilities of new public bodies, although the effect of such provisions is often merely to emphasise their existence rather than to confer any greater legal weight. The formulations vary, even within the same statute. Without prejudice to their general function of furthering the improvement of the environment,[14] Scottish Enterprise is obliged merely to "have regard to ... the desirability of safeguarding the environment",[15] whereas for Highlands and Islands Enterprise the duty is more fully expressed as being to

> "have regard to the desirability of safeguarding —
> (a) the natural beauty of the countryside in;
> (b) the flora and fauna of; and
> (c) the geological and geomorphological[16] features of special interest of,
> the Highlands and Islands."[17]

[9] Forestry Act 1967, s.1(3A) (added by Wildlife and Countryside (Amendment) Act 1985, s.4).

[10] See para. 2.3.4, below.

[11] Expressly stated to include the conservation of flora and fauna and geological and physiographical features.

[12] Agriculture Act 1986, s.17.

[13] Sea Fisheries (Wildlife Conservation) Act 1992, s.1.

[14] Enterprise and New Towns (Scotland) Act 1990, s.1.

[15] *Ibid.*, s.4(4).

[16] There is probably no practical significance in the use of "geomorphological" in place of the more usual "physiographical."

[17] Enterprise and New Towns (Scotland) Act 1990, s.5(3).

The fuller terms of the latter provision may result in environmental considerations appearing more significant, but it is unlikely that there is any difference in legal terms to the place of such issues in the authorities' deliberations.

2.2.6 More positive obligations are imposed on the authorities concerned with water resources and drainage in England and Wales.[18] One function of the National Rivers Authority in England and Wales is "to such extent as it considers desirable, generally to promote the conservation of ... flora and fauna which are dependent on an aquatic environment" and the conservation of the natural beauty and amenity of waters and associated land.[19] The ministers, the National Rivers Authority, internal drainage boards, and water and sewerage undertakers are all obliged not merely to have regard to the desirability of conservation, but (so far as is consistent with the relevant statutory functions) to exercise their powers so as to further the conservation and enhancement of natural beauty and the conservation of flora, fauna and geological or physiographical features of special interest, and to take into account the effect of their conduct on the beauty, wildlife and features of any affected area.[20] Such a formulation may somewhat increase the weight of environmental considerations, but as always the prime statutory functions of the authorities take priority. Provided that an authority can produce some justification for its conduct based on these functions and some evidence that the environmental impact was not wholly ignored, it is unlikely that a court would be willing to hold that an authority was in breach of such a broadly phrased duty.

2.2.7 As well as being attached to the general functions of particular authorities, balancing obligations appear in relation to a range of specific tasks. The desirability of preserving natural beauty and conserving flora, fauna and geological and physiographical features must be taken into account at all stages in the preparation and approval of proposals for new pipelines,[21] and

[18] See paras.2.6.4–2.6.7, below.
[19] Water Resources Act 1991, s.2(2).
[20] Water Industry Act 1991, s.3(2); Water Resources Act 1991, s.16(1); Land Drainage Act 1991, s.12(1).
[21] Pipelines Act 1962, s.43.

for the underground storage of gas,[22] while for opencast coal operations[23] and electricity generating stations and transmission lines,[24] there is the further requirement that the proposals include measures to mitigate any adverse effects on the environment. Housing authorities must bear in mind the effect of their proposals on the beauty of the landscape or countryside,[25] and in order to protect natural beauty and the environment additional conditions can be imposed on works otherwise automatically authorised under the Telecommunications Code[26] or approved for the Channel Tunnel.[27]

2.2.8 In many instances the presence of such balancing obligations is perhaps more symbolic than significant in view of the priority always granted to the main statutory functions of the bodies concerned, functions which may call for works and activities with serious adverse effects on the natural environment. However, the authorities cannot claim that they are not allowed to respond to the interests of nature conservation and cannot shut their eyes to the environmental impact of their activities nor their ears to the arguments of those pressing for conservation to be taken into account. There may be little likelihood of an authority ever being found to be in breach of such obligations, but their presence does give some legal weight to conservation interests.

CENTRAL GOVERNMENT

2.3.1 Although most of the detailed administration of nature conservation lies in the hands of specialist bodies, especially the conservancy councils which have succeeded the Nature Conservancy Council, central government is deeply involved in the making of overall policy and retains many significant powers to control or influence the way in which the law operates in

---

[22] Gas Act 1965, s.4(4).
[23] Opencast Coal Act 1958, s.3 (substituted by the Coal Industry Act 1990, s.5).
[24] Electricity Act 1989, Sched. 9, paras.1,3.
[25] Housing Act 1985, s.607; Housing (Scotland) Act 1987, s.6(1).
[26] Telecommunications Act 1984, s.10(4).
[27] Channel Tunnel Act 1987, Sched. 3, para. 2.

practice. The strength of the government's commitment to nature conservation will determine its place (usually fairly low) in relation to conflicting concerns, such as promoting economic development or expanding the motorway system, and to competing claims for public funds. The policy lead given by central government will be crucial in determining where the balance between various interests is to be struck, especially as so much of the law relies on discretionary powers. More fundamentally, central government is responsible for providing the funds for the various conservation bodies and for promoting the legislation under which they operate.

2.3.2 In addition to functions within the domestic system, the central authorities are responsible for handling conservation issues at European and international levels. It is the government, in the name of the Crown, which signs and ratifies international treaties. It is the government whose representatives on the Council of Ministers of the European Community negotiate and agree to European legislation, and it is the government which is responsible for ensuring that Community law is properly implemented and observed in this country. The fact that the government may ultimately have to answer before the European Court of Justice for the state of our law gives central government an added incentive to keep a close eye on what is happening, even where the prime responsibility lies with local authorities or other public bodies.

2.3.3 Within the government, responsibility is divided between a number of departments. Since the splitting of the Nature Conservancy Council,[28] in Scotland all significant matters fall within the scope of the Scottish Office; most matters are dealt with by the Scottish Office Environment Department,[29] although issues handled by the Agriculture and Fisheries Department are also significant. In England the Department of the Environment is the main department involved; in Wales some matters are dealt with by the Welsh Office, whilst others remain with the Department of the Environment.[30] These are

---

[28] See section 2.5, below.

[29] Abbreviated to SOEnD, to distinguish it from the Education Department, SOED.

[30] The distribution of functions between departments is achieved by orders under the Ministers of the Crown Act 1975, *e.g.* the Transfer of Functions (Wales) (No. 1) Order 1978, S.I. 1978 No. 272.

the departments responsible for nature conservation, town and country planning and pollution control.

2.3.4 The government's powers in relation to agriculture are frequently relevant to nature conservation, and here responsibility is again split geographically. The standard pattern is for legislation to refer to "the Minister," which is then defined so that responsibility lies for Scotland with the Secretary of State for Scotland, for England with the Minister of Agriculture and Fisheries, and for Wales with the Secretary of State for Wales,[31] and any reference here to "the agriculture ministers" should be interpreted in this way. Forestry matters are regulated by the same three ministers,[32] acting together where more than one country is affected, with the Secretary of State for Scotland being "the lead minister." Whatever the practical arrangements, the formal approach in all areas is for statutes to confer powers simply on "the Secretary of State," which means that any of Her Majesty's Principal Secretaries of State can lawfully exercise the power.[33]

2.3.5 The role of government ministers is often hidden behind the more obvious and direct official powers lying in the hands of the conservancy councils and other public bodies. However, although lying in the background, the power of central government should not be underestimated, especially in relation to the conservancy councils. This power comes in various forms. In the first place, it is the government which appoints the members of the councils,[34] and in so doing can obviously influence the general approach which is likely to be taken by them. Secondly, as the finances which are to be available to the councils are also determined by the government,[35] some control can be exercised over how much the councils are actually able to achieve in carrying out their functions, *e.g.* the extent to which funds are available will obviously have a direct effect on the number, scale and nature of management agreements which can be offered to landowners.[36] There is also the possibility of

---

[31] *e.g.* Agriculture Act 1986, ss.17(2), 18(11).

[32] Forestry Act 1967, s.49(1).

[33] Interpretation Act 1978, Sched. 1; *Agee* v. *Lord Advocate*, 1977 S.L.T. (Notes) 54.

[34] *E.g.*, NHSA, Sched. 1, para. 3.

[35] *E.g.*, *ibid.*, s.8.

[36] An issue highlighted after the decision in *Cameron* v. *Nature Conservancy Council*, 1991 S.L.T. (Lands Tr.) 85; see para. 5.4.12, below.

direct involvement through the power of government to issue to the councils directions which must be obeyed.[37]

2.3.6 In addition to these general powers over bodies such as the conservancy councils, the government exercises controls over their activities in other ways. The making of grants and loans by such bodies is usually subject to government approval,[38] as is the exercise of any power of compulsory purchase.[39] Bye-laws have to be confirmed by the Secretary of State,[40] and many of the significant designations of land for conservation purposes have to be made or confirmed by the Secretary of State.[41]

2.3.7 In other areas, such as agriculture and town and country planning, the role of government ministers is more direct. Regulations made by the ministers govern most aspects of agriculture, and the grant schemes which play such an important role in shaping the industry are created and administered by central government (within European Community guidelines).[42] In the planning system, the Secretaries of State make the detailed rules which exempt certain forms of development from the need for permission,[43] approve planning authorities' structure plans[44] and supervise other development plans,[45] decide appeals,[46] and can call in individual applications for their own determination.[47] The number of references throughout this book to "the Secretary of State" is itself testament to the extent of direct power enjoyed by ministers in matters relevant for conservation.

2.3.8 Central government is thus deeply involved in the handling of nature conservation. From the framing of the fundamental pieces of legislation to the determination of

[37] *E.g.* NHSA, s.11.
[38] *E.g. ibid.,* s.9.
[39] *E.g.* NPACA, s.103(1) (substituted by Nature Conservancy Council Act 1973, Sched. 1, para. 2 and amended by EPA Sched. 9, para. 1).
[40] *E.g. ibid.,* s.106.
[41] *E.g.* Nature Conservation Orders, Natural Heritage Areas; see sections 5.4, 5.8, below.
[42] *E.g.* Agriculture Act 1970, s.29 and schemes authorised thereunder.
[43] TCPSA, s.21; TCPA, s.59.
[44] *Ibid.,* s.7; *ibid.,* s.35.
[45] *Ibid.,* s.12; *ibid.,* ss.18, 44.
[46] *Ibid.,* s.33; *ibid.,* s.79.
[47] *Ibid.,* s.32; *ibid.,* s.77.

individual applications for grants or planning permission, the government can affect the whole form and direction of the law and policy throughout the country, a position strengthened by its control over the membership and finances of the public bodies established outside government to play the leading part in conservation matters. In practice governments have not generally exercised their powers so as to interfere with the detailed workings of the conservation bodies, but the extent of power and influence which lies in the hands of central government must always be remembered.

LOCAL AUTHORITIES

2.4.1 The range of powers and responsibilities exercised by local authorities means that they are heavily involved in matters affecting nature conservation. This involvement is divided between the two tiers of local government, occasionally being shared between tiers, while authorities may be allowed to support other public or voluntary bodies or other local authorities in their activities. Within authorities, though, the demands of nature conservation must compete with the many other demands placed on local government and it is not surprising if authorities at times view economic development as more important than nature conservation when it comes to determining land use, and education, housing and social services as more deserving when it comes to the allocation of resources. Nevertheless, the wide discretion and broad powers enjoyed by local authorities mean that there is much which an authority can do to further the interests of nature conservation if it is so minded.

2.4.2 Perhaps the most obvious part played by local authorities is in the operation of the system of town and country planning. As this subject is well covered in more specialised works, it is not the intention to deal with it in any detail in this book.[48] At present it is enough to note that as planning authorities,[49] local

---

[48] See section 8.2, below.
[49] Planning functions are divided between the two tiers of local government in most cases; Local Government (Scotland) Act 1973, s.172; TCPA, s.1.

authorities are responsible for the making of development plans for their areas[50] and for the approval of the individual applications for permission to carry out building, engineering or mining operations or to change the use of any land.[51] Within the scope of these powers, which exclude most agricultural and forestry matters,[52] the authorities have considerable control over changes in the use of land and thus on the sort of habitat which will be available within their areas, a control emphasised by the fact that a grant of planning permission can authorise activities in an SSSI, however damaging to its value as natural habitat.[53]

2.4.3 Direct powers over the countryside are also enjoyed by local authorities. In Scotland, these powers generally rest with the district or islands councils,[54] whereas in England and Wales the position is more complex, with a number of concurrent powers.[55] Local nature reserves can be created,[56] public access can be arranged through agreements or orders,[57] and management agreements can be made for the preservation and enhancement of the natural beauty of the countryside and the promotion of its enjoyment by the public.[58] Country parks (and in Scotland, regional parks) can be created[59] and there is a variety of powers to make byelaws[60] and appoint rangers or wardens[61] for areas where an authority has intervened in some way. The law also allows authorities more general powers which may be of relevance, *e.g.* in Scotland local authorities may undertake works for the preservation and enhancement of natural beauty.[62]

[50] TCPSA, Pt. II; TCPA, Pt. II.

[51] *Ibid.*, Pt. III; *ibid.*, Pt. III.

[52] *Ibid.*, s.19(2)(e); *ibid.*, s.55(2)(e).

[53] WCA, s.28(8); see section 5.4, below.

[54] Local Government and Planning (Scotland) Act 1982, Sched. 1.

[55] See the useful tables in Appendices A–C of S. Bailey, *Cross on Local Government Law* (8th ed., 1991).

[56] NPACA, s.21; see para. 5.2.10, below.

[57] CSA, Pt. II (this power is now shared with SNH; NHSA, s.13); NPACA, Pt. V.

[58] *Ibid.* s.49A(2) (added by Countryside (Scotland) Act 1981, s.9, amended by NHSA Sched. 10, para. 4); WCA, s.39.

[59] *Ibid.* ss.48, 48A (added *ibid.*, s.8); CA, s.7.

[60] *E.g.*, for country parks and areas covered by access agreements; NPACA, s.90, CSA, s.54, CA, s.41.

[61] NPACA s.92, CSA s.65 (amended by Countryside (Scotland) Act 1981, Sched. 1, para. 4).

[62] Local Government (Development and Finance) (Scotland) Act 1964, s.2 (amended by CSA, s.52).

2.4.4 An authority's other functions will also have an effect on habitat and nature conservation. Local authorities act as coast protection authorities,[63] as roads and highways authorities,[64] as waste disposal and regulation authorities,[65] in all of which capacities works with significant environmental impact can be undertaken or authorised. Involvement in aspects of public health[66] and pollution control[67] gives authorities a role in environmental issues. The responsibility for providing recreational facilities[68] could also be invoked to justify support for facilities for bird-watching, etc., whilst the way in which an authority treats the land under its direct control (schools, housing, cemeteries) will also be of importance in terms of habitat on a local level. As with central government, throughout this book the reference to local authorities in their many capacities illustrates the range of powers which they enjoy and which are of importance for nature conservation.

CONSERVANCY COUNCILS

2.5.1 Until 1991 responsibility for nature conservation and other countryside matters was divided along functional lines. There was a single body, the Nature Conservancy Council (NCC),[69] responsible for nature conservation throughout Great Britain, whilst separate bodies, the Countryside Commissions,[70] were responsible for the natural beauty of the countryside and promoting its enjoyment by the public. As the task of

[63] Coast Protection Act 1949, s.1 (amended by Local Government Act 1972, Sched. 30, Local Government (Scotland) Act 1973, Sched. 29 and applied by Local Government (Scotland) Act 1973, s.138); in Scotland regional and island councils are also responsible for flood prevention (Flood Prevention (Scotland) Act 1961, s.1 (amended and applied by Local Government (Scotland) Act 1973, s.137)).

[64] Roads (Scotland) Act 1984, s.151; Highways Act 1980 s.1.

[65] EPA, s.30.

[66] Public Health (Scotland) Act 1897, s.12 (substituted by Local Government (Scotland) Act 1973, Sched. 27 Pt. II para. 28); Public Health Act 1936, s.1 (amended by Local Government Act 1972, Sched. 14, para. 1).

[67] EPA, s.4.

[68] Local Government and Planning (Scotland) Act 1982, ss.14–18; Local Government (Miscellaneous Provisions) Act 1976 s.19.

[69] Established in its final form by the Nature Conservancy Council Act 1973.

[70] The Countryside Commission for Scotland, established under CSA, and the Countryside Commission which operated in England and Wales and was created by CA as successor to the National Parks Commission created by NPACA.

preserving the natural beauty of the countryside was expressly declared to include the conservation of its flora and fauna and its geological or physiographical features of special interest,[71] this division was somewhat artificial, but the NCC and the Commissions developed their own clear areas of activity.

2.5.2 This structure has now been transformed and the main division now is on a geographical basis. In Scotland and in Wales new bodies have been created, Scottish Natural Heritage (SNH)[72] and the Countryside Council for Wales (CCW),[73] which exercise the functions of both the NCC and the Countryside Commissions. Only in England does the division remain between the newly established Nature Conservancy Council for England (NCCE)[74] and the Countryside Commission, now restricted to operations in England.[75] The three successors to the NCC can conveniently be called the conservancy councils.

2.5.3 The aim of creating single bodies in Scotland and Wales was to provide the opportunity for an integrated approach to be taken to all conservation and countryside matters, and to recognise the fact that the issues and pressures affecting conservation in those countries are different from those in much of England.[76] In Scotland further elements were the desire to transfer the conservation body to the ambit of the Scottish Office[77] and the hope that a new body could establish better relations with local communities than had been the case with the NCC which had become involved in a number of very public controversies over land use during the 1980s.[78] The arguments for integration, however, were not seen as convincing enough for a similar merger to be carried out in England. The splitting

[71] CSA, s.78(2); CA, s.49(4).

[72] NHSA, Pt. I; for one year a separate Nature Conservancy Council for Scotland was in existence (EPA s.128) before the 1991 Act created SNH as the integrated body.

[73] EPA, ss.128, 130.

[74] *Ibid.*, s.128.

[75] *Ibid.*, s.130, Sched. 8.

[76] On the background to the changes see S. Tromans, *The Environmental Protection Act 1990* (1991), pp. 43.226–43.228; F. Reynolds & W.R. Sheate, "Reorganization of the Conservation Authorities" in W. Howarth & C.P. Rodgers (eds.), *Agriculture, Conservation and Land Use* (1992).

[77] All aspects of the NCC's work were under the supervision of the Department of the Environment.

[78] *E.g.* over the Flow Country and the management of geese on Islay.

of the NCC attracted much criticism as being likely to weaken the scientific base of the conservation authorities and as being an unhelpful fragmentation of responsibility when many issues required study and action at a British level,[79] to say nothing of the practical difficulties caused by dividing responsibility for such areas as the Solway Firth and Bristol Channel. The legislation was hotly debated, and the establishment of the Joint Nature Conservation Committee[80] did little to quieten the concern being expressed that the splitting of the NCC could only weaken the voice of nature conservation on important matters.

2.5.4 With only a few exceptions,[81] the structural changes in the administration of nature conservation have not affected the substantive rules to be applied. The new conservancy councils operate by means of the same provisions as governed the powers and functions of the NCC, and the law remains essentially the same throughout Great Britain. At an administrative level, the councils can also be largely discussed together since they share many features, indeed CCW and NCCE share the same constitutional provisions. The following paragraphs describe the common features of the councils, before examining the special aspects of each in turn and the role of the Joint Committee.

Common features

2.5.5 Each council has about a dozen members,[82] all of whom are appointed by the relevant Secretary of State[83] and on terms determined by him;[84] members may be removed in the event of

---

[79] As ever, Northern Ireland is treated separately and is regarded as a special case, although in this instance its geographical separation might in fact justify a different approach in any event.

[80] EPA, s.128(4); see paras.2.5.19–2.5.22, below.

[81] The most noticeable being the creation in Scotland of the Advisory Committee on SSSIs; see paras. 5.4.4–6, below.

[82] Between eight and twelve members for SNH and CCW, between ten and fourteen for NCCE (EPA, s.128(2), NHSA, Sched. 1, para. 3); the number of members can be varied by ministerial order (EPA, s.128(3), NHSA, Sched. 1, para. 8).

[83] EPA, s.128(2), NHSA, Sched. 1, para. 3; membership of a council is a disqualification from being an M.P. (for SNH, House of Commons Disqualification Act 1975, Sched. 1 Pt. II (amended by NHSA Sched. 10 para. 8); for CCW and NCCE, *ibid.* Sched. 1 Pt.III (amended by EPA, Sched. 6, para. 24) (members in receipt of remuneration only)).

[84] *Ibid.*, Sched. 6 para. 4, *ibid.*, Sched. 1, para. 7.

bankruptcy, prolonged absence from the council's business (unless permission has been granted) or other causes rendering them unfit or unable to continue.[85] For SNH the Secretary of State is bound to have regard to the desirability of ensuring so far as practicable that there are among the members persons of knowledge or experience of SNH's principal areas of activity,[86] and to satisfy himself that the members have no financial or other interest likely to be prejudicial to their performance in office.[87] In all cases a chairman and deputy chairman are appointed by the Secretary of State[88] while the chief officer is appointed by the council with the Secretary of State's approval.[89] Each council has control of its own procedure[90] and can appoint committees including outside members;[91] this latter power is especially significant for SNH which has four regional boards, established in an attempt to maintain close contacts with local communities.

2.5.6 Although independent of government departments, the councils remain under a degree of central supervision. Annual reports and accounts must be prepared and presented to the Secretary of State and forwarded by him to Parliament in the case of reports and to the Comptroller and Auditor General in the case of accounts.[92] As well as being able to influence the councils through the appointment of their members, the Secretary of State has the power to give the councils directions of a general or specific character with regard to the discharge of their functions, but not in relation to the detailed exercise of their nature conservation powers.[93] More significantly, the funds made available to the councils are determined by the Secretary of State acting with Treasury approval[94] and the grants and loans made by the councils must be authorised (specifically or

[85] *Ibid.*, Sched. 6, para. 6, *ibid.*, Sched. 1, para. 9; the English and Welsh provisions refer to six consecutive months' absence, the Scottish ones to three months' as well as including a power to dismiss members who are "unsuitable" as well as unable or unfit to continue in office.

[86] NHSA, Sched. 1, para. 4.

[87] *Ibid.*, Sched. 1, para. 5; for this purpose the Secretary of State can request information from members and potential members (*ibid.*, para. 6).

[88] EPA, Sched. 6, para. 4; NHSA, Sched. 1, para. 10.

[89] *Ibid.*, Sched. 6, para. 8; *ibid.*, Sched. 1, para. 12.

[90] *Ibid.*, Sched. 6, para. 12; *ibid.*, Sched. 1, para. 15.

[91] *Ibid.*, Sched. 6, para. 14; *ibid.*, Sched. 1, para. 16.

[92] *Ibid.*, Sched. 6, paras. 19–21; *ibid.*, s.10.

[93] *Ibid.*, s.131(4); *ibid.*, s.11.

[94] *Ibid.*, s.129; *ibid.*, s.8.

by means of a general authorisation) by the Secretary of State
again acting with Treasury approval.[95] The councils also fall
within the jurisdiction of the Ombudsman.[96] Although these
powers have not in fact been used to interfere with the workings
of the councils, or the NCC before them, it must be noted that
the independence of the councils could be undermined by the
existence of such provisions.

2.5.7 The conservancy councils are given a range of general
functions and powers to enable them to carry out their
responsibilities for nature conservation.[97] These functions
include the provision of advice to government ministers on the
development and implementation of policies for nature conservation, the provision of advice to any persons about nature
conservation, the dissemination of relevant knowledge, and the
commissioning and support (financial or other) of research.[98]
The general powers enable the councils to initiate and carry out
research themselves, to accept and apply gifts and contributions
for the achievement of their purposes, to hold land, to make
charges for their services and to do all other things incidental or
conducive to their functions.[99] These provisions are wide enough
to allow the councils to operate freely without continually
checking the limits of their legal powers and are in addition to
the specific measures contained in the detailed provisions on
nature conservation.

2.5.8 The substantive provisions are discussed in detail below,
but in summary, the councils are responsible for the designation
of nature reserves and the making of bye-laws and management
agreements for them, for the designation of SSSIs, the approval
of activities within them and the making of management
agreements for them, and for the licensing of activities relating
to protected species. The councils are also involved as
consultees in many official procedures and are charged with the
provision of advice to government at all levels on matters
relating to nature conservation, from the formulation of policy

[95] *Ibid.*, s.134; *ibid.*, s.9.
[96] Parliamentary Commissioner Act 1967, Sched. 2 (amended by EPA,
Sched. 6, para. 23; NHSA, Sched. 10, para. 3).
[97] Defined for this purpose as "the conservation of flora, fauna or geological
or physiographical features" (EPA, s.131(6)).
[98] EPA, s.132(1); NHSA, s.2(1).
[99] *Ibid.*, s.132(2); *ibid.*, s.2(1), (2): the Scottish legislation expressly includes
reference to the power to form partnerships and companies.

to the desirability of particular acts and the protection of individual species. For all of these tasks a major research effort is necessary.

Scottish Natural Heritage

2.5.9 Scottish Natural Heritage (SNH) was created by the Natural Heritage (Scotland) Act 1991, as the successor to both the Nature Conservancy Council for Scotland and the Country-side Commission for Scotland. Its general aims reflect those of its two predecessors, being

> "(a) to secure the conservation and enhancement of; and
> (b) to foster understanding and facilitate the enjoyment of,
> the natural heritage of Scotland."[1]

SNH is thus charged with the responsibility both for conservation and for recreation and amenity, a combination which offers the opportunity for an integrated approach to be taken on many countryside and environmental issues. However, much closer coordination with the authorities responsible for agriculture, forestry and other rural land uses is necessary before a truly integrated approach is possible,[2] while the present dual objectives of SNH may lead to internal conflicts in areas where recreational pressure is damaging fragile environments.

2.5.10 The legislation creating SNH contains two novelties. First, the concept of the "natural heritage" of Scotland is introduced. This is defined as including the flora and fauna of Scotland, its geological and physiographical features, and its natural beauty and amenity,[3] thereby combining and replacing the somewhat ungainly terms which have been used in previous conservation and countryside legislation.

2.5.11 The second novelty is the reference to the concept of sustainability. As part of its general aims, SNH is required to have regard to the desirability of ensuring that anything done in relation to the natural heritage of Scotland "is undertaken in a

---

[1] NHSA, s.1(1).
[2] Such cooperation is attempted, but on an essentially non-statutory basis, in Natural Heritage Areas; see section 5.9, below.
[3] NHSA, s.1(3).

manner which is sustainable."[4] The exact meaning and impact of this provision are far from clear, especially as no definition is provided of "sustainable". The most that was offered in the parliamentary debates was the quotation of very broad principles taken from a document prepared by the International Union for the Conservation of Nature.[5] The introduction of this concept can be viewed as either a strengthening or a weakening of the commitment to conservation. A strengthening may result from the test of sustainability being applied to all activities which in any way affect the natural heritage, assessing their acceptability in terms of their long-term impact on the natural environment. On the other hand the commitment to conservation could be weakened if a concentration on the sustainability of any new development leads to a presumption that any proposal which can claim a degree of sustainability should be approved, diverting attention from the issue of whether any development at all should be allowed to interfere with the status quo. Whatever one's approach, sustainability remains more of a political, economic and ethical principle than a legal standard by which conduct can be judged. In view of the lack of definition and the fact that SNH is merely required "to have regard to" the desirability of securing sustainability, arguments over the meaning and effect of this provision are likely to take place at the policy rather than the legal level.

2.5.12 In addition to having regard to the desirability of ensuring sustainability, SNH is required to pay heed to a number of other considerations, balancing the concerns of conservation with a range of other interests.[6] As with all such balancing obligations, the precise weight to be given to any consideration is left to the discretion of SNH in each instance, but the various factors must at least be borne in mind and will obviously exert some influence on the making of policy and determination of particular cases. In keeping with SNH's main responsibilities actual or possible ecological and other environmental changes to the natural heritage of Scotland must be considered,[7] and it is also to have regard to aspects of what is sometimes called the "cultural heritage," namely the need to

---

[4] *Ibid.*, s.1(1).
[5] A draft of *Caring for Our World — A Strategy for Sustainability*; H.C. 1990–91 First Scottish Standing Committee C, col. 55.
[6] NHSA, s.3(1).
[7] This is the only consideration to be taken into account in the exercise of functions relating to the Joint Nature Conservation Committee (*ibid.*, s.3(2)).

conserve sites and landscapes of archaeological and historical
interest. Such conservationist concerns are balanced by the duty
to consider the needs of agriculture, fisheries and forestry and
the need for social and economic development. There is also a
duty to consider the interests of owners and occupiers of land
and of local communities. These latter needs and interests will
obviously conflict at times with those of nature conservation
(and of promoting recreation), but any successful conservation
policy must pay heed to the concerns of the people who often
feel themselves as being the most endangered species in the
remote areas valued for their natural features. Nevertheless at
the time of the passing of the legislation fear was expressed that
these provisions will allow too much influence to be exercised
by interests unsympathetic to the main aims of SNH.

2.5.13 From the Nature Conservancy Council for Scotland,
SNH has inherited the detailed nature conservation functions
described later in this book as well as a role as official consultee
on many planning and related matters.[8] From the Countryside
Commission for Scotland, it has inherited a range of advisory
functions and concern for the promotion of public recreation in
the countryside. SNH's latter role has been enhanced by the
power for SNH itself to enter access agreements and to make
access orders to provide public access to areas of the
countryside for recreational purposes[9]; previously the Countryside Commission for Scotland had been restricted to an advisory
role, with the relevant legal powers being exclusively in the
hands of planning authorities.

2.5.14 The powers which the Countryside Commission for
Scotland enjoyed have been retained and broadened in scope,
both geographically, as they are no longer restricted to "the
countryside,"[10] and in terms of their use, as they can now be
exercised in connection with the full range of SNH's functions,
not merely those inherited from the Commission. There is a
general power to enter management agreements[11] and a power
to undertake and promote development schemes designed to

[8] Detailed amendments to the relevant legislation to take account of this
transfer of functions to SNH are made by EPA, Sched. 9 and NHSA, Sched. 2.
[9] NHSA, s.13 and Sched. 3, amending Pt. II of CSA 1967.
[10] The Commission was restricted to operating in "the countryside" as defined
by CSA, s.2.
[11] CSA, s.49A (added by Countryside (Scotland) Act 1981, s.9 and amended
by NHSA, Sched. 10, para. 4).

enhance or conserve or to foster understanding or enjoyment of the natural heritage.[12] Such schemes must involve the application of new techniques and methods or serve to illustrate the appropriateness of such schemes to particular areas,[13] and wide powers, including that of compulsory purchase of land, are provided to allow such schemes to be carried out.[14] From both predecessors SNH has acquired the power to make or propose bye-laws for areas where it is exercising various powers[15] and the ability to offer grants, loans and other forms of assistance to those furthering its objectives.[16]

Countryside Council for Wales

2.5.15 The Countryside Council for Wales (CCW) was created by the Environmental Protection Act 1990,[17] and like SNH is charged with the tasks previously carried out by separate conservation and countryside bodies. Responsibility for nature conservation in Wales and the relevant statutory powers and functions were transferred to CCW from the Nature Conservancy Council,[18] while it is provided that in Wales CCW is to exercise the functions of the Countryside Commission, which had previously operated in both England and Wales.[19] Thus, as in Scotland, there is in Wales a single body which should be able to offer a more integrated approach to countryside and conservation issues than was previously the case.

2.5.16 The conservation functions and powers of CCW are the same as those of the other conservancy councils, and the countryside ones as those of the Countryside Commission in England.[20] The latter powers are to be exercised for dual purposes.[21] Firstly, CCW is to act for the conservation and

---

[12] NHSA, s.5(1).

[13] *Ibid.*, s.5(2).

[14] *Ibid.*, s.5(3)–(11); any compulsory purchase of land must be approved by the Secretary of State and is subject to special parliamentary procedure.

[15] *e.g.* for nature reserves (NPACA, s.2) and for areas covered by access arrangements (CSA, s.54(4) (amended by NHSA, Sched. 10, para. 4)).

[16] Now governed by NHSA, s.9.

[17] EPA, ss.128, 130.

[18] The detailed amendments necessary to achieve this are contained in *ibid.*, Sched. 9.

[19] *Ibid.*, s.130; the detailed amendments necessary are contained in *ibid.*, Sched. 8, in particular substituting a new s.1 and adding ss.4A, 50A and 86A to NPACA.

[20] See paras.2.6.1–3, below.

[21] EPA, s.130(2).

enhancement of natural beauty in Wales[22] and of the natural beauty and amenity of the countryside in Wales, both in areas designated as National Parks and Areas of Outstanding Natural Beauty and elsewhere.[23] Secondly, CCW is to encourage the provision and improvement of facilities for the enjoyment of the Welsh countryside and of opportunities for open-air recreation and the study of nature. At the same time CCW is required to have regard to the social and economic interests of rural areas in Wales,[24] but there are no more detailed balancing obligations to mirror those imposed on SNH.[25] As described below, the powers acquired from the Countryside Commission are largely advisory and supportive, rather than offering scope for the implementation of major independent initiatives.

Nature Conservancy Council for England (English Nature)

2.5.17   The integration of conservation and countryside responsibilities which took place in Scotland and Wales did not take place in England, so that after the division of the NCC and the transfer to CCW of countryside functions in Wales, England has been left with two bodies, defined by both functional and geographical limits. In England, one body exercises responsibility for nature conservation, as successor to the NCC; this body's statutory name is the Nature Conservancy Council for England (NCCE) but it operates under the name English Nature. Meanwhile, the Countryside Commission continues as before to perform its functions in relation to the countryside and recreation, but now limited to activities in England.[26]

2.5.18   The Environmental Protection Act 1990 lays down the constitution and general functions of NCCE, as described above.[27] The functions of NCCE are the same as those conservation functions exercised by the other councils. These functions have been described in general terms above and are discussed in more detail throughout the following chapters.

---

[22] The conservation of natural beauty includes the conservation of flora and fauna and geological and physiographical features; *ibid.*, s.130(3).

[23] Earlier legislation had suggested that efforts should be concentrated on the designated areas by stating that the conservation and enhancement of natural beauty were to be sought "particularly" in the designated areas; NPACA, s.1 as originally enacted.

[24] EPA, s.130(2).

[25] See para. 2.5.12, above.

[26] EPA, s.130.

[27] *Ibid.*, ss.128–134, Sched. 6.

Joint Nature Conservation Committee

2.5.19 In order to counter some of the disadvantages of
splitting the NCC, the Environmental Protection Act 1990
requires the conservation councils to establish a Joint Nature
Conservation Committee (JNCC).[28] The Committee is comprised of eleven voting members, being a chairman and three
members appointed by the Secretary of State, the chairman and
one other member (chosen by the council itself) from each of
the conservancy councils, and the chairman of the Countryside
Commission, with two non-voting members appointed by the
Department of the Environment in Northern Ireland.[29] The
chairman and Secretary of State's appointees are not to be
members of any of the councils, and the appointees[30] are
required to be people appearing to the Secretary of State to
have experience in or scientific knowledge of nature conservation, chosen with regard to the recommendation of the chairman
of the Committee and after such consultations as the Secretary
of State considers appropriate.

2.5.20 The Committee shares the broad functions in relation to
nature conservation which the conservancy councils have
inherited from the NCC.[31] More specifically the councils are
entrusted with a range of "special functions" which can be
discharged only through the Committee, although the Secretary
of State can issue directions that the councils themselves should
act.[32] The Committee has control of its own procedure[33] and is
obliged to produce an annual report to the Secretary of State,
who shall lay it before Parliament, and to each of the councils.[34]
The Secretary of State in the exercise of his power to make
grants to the conservation councils can specify that sums are to
be used for the purposes of the Committee.[35]

2.5.21 The "special functions" to be discharged through the
Committee relate to matters at an international level or which

[28] *Ibid.*, s.128(4); this provision and others relating to the JNCC have been
amended by NHSA, s.4 to take account of the subsequent creation of SNH.
[29] *Ibid.*, Sched. 7, paras.2–4.
[30] But not the chairman.
[31] EPA, s.131(5).
[32] *Ibid.*, s.133.
[33] *Ibid.*, Sched. 7, para. 8.
[34] *Ibid.*, Sched. 7, para. 10.
[35] *Ibid.*, s.129(2).

affect Great Britain as whole, thereby seeking to ensure that despite the splitting of the NCC there continues to be consistency and coherence on matters of more than local interest. In particular it is useful for there to be a single body providing advice and information on dealings outside the United Kingdom, a matter of growing importance as the government becomes involved in more European Community and international measures, which increasingly contain obligations for regular monitoring and reporting. These functions[36] are, firstly, the provision of advice to the government on policies for or affecting nature conservation in Great Britain as a whole[37] or outside Great Britain, and, secondly, the provision of advice and dissemination of knowledge to anyone about the same matters. A matter concerns Great Britain as a whole if it is of national[38] or international importance or otherwise affects the interests of Great Britain as a whole (tests which can be satisfied by matters arising in only one of the constituent parts of Great Britain) or if it is a matter arising throughout Great Britain and raising issues common to all three parts. A third special function for the Committee is the establishment of common standards throughout Great Britain for the monitoring of and research into nature conservation and the analysis of the resulting information. Fourthly, and most particularly, the Committee is charged with the periodic review and making of recommendations for change to the lists of wild plants and animals given protection by virtue of Schedules 5 and 8 of the Wildlife and Countryside Act 1981.[39] The Committee can also commission or support research which in its opinion relates to any of the above matters. Advice and information can further be given to any of the conservancy councils on matters which in the opinion of the Committee concern nature conservation for Great Britain as a whole or outside Great Britain.

2.5.22 As these functions are very broadly defined, and the Committee shares the other functions of the conservancy councils, it will take some time before it is clear exactly what the Committee's tasks will be. The legislative framework would allow the relationship between the Committee and the councils to take several forms, and perhaps it is only after the new

---

[36] *Ibid.*, s.133.
[37] *I.e.* Scotland, England and Wales.
[38] Presumably the United Kingdom is the "nation" in mind.
[39] WCA, ss.22(3), 24(1) (amended by EPA, Sched. 9, para. 11); see paras.3.4.2, 6.2.4, below.

councils have come to terms with their own functions that the true role of the Committee will be addressed.

OTHER PUBLIC BODIES

Countryside Commission

2.6.1 The Countryside Commission was constituted in its present form by the Wildlife and Countryside Act 1981,[40] after the Countryside Act 1968[41] had transformed the original National Parks Commission established in 1949[42] by giving it responsibility for the countryside in general and its new name. All of the relevant legislation has now been amended to take account of the fact that it is now CCW which carries out countryside functions in Wales and consequently restricting the Countryside Commission to England.[43] The Commission's status and administration are essentially the same as for the conservancy councils, with Commissioners appointed by the Secretary of State, and the Commission is subject to similar provisions on ministerial directions, annual reports and accounts.[44] Its funds come from the government[45] and the Secretary of State and Treasury must approve arrangements for the grants and loans which it makes to others.[46]

2.6.2 The Commission's functions are the preservation and enhancement of natural beauty[47] and amenity in the countryside and the encouragement of the provision of facilities for the enjoyment of the countryside and open-air enjoyment therein.[48] Included in this is a concern for the need to secure public access to the countryside for recreational purposes and the study of nature.[49] In the exercise of its functions, the Commission must have due regard to the needs of agriculture and forestry and to

---

[40] *Ibid.*, Sched. 13.
[41] CA, ss.1–2.
[42] NPACA, s.1 (as originally enacted).
[43] EPA, Sched. 8.
[44] WCA, Sched. 13.
[45] *Ibid.*, s.47(2).
[46] Local Government Act 1974, s.9.
[47] This includes conservation of flora and fauna and geological and physiographical features; NPACA, s.114(2) (amended by CA, s.21(7)).
[48] CA, s.1(2) (substituted by EPA, Sched. 8, para. 1).
[49] *Ibid.*, s.2(2) (amended by *ibid.* Sched. 8, para. 2).

the economic and social interests of rural areas.[50] The Commission is the body primarily responsible for the designation of National Parks and Areas of Outstanding Natural Beauty, and within the former plays a major consultative and advisory role in relation to the park authorities.[51] Other than in the provision of information and publicity about the countryside and for the benefit of visitors to it,[52] it is only really in relation to experimental schemes demonstrating the application of new techniques or approaches that the Commission can take an executive role.[53] In other areas, particularly the promotion of public access by means of access and public path agreements and orders,[54] the Commission can make initiatives and offer advice, but ultimately depends on planning authorities and others to implement its ideas.[55] The Commission is charged with the task of advising government at all levels on countryside matters, acting on its own initiative as well as in response to formal requests,[56] and is a consultee in many official procedures.

2.6.3 As far as nature conservation is concerned, the Commission's major influence is likely to be in its encouragement of the preservation of habitat, particularly in National Parks, but more generally through its promotion of the countryside as a place to enjoy for its natural beauty. However, the growth of recreational use of areas of the countryside in turn produces new threats of disturbance and damage to habitats, and the Commission will have to balance its twin aims of conserving natural beauty and encouraging recreation. The resolution of such conflicts and debate on them may be more open and subject to greater public scrutiny in England, where there are separate bodies to put forward the arguments for recreation and for nature conservation, than in Scotland and Wales where in the first instance such arguments must take place internally within a single organisation. On the other hand, the ability of SNH and CCW to take a more integrated approach to the countryside, offers advantages over the English position.

---

[50] *Ibid.*, s.37.
[51] NPACA, ss.5–6, 87; see sections 5.10, 5.11, below.
[52] CA, s.2(8).
[53] *Ibid.*, s.4, (partly substituted by WCA, s.40).
[54] NPACA, Pt. V.
[55] As well as advice it can provide practical help in the form of specially skilled staff; CA, s.2(5).
[56] *Ibid.*, s.2(4).

Water

2.6.4 The authorities with responsibility for rivers and other aspects of the aquatic environment can also play a significant part in nature conservation. This is not the place for a detailed examination of water law in all its complexity[57]; all that the following paragraphs aim to do is to identify which authorities have responsibility for the major activities in this field.[58]

2.6.5 In England and Wales the position has been simplified by the restructuring of the water industry.[59] This involved the creation of the National Rivers Authority (NRA) to safeguard and manage water resources.[60] The NRA is a public authority enjoying a relationship to government similar to that of the conservancy councils[61] and charged with a broad range of tasks relating to the management of water resources, the control of pollution, flood control, land drainage, fisheries and navigation.[62] In its operation it is assisted by an advisory committee for Wales, regional rivers advisory committees, regional and local advisory committees on fisheries and regional and local flood defence committees.[63] Under various provisions the NRA has a general duty (to such extent as it considers desirable) to promote the conservation and enhancement of the natural beauty and amenity of inland and coastal waters and associated land, and the conservation of flora and fauna dependent on the aquatic environment,[64] and (so far as may be compatible with the purpose of the relevant enactments) to exercise its statutory powers in such a way as to further these ends.[65] The NRA is also bound to consult the conservancy councils or the National Park authorities in the event of works which it carries out or

---

[57] See *Stair Memorial Encyclopaedia of the Laws of Scotland* (1989), Vol. 25, "Water and Water Rights," "Water Supply"; W. Howarth, *The Law of the National Rivers Authority* (1990); W. Howarth, *Wisdom's Law of Watercourses* (5th ed., 1992); J.H. Bates, *Water and Drainage Law* (1990).

[58] See further section 8.6, below.

[59] The restructuring was carried out by the Water Act 1989, but the relevant legislation has since been consolidated in the Water Industry Act 1991, the Water Resources Act 1991, the Statutory Water Companies Act 1991, the Land Drainage Act 1991 and the Water Consolidation (Consequential Provisions) Act 1991.

[60] Water Resources Act 1991, s.1.

[61] See in particular, *ibid.*, ss.1, 5, 187 and Sched. 1.

[62] *Ibid.*, s.2.

[63] *Ibid.*, ss.6–14.

[64] *Ibid.*, s.2(2).

[65] *Ibid.*, s.16; Land Drainage Act 1991, s.12.

authorises posing a threat to sites which these bodies have notified as being of special importance.[66]

2.6.6 The NRA can impose restrictions on the abstraction or impounding of water,[67] setting a minimum acceptable flow for specific waters,[68] and imposing further restrictions in the event of drought.[69] It is responsible for issuing consents where activities are likely to lead to the entry (direct or indirect) of polluting matter into waters and for other pollution control measures,[70] and for the general supervision of flood defence.[71] The NRA is under a duty to maintain, improve and develop fisheries[72] and may have navigation functions transferred to it from existing navigation and harbour authorities.[73] Land drainage is also under the supervision of the NRA,[74] although in most circumstances immediate responsibility lies with the internal drainage boards comprised of elected and appointed members under the Land Drainage Act 1991.[75] All of these responsibilities can obviously have a major impact on the survival and quality of the habitat necessary for communities of aquatic plants and animals.

2.6.7 In Scotland similar powers exist, but they are distributed between a variety of authorities. A general duty to promote the conservation of water resources is imposed on the Secretary of State.[76] The maintenance of water quality is a task for the river purification authorities, namely the islands councils and on the mainland the river purification boards, comprising representatives from the local authorities in the area and members appointed by the Secretary of State.[77] These authorities are also responsible for the management of water resources,[78] including

[66] *Ibid.*, s.17; *ibid.* s.13.
[67] *Ibid.*, Pt. II, Chap.II.
[68] *Ibid.*, Pt. II, Chap. I.
[69] *Ibid.*, Pt. II, Chap. III.
[70] *Ibid.*, Pt. III.
[71] *Ibid.*, Pt. IV.
[72] *Ibid.*, Pt. V.
[73] *Ibid.*, s.2 and Sched. 2.
[74] Land Drainage Act 1991, s.7.
[75] *Ibid.*, s.1 and Scheds.1,2.
[76] Water (Scotland) Act 1980, s.1.
[77] Rivers (Prevention of Pollution) (Scotland) Act 1951, s.17 (amended by Local Government (Scotland) Act 1973, Sched. 16, para. 5; Control of Pollution Act 1974, Sched. 3, para. 13; NHSA Sched. 10, para. 1); Local Government (Scotland) Act 1973, ss.135,135A (added by NHSA, Sched. 10, para. 6).
[78] Rivers (Prevention of Pollution) (Scotland) Act 1951, s.17.

controls on the abstraction of water for irrigation.[79] The maintenance of water supplies is the responsibility of the regional and island councils as water authorities[80] (supplemented by the work of water development boards[81]), *e.g.* it is they who can initiate the procedure for drought orders.[82] Flood prevention is a matter for regional and islands councils.[83] Statutory control of land drainage is primarily in ministerial hands,[84] while matters affecting fisheries are dealt with by the Secretary of State, proprietors and district salmon fishery boards.[85] Responsibility for the aquatic environment is thus much more fragmented in Scotland, and the activities of a range of authorities can affect the habitat for aquatic life.

Forestry

2.6.8 In view of the large areas affected and the dramatic impact on wildlife habitat caused by the planting or felling of trees on a large scale, the actions of the Forestry Commission can be of considerable significance for nature conservation, a fact amply demonstrated in the controversy over afforestation in the Flow Country of Sutherland. The Commission fulfils a dual role, being responsible for the management of the large areas of productive woodland still in public ownership, and for encouraging and regulating the development of private forestry. To cope with these potentially conflicting functions, the Commission is now organised as two branches, Forest Enterprise, managing plantations, and the Forestry Authority, exercising the regulatory function. In the past the Commission itself was active in the establishment of new plantations, but government policy in recent years has moved the main responsibility for extending afforestation to the private sector, guided by the Commission's supervisory powers.

2.6.9 There are up to ten Commissioners, appointed by the Crown, and including at least three with knowledge and experience of forestry, one with relevant scientific attainments

[79] NHSA, Pt. II.
[80] Water (Scotland) Act 1980, s.3.
[81] *Ibid.*, Pt. VIII.
[82] NHSA, Pt. III.
[83] Flood Prevention (Scotland) Act 1961, s.1 (amended by Local Government (Scotland) Act 1973, s.137).
[84] Land Drainage (Scotland) Acts 1930, 1941 and 1958.
[85] Constituted under the Salmon Act 1986.

and one with experience of the timber trade.[86] The Commission
is subject to fairly standard provisions on preparing annual
reports and accounts, and is subject to ministerial direction.[87]
The Commission's duty is to promote the interests of forestry,
the development of afforestation and the production and supply
of timber and other forest products,[88] but this is now tempered
by an obligation to endeavour to achieve a reasonable balance
between these aims and the conservation and enhancement of
natural beauty and the conservation of flora and fauna and
geological and physiographical features of special interest.[89] This
obligation reflected a growing appreciation within the Commission of environmental matters, and there has been a very
significant shift in policies during the last decade or so, although
as trees grow only slowly, the effects of this will not be apparent
for some time.

2.6.10   The Forestry Commission's control over private forestry
is achieved in two ways, discussed more fully in Chapter 6.[90] As
far as felling is concerned, there is a full statutory scheme which
imposes a requirement for a felling licence to be obtained
before any significant felling is carried out. For planting, there
are no statutory restrictions, but control is exercised through
grant schemes operating in an economic context which means
that no major planting will be economically viable without grant
support. These grant schemes now take into account considerations of habitat diversity, environmental protection and amenity
as well as commercial timber production. Proposals for new
planting in sensitive areas may also be subject to an
environmental assessment.[91] These arrangements mean that the
Commission will be involved in considering the desirability of
any major forestry activities and is in a position to ensure that
conservation matters are at least taken into account.

2.6.11   The Commission encourages visitors to parts of its land
and has the power to provide facilities for them,[92] including in

[86] Forestry Act 1967, s.2 (amended by Forestry Act 1981, s.5).
[87] See especially *ibid.*, ss.1(4),44,45 and Sched. 1.
[88] *Ibid.*, s.1(2).
[89] *Ibid.*, s.1(3A) (added by Wildlife and Countryside (Amendment) Act 1985,
s.4).
[90] See section 6.3, below.
[91] Environmental Assessment (Afforestation) Regulations 1988, SI 1988
No. 1207; see paras.6.3.12–6.3.13, below.
[92] CSA, s.58; CA, s.23.

Scotland the express power to appoint rangers.[93] There is also a power to make bye-laws to regulate the conduct of those on land managed by the Commission,[94] and bye-laws have been made prohibiting the lighting of fires, any form of damage to trees and plants, the wilful disturbance of animals and their lairs of all sorts and the catching of butterflies, moths and dragonflies (one of the few legislative measures to make special mention of insects of any sort).[95] In other words, visitors must ensure that the natural environment in the woodland is disturbed as little as possible by their presence, so that on Forestry Commission land the general laws protecting plants and animals are considerably strengthened.

Crown Estate Commission

2.6.12 The Crown Estate Commissioners are responsible for administering the rights of the Crown in areas of land where the Crown retains a major interest,[96] most noticeably the foreshore and seabed.[97] Any activity, *e.g.* fish farming, which involves the positioning of structures on or over the seabed will require their permission. The Commissioners are appointed by the Crown,[98] are subject to ministerial direction[99] and report annually to Her Majesty and Parliament.[1] Regulations can be made to control the conduct of the public granted access to Crown land.[2] The general duty of the Commissioners is, while maintaining the Crown Estate as an estate in land, to maintain and enhance its value and the return obtained from it, but with due regard to the requirements of good management.[3] No specific environmental duty is placed on the Commissioners, but they are bound by the general balancing duties applicable to all public bodies.[4] Other than the requirement for environmental assessment of

---

[93] *Ibid.*, s.65 (amended by Countryside (Scotland) Act 1981, Sched. 1, para. 4).

[94] Forestry Act 1967, s.46.

[95] Forestry Commission Byelaws 1982, S.I. 1982 No. 648.

[96] Crown Estates Act 1961, s.1.

[97] See generally M.E. Deans, "The Crown Estate Commissioners — Their Role and Responsibilities in respect of the Foreshore and Sea-bed around Scotland" — (1986) 4 *Journal of Energy and Natural Resources Law* 166.

[98] Crown Estates Act 1961, Sched. 1, para. 1.

[99] *Ibid.*, s.1(4).

[1] *Ibid.*, s.2.

[2] *Ibid.*, s.6.

[3] *Ibid.*, s.1(2).

[4] CSA, s.66; CA, s.11; see para. 2.2.2, above.

certain marine salmon farming developments,[5] there are no other legal restrictions specifically imposed on the Commissioners for environmental or conservation grounds, and they enjoy a wide immunity from legal challenge to the exercise of their powers.[6] This lack of legal control and a lack of openness in their proceedings have often been criticised.

Red Deer Commission

2.6.13 In Scotland the Red Deer Commission has general responsibility for the conservation and control of deer, initially limited to red deer but subsequently extended to other species.[7] The Commission is appointed by the Secretary of State and comprises a chairman and twelve members drawn from nominees put forward by organisations representing the following groups: one each from SNH and the National Environmental Research Council, three from the owners of land used for agriculture and forestry, two from sporting interests in deer, three from farmers and crofters (at least one from each category), and two from hill sheep farmers.[8] Local panels, again reflecting a balance of interests can be established to carry out the Commission's tasks in particular localities.[9] An annual report must be presented to the Secretary of State.[10]

2.6.14 The Commission advises both the Secretary of State[11] and landowners, collaborates with scientific investigations and supports or carries out its own research into matters affecting deer in Scotland.[12] It has power to deal with marauding deer and to introduce wider deer control schemes,[13] and can provide services and equipment to those involved in the control of deer.[14] Authority from the Commission acts as an exemption

[5] Environmental Assessment (Salmon Farming in Marine Waters) Regulations 1988, S.I. 1988 No. 1218; see para. 8.3.7, below.
[6] Crown Estates Act 1961, s.1(5); see *Walford* v. *Crown Estates Commissioners*, 1988 S.L.T. 377.
[7] Deer (Scotland) Act 1959, almost every section of which has been amended by the Deer (Amendment) (Scotland) Act 1982.
[8] *Ibid.*, s.1(3),(4) (amended by Nature Conservancy Council Act 1973, Sched. 1, para. 4; NHSA, Sched. 2, para. 2).
[9] *Ibid.*, s.2.
[10] *Ibid.*, s.3(2).
[11] *Ibid.*, s.3(1).
[12] *Ibid.*, s.4.
[13] *Ibid.*, ss.6–7 (significantly amended by Deer (Scotland) Act 1982).
[14] *Ibid.*, s.12.

from the normal requirements for game licences to kill deer.[15]
The details of the Commission's powers are discussed in relation
to the law on deer generally.[16]

Natural Environment Research Council

2.6.15 The Natural Environment Research Council plays a
major role in research relevant to nature conservation.
Established under royal charter and the Science and Technology
Act 1965, its statutory functions are to carry out research in
earth sciences and ecology, to facilitate, encourage and support
such research by other institutions and people, and to
disseminate knowledge and provide advice on these subjects.[17]
It has no legal powers to intervene directly for the benefit of
nature conservation, although it is represented on some other
bodies which do have direct powers and must be consulted in
some circumstances. However the research which it carries out
in its own institutes and supports elsewhere is of major
significance, and it is the parent body for, among others, the
British Antarctic Survey, the British Geological Survey, the
Institute of Terrestrial Ecology and the Institute of Freshwater
Ecology.[18]

NON-GOVERNMENTAL BODIES

2.7.1 Non-governmental bodies have played a major part in
the development of concern for nature conservation and in the
achievement of practical measures to this end. A large number
of charitable bodies have been active in this field, providing a
voice for those concerned for nature and actively seeking ways
of preserving threatened habitat and species. Much can be
achieved by small groups and even individuals in relation to
particular sites, and apparently insignificant tasks such as the
recording of the distribution and preferred habitat of species in
an area provide essential information for the creation of the

[15] *Ibid.*, s.14.
[16] See paras.4.2.17–4.2.22, below.
[17] Science and Technology Act 1965, s.1(3).
[18] See J. Sheail, *Natural Environment Research Council: A History* (1992).

scientific base on which major decisions can be founded. The contribution made by such voluntary efforts to nature conservation in Britain is immense.

2.7.2 There is a large number of ways in which such activities can be organised, and few raise any legal issues specific to this area. The general law of trusts, charities and unincorporated associations must however be borne in mind, especially if an organisation wishes to acquire an interest in land or to enter other formal legal relationships in order to secure its aims. Careful attention to the legal formalities is essential if any effective long-term arrangements are to be made.

2.7.3 A number of charities, most notably the Royal Society for the Protection of Birds, do own and manage significant areas of land as nature reserves and this is one place where the law does come into contact with the activities of such voluntary bodies. Land which is being managed as a nature reserve by any body approved by a conservancy council and which the council considers to be of national importance can be declared by it to be a National Nature Reserve[19]; this means that the council can make bye-laws for the protection of the reserve in the same way as it can for those which it manages itself.[20] This power provides a means by which the voluntary efforts in this field can be integrated with the official ones and offers official recognition of the efforts made by the voluntary bodies to support those of the public conservation bodies.

National Trusts

2.7.4 The National Trusts occupy a position halfway between official and private organisations, in that although in no way governmental bodies, they do enjoy some statutory recognition. The National Trust was incorporated under a private Act of Parliament in 1907,[21] and the National Trust for Scotland likewise in 1935,[22] and their constitutions are embodied in statute. Both have among their purposes

[19] WCA, s.35.
[20] NPACA, s.20; see section 5.2, below.
[21] National Trust Act 1907; see also National Trust Charity Scheme Confirmation Act 1919 and National Trust Acts 1937, 1939, 1953, 1971.
[22] National Trust for Scotland Order Confirmation Act 1935; see also National Trust for Scotland Order Confirmation Acts 1938, 1947, 1952, 1961, 1973.

"the permanent preservation for the benefit of the nation of lands ... of beauty or historic interest and ... the preservation (so far as practicable) of their natural aspect and features and animal and plant life"[23]

so that nature conservation does fall within the purposes for which the Trusts can act.

2.7.5 Certain land which is held by the Trusts is declared to be inalienable,[24] so that there is a guarantee that it will continue to be used in accordance with the Trusts' purposes. Such land is accorded special treatment in other legislation, *e.g.* special procedures are required for its compulsory purchase.[25] On land in which they have an interest, the Trusts have the power to make bye-laws, including ones to prevent any damage or disturbance to plants or animals,[26] and in England and Wales the power[27] to make and enforce restrictive covenants even though no adjacent land is held may allow something akin to a management agreement.[28] As the Trusts are significant land-owners, particularly in areas of scenic beauty, considerable benefits for nature conservation can arise from these provisions.

EUROPEAN COMMUNITY

2.8.1 Although the European Community had been active on environmental issues for many years previously, it was only in 1987 that it was given express competence to act in this field. The impact of the Community is felt through its legislation on environmental topics and through the influence of its policies in other areas, particularly agriculture, which play a major part in shaping the way in which individuals and businesses act within the UK. An awareness of the European dimension is essential for a full understanding of the law on nature conservation; while the substantive rules are described where relevant in other

[23] National Trust Act 1907, s.4(1); National Trust for Scotland Order Confirmation Act 1935, Sched., s.4.
[24] *Ibid.*, s.21; *ibid.*, s.22.
[25] Acquisition of Land (Authorisation Procedure) (Scotland) Act 1947, s.1(2); Acquisition of Land Act 1981, s.18.
[26] National Trust Act 1971, s.24; National Trust for Scotland Order Confirmation Act 1935, Sched., s.33.
[27] National Trust Act 1937, s.8.
[28] See para. 5.1.5, below.

chapters below, especially Chapter 7, this section offers a brief outline of the basic framework of Community involvement in conservation matters.[29]

2.8.2 The powers and competence of the Community depend upon the treaties which create it, and at first there was no reference in these to environmental matters. However, this did not prevent the Community from taking an interest in such issues and in addition to environmental considerations affecting its activities in other areas, a range of specifically environmental measures[30] were produced under the authority of two general provisions of the EEC Treaty: Art. 100 which provides for the approximation (or harmonisation) of laws affecting the establishment or functioning of the common market, and Art. 235 which allows measures to be taken where necessary for the attainment of the Community's objectives and where the Treaty has not specifically provided the necessary powers. These were not an altogether satisfactory basis for Community activity in this field and when the treaties were amended by the Single European Act which took effect in 1987, a new title was added conferring on the Community powers relating to the environment.[31] These provisions are amended by the Treaty on European Union (the Maastricht Agreement).

2.8.3 The new provisions allow the Community to take action with the objectives of preserving, protecting and improving the environment, contributing towards the protection of human health and ensuring the prudent and rational utilisation of natural resources,[32] and require that environmental protection be a component of the Community's other policies.[33] Community action should be based on the principles that preventive action should be taken, that environmental damage should be rectified at source and that the polluter should pay; the precautionary principle is added to this list by the Treaty on

---

[29] See generally L. Krämer, *EEC Treaty and Environmental Protection* (1990).
[30] *e.g.* the Directive on the Conservation of Wild Birds (79/409) made in 1979; see section 7.4, below.
[31] Title VII of the EEC Treaty (Arts. 130r–130t), added by Art. 25 of the Single European Act; for a detailed account of these provisions see Krämer, *op. cit.*.
[32] EEC Treaty, Art. 130r(1).
[33] *Ibid.*, Art 130r(2); the amendments in the Treaty on European Union strengthen this by stating that stating that "environmental protection requirements must be integrated into the definition and implementation of other Community policies."

European Union.[34] The action to be taken is to be decided by the Council of Ministers acting on proposals from the Commission[35] and in consultation with the Parliament and Economic and Social Committee; the Council may define certain matters as ones which can be dealt with by a qualified majority within the Council as opposed to requiring unanimous support.[36] Member States remain free to adopt more stringent protective measures for themselves, provided that these are compatible with their broader Community obligations.[37] A number of proposals have been made resting on the authority of these new treaty provisions, and more can be expected in future years.[38]

2.8.4 Legislation from the Community comes in the form of Regulations and Directives. Regulations automatically become part of the domestic law of the Member States and must be followed and enforced in the same way as other laws within the national legal system. Directives are addressed to the Member States which are required to take whatever measures are necessary to ensure that the objectives set out in Directive are achieved within their own national legal systems within the period specified in the Directive. Therefore where the national law does not already provide for the requirements of the Directive, new national legislation should be introduced, and in the UK this can be achieved by delegated legislation under the European Communities Act 1972.[39] Any implementing measures are to be interpreted so far as possible to ensure that the terms of the Directive are in fact completely satisfied.[40]

2.8.5 If a Directive has not been fully or properly implemented, the European Commission (frequently acting on the basis of a complaint from an individual) can take steps to ensure

[34] *Ibid.*, Art. 130r(2) as amended by the Treaty on European Union.

[35] Directorate General XI of the Commission has responsibility for the Environment, Nuclear Safety and Civil Protection.

[36] EEC Treaty, Art. 130s; the procedures are amended by the Treaty on European Union.

[37] *Ibid.*, Art. 130t.

[38] All of the Community's legislation on environmental matters is printed in a form as amended up until September 1991 in *European Community Environment Legislation* (1992); Vol. 4 deals with "Nature."

[39] European Communities Act 1972 s.2(2); to give one example, it was under this authority that the various regulations were made to implement the Directive on environmental assessment, see section 8.3, below.

[40] *Litster* v. *Forth Dry Dock and Engineering Co. Ltd.*, 1989 S.L.T. 540.

that the defaulting state does fulfil its obligation to give effect to the Directive, a process which can lead ultimately to an action before the European Court of Justice. Such actions have been necessary on several occasions to enforce the implementation of the Directive on the Conservation of Wild Birds.[41] A Directive which has not been implemented by the due date may also have direct effect.[42] This means that an individual can rely on its terms as if they were part of the national law in any dealings with a branch of defaulting state[43] (but not against other individuals),[44] provided that the relevant provisions are sufficiently precise and unconditional for it to be clear exactly what the legal position would have been had the Directive been properly implemented.[45] It is thus important to know what is provided in Community Law, both as a guide to the proper interpretation of domestic law implementing its terms and as a source of law which may supplement or override[46] domestic provisions. An individual who has suffered harm as a direct result of a Member State failing to implement a Directive may also be entitled to claim compensation from that state.[47] Although some of the measures on the protection of particular species are precise enough to be given direct effect, much of the legislation on nature conservation contains too great an element of discretion on the part of the Member State to be given direct effect,[48] and it is unlikely that any individual will be able to demonstrate a sufficiently direct loss to benefit from the potential for compensation.

[41] Directive 79/409; see para. 7.4.10, below.

[42] *Van Duyn* v. *Home Office* (41/74) [1974] E.C.R. 1337, *Pubblico Ministero* v. *Ratti* (148/78) [1979] E.C.R. 1629.

[43] This covers all public authorities and other bodies given powers or responsibilities over and above those of private individuals and companies; *Foster* v. *British Gas plc* (C–188/89) [1990] E.C.R. I–3313, [1991] Q.B. 405.

[44] *Marshall* v. *Southampton and South West Hampshire Area Health Authority (Teaching)* (152/84) [1986] E.C.R. 723, [1986] Q.B. 401.

[45] *Becker* v. *Finanzamt Münster-Innenstadt* (8/81) [1982] E.C.R. 53; for a discussion of direct effect in an environmental context see C.T. Reid & J.D. Hunter, "Forestry, Environment and Europe" 1991 S.L.T. (News) 274; L. Krämer, "The Implementation of Community Environmental Directives within Member States: Some Implications of the Direct Effect Doctrine" (1991) 3 J.E.L. 39; R. Macrory, "Environmental Assessment and Community Law" (1992) 4 J.E.L. 298.

[46] *R.* v. *Secretary of State for Transport, ex p. Factortame Ltd. (No. 2)* [1991] 1 A.C. 603.

[47] *Francovich, Bonifaci and Others* v. *Italy* (C–6/90, C–9/90) [1993] 2 C.M.L.R. 66.

[48] See comments on the Birds Directive in *Kincardine and Deeside District Council* v. *Forestry Commissioners*, 1992 S.L.T. 1180.

2.8.6 Community law has had a major impact on all aspects of environmental law in Great Britain. As far as nature conservation is concerned, the need to comply with the Birds Directive was one of the factors which led to the Wildlife and Countryside Act 1981, and the details of the law continue to be refined to ensure adequate compliance.[49] The new Directive on Habitats and Species[50] will provide a further standard against which the adequacy of the British law will be rigorously tested. Even if the Community law cannot be given direct effect to override the domestic legislation, the threat of enforcement action before the European Court and the publicity which even the consideration of the issue by the Commission can attract, mean that Community law acts as an important constraint on the development and operation of the law in Great Britain. The provisions of Community law should be studied and taken into account as thoroughly as those of Parliament.

---

[49] See the recent changes affecting pest species of bird; para. 3.3.7, below.
[50] Directive 92/43; see paras.7.4.12–7.4.35, below.

3. Protection of Wild Animals

3.1.1 The most straightforward legal approach to protecting wildlife is to enact laws punishing people who cause it direct harm. Most of the early legislation designed to preserve game and other species considered to be of value took this form, and similar laws continue to play a major role in nature conservation, although increasingly supported by measures to protect the habitat necessary for the continued survival of the protected species. The decline of many species is the direct result of man's deliberate conduct in exterminating them, for food, fur and feathers, for sport or display, or to prevent harm to more valued species. Putting an end to such direct assaults is an obvious and essential first step in seeking to protect wildlife.

3.1.2 Such laws can be relatively simple. Certain actions directed towards certain specified animals are prohibited; the law affects everybody and is of general application. The straightforward nature of such measures means that they can be simple to understand, with real benefits in terms of publicity and education. Although detracting from the simplicity of the law, a further advantage of structuring the law on the basis of prohibiting direct harm to wildlife is that the particular threats to each species can be specifically addressed. Some creatures are in need of more protection than others; some are the special victims of particular conduct. In other cases a degree of exploitation may be tolerated whilst protection is also required in some situations. Enacting a separate law for each species would achieve the maximum of individual attention, but this would be quite unacceptable in terms of the legislative time and effort required, to say nothing of producing an unworkably fragmented system. To reduce this problem, species can be grouped into a handful of categories, and different regimes designed for each category, offering different levels of protection whilst leaving the law in a relatively manageable state.

3.1.3 Aside from the risk of excessive fragmentation, three factors may reduce the effectiveness of this very direct approach to conservation legislation. By requiring the express prohibition of the undesired conduct, there is a risk that some forms of harm, or some species in need of protection, will be omitted, or will come to be appreciated only after the law is in place. The presence of gaps and possible loopholes may undermine the law, and it may be difficult to persuade the legislators to make the effort to enact the necessary amendments promptly. In the second place, such legislation is likely to favour the large and "cuddly" animals. More tends to be known about such animals, they are more in the public's eye, and elected legislators are more likely to act on behalf of those creatures which enjoy public sympathy than those whose importance or value is not widely appreciated.[1] Thus there is in Britain special legislation for badgers and seals, but no Woodlice Act is readily conceivable, however endangered or ecologically vital some species of woodlice may be in the wild.

3.1.4 The third feature which besets specific legislation is that of identifying the creatures and plants to which protection is given. A law which makes it a criminal offence to disturb certain species will only work if potential offenders can identify those species and moderate their conduct accordingly. How many people can tell the difference between the reed warbler and the strictly protected marsh warbler,[2] between the black-headed gull and the protected little and Mediterranean gulls? This is a problem which is even more severe in relation to the law on plants and invertebrates. The good intentions of such legislation may be undermined by a lack of public knowledge which makes a nonsense of the attempt to categorise species carefully.

3.1.5 The law relating to wildlife is, however, not concerned only with its protection. It is also concerned to permit and regulate the exploitation of wild creatures through various forms of hunting, and to secure the destruction of those creatures viewed as pests. There are thus provisions imposing require-ments to destroy damaging species, regulating who can hunt for

---

[1] See, for example, the leader in *The Times* (January 4, 1991) and subsequent letters (January 12, 1991) after adders were given statutory protection.

[2] A leading field guide to birds describes the marsh warbler as "Virtually impossible to distinguish from Reed Warblers ... in the field except by song", H. Heinzel, *et al.*, *The Birds of Britain and Europe* (1972), p. 224.

animals and controlling the means which can be used to kill or take animals and birds. Any attempt to present an overall picture of the law regulating the harm which can be done to wildlife must therefore bring together provisions from these somewhat different areas. It may seem odd in a book on nature conservation to discuss laws designed to allow, or even require, the destruction of wildlife, but such measures play an essential part in the overall legal background for conservation, and even the law on hunting plays a part in conservation by imposing a degree of regulation as opposed to allowing a destructive or indiscriminate free-for-all. Moreover, such measures may be used to achieve incidental benefits for wildlife generally, *e.g.* by acquiring but not exercising the right to hunt game, interested parties can offer some protection to animals and birds in a particular area.

3.1.6 The law remains fragmented, and this chapter and the next endeavour to integrate the various threads of the law, presenting a picture based on the eventual legal results, rather than the structure of the legislation. The arrangement which follows draws a general distinction between measures which have as their primary objective the conservation of wildlife, those which seek primarily to regulate the exploitation of particular species, those which restrict the means by which creatures can be killed or caught, and those which require the destruction of species. This distinction is artificial, since the law in most cases contains elements of all four functions, but it does offer a rough framework on which to structure what would otherwise be a compilation of isolated pieces of legislation in either chronological or some arbitrary order. A degree of repetition has been inevitable in the attempt to present as coherent a guide as possible to this jumble of law.

WILDLIFE AND COUNTRYSIDE ACT 1981

3.2.1 The single most important statute relating to the protection of wildlife is the Wildlife and Countryside Act 1981, which creates a large number of offences relating to the killing and taking of birds, other animals and plants. These provisions, contained in Part I of the Act, will be considered in detail below,[3] but some points of general application can usefully be considered at this stage.

3.2.2 The Act relies heavily on the use of schedules to identify categories of species which are to enjoy differing levels of protection under the Act. In this way the needs of many species can be catered for without the Act becoming too fragmented or even more complex. This approach also has the advantage that whilst the basic provisions are contained in parliamentary legislation, their detailed application is determined by the content of the schedules, which can be more easily amended. The Secretary of State is given wide powers to alter the various schedules, and many of the other details of the legislation, by means of statutory instruments,[4] in most cases involving Parliament only through the possibility of annulment by either House.[5] This enables the law to retain some flexibility and to respond to changing pressures or scientific appreciation of the status of particular species. There is an obligation on the conservancy councils, acting jointly through the JNCC, to review the schedules of protected animals and plants every five years.[6] A common feature is that offences in relation to the species given additional protection attract a "special penalty," more severe than if other species are involved.[7]

3.2.3 The central provisions in Part I of the Act outlawing the killing and taking of animals, birds and their eggs are backed up by a number of other provisions to overcome the difficulty of proving all of the elements of such offences. When a dead eagle, an osprey's egg or an otter's pelt is discovered, it may be impossible for anyone but the persons involved to know exactly when and in what circumstances it was killed or taken. The difficulties of providing legal proof of deliberate killing, etc., are so great that most offenders would probably escape were it not for the supporting provisions which exist. It is therefore made an offence simply to possess wild birds and animals, and strict

[3] See section 6.2, below in relation to plants.

[4] WCA, s.22.

[5] *Ibid.*, s.26; express parliamentary approval is required for amendments to the provisions on the methods of killing or taking birds or animals (s.26(3)).

[6] *Ibid.*, s.24(1) (amended by EPA, Sched. 9 para. 11).

[7] Fines at level 5 as opposed to level 3; *ibid.*, s.21 (amended for Scotland by Criminal Procedure (Scotland) Act 1975, s.289G (added by Criminal Justice Act 1982, s.54); for England and Wales by Criminal Justice Act 1982, s.46).

liability is employed. The strict liability is mitigated by a number of defences, but the onus is placed on the accused to show that his conduct has been innocent, a reflection both of the fact that he alone is likely to be in a position to provide evidence on such matters, and of the policy that those who wish to keep wild animals or birds (alive or dead) or birds' eggs should do so at their own risk.[8]

3.2.4 The enforcement of the law is assisted by a range of powers granted under s.19 of the Act.[9] A police officer who reasonably suspects that a person is committing or has committed an offence under Part I of the Act and reasonably suspects that evidence of the commission of the offence may be found, is authorised without warrant to stop and search the person, and to search or examine anything which the suspect is using or has in his possession. There is also a power to seize and detain anything which may be evidence of the commission of an offence; it has been held that this power is of general application, and is not restricted to circumstances where there has been a search under the previous provisions.[10] A suspect who fails to give his name and address to the police officer's satisfaction may be arrested without warrant.[11] In order to exercise these powers, a power of entry to land other than a dwelling house is given where the suspicion is that an offence is currently being committed. Warrants are available from justices of the peace[12] to authorise entry and search in other circumstances.

3.2.5 A further general feature is the possibility for exemptions to be granted from many of the Act's provisions, over and above the general defences which exist. Licences which authorise conduct which would otherwise be an offence may be obtained for a variety of reasons, from the Secretary of State, the agriculture ministers or the conservancy councils.[13] These licences may be conditional, may be general or specific, may be

---

[8] See *Kirkland* v. *Robinson* [1987] Crim.L.R. 643.
[9] As amended by Police and Criminal Evidence Act 1984, Sched. 6 para. 25, Sched. 7.
[10] *Whitelaw* v. *Haining*, 1992 S.L.T. 956.
[11] WCA, s.19(1)(c) for Scotland; for England and Wales this provision has been repealed by the Police and Criminal Evidence Act 1984, Sched. 7, but the general power of arrest under s.25 of that Act is available.
[12] Expressly including sheriffs in Scotland.
[13] WCA, s.16.

personal or in favour of a class of people and will be of fixed duration.[14] A table of which authorities can grant a licence and for what purposes appears as Appendix C below. The possibility of obtaining a licence must always be borne in mind when the prohibitions in the Act are being considered, and the scope and availability of licences can considerably alter the effect of the law in practice.[15]

3.2.6 One definition of general application can also be conveniently discussed here. In several places the Act declares that it is permissible for an "authorised person" to do acts which are otherwise criminal. For these purposes an authorised person is defined as: the owner or occupier of the land where the action takes place or someone authorised by him, a person authorised in writing by the local authority (either tier) for the area, or a person authorised in writing by the National Rivers Authority, a water undertaker or a sewerage undertaker. In relation to birds, authorisation in writing can also be provided by the conservancy councils, a district salmon fishery board in Scotland or a local fisheries committee in England and Wales.[16]

3.2.7 A final point to mention in passing is that although in some contexts references to the taking of animals includes references to their taking by killing (especially in the context of the taking of game), in the legal context "taking" appears to mean only their capture.[17] This contrasts with the position in the U.S.A. where the legislation protecting endangered species prohibits their "taking" and gives this term the wide definition of "harass, harm, pursue, hunt, shoot, wound, kill, trap, capture or collect,"[18] such that there is debate over the extent to which this broad view of taking can extend to cover habitat damage which harms a creature's chances of survival.[19]

[14] *Ibid.*, s.16(5); licences authorising the killing of birds or animals must specify the area and method of killing and have a maximum validity of two years (s.16(6)).
[15] *E.g.*, in relation to pest species of birds; see paras. 3.3.7–3.3.8, below.
[16] WCA, s.27 (amended by Water Act 1989, Sched. 25 para. 66, Sched. 27; Local Government Act 1985, Sched. 17; EPA, Sched. 9 para. 11.).
[17] The legislation consistently uses separate words for killing and taking; *cf. Wells* v. *Hardy* [1964] 2 Q.B. 447, catching and returning fish is not "taking" for the Larceny Act 1861.
[18] Endangered Species Act 1973 (U.S.A.), s.3.
[19] M.E. Field, "The Evolution of the Wildlife Taking Concept from its Beginning to its Culmination in the Endangered Species Act" (1984) 21 Hous. L.R. 457.

Capturing animals (whether to kill them or to keep them) in theory poses different problems from direct killing in terms of legal control, but since in almost all cases the taking of animals is regulated along with their killing, it is possible to deal with both together.

BIRDS AND EGGS

3.3.1 The main legislation concerning birds is to be found in Part I of the Wildlife and Countryside Act 1981 which replaced the previous legislation protecting birds. The starting point for the law is the simple statement in s.1(1) that it is an offence for any person intentionally to kill, injure or take any wild bird. However, in order to meet the requirements of different species, birds are divided into various categories: some are covered simply by the general law, some given added protection, others are given protection during a close season only and pest species are in practice deprived of the general protection granted to others. In all cases it must be remembered that licences may be granted allowing exemptions from the various prohibitions in the 1981 Act, but the methods by which birds can be killed or taken are always controlled.[20] Legal protection for birds is also granted by the provisions of the European Community's Birds Directive,[21] discussed in Chapter 7, and separate rules apply to game birds.[22]

The general position

3.3.2 It is an offence for any person intentionally to do any of the following: to kill, injure or take any wild bird, to take, damage or destroy the nest of a wild bird while it is in use or being built, or to take or destroy the egg of any wild bird.[23] A wild bird is defined as being any bird ordinarily resident in or a visitor to Great Britain in a wild state, other than poultry or game birds, and anything calculated to prevent the hatching of an egg is included within the meaning of destroying eggs.[24] The

[20] See paras. 4.4.15–4.4.17, below.
[21] Directive 79/409; see section 7.4, below.
[22] See section 4.2, below.
[23] WCA, s.1(1).
[24] *Ibid.*, s.27.

offence does not apply to birds shown to have been bred in captivity.[25] It is not clear whether the intention applies only to the killing, etc. or extends to require knowledge that the bird was "wild" for the purposes of the Act. In relation to the taking or destruction of eggs, the law of corroboration is relaxed in Scotland so that a person may be convicted on the evidence of one witness.[26-27]

3.3.3 A number of defences are provided to limit the scope of this general prohibition. A person's taking of disabled birds in order to tend and release them is excluded, as is the mercy killing of seriously disabled birds with no reasonable chance of recovery, provided in both cases that the original injury was not the result of that person's unlawful act.[28] A more general defence excludes acts which are the incidental result of a lawful operation and could not reasonably have been avoided, *e.g.* the destruction of nests when felling woodland.[29] In each of these cases the onus is on the acused to show that he falls within the terms of the defence. Further allowances are made for authorised persons.[30] They are allowed a defence if they can show that their action was necessary for the purpose of preserving public health, public safety or air safety, for preventing the spread of disease, or for preventing serious damage to livestock, crops, fruit, growing timber or fisheries.[31] A more specific exemption allows the gathering for human consumption of gannets on Sula Sgeir, gull's eggs, and (before April 15th each year) lapwings' eggs, provided that this is done in accordance with a licence from the Secretary of State.[32]

3.3.4 No offence is committed[33] if the action in question is required by ministers in the exercise of their powers relating to agricultural pest control,[34] or is done under the Animal Health Act 1981 or an order made under it.[35] As noted above, the

[25] *Ibid.*, s.1(6).
[26-27] *Ibid.*, s.19A (added by Prisoners and Criminal Proceedings (Scotland) Act 1993, s.36).
[28] *Ibid.*, s.4(2)(a), (b).
[29] *Ibid.*, s.4(2)(c).
[30] See para. 3.2.6, above.
[31] WCA, s.4(3).
[32] *Ibid.*, s.16(2).
[33] *Ibid.*, s.4(1).
[34] Agriculture Act 1947, s.98; Agriculture (Scotland) Act 1948, s.39; see para. 4.5.2, below.
[35] See para. 4.5.11, below.

definition of "wild bird" means that poultry (domestic fowls, geese, ducks, guinea fowls, pigeons, quails and turkeys) and game birds (pheasant, partridge, grouse (moor game), black (heath) game and ptarmigan) fall outside the range of this protection,[36] as do birds shown to have been bred in captivity.[37]

Protected birds

3.3.5 A number of birds listed in Schedule 1 to the 1981 Act enjoy enhanced protection. Almost 100 species are listed.[38] The general position is modified in three ways in relation to such birds. Firstly, in addition to the offences mentioned above, it is an offence intentionally to disturb any wild bird included in Schedule 1 whilst it is building a nest or is at or near its nest containing eggs or young, or intentionally to disturb the dependent young of such a bird.[39] Over-zealous photographers and birdwatchers may be in danger of falling foul of this provision. Secondly, anyone convicted of offences in relation to these birds is liable to a significantly increased penalty.[40] Thirdly, some of the defences noted above do not apply in relation to Schedule 1 of birds. The exemption for acts done under the Animal Health Act 1981 is restricted to acts done in pursuance of orders made under sections 21 and 22 of that Act (wildlife destruction orders),[41] and none of the further defences available to authorised persons apply.[42] In the case of three species of bird which are listed in Schedule 1 but may be hunted,[43] the special rules apply only during the close season.[44] The birds concerned are goldeneye, pintail, and (in parts of northwest Scotland only) greylag geese.

Birds which may be hunted

3.3.6 Game birds are excluded from the scope of most of the 1981 Act and the general position described above is modified

---

[36] WCA, s.27.

[37] *Ibid.*, s.1(6).

[38] See Appendix A.

[39] WCA, s.1(5).

[40] *Ibid.*, s.1(4); see para. 3.2.2, above.

[41] *Ibid.*, s.4(1); see para. 4.5.11, below.

[42] *Ibid.*, s.4(3).

[43] *Ibid.*, Sched. 1, Pt. II; see Appendix A.

[44] *Ibid.*, s.1(7); the close season is February 21–August 31 for areas below high-water mark, February 1–August 31 for other areas (*ibid.*, s.2(4)); see Appendix B.

in order to allow the hunting of a number of other species of birds, listed in Part I of Schedule 2 to the Act.[45] No offence is committed by killing or taking such birds outside the close season, or by injuring them in the attempt to kill them,[46] although certain methods are prohibited in relation to all birds,[47] and it remains an offence to injure such a bird deliberately, except in the course of trying to kill it. The various close seasons are defined in the Act[48] and hunting is not permitted in Scotland on Sundays or on Christmas Day, nor on Sundays in any area of England and Wales prescribed by the Secretary of State.[49] The Secretary of State has the power to make orders varying the close seasons.[50] After consulting a representative of shooting interests he may also make orders offering any birds listed in Part II of Schedule 1 or Part I of Schedule 2 special protection for a period of up to 14 days at a time. These orders, intended for periods of exceptionally severe weather or other temporary crises for the birds, operate so as to apply the rules for the close season during the period of special protection, and may affect all or only part of the country.[51] In England and Wales, some of these birds enjoy further protection in that it is an offence for anyone to take or destroy their eggs unless authorised by the person with the right to kill game on the land in question.[52]

Pests

3.3.7 The statutory provisions used to contain a considerable relaxation of the general protection for wild birds to allow authorised persons to deal with birds widely regarded as pests. The birds were listed in Part II of Schedule 2 and no offence was committed by an authorised person who killed or took such a bird, destroyed, damaged or took its nest or destroyed or took

---

[45] See Appendix A; the three species listed in Part II of Schedule 1 and thereby enjoying enhanced protection during the close season also appear in Part I of Schedule 2.

[46] WCA, s.2(1); see Appendix B for a table of close seasons for the birds covered here and for game birds.

[47] See paras. 4.4.15–4.4.17, below.

[48] WCA, s.2(4).

[49] *Ibid.*, s.2(3). The Wild Birds (Sundays) Orders made under s.2 of the Protection of Birds Act 1954 presumably continue in effect in prescribing such areas; S.I.s 1955 No. 1286, 1956 No. 1310, 1957 No. 429, 1963 No. 1700.

[50] *Ibid.*, s.2(5).

[51] *Ibid.*, s.2(6).

[52] Game Act 1831, s.24, applying to game and "any swan, wild duck, teal and widgeon."

its eggs.[52a] However this legislative exception for pest species was considered to fall foul of the terms of the EC Directive on Wild Birds[53] which imposes a prohibition on the killing and taking of *all* wild birds[54] and permits derogations only where certain criteria are met.[55] Accordingly, all of the species have now been removed from Part II of Schedule 2 and in its place a number of licences have been issued by the Scottish and Welsh Offices and by the Department of the Environment under s.16 of the 1981 Act.[56]

3.3.8 These licences permit authorised persons to kill or take the listed species[57] or their eggs for a variety of purposes, including the protection of other wild birds, the prevention of the spread of disease, the prevention of serious damage to livestock, foodstuffs, crops, vegetables or fruit and the preservation of public health or public or air safety. The licences are annual but apply to all authorised persons, so that there is no need for individual applications to be made. This change of form does not have any real impact on the practical effect of the law, but makes it even harder for anyone to find out exactly what they are or are not permitted to do (and therefore whether or not they are committing a crime), and removes the details of the law from any direct parliamentary scrutiny.

Possession

3.3.9 In view of the difficulty of proving that someone has intentionally killed a wild bird, and in order to suppress the demand for birds and their eggs, the 1981 Act renders their possession unlawful. It is a criminal offence to possess any live or dead wild bird or anything derived from one, or to possess the egg of any wild bird or part of an egg.[58] Unlike the earlier legislation,[59] the offences are not limited to birds which have been recently killed or taken, and a stuffed and mounted bird

---

[52a] WCA, s.2(2).

[53] Directive 79/409; see paras. 7.4.3–7.4.11, below.

[54] *Ibid.*, Art. 5.

[55] *Ibid.*, Art. 9.

[56] See para. 3.2.5, above.

[57] The species covered are; crow, great black-backed gull, lesser black-backed gull, herring gull, jackdaw, jay, magpie, feral pigeon, rook, collared dove, house sparrow, starling, woodpigeon. The last four species are not covered by the licences authorising action for the conservation of other species of bird.

[58] WCA, s.1(2).

[59] Protection of Birds Act 1954, s.1.

continues to be a "dead wild bird" whose possession may be a criminal offence.[60] Subject to the exceptions noted below, these are offences of strict liability, as decided in *Kirkland* v. *Robinson*.[61] In deciding that the law did impose strict liability the court was influenced by the contrast with the other offences created by the same section, *e.g.* killing birds, which expressly require intentional conduct, by the presence of statutory defences to mitigate the potential harshness of strict liability, and by the importance of environmental protection. It was right that those who chose to possess wild birds should do so at their own risk.

3.3.10 The offence of possession is widely drawn, rendering it unlawful for any person to have in his possession or control any live or dead wild bird, any part of one, anything derived from such a bird or any egg (whole or part) of a wild bird.[62] Where the bird is protected under Schedule 1 to the Act, the penalties for offenders are increased.[63] The person in possession of the bird or egg can establish a defence if he can show that the bird or egg had not been killed or taken (in other words had come under his control by natural means), or had been killed or taken otherwise than in contravention of the 1981 Act or its predecessors[64] (in other words was the product of lawful activity or had been taken before 1954). A defence is also available if it can be shown that the bird or egg had at some stage been sold otherwise than in contravention of the 1981 Act or its predecessors.[65] The offences do not apply in relation to any bird shown to have been bred in captivity.[66]

Keeping

3.3.11 The keeping of certain live wild birds is covered by the general possession offence described above, but a number of other provisions exist to regulate the keeping of birds, and the conditions in which they are kept. For many species a person with a bird in his possession or control must ensure that the bird is registered and ringed or marked in accordance with

---

[60] *Robinson* v. *Everett* [1988] Crim.L.R. 699.
[61] [1987] Crim.L.R. 643.
[62] WCA, s.1(2).
[63] *Ibid.*, s.1(4).
[64] Protection of Birds Acts 1954–1967.
[65] WCA, s.1(3).
[66] *Ibid.*, s.1(6).

regulations made by the Secretary of State.[67] The species to which this provision may apply are listed in Schedule 4 to the 1981 Act.[68]

3.3.12 In order to ensure proper compliance with these rules, those authorised by the Secretary of State enjoy powers of entry to inspect premises where birds covered by Schedule 4 are being kept, and obstruction of such inspectors is an offence.[69] The law here is particularly severe on persistent offenders. Regardless of whether the bird is registered and ringed, it is an offence for a bird listed in Schedule 4 to be kept by any person who has been convicted within the last five years of an offence attracting a special penalty under Part I of the 1981 (*e.g.* in relation to the birds given extra protection under Schedule I), or within the last three years of an offence relating to the protection of birds or other animals or their ill-treatment.[70] It is also an offence for anybody knowingly to dispose or offer to dispose of a Schedule 4 bird to anyone falling within these categories of past offenders.[71]

3.3.13 It is an offence to cause or permit certain birds to be shown for the purposes of competitions or at premises where a competition is taking place.[72] This prohibition applies to any live wild bird, or bird which has a wild bird as a parent, other than the species listed in Part I of Schedule 3 and ringed or marked in accordance with regulations made by the Secretary of State.[73] Increased penalties apply if the offence is committed in relation to a Schedule 1 bird.[74]

3.3.14 In order to prevent unecessary suffering, the general rule is laid down that if birds are kept it must be in a cage or other receptacle which is large enough to allow the bird to stretch its wings freely. Failure to comply with this rule is an

---

[67] *Ibid.*, s.7(1); Wildlife and Countryside (Registration and Ringing of Certain Captive Birds) Regulations 1982, S.I. 1982 No. 1221 (amended by Wildlife and Countryside (Registration and Ringing of Certain Captive Birds (Amendment) Regulations 1991, S.I. 1991 No. 478).
[68] See Appendix A.
[69] WCA, s.7(6), (7).
[70] *Ibid.*, s.7(3); spent convictions under the Rehabilitation of Offenders Act 1974 are to disregarded (*ibid.*, s.7(5)).
[71] *Ibid.*, s.7(4).
[72] *Ibid.*, s.6(3).
[73] *Ibid.*, s.6(5); Wildlife and Countryside (Ringing of Certain Birds) Regulations 1982, S.I. 1982 No. 1220.
[74] *Ibid.*, s.6(4).

offence attracting a special penalty.[75] This rule applies to all birds, not just wild birds, with the exceptions of poultry, birds in the course of conveyance, birds undergoing examination or treatment by a veterinary practitioner, and birds being shown at a public exhibition or competition provided that the bird is not confined in the smaller cage for more than 72 hours.[76] A special penalty is also imposed on anyone who promotes, takes part in or organises an event in which captive birds are liberated for the purpose of being shot immediately after they have been freed.[77] The owners and occupiers of land used for this purpose are likewise liable.

Sale

3.3.15 The sale of birds and their eggs is also strictly controlled. The provisions on sale are expressed so as to cover not merely the sale of birds or eggs, a requirement which may be difficult to prove and prevent early intervention by the authorities, but also offering or exposing for sale, possessing or transporting for the purpose of sale, and publishing or causing to be published an advertisement likely to be understood as meaning that a person does or intends to buy or sell.[78] In this way all activities relating to a sale should be covered and there should be little if any room for defences based on technicalities or a failure to prove that a formal legal sale has taken place.

3.3.16 There is a complete prohibition on the sale of the eggs of wild birds or of live wild birds other than those listed in Part I of Schedule 3,[79] and only then provided that they have been bred in captivity and are ringed or marked in accordance with regulations made by the Secretary of State.[80] For dead wild birds and things derived from them, the prohibition extends to all species apart from those listed in Parts II and III of Schedule 3, but these may be sold only by a registered dealer.[81] For dead

---

[75] *Ibid.*, s.8(1).
[76] *Ibid.*, s.8(2).
[77] *Ibid.*, s.8(3).
[78] *Ibid.*, s.6(1), (2).
[79] *Ibid.*, s.6(1); see Appendix A.
[80] *Ibid.*, s.6(5); Wildlife and Countryside (Ringing of Certain Birds) Regulations 1982, S.I. 1982 No. 1220.
[81] *Ibid.*, s.6(2); Wildlife and Countryside (Registration to Sell, etc., Certain Dead Wild Birds) Regulations 1982, S.I. 1982 No. 1219 (amended by Wildlife and Countryside (Registration to Sell, etc., Certain Dead Wild Birds) (Amendment) Regulations 1991, S.I. 1991 No. 479).

birds listed in Part III of the Schedule sale is permitted only during the shooting season, from September 1—February 28.[82] Registration for the purposes of selling dead birds is not available to anyone within five years of being convicted of an offence under Part I of the 1981 Act attracting a special penalty, or within three years of a conviction for an offence concerning the protection or ill-treatment of birds or other animals.[83] The Secretary of State may authorise people to enter and inspect premises where a registered person keeps wild birds, and obstruction of such inspectors is an offence.[84] The sale of game birds is subject to separate licensing requirements.[85]

ANIMALS

3.4.1 The law relating to other animals is more fragmented than that concerned with birds. In addition to the provisions of the Wildlife and Countryside Act 1981, there is older legislation dealing with pests and game, and a sizeable number of provisions which relate to individual species, *e.g.* the Protection of Badgers Act 1992. The law on animals generally is blighted by the profileration of different legislative definitions of "animal," sometimes referring to domestic animals only and frequently defying any scientific classification. In every case where a statute refers to "animals" it is wise to check that the animal which one has in mind is in the particular circumstances an animal for the purposes of the provision in question.

Protected animals

3.4.2 Under the Wildlife and Countryside Act 1981, a number of animals are given protection similar to that given to those birds listed in Schedule 1 to the Act. The protected animals are listed in Schedule 5[86] and it is an offence for any person intentionally to kill, injure or take a wild animal of those species.[87] It is an offence to have in one's possession or control

---

[82] *Ibid.*, s.6(6).
[83] *Ibid.*, s.6(8); spent convictions under the Rehabilitation of Offenders Act 1974 are to be disregarded.
[84] *Ibid.*, s.6(9), (10).
[85] See para. 4.2.9, below.
[86] See Appendix A.
[87] WCA, s.9(1).

any such animal, whether alive or dead, or anything derived from one.[88] As is the case with birds, it is a defence to show that the animal was not killed or taken, or was not killed or taken in contravention of the 1981 Act or its predecessor (the Conservation of Wild Creatures and Wild Plants Act 1975) or had been sold without contravening those provisions.[89] It is a further offence for anyone intentionally to damage, destroy or obstruct access to any place a wild animal included in Schedule 5 uses for shelter or protection, or intentionally to disturb an animal while using such a place.[90] However this latter offence does not apply to anything done within a dwelling-house, where it is permissible to evict or disturb protected animals, with the exception of bats which enjoy the benefits of special protection in this regard.[91] The sale, offer for sale, etc., or advertising of protected animals is also prohibited.[92] In any proceedings a particular animal is generally presumed to be wild unless the contrary is shown.[93]

3.4.3 The above provisions do not apply in certain circumstances. It is not an offence for a person to take a disabled animal for the purpose of treating it and releasing it, nor to kill an animal so severely disabled as to have no reasonable chance of recovery, provided in both cases that it was not that person's unlawful act which caused the disability.[94] More generally, no offence is committed where the otherwise unlawful conduct towards the animal is the incidental result of a lawful operation and could not reasonably have been avoided, *e.g.* the disturbance entailed in lawful agricultural or forestry operations.[95] No offence is committed by actions done under a ministerial requirement relating to agricultural pest control[96] or under the Animal Health Act 1981.[97] A further defence is available to "authorised persons,"[98] who are allowed to kill or

[88] *Ibid.*, s.9(2).
[89] *Ibid.*, s.9(3).
[90] *Ibid.*, s.9(4).
[91] *Ibid.*, s.10(2), (5); see para. 3.4.5, below.
[92] *Ibid.*, s.9(5).
[93] *Ibid.*, s.9(6); the presumption applies to offences under subss. (1), (2), (5(a)).
[94] *Ibid.*, s.10(3)(a), (b).
[95] *Ibid.*, s.10(3)(c).
[96] Agriculture Act 1947, s.98; Agriculture (Scotland) Act 1948, s.39; see para. 4.5.2, below.
[97] WCA, s.10(1); see para. 4.5.11, below.
[98] See para. 3.2.6, above.

injure animals where it can shown that the action was necessary to prevent serious damage to livestock, food for livestock, crops, fruit, growing timber or other forms of property or fisheries.[99] This defence is not available if the need for the action became apparent beforehand, unless an application has been made for a licence to authorise the conduct and that application is still being considered.[1] As with the rest of Part I of the 1981 Act, licences may be obtained authorising actions which would otherwise constitute offences.[2]

3.4.4 A lesser degree of protection is granted to the animals listed in Schedule 6 to the 1981 Act.[3] Their protection is limited to a prohibition on the use of certain methods of killing or taking them.[4] These include the use of the following devices in killing or taking the listed animals,[5] or their setting (for whatever purpose) in circumstances calculated to cause bodily injury to such animals:[6] traps or snares, electrical devices for killing or stunning, poisonous, poisoned or stupefying substances, or nets.[7] A limited defence is available in relation to the setting of the prohibited devices in that no offence is committed if the accused can show that the article was set for the purpose of the lawful killing of animals in the interests of public health, agriculture, forestry, fisheries or nature conservation, and all reasonable precautions were taken to prevent injury to the animals protected under Schedule 6.[8] Also prohibited is the use of: automatic or semi-automatic weapons, devices for illuminating a target, sighting devices for night shooting, artificial lights, mirrors or dazzling devices, gas or smoke, sound recordings employed as decoys, and mechanically propelled vehicles used in immediate pursuit of animals, for the purpose of driving, killing or taking them.[9] A person who knowingly causes or permits the acts rendered unlawful by these

[99] WCA, s.10(4).

[1] *Ibid.*, s.10(6); if the application is granted, the licence will authorise the action taken, if refused, the action is unlawful.

[2] *Ibid.*, s.16; see para. 3.2.5, above and Appendix C.

[3] See Appendix A.

[4] WCA, s.11(2); see section 4.4, below for the general law on methods of killing and taking animals.

[5] *Ibid.*, s.11(2)(b).

[6] *Ibid.*, s.11(2)(a).

[7] The setting of nets is not itself prohibited.

[8] WCA, s.11(6), (7) (added by Wildlife and Countryside (Amendment) Act 1991, s.2).

[9] *Ibid.*, s.11(2)(c)–(e).

provisions is also guilty of an offence,[10] so that a landowner who deliberately does nothing to stop his gamekeeper offending may himself be prosecuted.

Bats

3.4.5 Bats are given full protection under Schedules 5 and 6 to the 1981 Act, and are further protected by a restriction of the exemptions normally permitting action against protected species. In general no offence is committed by the killing, injuring or taking of a protected animal or the disturbance of its shelter if the action in question is carried out in a dwelling-house, or is the incidental result of a lawful operation and could not reasonably be avoided.[11] In relation to bats however, these defences are limited to action taken within the living area of a dwelling-house (in other words the inhabited rooms, not a loft or outbuilding), or taken after the relevant conservancy council has been notified of the intended action.[12] In the latter case, the council must be given a reasonable time to advise whether the action should be carried out and if so, how. This provision is intended particularly to protect bats from the harmful effects of wood treatments and preservatives applied in roof-spaces where they may be roosting.

Badgers

3.4.6 The badger is protected against being killed or taken by certain means under Schedule 6 to the Wildlife and Countryside Act 1981,[13] but receives more general protection under the Protection of Badgers Act 1992.[14] The structure and provisions of the 1992 Act are broadly similar to those for protected species under the 1981 Act, with generally worded prohibitions on killing and taking being supported by provisions on possession and sale, and qualified by a number of defences, but the scope and, in particular, the wording of the two Acts differ so that where badgers are involved the precise wording of the 1992 Act must be carefully studied.

[10] *Ibid.*, s.11(2)(d) (added by Wildlife and Countryside (Amendment) Act 1991, s.2).
[11] *Ibid.*, s.10(2), (3)(c), offering defences to s.9.
[12] *Ibid.*, s.10(5).
[13] See para. 3.4.4, above.
[14] Consolidating the Badgers Act 1973, which had been amended on several occasions, the Badgers Act 1991 and the Badgers (Further Protection) Act 1991.

3.4.7 It is an offence wilfully to kill, injure or take a badger, or to attempt to do so, otherwise than as permitted under the Act.[15] Moreover, the onus of proof is reversed in relation to this offence, in that where someone is charged with attempting to kill, injure or take a badger, and there is evidence from which it can reasonably be concluded that he was involved in such an attempt, he is presumed to have been so involved unless the contrary is shown.[16] It is also an offence[17] cruelly to ill-treat a badger, to use any badger tongs in the course of killing or taking a badger or attempting to do so, to use against badgers any firearm other than one of the specified size and power,[18] or to dig for badgers. In relation to digging for badgers, the onus of proof is again reversed, with evidence from which it could reasonably be concluded that a person was digging for a badger giving rise to a presumption that he was so doing unless the contrary is shown.[19]

3.4.8. These prohibitions designed to protect badgers are subject to a number of exceptions. They do not apply to a person taking or attempting to take a badger in order to tend it when it has been disabled otherwise than by his own act, to the killing or attempted killing of a badger appearing to be so seriously injured or in such a condition that killing it would be an act of mercy, nor to the unavoidable killing or injuring of a badger as an incidental result of a lawful action.[20] Conduct authorised under the Animals (Scientific Procedures) Act 1986 is also exempt. Killing a badger, taking one or injuring one while attempting to kill or take it is not an offence if the accused can show that his conduct was necessary for the purpose of preventing serious damage to land, crops, poultry or other forms of property.[21] However, the benefit of this provision is not available if the need for such action became apparent beforehand unless an application for a licence authorising the action has been made and is still under consideration.[22]

[15] Protection of Badgers Act 1992, s.1(1).
[16] *Ibid.*, s.1(2).
[17] *Ibid.*, s.2(1).
[18] A smooth bore weapon of not less than 20 bore or a rifle using ammunition having a muzzle energy of not less than 160 footpounds and a bullet weighing not less than 38 grains; *ibid.*, s.2(1)(d).
[19] *Ibid.*, s.2(2).
[20] *Ibid.*, s.6.
[21] *Ibid.*, s.7(1).
[22] *Ibid.*, s.7(2).

3.4.9. In order to back up these offences, it is further provided that it is an offence to have in one's possession or control a dead badger, or any part of one or anything derived from one.[23] This is an offence of strict liablity, but specific defences are provided if it can be shown that the badger had not been killed or had been killed otherwise than in contravention of the Act or the Badgers Act 1973, or that the badger or other article had at some stage been sold in circumstances such that the purchaser had no reason to believe that the badger had been killed in contravention of the Acts.[24] A person commits a crime by selling or offering for sale a live badger, or by having one in his possession or under his control,[25] unless he has possession or control of it in the course of his business as a carrier, or unless it was disabled otherwise than by his own act and is being kept to be tended.[26] Ringing or otherwise marking a badger is also an offence unless a licence is obtained.[27]

3.4.10 Protection is extended to badger setts, defined for the purposes of the Act "any structure or place which displays signs indicating current use by a badger."[28] It is an offence intentionally or recklessly[29] to interfere with a badger sett by damaging or destroying it, by obstructing access to it, by causing a dog to enter it or by disturbing a badger in occupation. A defence is provided for action necessary to prevent serious damage to land, crops, poultry or other forms of property,[30] provided that if the need for such action was known in advance a licence had been applied for and is still under consideration.[31] It is a defence that the conduct was the incidental result of a lawful operation and could not reasonably have been avoided,[32] but this does not apply to interference in the form of causing a dog to enter the sett or the destruction of the sett. It follows that a licence is required for the destruction of a sett, even if this is merely incidental to some lawful operation, *e.g.*

---

[23] *Ibid.*, s.1(3).
[24] *Ibid.*, s.1(4).
[25] *Ibid.*, s.3.
[26] *Ibid.*, s.9.
[27] *Ibid.*, s.5.
[28] *Ibid.*, s.14.
[29] In England and Wales this probably means recklessly in the more objective sense established in *R.* v. *Caldwell* [1982] A.C. 341; Scots law probably also interprets this in an objective sense, *Allen* v. *Patterson*, 1980 J.C. 57.
[30] Protection of Badgers Act 1992, s.8(1).
[31] *Ibid.*, s.8(2) applying s.7(2).
[32] *Ibid.*, s.8(3).

development authorised by planning permission. Subject to restrictions as to the methods and materials used, obstruction of the entrance to a badger sett for the purpose of hunting foxes with hounds is no offence, provided that it is authorised by the owner or occupier of the land and a recognised Hunt.[33]

3.4.11 Licences authorising conduct prohibited under the Act are available from the conservancy councils and the agriculture ministers. The councils can grant licences in relation to any action taken for scientific or educational purposes, for the purpose of the conservation of badgers, for the purpose of zoological gardens, or for marking badgers. The councils can also grant licences permitting interference with badger setts for the purposes of development authorised under the town and country planning legislation, for preserving scheduled ancient monuments[34] or carrying out archaeological investigations of them, and for investigations into any offence or for gathering evidence for any court proceedings.[35] Both the councils and the ministers can grant licences to interfere with setts for the purpose of controlling foxes in order to protect livestock, game or wild life.[36]

3.4.12 The agriculture ministers can grant licences for the killing or taking of badgers in order to prevent the spread of disease or to prevent serious damage to land, crops, poultry or other forms of property. Licences for interference with badger setts can be granted for the same purposes and for any agricultural or forestry operation or for drainage works.[37] Each minister must consult the appropriate conservancy council on the exercise of his functions under this provision and must not grant a licence unless he has received the council's general advice of the circumstances in which such licences should be granted.[38] In Scotland this provision is restricted to licences granted for the protection of land and property[39]; in England and Wales it extends to licences granted for any of the above purposes except for preventing the spread of disease.[40]

[33] *Ibid.*, s.8(4)–(9).
[34] Under the Ancient Monuments and Archaeological Areas Act 1979.
[35] Protection of Badgers Act 1992, s.10(1).
[36] *Ibid.*, s.10(3).
[37] *Ibid.*, s.10(2).
[38] *Ibid.*, s.10(6).
[39] *Ibid.*, s.10(7).
[40] *Ibid.*, s.10(6).

3.4.13 Licences can be revoked at any time by the authority which granted them,[41] but are not to be unreasonably withheld or revoked.[42] Action authorised under a licence can not constitute an offence under the general restrictions on the placing of poison,[43] but failure to adhere to the conditions in a licence is itself an offence, regardless of any other liability.[44]

3.4.14 A number of provisions exist to assist in the enforcement of the law protecting badgers. Anyone found on any land committing an offence of killing, injuring or taking a badger or in possession of a dead badger can be required to leave the land by the owner or occupier (or their servants), or by a constable and required to give his full name and address. Wilful refusal to comply with these requirements is an offence.[45] The police are also given powers to stop and search suspected offenders, to arrest them and to seize anything which may be evidence of the commission of an offence. The power of seizure extends to articles liable to forfeit under the further provisions which state that on conviction the court shall order the forfeiture of any badger or skin which was the subject of the offence and may order the forfeiture of any weapon or item used in the commission of the offence.[46] Further provisions authorise the destruction or disposal of any dog used in committing an offence and the disqualification of the offender from having custody of a dog.[47]

Seals

3.4.15 The Conservation of Seals Act 1970 offers legal protection to seals in a number of ways. As usual, though, there are a number of exceptions and the possibility of licences being granted to authorise for certain purposes action which is normally prohibited.

3.4.16 In the first place, there is a prohibition on the use of poison of any sort for killing or taking seals, and it is an offence

---

[41] *Ibid.*, s.10(8).
[42] *Ibid.*, s.10(9).
[43] *Ibid.*, s.10(10), referring to Protection of Animals Act 1911, s.8, and Protection of Animals (Scotland) Act 1912, s.7; see para. 4.4.3, below.
[44] *Ibid.*, s.10(8).
[45] *Ibid.*, s.1(5).
[46] *Ibid.*, s.11.
[47] *Ibid.*, s.13.

to use firearms other than those of prescribed power to kill, injure or take a seal.[48] The possession of poison or prohibited firearms or ammunition with intent to kill or take a seal is itself an offence.[49] The rules restricting the means of killing do not apply to a person's mercy killing of a seal so seriously disabled that it has no reasonable chance of recovery, provided that it was not his own act that disabled it in the first place.[50]

3.4.17 A close season is laid down for both species of seal found in British waters and it is an offence wilfully to kill, injure or take a seal during the close seasons. For grey seals the close season is September 1–December 31, for common seals June 1–August 31.[51] The effect of these close seasons can be extended by orders made by the Secretary of State where it appears necessary for the proper conservation of seals. Such orders can apply to specific areas and to either or both species,[52] and in practice greatly extend the protection offered to seals. In particular this protection was considerably extended following the epidemic in 1988 which killed many seals in the North Sea, the extensions applying initially for a few years at a time.[53] Until December 1993 there was a general ban on killing either species of seal on the North Sea coast of England[54] and there is an indefinite ban on killing common seals around Shetland.[55]

3.4.18 A number of defences are available. No offence is committed by the taking of a disabled seal in order to tend it (provided that the tender did not cause the injury), by a mercy killing, by the unavoidable killing or injuring of a seal as an incidental result of a lawful action, or by the killing or injuring of a seal in order to prevent damage to a fishing net or tackle,

---

[48] Conservation of Seals Act 1970, s.1; the permitted firearms are rifles using ammunition of muzzle energy of not less than 600 footpounds and bullets weighing not less than 45 grains; the Secretary of State can amend this prescription by statutory instrument (*ibid.*, s.1(2)).

[49] *Ibid.*, s.8(2).

[50] *Ibid.*, s.9(2).

[51] *Ibid.*, s.2.

[52] *Ibid.*, s.3.

[53] *E.g.*, Conservation of Seals (Common Seals) Order 1988, S.I. 1988 No. 2023; Conservation of Seals (England and Wales) Order 1988, S.I. 1988 No. 2024.

[54] Conservation of Seals (No. 2) Order 1990, S.I. 1990 No. 2500.

[55] Conservation of Seals (Shetland Islands Area) Order 1991, S.I. 1991 No. 2638.

or to fish which are in a net.[56] This last defence is available only when the seal is in the vicinity of fishing net or tackle, and only to the person in possession of the equipment or someone acting at his request. It does not allow those seeking to reduce competition for fish stocks to kill seals which are not immediately threatening fishery operations.[57]

3.4.19 Licences may be granted by the Secretary of State for a number of purposes authorising the killing or taking of seals, but in no case can the use of strychnine be authorised.[58] The licences can be granted for scientific or educational purposes, for the purposes of a zoo or other collection, for the prevention of damage to fisheries, for the reduction of a population surplus of seals either for management purposes or to use them as a resource, or for the protection of flora or fauna in nature reserves, marine nature reserves, SSSIs and land protected by a Nature Conservation Order. Before granting licences, the Secreatry of State is to consult with the Natural Environment Research Council, and he must have the consent of the relevant conservancy council before granting a licence for a nature reserve or SSSI.[59] Contravening the conditions in a licence is itself an offence, regardless of other liabilities.[60]

3.4.20 In order to assist in the enforcement of the Act and to allow any authorised culling to take place, there are provisions for powers of entry,[61] for powers of arrest, search and seizure,[62] for the forfeiture of unlawfully taken seals or sealskin and of firearms, etc. used in committing offences,[63] and provisions regulating the jurisdiction of courts where offences are committed on the coast or at sea.[64] The Natural Environment Research Council is to provide the Secretary of State with scientific advice on the management of seal populations.[65]

---

[56] Conservation of Seals Act 1970, s.9.
[57] For the position affecting fish farms see W. Howath, *The Law of Aquaculture* (1990), pp. 149–152.
[58] Conservation of Seals Act 1970, s.10 (amended by WCA, Sched. 7 para. 7).
[59] *Ibid.*, s.10(3).
[60] *Ibid.*, s.10(2).
[61] *Ibid.*, s.11.
[62] *Ibid.*, s.4 (amended for England and Wales by the Police and Criminal Evidence Act 1984, Sched. 7 Pt. I).
[63] *Ibid.*, s.6.
[64] *Ibid.*, s.7.
[65] *Ibid.*, s.13.

Whales

3.4.21 All species of whales, dolphins and porpoises are given protection under Schedule 5 to the Wildlife and Countryside Act 1981,[66] but a number of other provisions also exist. The catching of all species of cetacean or their treatment once caught, is prohibited within the coastal waters of the United Kingdom.[67] Any British ship involved in the catching or treatment of whales or any factory treating whales or producing whale oil must have a licence from the Secretary of State, and no such licences are currently in force.[68] However, the Secretary of State may issue permits granting exemptions from these provisions for scientific or other exceptional purposes.[69] It is also an offence to drive ashore in Scotland any of the smaller types of whale commonly known as bottlenose or pilot whales.[70]

Fish

3.4.22 Fish do not have the same place in the public's affection as seals and whales and the hunting of fish is still widely accepted as a legitimate pastime, as well as a commercial activity. The protection of fish has thus attracted considerably less attention than that devoted to marine mammals, but the law has not ignored fish. Fish can benefit directly from the more general legislation on nature conservation, and a few species of fish are protected under Schedule 5 to the Wildlife and Countryside Act 1981.[71] However, the majority of the legislation is designed to regulate the exploitation of fish stocks and is discussed in Chapter 4.

3.4.23 The law on fishing, as well as trying to regulate the catching of certain species so as protect future stocks, can have incidental benefits for the conservation of aquatic fauna. The restrictions on when and how fishing can take place serve to provide some protection for fish and aquatic animals in generally. In particular, the prohibitions on the use of indiscriminate and destructive methods of fishing, such as

---

[66] See para. 3.4.2, above.
[67] Whaling Industry (Regulation) Act 1934, ss.1, 2 (amended by the Fisheries Act 1981, s.35).
[68] *Ibid.*, s.4.
[69] *Ibid.*, s.7.
[70] Fisheries Act 1981, s.36.
[71] See para. 3.4.2, above.

electric devices and poison, will obviously benefit all forms of aquatic life.[72] Moreover, the value of waters for fishing can provide a strong incentive for their retention in an unpolluted state, to the benefit of animal and plant life generally.

[72] See paras. 4.3.10–4.3.12, below.

4. Exploitation and Destruction of Wildlife

4.1.1. Animals and birds have been hunted for food since the beginning of human existence, and more recently for sport. It was in order to protect wildlife for such purposes that the first laws affecting them were made, and the law regulating hunting and fishing continues to play a major role in controlling what can be done to wildlife. It therefore deserves to be considered in a book on nature conservation. An account of the full complexities of the law in this field, especially in relation to administration and detailed control of fishing, inland and marine, would take this book beyond reasonable size, and what follows is a brief guide, with an emphasis on those parts of the law which may have most impact on nature conservation. Fuller accounts exist of the law on game and inland fisheries, but unfortunately there is no straightforward guide to the ever-changing mass of legislation, national and European, on offshore fishing.[1]

4.1.2 Although the law dealt with in this chapter is designed to allow the killing and taking of wildlife, it may be of considerable benefit to nature conservation. It was in order to preserve deer for royal hunting that areas of forest were shut off from agricultural or forestry use, with lasting benefits to many forms of plant and animal life. The law stipulating close seasons, etc., seeks at least to ensure that the species concerned are not exterminated, albeit with a view only to their future exploitation, and other controls may serve to limit the likelihood of harm afflicting species other then the intended targets. On a more practical level, the economic potential of shooting rights, etc., may help to prevent areas of "natural" countryside being destroyed by other forms of exploitation. Moreover, the offences created to punish those hunting particular species by unauthorised means, in unauthorised places or at unauthorised

---

[1] See references in the relevant section, below.

times may also offer a means of taking action against those engaged in activities which are harmful to other species, *e.g.* the likelihood of game being caught might allow the game laws to be invoked against those using nets to catch wildlife, even though game was not their intended target. By acquiring but then not exercising game rights over land those interested in nature conservation may be able to achieve a degree of protection for some species in the area, otherwise possible only at the expense of acquiring the land itself.

4.1.3 The legal provisions requiring the destruction of animals are not so likely to produce such incidental benefits. Some pest control measures may be of benefit to other species, but generally the significance of the law lies not in any potential benefits for nature conservation, but in the ways in which it can conflict with and even override other measures adopted to further conservation, *e.g.* requiring the destruction of wild animals even within nature reserves.

4.1.4 This chapter is organised in an attempt to bring some order to a very fragmented area of law. First the law on hunting, shooting and fishing is considered for its effect in regulating who is permitted to kill or take wildlife and in what circumstances. Then the various provisions affecting the methods which can be used for killing and catching animals are considered. Finally the law requiring or permitting the destruction of wildlife is examined.

HUNTING AND SHOOTING

Game laws

4.2.1 Although the broad objectives and basic structure of the law of game are the same in Scotland and in England and Wales, there are many differences of considerable importance.[2] The law is further complicated by the existence of a number of overlapping provisions. One initial problem common to both jurisdictions is the absence of clear and consistent definitions of what is meant by "game."

[2] See generally, S. Scott Robinson, *The Law of Game, Salmon and Freshwater Fishing in Scotland* (1990); C. Parkes & J. Thornley, *Fair Game* (1987).

The meaning of game

4.2.2 There is no single definition of "game" in either Scotland or England and Wales. Different statutes provide their own definitions, definitions which themselves give rise to doubts since they usually state that game "includes" the species which are listed rather than offering a complete definition. In both jurisidictions it is clear that the term "ground game" refers to hares and rabbits only,[3] but the broader position is less clear. As a common core, though, it can be said that the following will be regarded as game in virtually all circumstances: hares, pheasants, partridges, grouse, heath or moor game and black game.[4]

4.2.3 The position in Scotland is particularly complex. The Game (Scotland) Act 1772 contains provisions affecting hares, partridges, pheasants, muir fowl, tarmagans (ptarmigan), heath fowl and snipe.[5] The Night Poaching Act 1828 defines game as including the species listed in the core definition given above, with the addition of bustards,[6] and also applies to rabbits.[7] The Game (Scotland) Act 1832 applies to game, woodcock, snipe, wild ducks and conies (rabbits); no definition of game is given, but that in the 1828 Act is generally accepted to apply here.[8] It has also been held that capercailzie are game for the purposes of the 1832 Act.[9] The Game Licences Act 1860 requires a licence for hunting game (again the 1828 definition is accepted in the absence of a definition in the Act),[10] woodcock, snipe, rabbits and deer.[11] For the Poaching Prevention Act 1862, game includes the species in the core definition above, the eggs of the birds listed there, woodcock, snipe and rabbits.[12] Only deer, pheasants, partridges, grouse and black game qualify as game

---

[3] Ground Game Act 1880, s.8.

[4] Heath, moor and black game are terms covering the red and black grouse and ptarmigan.

[5] Game (Scotland) Act 1772, ss.1, 3.

[6] Night Poaching Act 1828, s.13.

[7] *Ibid.*, s.1.

[8] Scott-Robinson, *op. cit.*, p. 9; deer were originally included in the 1832 Act but removed by the Deer (Scotland) Act 1959, Sched. 3.

[9] *Colquhoun's Trs.* v. *Lee*, 1957 S.L.T. (Sh.Ct.) 50; the status of the capercailzie is complicated by the fact that it became extinct in Britain during the second half of the eighteenth century, but it was reintroduced to Scotland from Sweden in 1837.

[10] Scott Robinson, *op. cit.*, p. 14.

[11] Game Licences Act 1860, ss.2, 4.

[12] Poaching Prevention Act 1862, s.1.

for the purpose of compensating agricultural tenants for damage caused by game;[13] the control of rabbits and hares lies within the hands of the tenants.[14]

4.2.4 In England and Wales, the core definition noted above is the one which appears in the Game Act 1831.[15] The Night Poaching Act 1828 includes bustards within the definition,[16] and the Poaching Prevention Act 1862 applies to the core species and to rabbits, woodcock, snipe and the eggs of the birds in the core definition.[17] The Game Licences Act 1860 requires a licence for the hunting of game (undefined, but probably the core definition with the inclusion of bustards as in the 1828 Act) and of deer, rabbits, woodcock and snipe.[18]

4.2.5 Game birds are excluded from the provisions of Part I of the Wildlife and Countryside Act 1981 which give protection to wild birds, and are defined for that purpose as pheasant, partridge, grouse (or moor game), black (or heath) game, or ptarmigan.[19] The other species of wildfowl (ducks and geese) which are hunted do fall within the 1981 Act and their hunting is regulated by the provisions there.[20]

Killing and taking game

4.2.6 The right to take and kill game is one of the incidents of the ownership of land. The animals and birds themselves are *res nullius*, capable of appropriation by anyone who can take them, but no one has the right to enter land to take game in the absence of permission from the owner. This position at common law is backed up by a large number of statutory provisions creating offences relating to trespass in pursuit of game. The right to take game may, however, be severed from

---

[13] Agricultural Holdings (Scotland) Act 1991, s.53; the equivalent English legislation no longer refers to "damage from game" but to "damage from wild animals or birds the right to kill and take which is vested in the landlord or anyone (other than the tenant himself) claiming under the landlord" (Agricultural Holdings Act 1986, s.20).

[14] Ground Game Act 1880; see para. 4.2.8, below.

[15] Game Act 1831, s.2.

[16] Night Poaching Act 1828, s.13.

[17] Poaching Prevention Act 1862, s.1.

[18] Game Licences Act 1860, ss.2, 4.

[19] WCA, s.27.

[20] See para. 4.2.15, below.

other rights in the land and is frequently the subject of a separate lease or is reserved, for his own use or for separate leasing, when the proprietor allows a tenant to occupy the land. The particular extent of the rights granted or reserved, and other matters relating to the management of the land will depend on the terms of individual agreements.

4.2.7 The holder of the right to take game is entitled to access to the land to exercise his right, and can authorise other people to exercise the right with him or in his stead. Those involved in killing or taking game, deer, woodcock and snipe must have a game licence under the Game Licences Act 1860.[21] A number of exceptions exist including: the taking of woodcock by nets or springes, the hunting of hares with hounds, the taking of rabbits on enclosed land by or with the permission of the proprietor or tenant, the taking or killing of deer in enclosed lands by or with the permission of the owner or occupier.[22] No licence is required for the killing of hares by the owner or occupier of the land,[23] and the law also provides that members of the Royal Family and gamekeepers appointed by the Queen are exempt from the licensing requirements.[24] When someone is discovered doing acts requiring a licence, the licence must be displayed on request from an Inland Revenue officer, gamekeeper, owner or occupier of the land or the holder of a game licence.[25] A licence is valid for the whole United Kingdom unless it has been taken out solely in a person's capacity as a gamekeeper.[26]

4.2.8 The occupier of land does however have the right to take and kill ground game (*i.e.* rabbits and hares) on his land.[27] This right is inseparable from the occupation of the land but may be exercised only by the occupier and those authorised by him in writing. Only the occupier and one other person (who must fall within certain categories) are allowed to use firearms. No game licence is required for the exercise of this right.[28]

---

[21] Game Licences Act 1860, s.4 (amended by Protection of Birds Act 1954, Sched. 6).

[22] *Ibid.*, s.5; for deer see paras. 4.2.16–4.2.27, below.

[23] *Ibid.*; this exception applies to those authorised under the provisions (which are differently worded) of the Hares Act 1848, s.1 (England and Wales), and the Hares (Scotland) Act 1848, s.1.

[24] *Ibid.*, s.5.

[25] *Ibid.*, s.10.

[26] *Ibid.*, s.18.

[27] Ground Game Act 1880, s.1.

[28] *Ibid.*, s.4.

4.2.9 There are also limits on who can sell game. A dealer in game must obtain both a licence from the district council (or equivalent local authority)[29] and an excise licence.[30]

Close seasons and methods of taking
4.2.10 The taking and killing of game is prohibited during the close seasons. A table showing the open seasons for game appears below.[31] In England the taking or killing of game on Sundays and on Christmas Day is prohibited[32] but no such *legal* prohibition applies to game in Scotland.[33] There is no close season on the killing of rabbits and hares, although rights under the Ground Game Act 1880 may be exercised on open moorland and unenclosed land in England and Wales only between September 1–March 31, with the use of firearms permitted only between December 11–March 31 unless all interested parties agree to waive this further restriction.[34] In Scotland such rights may be exercised all year, but the use of firearms is not permitted in April, May or June.[35] The close seasons do not apply in Scotland to the taking of pheasants and partridges for breeding purposes.[36] The means by which it is permissible to kill and take game are dealt with later.[37]

4.2.11 Close seasons also apply to the sale of game. Game birds cannot be bought or sold ten days after the start of their close seasons.[38] The sale of indigenous hares is prohibited in the months of March, April, May, June and July.[39]

Poaching
4.2.12 It is a criminal offence unlawfully to take or kill game or rabbits at night,[40] to enter land with any gun, net or other

[29] Game Act 1831, s.18, extended to apply to Scotland by Game Licences Act 1860, s.13.
[30] Game Licences Act 1860, s.14.
[31] Appendix B.
[32] Game Act 1831, s.3.
[33] See Parkes & Thornley, *op. cit.*, p. 57; *cf.* the position for wildfowl, para. 4.2.15, below.
[34] Ground Game Act 1880, s.1(2); Ground Game Act 1906, ss.1, 2.
[35] Ground Game Act 1880, s.1(2) (amended by Agriculture (Scotland) Act 1948, s.48).
[36] Game (Scotland) Act 1772, s.2.
[37] See section 4.4, below.
[38] Game Act 1831, s.4 (amended by Game Act 1970, s.1).
[39] Hares Preservation Act 1892, s.2.
[40] Night Poaching Act 1828, s.1, extended to apply to roads and highways by Night Poaching Act 1844, s.1.

instrument in pursuit of game at night,[41] or trespass in pursuit of game, woodcock, snipe or rabbits during the day.[42] Greater penalties are incurred if at night there are three or more offenders or they are armed,[43] and by day if there are five or more offenders or (in Scotland only) if the offender has a blackened or otherwise disguised face.[44] These provisions do not apply to those hunting with hounds for hares, foxes or (in England and Wales only) deer.[45] In England and Wales it is also an offence for a person without the right to take game, to remove or destroy the eggs of any game bird, swan, wild duck, teal or widgeon.[46]

Enforcement

4.2.13 Any person found trespassing in pursuit of game can be required by the person holding the game rights, the occupier of the land or their servants to give his name and address and to leave the land. If he fails to comply with such a request he can be apprehended by the same people; at night he can be apprehended immediately, without preliminaries.[47] Any game found on such a suspected offender can be seized,[48] and any assault on those exercising such powers is an offence.[49] Where an accused argues that he is in fact authorised in his conduct, the onus of proving any licence, etc., lies on him.[50]

Wildfowl

4.2.14 Wild ducks and geese generally fall outwith the scope of the game legislation, although wild ducks are included in the scope of some provisions. In Scotland it is an offence to trespass during the day in pursuit of wild ducks,[51] and in England and Wales it is an offence for someone with no game rights on the land to remove or destroy their eggs.[52] Snipe and woodcock are

---

[41] Night Poaching Act 1828, s.1.
[42] Game Act 1831, s.30; Game (Scotland) Act 1832, s.1.
[43] Night Poaching Act 1828, s.9.
[44] Game Act 1831, s.30; Game (Scotland) Act 1832, s.1.
[45] *Ibid.*, s.35; *ibid.*, s.4.
[46] Game Act 1831, s.24; see also para. 3.3.6, above.
[47] *Ibid.*, s.31; Game (Scotland) Act 1832, s.2; Night Poaching Act 1828, s.2.
[48] Game Act 1831 s.36; Game (Scotland) Act 1832, s.5.
[49] *Ibid.*, s.32; *ibid.*, s.6.
[50] *Ibid.*, s.42; *ibid.*, s.12.
[51] Game (Scotland) Act 1832, s.1.
[52] Game Act 1831, s.24.

similarly covered by some of the provisions on game discussed above. No game licence is required to shoot wildfowl. Landlowners may restrict access to their land, and there is some uncertainty on the use of the foreshore for this purpose.[53]

4.2.15 Wild ducks, wild geese, snipe, woodcock and other birds which do not count as "game" do, however, fall within the provisions of Part I of the Wildlife and Countryside Act 1981. This imposes a general prohibition on any intentional killing or taking of wild birds, except for those species listed in Part I of Schedule 2 to the Act. These may be killed or taken except during the close seasons, on Sundays and Christmas Day in Scotland, and on Sundays in areas of England and Wales prescribed by the Secretary of State.[54] The means by which these and all other sorts of wild bird may be killed or taken are also regulated.[55]

Deer

4.2.16 The law concerning deer offers these animals protection at some times of the year and in some circumstances, regulates their hunting, controls the means by which they can be killed or taken and provides for their destruction as pests. As the law is found in modern legislation providing more or less comprehensive codes, it is sensible to examine all aspects of the law together. The law in Scotland is somewhat different from that in England and Wales, and suffers from the fact that the neatness of having a fairly modern restatement of the law has been lost by more recent amendments, whereas the English legislation has recently been consolidated. The overall effect of the two sets of lesgislation is broadly similar, but the existence of the Red Deer Commission in Scotland and the many detailed differences mean that the two jurisdictions have to be treated separately.

Scotland

4.2.17 The relevant legislation in Scotland is the Deer (Scotland) Act 1959, amended primarily by the Deer (Amendment) (Scotland) Acts 1967 and 1982. The control and

---

[53] See Parkes & Thornley, *op. cit.*, pp. 211–213.
[54] WCA, ss.1, 2; see paras. 3.3.1–3.3.7, above.
[55] See paras. 4.4.15–4.4.17, below.

conservation of red and sika deer[56] is supervised by the Red Deer Commission,[57] and the Commission may grant authority for its own staff or others to kill deer in certain circumstances. Generally though, as with game, the right to take or kill deer is a right enjoyed by the owner of the land or those to whom he has transferred this right. A game licence is required to take or kill deer,[58] except where the deer are killed or taken on enclosed land by or with the permission of the owner or occupier,[59] or through the actions of those authorised or required to take action against red or sika deer by the Red Deer Commission.[60] Licences are also required for dealing in venison.[61]

4.2.18 There are close seasons for four species of deer in Scotland, set out in Appendix B,[62] and during the close season it is an offence to take or wilfully to kill or injure any deer.[63] This prohibition does not apply to farmed deer which are enclosed and properly marked,[64] nor to action required or authorised by the Red Deer Commission in relation to deer causing damage.[65] Also excluded is action taken by the occupier of agricultural land or enclosed woodland or others authorised by him[66] where deer are found on arable land, garden ground or enclosed grassland or woodland, and where the occupier has reasonable cause to believe that serious damage will be caused to crops, pasture, trees, animal or human food stuffs unless the deer are killed.[67] Licences granted for scientific purposes by the

[56] Hybrids between the two species are also covered: Deer (Scotland) Act 1959 s.33(4E) (added by Deer (Amendment) (Scotland) Act 1982, s.13).
[57] Deer (Scotland) Act 1959, s.1 (amended by Deer (Amendment) (Scotland) Act 1982, s.1); see paras. 2.6.13–2.6.14, above. The Commission's powers can be extended to other species by the Secretary of State.
[58] Game Licences Act 1860, s.4.
[59] *Ibid.*, s.5.
[60] Deer (Scotland) Act 1959, s.14.
[61] *Ibid.*, ss.25A–25F (added by Deer (Amendment) (Scotland) Act 1982, s.11).
[62] *Ibid.*, s.21(1), (2) (amended by Deer (Amendment) (Scotland) Act 1982, s.6); Deer (Close Seasons) (Scotland) Order 1984, S.I. 1984 No. 76; see Appendix B.
[63] *Ibid.*, s.21(1).
[64] *Ibid.*, s.21(5A) (added by Deer (Amendment) (Scotland) Act 1982, s.7).
[65] *Ibid.*, s.33(2) (substituted by Deer (Amendment) (Scotland) Act 1967, s.2).
[66] Only certain categories of person can be authorised without the approval of the Red Deer Commission.
[67] Deer (Scotland) Act 1959, s.33(3) (substituted by Deer (Amendment) (Scotland) Act 1982, s.13).

Secretary of State can also authorise conduct normally prohibited during the close season.[68] It is also lawful to do acts in order to prevent suffering by injured or diseased deer or by a calf or fawn deprived of its mother.[69]

4.2.19 The capture of live deer is permitted in any manner not causing unnecessary suffering,[70] but otherwise the only lawful method of taking, killing or injuring a deer is by shooting with a firearm.[71] The permitted categories of firearms and ammunition are prescribed in regulations made by the Secretary of State, which also prohibit the use of certain forms of sights, and allow him to grant special exemptions.[72] The use of shotguns is permitted in the case of action against deer causing serious damage, etc., but only with the specified forms of ammunition. Taking, killing or injuring a deer at night is unlawful,[73] unless the action is to avoid suffering,[74] is taken on the authority of the Red Deer Commission to control damage,[75] or is taken by the occupier of agricultural land or enclosed woodland in relation to red or sika deer where he has reasonable grounds for believing that serious damage to his crops or trees will be caused if the deer are not killed.[76] The discharge of any firearm or missile at a deer from any aircraft is prohibited, as is the use of aircraft to transport live deer unless the animal is inside the aircraft or the operation is approved by a veterinary practitioner.[77] Also prohibited is the use of vehicles to drive deer on unenclosed land with a view to killing or injuring the deer, or to taking

---

[68] *Ibid.*, s.33(3B) (added by *ibid.*).

[69] *Ibid.*, s.33(1) (amended by Deer (Amendment) (Scotland) Act 1967, s.2; Deer (Amendment) (Scotland) Act 1982, s.12); unlike the "mercy killing" provisions in the Wildlife and Countryside Act 1981 and in relation to seals and badgers, this is not qualified to deny the benefit of the exception to a person who caused the suffering in the first place, although that initial act may well itself be an offence unprotected by the exception.

[70] *Ibid.*, s.23(5).

[71] *Ibid.*, s.23(2).

[72] *Ibid.*, s.23A (added by Deer (Amendment) (Scotland) Act 1982, s.10); Deer (Firearms) (Scotland) Order 1985, S.I. 1985 No. 1168; see Appendix B.

[73] *Ibid.*, s.23(1) (amended by Deer (Amendment) (Scotland) Act 1982, s.6).

[74] *Ibid.*, s.33(1) (amended by Deer (Amendment) (Scotland) Act 1967, s.2; Deer (Amendment) (Scotland) Act 1982, s.12).

[75] *Ibid.*, s.33(2)(a) (substituted by Deer (Amendment) (Scotland) Act 1967, s.2), (4A) (added by Deer (Amendment) (Scotland) Act 1982, s.13).

[76] *Ibid.*, s.33(4) (substituted by Deer (Amendment) (Scotland) Act 1982, s.13).

[77] *Ibid.*, s.23(2A)–(2C) (added by Deer (Amendment) (Scotland) Act 1982, s.8); the latter provision is to prevent the carriage of deer in nets suspended below helicopters.

them alive (unless no unnecessary suffering is caused).[78] The wilful injury of any deer with a firearm is an offence.[79]

4.2.20 As noted above, the law is relaxed in relation to the close seasons in order to allow occupiers to take action to control deer which are causing serious damage to agriculture or forestry, and is similarly relaxed to allow for control measures authorised by the Red Deer Commission. The Commission can authorise the killing of red or sika deer where it is satisfied that such deer on agricultural land, woodland or garden ground are causing damage to crops, forestry or farm animals (including serious overgrazing) and that the killing is necessary to prevent the damage.[80] Any competent person can be authorised for this purpose, the authorisation lasting for 28 days, and where the power is exercised the landowner must be notified and people likely to be on the land warned. Where the deer are coming from particular land, the person with the right to kill deer there must first be requested to take the necessary action (provided that the Commission is satisfied that he will act forthwith) and authorisation for others to act can only be given once he has proved unable or unwilling to satisfy the request. In relation to other species of deer similar powers exist but only the servants of the Commission acting with the consent of the occupier can be authorised to kill.[81]

4.2.21 More general control measures can be introduced by means of a control scheme for the reduction in numbers or extermination or red or sika deer in a locality where they are causing damage to agriculture or forestry. The Red Deer Commission is to determine the necessary measures and consult with the owners and occupiers before introducing an agreed scheme or making a scheme to take effect once confirmed by the Secretary of State.[82] The scheme will set out the aims of the scheme, the area and duration of its operation, the number and kind of deer to be killed and the measures to be taken to execute the scheme (which cannot include a requirement to construct fences).[83] Owners and occupiers are under a duty to

[78] *Ibid.*, s.23(3A), (5) (amended by Deer (Amendment) (Scotland) Act 1982, s.9).
[79] *Ibid.*, s.23A(5) (added by Deer (Amendment) (Scotland) Act 1982, s.10).
[80] *Ibid.*, s.6 (amended by Deer (Amendment) (Scotland) Act 1982, s.3).
[81] *Ibid.*, s.6A (added by *ibid.*, s.4).
[82] *Ibid.*, s.7 (amended by *ibid.* s.1).
[83] *Ibid.*, s.8 (amended by *ibid.*).

take the measures required by the scheme.[84] Wilful failure to comply is a criminal offence,[85] and in the event of any failure the Commission must itself carry out any requirements of the scheme which it is satisfied are still necessary, recovering the cost through the sale of the deer killed and, for any sum still outstanding, from the owner or occupier.[86] A person authorised to kill deer under these provisions does not require a game licence,[87] and powers of entry are provided to ensure that the Commission can carry out its tasks effectively.[88]

4.2.22 The enforcement of the law relating to deer is assisted by a number of provisions. It is an offence for anyone who has no right to do so to take, kill or injure deer or to remove a deer carcase,[89] and where more than one person is acting together the penalties for this and the other offences noted above relating to killing or taking deer at unlawful times or by unlawful means are increased.[90] Trespassing in pursuit of deer is not itself an offence, but it is likely that a firearms offence will be involved.[91] The possession of deer in circumstances where there are reasonable grounds for suspecting that it has been unlawfully taken is an offence, as is the unlawful possession of firearms for this purpose.[92] Powers of arrest, search and seizure are conferred,[93] and for some offences a single witness suffices for conviction.[94]

England and Wales
4.2.23 The legislation for England and Wales has been recently consolidated in the Deer Act 1991.[95] As in Scotland, the right to take deer lies primarily with the owner of the land, but this right can be transferred separately and occupiers are given some rights in relation to deer causing damage. A game licence is

[84] *Ibid.*, s.9(1).
[85] *Ibid.*, s.(2).
[86] *Ibid.*, ss.10, 11.
[87] *Ibid.*, s.14 (amended by Deer (Amendment) (Scotland) Act 1982, s.1).
[88] *Ibid.*, s.15 (amended by Deer (Amendment) (Scotland) Act 1967, s.1; Deer (Amendment) (Scotland) Act 1982, s.1).
[89] *Ibid.*, s.22 (amended by Deer (Amendment) (Scotland) Act 1982, ss.6, 14).
[90] *Ibid.*, s.24 (amended by *ibid.*, s.14).
[91] *Ferguson* v.*Macphail*, 1987 S.C.C.R. 52.
[92] Deer (Scotland) Act 1959, s.25.
[93] *Ibid.*, ss.27–28.
[94] *Ibid.*, s.25(4).
[95] Replacing the Deer Act 1963, as amended by the Wildlife and Countryside Act 1981 and by the Deer Act 1987, and the Deer Act 1980.

required except for the taking or killing of deer on enclosed land by or with the permission of the owner or occupier.[96] Only licensed game dealers can deal in venison.[97]

4.2.24 For the four main species of deer close seasons are specified, different from those in Scotland.[98] It is an offence to take or intentionally to kill any deer during the close season,[99] except for action taken to prevent the suffering of diseased or injured deer,[1] to meet the requirements of an order for agricultural pest control,[2] or where a person falling within certain limited categories acts to prevent damage by deer on cultivated land, pasture or enclosed woodland.[3] The close season does not apply to deer farms where the deer are clearly marked and kept on enclosed land,[4] and the Countryside Council for Wales and the Nature Conservancy Council for England can grant licences for removing live deer from one area to another or for the taking of live deer for scientific or educational purposes.[5]

4.2.25 It is an offence to set any trap or snare or to lay any poison in positions likely to cause bodily injury to deer, or to use these methods or a net to take or kill a deer.[6] Also prohibited is the use of any firearm other than those permitted by the Secretary of State (different from those allowed in Scotland),[7] any arrow, spear or similar missile or any drugged or poisoned missile.[8] Motor vehicles cannot be used to drive deer or for the discharge of any firearm or missile, unless in relation to enclosed land where deer are normally kept and with the occupier's written permission.[9] It is also an offence to take or wilfully kill deer at night,[10] except in the case of deer taken

[96] Game Licences Act 1860, ss.4, 5.
[97] Deer Act 1991, s.10.
[98] *Ibid.*, s.2 and Sched, 1; see Appendix B.
[99] *Ibid.*, s.2(1).
[1] *Ibid.*, s.6(2).
[2] *Ibid.*, s.6(1), referring to action required under s.98 of the Agriculture Act 1948; see para. 4.5.2, below.
[3] *Ibid.*, s.7; see para. 4.2.26, below.
[4] *Ibid.*, s.2(3).
[5] *Ibid.*, s.8.
[6] *Ibid.*, s.4(1).
[7] Specified *ibid.*, Sched. 2; see Appendix B.
[8] *Ibid.*, s.4(2).
[9] *Ibid.*, s.4(4), (5).
[10] *Ibid.*, s.3.

in accordance with requirements for agricultural pest control.[11] Action taken to relieve the suffering of diseased or injured deer is exempt from the prohibitions on night shooting and the use of traps and nets, and a wider range of firearms can be used.[12] The use of nets, traps and devices to project these can be authorised by the conservancy councils in relation to live deer for scientific and educational purposes or for the purpose of removing deer from one area to another.[13]

4.2.26 The control of deer as pests can be undertaken under the more general rules on pest control under s.98 of the Agriculture Act 1948 by which the agriculture ministers can make pest control orders requiring measures to combat deer and other pests.[14] More generally and as noted above, the law on the close seasons and night shooting are relaxed to allow action to be taken against deer causing damage.[15] The relaxation is available only to the occupier of the land,[16] members of his household or staff authorised by him and the person who has the right to kill deer on the land (if different from the occupier),[17] and covers the shooting of deer with prescribed firearms[18] on cultivated land, pasture or enclosed woodland.[19] It applies where it can be shown that there is reasonable cause to suspect deer of the same species of causing damage to crops, vegetables, fruit, growing timber or other forms of property, that it is likely that further serious damage will be caused, and that the killing is necessary to prevent such damage.[20] This provision may, however, be restricted by the Secretary of State in relation to particular species or particular areas.[21]

4.2.27 Trespass in search or pursuit of deer with the intention of killing or injuring it is an offence, as is any intentional taking, killing or injuring of deer, pursuit of deer or removal of carcases

---

[11] *Ibid.*, s.6(1).
[12] *Ibid.*, s.6(3), (4).
[13] *Ibid.*, s.8.
[14] See para. 4.5.2, below.
[15] Deer Act 1991, s.7.
[16] *I.e.* the occupier of the land on which the shooting takes place, *Traill* v. *Buckingham* [1972] 1 W.L.R. 459.
[17] Deer Act 1991, s.7(4).
[18] For this purpose including shotguns using specified ammunition; *ibid.*, s.7(2); see Appendix B.
[19] *Ibid.*, s.7(1).
[20] *Ibid.*, s.7(3).
[21] *Ibid.*, s.7(5).

without the consent of the owner or occupier of the land or other lawful authority.[22] An authorised person may require a person suspected of committing these offences to give his name and address and to quit the land,[23] and more general powers of search and seizure are provided to assist in the enforcement of the Act.[24]

FISHING

4.3.1 Fish and fishing are the subject of considerable legal attention. Although there are few measures which are expressly conservationist in intention, the measures designed to protect stocks from over-exploitation and to protect private fishing rights do operate to the benefit of aquatic species generally and are the main way (other than pollution controls[25]) in which the law intervenes with the aquatic environment. Moreover, as with game rights, the economic value of fishing rights can provide a strong incentive for their owners to take steps to protect the quality of waters to the benefit of wildlife more generally. The following paragraphs offer an outline of the law on issues which are most likely to have consequences for nature conservation.

4.3.2 Inland fishing is burdened with considerable legal controls, with significant differences between Scotland and England and Wales; special regimes apply to the Tweed and Solway.[26] As with taking and killing game, the right to catch fish is largely an incident of the ownership of land, but can be sold and leased separately. In addition to any restrictions imposed by proprietors, the law lays down some general rules relating to closed times and means of fishing, but to some extent the details of the regulation of fisheries is left to the bye-laws of the administrative bodies vested with powers in this area. In England and Wales the National Rivers Authority inherited this

---

[22] *Ibid.*, s.1(1), (2); belief that one has consent or other lawful authority, or that consent would be given were the circumstances known, is a defence (s.1(3)).

[23] *Ibid.*, s.1(4).

[24] *Ibid.*, s.12.

[25] See section 8.5, below.

[26] See generally, S. Scott Robinson, *The Law of Game, Salmon and Freshwater Fishing in Scotland* (1990); W.M. Gordon, *Scottish Land Law* (1989), Chap. 8; W. Howarth, *Freshwater Fishery Law* (1987); R.I. Millichamp, *A Guide to Angling Law* (1990).

function from the water authorities abolished by the Water Act 1989.[27] Fish farms and other waters where fish are kept in captivity and artifically reared are exempt from many of the provisions noted below.[28]

4.3.3 In Scotland, the law concerning salmon fishing is different from that for other sorts of fish. The right to catch salmon originally lay with the Crown as part of the *regalia minora* (except in Orkney and Shetland where udal law provided differently), but in very many instances the right has been granted to others. Salmon fishings can constitute a separate heritable tenement which can be held independently of any proprietorial rights in the land affected. In relation to other fish, the general rule is that in rivers which are navigable and tidal, and in some large lochs which are also used for public navigation, the right to catch fish is enjoyed by the public at large. In other waters fishing rights lie within the riparian proprietors, but may be expressly transferred to others, although not as a separate holding. In England and Wales, the right to fish for salmon is not treated separately. The general distinction between public and private fisheries exists, but the National Rivers Authority[29] operates a licensing scheme to regulate fishing for salmon, trout, freshwater fish and eels.[30] In both jurisdictions the rights of the public may be considerably curtailed in practical terms by the absence of any means of access to the waters where fishing may be permissible.

4.3.4 In Scotland, the proprietors of salmon fisheries in a district may form a district salmon fishery board, now regulated by the Salmon Act 1986. Such boards may do such acts, execute such works and incur such expenditure as appears expedient for the protection and improvement of fisheries in their district, for the increase of salmon and the stocking of waters with salmon.[31] The boards can raise money by means of an assessment on the fisheries in the district.[32] For other sorts of fish, the Secretary of State can make Protection Orders regulating and imposing

[27] Water Act 1989, s.141, Sched. 17; see now Water Resources Act 1991, Pt. V.

[28] See generally W. Howarth, *The Law of Aquaculture* (1990).

[29] By virtue of the Water Act 1989, Sched. 17, the NRA exercises the functions of the water authorities in relation to fishing and all earlier statutes are to be read in this way.

[30] Salmon and Freshwater Fisheries Act 1975, s.25.

[31] Salmon Act 1986, s.16.

[32] *Ibid.*, s.15.

controls and charges on fishing in specified areas and authorising wardens to exercise enforcement powers.[33] In England and Wales, in addition to operating the licensing scheme, the National Rivers Authority is responsible for maintaining, improving and developing fisheries for salmon, trout and other species,[34] whilst the Secretary of State may make general regulations.[35]

4.3.5 In Scotland, it is an offence to fish for or take any unclean salmon (*i.e.* one which has spawned or is about to spawn) unless it is taken by accident and returned to the water with the least possible injury.[36] It is also unlawful knowingly to take any smolt or fry (*i.e.* young salmon before their migration to the sea), or to obstruct the passage of smolt or fry or the passage of mature salmon to spawning grounds during the annual close time, or to injure any spawn or spawning bed or shallow where spawn might be.[37] These prohibitions do not extend to action taken for the propagation of salmon or other scientific purposes nor to the incidental results of the cleaning of any dam or lade or exercise of property rights over the bed of a watercourse.[38] It is also lawful for a salmon fishery district board to take measures to prevent salmon reaching beds where from the nature of the stream their spawn might be destroyed.[39] Fixed engines (*i.e.* fixed nets or traps of any sort) are prohibited in inland waters,[40] and the construction and use of dams, sluices and gratings is also controlled.[41]

4.3.6 In England and Wales the intentional killing or taking of any immature or unclean (*i.e.* about to spawn or not yet recovered from spawning) fish is an offence.[42] It is also an offence wilfully to disturb any spawn or spawning fish or any

---

[33] Freshwater and Salmon Fisheries (Scotland) Act 1976, s.1.

[34] Water Resources Act 1991, s.114.

[35] *Ibid.*, s.115 (Agriculture Minister in England, Secretary of State in Wales).

[36] Salmon Fisheries (Scotland) Act 1868, s.20.

[37] *Ibid.*, s.19; this provision has been used to prevent an attempt to raft down a salmon river which might have disturbed shallows used by spawning slamon.

[38] *Ibid.*

[39] *Ibid.*

[40] Salmon and Freshwater Fisheries (Protection) (Scotland) Act 1951, s.2(1); a handful of long-standing cruives may remain in legitimate use; see Scott Robinson, *op. cit.*, p. 102.

[41] Salmon Fisheries (Scotland) Act 1862, Bye-law G.

[42] Salmon and Freshwater Fisheries Act 1975, s.2(2), (3); see *Pyle* v. *Welsh Water Authority* (unreported, noted in Howarth, *Freshwater Fishery Law* (1987) p. 36).

bed, bank or shallow where spawn or spawning fish might be, except in the exercise of a legal right to extract material (*e.g.* gravel) from the waters or in cases authorised by the National Rivers authority for the purposes of artificial propagation, scientific activities or the development of private fisheries.[43] Fish passes in English and Welsh waters containing salmon or migratory trout are controlled by the National Rivers Authority, which can require their construction and maintenance when dams are being built or altered, or itself (with ministerial approval) build fish passes.[44] The wilful alteration or injury to a fish pass, and any act obstructing the use of one or scaring, hindering or preventing fish from using it is an offence, as is a failure on the part of the owner or occupier to comply with a notice from the National Rivers Authority to restore a fish pass which has fallen into disrepair.[45] The law also regulates the use of sluices and provides for gratings to be installed and maintained to protect fish from being caught in mill races etc.[46] Fixed engines (*i.e.* any form of fixed net or trap for catching fish) and fishing weirs are also prohibited unless expressly authorised.[47]

4.3.7 In both jurisdictions, fishing is prohibited during the close times and there are also requirements relating to the removal of nets and other equipment during the close times to reduce the likelihood of their being improperly used.[48] In Scotland there is in relation to salmon a weekly close time, from 6.00 pm on Friday until 6.00 am on Monday, during which it is illegal to fish by nets whilst fishing by rod and line is unlawful on a Sunday.[49] There is also an annual close time of at least 168 days during which fishing is prohibited, although for fishing by rod and line a shorter period may be prescribed.[50] Each district or part of a district may have a different period set and there are considerable variations throughout Scotland. For trout the

---

[43] *Ibid.*, s.2(4), (5); *National Rivers Authority* v. *Jones* (unreported, see *The Times* March 10, 1992).
[44] Salmon and Freshwater Fisheries Act 1975, ss.9, 10.
[45] *Ibid.*, s.12.
[46] *Ibid.*, ss.13–15.
[47] *Ibid.*, ss.6–7.
[48] *e.g.*, Salmon Fisheries (Scotland) Act 1868, s.23.
[49] Salmon and Freshwater Fisheries (Protection) (Scotland) Act 1951, s.13 (as amended by Freshwater and Salmon Fisheries (Scotland) Act 1976, s.7 and Sched. 3) and Salmon (Weekly Close Time) (Scotland) Regulations 1988, S.I. 1988 No. 390.
[50] Salmon Act 1986, s.6.

close season runs October 7–March 14,[51] with no weekly close time.

4.3.8 In England and Wales the close time can be set by local bye-laws made by the National Rivers Authority, but in accordance with minimum times provided by statute, which also specifies the dates and times to be applied in the absence of local rules.[52] For salmon there must be an annual close time of at least 153 days for nets, etc.,[53] and 92 days for rod and line[54] and a weekly close time of 42 hours.[55] For trout the minimum close times are 181 and 153 days[56] with a 42 hour weekly close time as for salmon. For other freshwater fish and rainbow trout the close time can be dispensed with by bye-laws, but otherwise extends for at least 93 days.[57] The close season for catching salmon and trout by putt and putcher (a form of fixed trap) is set at 242 days.[58]

4.3.9 The law also restricts the possession and sale of fish during the close seasons and provides wide enforcement powers to allow for the search and seizure of unlawfully taken fish and equipment used. Provisions exist for the introduction of a scheme for licensing salmon dealers.[59]

4.3.10 Only a limited number of methods are permissible in the catching of fish. In addition to the prohibition of the use of poison discussed more fully below,[60] there are prohibitions in both jurisdictions on the use of explosive or electrical devices.[61] In relation to these and the other activities mentioned below, authorisation for their use can be given for scientific purposes or the development of fisheries by the salmon fishery district board (in some cases only) or the Secretary of State in Scotland, or by the National Rivers Authority in England and Wales.[62] In

---

[51] Freshwater Fisheries (Scotland) Act 1902, s.1 (amended by Trout (Scotland) Act 1933, s.1).
[52] Salmon and Freshwater Fisheries Act 1975, s.19 and Sched, 1.
[53] Aug. 31–Feb. 1.
[54] Oct. 31–Feb. 1.
[55] 6.00am Saturday–6.00am Monday.
[56] Aug. 31 and Sep. 30 until March 1.
[57] March 14–June 16.
[58] Aug. 31–May 1.
[59] Salmon Act 1986, ss. 20, 31.
[60] See paras. 4.4.10–4.4.11, below.
[61] Salmon and Freshwater Fisheries (Protection) (Scotland) Act 1951, s.4; Salmon and Freshwater Fisheries Act 1975, s.5.
[62] *Ibid.*, s.9; *ibid.*, ss.1, 2.

relation to salmon in Scotland, authorisation may also be granted for the purpose of conserving any creature or other living thing.[63]

4.3.11 The only lawful methods of taking salmon in Scotland are by rod and line or by net and coble in relation to inland waters, with bag nets, fly nets or other stake nets being permissible in the other waters of a salmon fishery district.[64] Regulations made by the Secretary of State can define what is meant by the various means of netting[65] and specify for particular areas certain forms of bait and lure for the purposes of the definition of "rod and line."[66] For other fish in inland waters the only permitted method of catching fish is by rod and line, except that where all the proprietors agree nets may be used in a loch or pond and that the proprietor or occupier may catch fish other than trout or salmon with nets or traps.[67] These rules do not prevent the use of a gaff or landing net in conjunction with rod and line.[68] Contravening these provisions is an offence, and the penalties are increased if two or more offenders are involved.[69] The taking of salmon leaping at or trying to ascend falls or going through a fish pass is also an offence.[70]

4.3.12 In England and Wales, the approach of the legislation is to ban the unlawful methods of fishing rather than to specify the lawful ones. The prohibited methods include the use of firearms, wires, spears, lights, and the use of stones or missiles to facilitate the catching of fish.[71] Also prohibited is the use of

[63] Salmon Act 1986, s.28.
[64] Salmon and Freshwater Fisheries (Protection) (Scotland) Act 1951, s.2(1), (1A) (added by Salmon Act 1986, s.21); the boards' waters extend seaward three miles from the mean low-water springs (Salmon Act 1986, s.1(1)).
[65] *Ibid.*, s.2(2A) (added by Salmon Act 1986, s.21); Salmon (Definition of Methods of Net Fishing and Construction of Nets) (Scotland) Regulations 1992, S.I. 1992 No. 1974; Salmon (Definition of Methods of Net Fishing and Construction of Nets) (Scotland) (Amendment) Regulations 1993, S.I. 1993 No. 257.
[66] Salmon Act 1986, s.8, relating to the definition in Salmon and Freshwater Fisheries (Protection) (Scotland) Act 1951, s.24.
[67] Salmon and Freshwater Fisheries (Protection) (Scotland) Act 1951, s.2(2).
[68] *Ibid.*, s.2(3).
[69] *Ibid.*, s.3.
[70] Salmon Fisheries (Scotland) Act 1868, s.15.
[71] Salmon and Freshwater Fisheries Act 1975, s.1; possession of such implements with the intention of using them to catch fish is itself an offence, but gaffs used as an auxiliary to rod and line are permitted.

fish roe[72] and in relation to salmon or migratory trout the use of nets which stretch across more than three-quarters of the width of a stream or have too small a mesh.[73] Fixed engines, fishing weirs, mills and dams are also prohibited unless authorised through being lawfully in use in 1861 by ancient right and containing the requisite gaps, etc., to allow the passage of fish and protect the flow of water.[74]

4.3.13 At sea, different rules apply, arising both from the salmon legislation and the rules on marine fishing. As noted above, fishing on the Tweed and Solway is the subject of separate legislation.

4.3.14 For marine fishing generally, the law is mostly of recent origin and is designed to protect stocks from the depredations of fishing fleets which have become extremely, perhaps excessively, efficient, whilst at the same time balancing the competing economic and social interests of a large number of states within and outwith the European Community. Regulations emerge in shoals from Brussels to regulate the total allowable catches and the allocation and the use of national quotas, banning the fishing for particular species in particular places by boats from particular countries at particular times, as well as controlling the types of fishing gear, vessels and methods of fishing which are permitted, and now even the number of days during which fishermen can be at sea.

4.3.15 At national level there are wide powers for ministers to make orders regulating the minimum sizes of fish which can be caught and landed, the types of fishing gear permissible, and the areas and seasons in which fishing can take place, while there are licensing arrangements for fishing boats. In the exercise of these powers ministers must have regard to the conservation of marine flora and fauna and seek a reasonable balance between conservation and their other concerns under the fisheries legislation.[75]

4.3.16 All of these measures, by controlling the volume, nature and location of fishing activity, have considerable

---

[72] *Ibid.*, s.2.
[73] *Ibid.*, s.3; landing nets used as an auxillary to rod and line are permitted.
[74] *Ibid.*, ss.6–8; see most recently *Gray* v. *Blamey* [1991] 1 All E.R. 1.
[75] Sea Fisheries (Wildlife Conservation) Act 1992, s.1.

significance for the conservation of marine species, albeit with the traditional aim of ensuring continued exploitation rather than seeking to conserve the environment. The details of this very rapidly changing mass of legislation lie beyond the scope of this work, but those concerned with nature conservation should be aware of the existence of this legal structure which offers potential for furthering conservationist aims, *e.g.* restrictions on inshore fishing may have a major impact on the food supply for nesting sea-birds, and certain forms of fishing gear can have destructive side-effects for other species.[76]

4.3.17 The taking of shellfish is also surrounded by legislation. Private fisheries can be established for oysters, mussels, cockles, clams, scallops and queens and within these the holders of the right to take shellfish can regulate fishing.[77] Private fisheries for oysters and mussels are also protected in Scotland by older legislation prohibiting others from dredging or otherwise disturbing or taking shellfish from such beds.[78] In addition to making provision for the minimum permissible size of creatures to be caught,[79] general rules lay down close seasons for the sale of indigenous oysters,[80] ban the possession or sale of edible crabs which are carrying spawn or have just cast their shells,[81] and allow for regulations to prohibit the landing of lobsters carrying spawn.[82]

4.3.18 On a related issue, it has been held that in England and Wales there is a public right to dig for bait (usually worms) on the foreshore, as an ancillary to the public right of fishing there.[83] It was stressed however, that this right is just an

[76] For an account of the legal regime, see the entries on "Fisheries", *Stair Memorial Encyclopaedia of The Laws of Scotland* (1990), Vol. 11, and *Halsbury's Laws of England* (4th ed., 1977), Vol. 18; and especially the relevant Supplements.
[77] Sea Fisheries (Shellfish) Act 1967, ss.1–3 (amended by Sea Fisheries Act 1968, s.15, extended by Shellfish (Specification of Molluscs) Regualtions 1987, S.I. 1987 No. 218).
[78] Oyster Fisheries (Scotland) Act 1840; Mussel Fisheries (Scotland) Act 1847.
[79] Sea Fish (Conservation) Act 1967, s.1; e.g. the Under-sized Lobsters Order 1993, S.I. 1993 No. 1178.
[80] Sea Fisheries (Shellfish) Act 1967, s.16.
[81] *Ibid.*, s.17; this does not apply if it can be shown that the crabs are for use as bait.
[82] *Ibid.*, s.17(3) (no such regulations have been made).
[83] *Anderson v. Alnwick District Council* [1993] 1 W.L.R. 1156.

ancillary one and that no taking of bait for commerical purposes would be legitimate.

METHODS OF KILLING AND TAKING

4.4.1 The means by which wild creatures can be caught and killed is the subject of considerable legislation which prohibits or controls the use of poison and traps as well as the use of certain aids to taking animals. More specific rules apply to particular species, e.g. badgers, seals and deer where there are strict controls on the sort of firearms and ammunition which can be used in hunting them.[84]

Poison

4.4.2 The use of poisons is controlled in various ways. Pesticides and their use are controlled generally by Part III of the Food and Environment Protection Act 1985 and the regulations made under it.[85] The basic conditions for the supply, storage and use of pesticides require that all reasonable precautions are taken to protect the health of human beings, creatures and plants and to safeguard the environment,[86] while notification must be given to various authorities before any aerial applications.[87] Similarly, the release of many poisonous substances is controlled by the laws regulating pollution.[88] The discharge and deposit of waste in liquid, gas or solid form are all controlled, with licences or other forms of approval being required for a large range of activities. These provisions should offer protection against conduct which would cause harm to the environment.

Animals
4.4.3 For the more specific legislation, perhaps the most convenient starting point is offered by the general provisions in s.8 of the Protection of Animals Act 1911[89] and s.7 of the

---

[84] See paras. 3.4.7, 3.4.16, 4.2.19, 4.2.25, above.
[85] Control of Pesticides Regulations 1986, S.I. 1986 No. 1510; Pesticides (Maximum Residue Levels in Food) Regulations 1988, S.I. 1988 No. 1378.
[86] Control of Pesticides Regualtions 1986, Sched. 2 para. 1, Sched. 3 para. 1.
[87] *Ibid.*, Sched. 4.
[88] See generally, C.T. Reid (ed.), *Green's Guide to Environmental Law in Scotland* (1992); S. Ball & S. Bell, *Environmental Law* (2nd ed., 1994).
[89] As amended by the Protection of Animals (Amendment) Act 1927, s.1.

Protection of Animals (Scotland) Act 1912. These sections make it an offence knowingly to place, or cause to be placed, on any land or in any building any poison or any fluid or edible matter (other than sown seed or grain) which has been rendered poisonous. This general prohibition on the laying of poison is however qualified by the existence of a defence if the poison is placed in order to destroy vermin in the interests of public health, agriculture or the protection of other animals or for manuring the land, provided that all reasonable precautions are taken to protect dogs, cats, fowls and other domestic animals.[90] These sections also prohibit the sale of any seed or grain which has been rendered poisonous, except for their bona fide use in agriculture.

4.4.4 The use of a particular poison can be prohibited or restricted by the Secretary of State if he is satisfied that it cannot be used for destroying animals or particular kinds of animals without causing undue suffering and that there are suitable alternative methods for destroying them which are adequate.[91] Only mammals count as "animals" for the purposes of this provision.[92] The effect of the regulations is to take the use of such poisons outwith the scope of the defences provided in s.8 of the Protection of Animals Act 1911 and s.7 of the Protection of Animals (Scotland) Act 1912, so that their use is a criminal offence. This power has been exercised so as to prohibit the use of phosphorous and red squill in all cases and the use of strychnine for all mammals except moles.[93]

4.4.5 Just as the use of a poison can be expressly taken outwith the scope of the defences in the 1911 and 1912 Acts, the use of poisons can be expressly brought within their scope. This can be achieved by ministerial approvals under the Food and Environment Protection Act 1985.[94] More specifically, the use

[90] The wording of the two provisions differs slightly: the Scottish provision refers simply to the destruction of "vermin," whereas the English one refers to "insects and other invertebrates, rats, mice, or other small ground vermin"; the Scottish provision refers to precautions to "prevent access" to the poison by dogs, etc., whereas the English one refers to precautions to "prevent injury" by the poison and includes wild birds within the categories entitled to protection.

[91] Animals (Cruel Poisons) Act 1962, s.2.

[92] *Ibid.*, s.3.

[93] Animals (Cruel Poisons) Regulations 1963, S.I. 1963 No. 1278; phosphorous is elementary yellow phosphorous and red squill is any powder or extract made from the plant *Urginea maritima* (L.) Baker (the sea squill).

[94] Food and Environment Protection Act 1985, s.16(14).

of particular poisons against grey squirrels and coypus can be authorised by the agriculture ministers in particular circumstances[95]; regulations have been made in the exercise of this power to permit the use of warfarin in destroying grey squirrels throughout England and Wales.[96]

4.4.6 The use of poison against rabbits and hares used to be prohibited throughout Great Britain under s.6 of the Ground Game Act 1880. For Scotland this provision has been repealed,[97] but it would appear that the prohibition on using poison to kill hares, contained in the Hares (Scotland) Act 1848,[98] remains in force. In England and Wales, the relevant part of s.6 of the 1880 Act has also ceased to have effect,[99] but again there is older legislation relating to hares.[1] It is expressly stated that it is not an offence under the Protection of Animals Act 1911 to use poisonous gas in rabbit holes[2] or in other burrows, etc. for the purpose of killing rodents of all sorts, foxes and moles under the agricultural pest control provisions of s.98 of the Agricultural Act 1947.[3] A similar provision allows the use of poisonous gas in agricultural pest control in Scotland.[4] It is an offence knowingly to use or to permit the use of a rabbit infected with myxomatosis to spread the disease to unaffected rabbits.[5]

4.4.7 In relation to other particular species, the use of poison will not be an offence under the 1911 and 1912 Acts if its use falls within the scope of a licence granted by the conservancy councils under the Protection of Badgers Act 1992 for scientific or educational purposes, or for the conservation of badgers.[6] The use of poison to kill seals is an offence,[7] as is its use against

---

[95] Agriculture (Miscellaneous Provisions) Act 1972, s.19.
[96] Grey Squirrels (Warfarin) Order 1973, S.I. 1973 No. 744; the laying of warfarin inside buildings is authorised throughout England and Wales, and its use outdoors in specified areas.
[97] Agriculture (Scotland) Act 1948, Sched. 10.
[98] Hares (Scotland) Act 1848, s.4.
[99] Prevention of Damage by Rabbits Act 1939, s.5(2); this repeal did not however extend to Greater London.
[1] Hares Act 1848, s.5.
[2] Prevention of Damage by Rabbits Act 1939, s.4.
[3] See para. 4.5.2, below.
[4] Agriculture (Scotland) Act 1948, s.49.
[5] Pests Act 1954, s.12.
[6] Protection of Badgers Act 1992, s.10(10); see para.3.4.11, above.
[7] Conservation of Seals Act 1970, s.1(1): licences may be granted to allow the use of poisons other than strychnine (s.10(1)); see para. 3.4.16, above.

deer.[8] The use of poison is prohibited in relation to those species given protection under Schedule 6 to the Wildlife and Countryside Act 1981.[9]

Birds

4.4.8 In addition to benefitting from the general restrictions on the use of poisons described above, the use of poisonous, poisoned or stupefying substances to kill or take wild birds is expressly prohibited.[10] The offence lies in setting such subtances in such a place that they are calculated to cause bodily injury to any wild bird, even though birds may not be the intended victims. For the purpose of this provision, game birds are included within the definition of "wild birds."[11] Those who knowingly cause or permit such action are also guilty, but there is a defence for the setting of substances to kill or take in the interests of public health, agriculture, forestry, fisheries or nature conservation any wild animals which can lawfully be killed or taken in that way. This defence applies, however, only where all reasonable precautions have been taken to prevent injury to wild birds.[12] It has been held that this provision creates three separate offences, of using poisonous, using poisoned and using stupefying substances, and a charge of using a poisoned substance failed when it was held that the substance in question was properly described as a narcotic and hence stupefying, not poisoned, substance.[13]

4.4.9 A further measure intended to protect wild birds is that the import and supply, but not the use, of lead weights for fishing is prohibited, a measure intended to reduce the danger to birds which risk being poisoned when such weights are ingested and worn down in their craw.[14]

---

[8] In England and Wales this is expressly provided in s.4 of the Deer Act 1991, whereas in Scotland it is included in the general prohibition on using any method other than shooting with a firearm to kill deer (Deer (Scotland) Act 1959, s.23(2)); see paras. 4.2.19, 4.2.25, above.

[9] WCA, s.11(2) (amended by Wildlife and Countryside (Amendment) Act 1991, s.2); see para. 3.4.4, above.

[10] *Ibid.*, s.5(1) (amended *ibid.*, s.1).

[11] *Ibid.*, s.27(1).

[12] *Ibid.*, s.5(4), (4A) (added *ibid.*, s.1).

[13] *Robinson* v. *Hughes* [1987] Crim.L. R. 644.

[14] Control of Pollution (Anglers' Lead Weights) Regulations 1986, S.I. 1986 No. 1992 (amended by Control of Pollution (Anglers' Lead Weights) (Amendment) Regulations 1993, S.I. 1993 No. 49); very large (over 28.35gm.) and very small (under 0.06gm.) weights are excluded.

Fish

4.4.10 The use of poison against fish is strictly prohibited. In Scotland it is an offence to put poison or any noxious substance in or near water with the aim of taking fish,[15] and it is also unlawful to possess poison for this purpose.[16] Permission can be granted by the Secretary of State for the use of poison for scientific purposes or to protect or develop stocks of fish, or (in relation to salmon only) to conserve any creature or other living thing.[17]

4.4.11 In England and Wales the same offence exists,[18] as does a broader offence of causing of knowingly permitting to be put into waters which contain fish any matter which causes the water to become poisonous or injurious to fish, their spawn, spawning grounds or food.[19] The very broad terms of that offence are qualified so as not to apply to actions authorised by law (*e.g.* licensed discharges of waste) provided that the best practicable means within reasonable costs are used to prevent the matter causing injury.[20] Prosecutions may be raised only by the National Rivers Authority or a person certified by the minister as having a material interest in the waters affected, a provision which limits the scope for environmental groups to utilise this provision to act against any pollution of waters.[21] The National Rivers Authority, acting with the approval of the ministers, may authorise the use of noxious substances for scientific purposes or in order to improve stocks of fish.[22]

Traps and Other Methods

Animals

4.4.12 The law controls both the sort of traps which can be used in catching animals and how they can be used. It is an offence to use or knowingly to permit the use of any spring trap other than one approved under regulations made by the Secretary of State and used in circumstances covered by its

---

[15] Salmon and Freshwater Fisheries (Protection) (Scotland) Act 1951, s.4.
[16] *Ibid.*, s.7.
[17] *Ibid.*, s.9; Salmon Act 1986, s.28.
[18] Salmon and Freshwater Fisheries Act 1975, s.5.
[19] *Ibid.*, s.4.
[20] *Ibid.*, s.4(2).
[21] *Ibid.*, s.4(3).
[22] *Ibid.*, s.5.

approval.[23] The approval for a trap may be general or subject to conditions as to the circumstances of its use or the animals against which it is used, and the Secretary of State may also grant licences authorising the experimental use of traps. The prohibition of the use of spring traps does not extend to those specified in regulations as being adapted solely for the destruction of rats, mice or other small ground vermin.[24] It is also an offence to sell or expose for sale any spring trap with a view to its use other than in accordance with the formal approvals, or to possess any spring trap for a purpose which is unlawful.[25]

4.4.13 Where a spring trap is used against hares or rabbits, it must be placed in a rabbit hole, and it is an offence to use or knowingly permit its use elsewhere.[26] The use of traps in accordance with a licence from the agriculture minister is outside this prohibition, and a licence to this effect may be embodied in a rabbit clearance order[27] or a notice served for the purpose of agricultural pest control.[28] Somewhat surprisingly, the meaning of "in a rabbit hole" has been the subject of decisions of the appellate courts.[29] Where spring traps are used against hares and rabbits, the traps must be inspected at least once a day.[30]

4.4.14 A number of other means of taking animals is also prohibited. It is an offence to place any self-locking snare so

[23] Agriculture (Scotland) Act 1948, s.50 (substituted by Pests Act 1954, s.10); Pests Act 1954, s.8.
[24] The current regulations are: for Scotland—Spring Traps Approval (Scotland) Order 1975, S.I. 1975 No. 1772; Spring Traps Approval (Scotland) (Variation) Orders 1982, 1988, 1993, S.I.s 1982 No. 91, 1988 No. 2213, 1993 No. 167; Small Ground Vermin Traps (Scotland) Order 1958, S.I. 1958 No. 1779; under the Agriculture (Spring Traps) (Scotland) Order 1969, S.I. No. 876 it is lawful to use unapproved spring traps against foxes; for England and Wales–Spring Traps Approval Order 1975 S.I. No. 1647; Spring Traps Approval (Variation) Orders 1982, 1988, 1993, S.I.s 1982 No. 53, 1988 No. 2111, 1993 No. 189; Small Ground Vermin Traps Order 1958, S.I. 1958 No. 24.
[25] Agriculture (Scotland) Act 1948; Pests Act 1954, s.8.
[26] Agriculture (Scotland) Act 1948, s.50A (added by Pests Act 1954, s.10); Pests Act 1954, s.9.
[27] Pests Act 1954, s.1; see para. 4.5.5, below.
[28] Agriculture Act 1947, s.98; Agriculture (Scotland) Act 1948, s.39; see para. 4.5.2, below.
[29] *Brown* v. *Thompson* (1882) 9 R. 1183, *Fraser* v. *Lawson* (1882) 10 R. 396, both considering the equivalent provision in the Ground Game Act 1880, s.6.
[30] Protection of Animals Act 1911, s.10; Protection of Animals (Scotland) Act 1912, s.9.

as to cause injury to any wild animal coming into contact with it, or to use a self-locking snare in any way in order to kill or take a wild animal.[31] Also prohibited are the use of any live mammal or bird as a decoy, any bow or crossbow, or explosive other than ammunition for a firearm.[32] A person who knowingly causes or permits the use of such methods is also guilty of an offence. A wider range of devices are prohibited in relation to those animals given enhanced protection under Schedule 6 to the Wildlife and Countryside Act 1981, and there is further legislation relating to badgers, deer and seals.[33]

Birds
4.4.15 The use of a large number of methods of killing and taking wild birds, which for this purpose includes game birds, is prohibited under the Wildlife and Countryside Act 1981, the list of prohibitions being subject to alteration by an order of the Secretary of State.[34] Such orders can only be made after a draft of the order has been approved by both Houses of Parliament,[35] and changes can be made to the rules affecting firearms only in order to comply with Britain's international obligations.[36]

4.4.16 It is an offence to use any of the following[37]:

   (a) a springe, trap, gin, snare, hook and line;
   (b) an electrical device for killing, stupefying or frightening;
   (c) a poisonous, poisoned or stupefying substance[38];
   (d) a baited board or bird lime or any similar substance;
   (e) a bow or crossbow;
   (f) an explosive other than ammunition for a firearm;
   (g) an automatic or semi-automatic weapon or shot-gun with a barrel or more than 1.25 inches at the muzzle;
   (h) a device for illuminating a target, any form of artifical lighting, any mirror or dazzling device or any sighting device for night shooting;
   (i) a gas or smoke;
   (j) a chemical wetting agent;

---

[31] WCA, s.11(1) (amended by Wildlife and Countryside (Amendment) Act 1991, s.2).
[32] *Ibid.*
[33] See section 3.4, above.
[34] WCA, s.5(2).
[35] *Ibid.*, s.26(3).
[36] *Ibid.*, s.5(3).
[37] *Ibid.*, s.5(1) (amended by Wildlife and Countryside (Amendment) Act 1991, s.1).
[38] See para. 4.4.8, above.

(k)   a decoy in the form of a sound recording or any live bird or animal which is in any way tethered, secured or maimed;

(l)   a mechanically propelled vehicle in immediate pursuit of a bird.

In relation to items (a)–(c), the offence depends on the offending article being of such a nature and being so placed that it is calculated to cause injury to any wild bird coming into contact with it, in relation to the others what is covered is the use of the banned method for killing or taking a wild bird.[39] The offences extend to those who knowingly cause or permit the prohibited actions. It is also an offence to be involved in any way with an event where captive birds are liberated for the purpose of being shot immediately after their release.[40]

4.4.17   The ban on the use of nets or traps does not extend to their use by an authorised person in order to catch pest species which may be listed in Part II of Schedule 2 to the Act, and their use is permitted in the licences which have in effect replaced Part II of Schedule 2.[41] Nets and traps may also be used to capture game birds when it is shown that the taking of the bird is solely for breeding purposes, and also legitimate is the use of nets in a duck decoy which was in use in 1954, immediately before the passing of the Protection of Birds Act 1954. These exceptions however, do not permit the use of nets for taking birds in flight, nor the use of any net propelled otherwise than by hand.[42] In relation to the offences of setting articles such that they are likely to cause injury, a defence is available if it can be shown that they were positioned for the lawful killing of any wild animal in the interests of public health, agriculture, forestry, fisheries or nature conservation, and that all reasonable precautions were taken to prevent injury to wild birds.[43]

Fish
4.4.18   Only a limited number of methods are permissible in the catching of fish. These have been discussed above.[44]

---

[39] WCA, s.5(1).
[40] *Ibid.*, s.8(3).
[41] See paras. 3.3.7–3.3.8, above.
[42] WCA, s.5(5).
[43] *Ibid.*, s.5(4A) (added by Wildlife and Countryside (Amendment) Act 1991, s.1).
[44] See section 4.3., above.

DESTRUCTION OF WILDLIFE

4.5.1 The control of pests has been a concern of the law for centuries, and until comparatively recently the total extermination of many species would have been regarded as a legitimate aim. Today, although the law does to a considerable extent provide protection to wildlife, regard must also be had to the law regulating its destruction, as such measures can have a significant effect on what can and cannot be done to kill or capture wild animals. The controls on the use of poison and many of the other matters already considered serve to regulate how many pest control operations can be carried out, and in several places exceptions to the law have been noted, whereby the occupiers of land and other limited classes of people are permitted, for the purposes of protecting human, animal and plant health and of protecting property, to take steps normally forbidden by measures enacted to further the interests of nature conservation. There also exists a fragmented mass of provisions specifically directed at the control of pests. Most of these are rarely, if ever, invoked, but they could require action directly contrary to the interests of nature conservation.

4.5.2 One major power is that of the agriculture ministers to serve notices requiring steps to be taken to take or destroy pests.[45] This power can be exercised where it appears expedient for preventing damage to crops, pasture, animal or human foodstuffs, livestock, trees, hedges, banks or works on land and can require action against rabbits, hares, other rodents, foxes, moles, wild birds (other than those enjoying special protection)[46] and deer.[47] The notice is to be served on the person who

---

[45] Agriculture Act 1947, s.98 (amended by Pests Act 1954, s.2 and Sched.; Protection of Birds Act 1954, Sched. 3, para. 1; Agriculture Act 1958, Sched. 3); Agriculture (Scotland) Act 1948, s.39 (amended by Pests Act 1954, s.2 and Sched.; WCA, s.72(4)).

[46] The Scottish Act has been amended to refer to WCA, Schedule 1 whereas the English one appears still to refer to the Protection of Birds Act 1954, repealed by WCA; however the provisions of WCA, s.4, setting the limits on the defences available to those acting in accordance with notices as described here ensures that the law is in fact the same (see paras. 3.3.4–3.3.5, above).

[47] Red and sika deer (and hybrids) were removed from the scope of this provision in Scotland by the Deer (Scotland) Act 1959, Sched. 3 and the Deer (Amendment) (Scotland) Act 1982, Sched. 3.

is entitled to take the specified action, who will usually be the owner or the occupier of the land but may be someone different if game and shooting rights are held separately. The specified measures may not include any killing which is otherwise prohibited by law, with the exception of the killing of game which may be required during the close season.[48] A notice under these provisions may also call for the destruction or reduction of breeding places or cover for rabbits, or for steps to limit their movement.[49]

4.5.3 There is no right of appeal against such a notice, and failure to comply with one within the specified time is an offence.[50] Moreover, in the event of a failure to comply, the minister may arrange for the necessary steps to be taken and recover the expenses incurred.[51] Powers of entry and inspection are provided to assist the ministers in the exercise of their functions under these provisions.[52] The ministers may also provide (at a reasonable charge) services and equipment to assist in compliance with a notice,[53] and anyone who has incurred costs in complying can apply to have these shared on a just and equitable basis with others who have an interest in the land.[54]

4.5.4 The Forestry Commissioners also enjoy the power to take action to control pests.[55] The Commissioners may act where they are satisfied that trees are being or are likely to be damaged by rabbits, hares or vermin (including squirrels)[56] owing to the failure of an occupier of land to take adequate steps to destroy the animals or prevent their causing damage. The owner and occupier of the land must be given an

---

[48] As specified in the Game (Scotland) Act 1772 and the Game Act 1831, s.3; see para. 4.2.10, above.

[49] Agriculture Act 1947, s.98(7); Agriculture (Scotland) Act 1948, s.39(5) (both added by Pests Act 1954, s.2).

[50] *Ibid.*, s.100(1); *ibid.*, s.41(1).

[51] *Ibid.*, s.100(2); *ibid.*, s.41(2).

[52] *Ibid.*, s.106; *ibid.*, s.82.

[53] *Ibid.*, s.101; *ibid.*, s.42.

[54] Applications are to the county court in England and Wales (*ibid.*, s.100(5)) and to the Land Court in Scotland (*ibid.*, s.41(4)).

[55] Forestry Act 1967, s.7.

[56] The red squirrel is protected under Sched. 5 to the Wildlife and Countryside Act 1981, and no exemption is allowed for action against protected animals under these forestry provisions, in contrast to the exceptions allowed for agricultural pest control (WCA, s.10(1)); see para. 3.4.3, above.

opportunity to take the requisite action before the Commissioners take steps themselves, but the costs of such steps can be recovered by the Commissioners from the occupier.

4.5.5 In addition to the measures requiring the clearance of land offering them cover,[57] further attention is given to rabbits. Rabbit clearance areas may be designated by the agriculture ministers after consultation with local representatives of farmers, landowners, other farm and forestry interests and after local publicity for the proposal.[58] Within these areas, the occupiers of land have an obligation to take the necessary steps to kill or take wild rabbits, or where destruction is not reasonably practicable, to prevent their causing damage.[59] The existence of a rabbit clearance order does not entitle the occupier of the land to any right to kill rabbits with firearms additional to that conferred by the Ground Game Act 1880,[60] but authorisation for the additional use of firearms can be given by the ministers where such measures are necessary and the person entitled to grant authorisation has unreasonably withheld it.[61]

4.5.6 Rats and mice come under the responsibility of district councils by virtue of the Prevention of Damage by Pests Act 1949.[62] The councils are under a duty to keep their areas free from rats and mice, and in particular should inspect their areas for such creatures, destroy them on their own land and enforce the duties placed on the occupiers of land by the 1949 Act.[63] Occupiers of land[64] must forthwith notify the council when it comes to their knowledge that rats or mice are resorting to or living on their land in significant numbers.[65] If the council considers it necessary, notices may be served requiring the occupier to take reasonable steps as specified to destroy rats and mice on their land. Failure to comply with a notice is an

---

[57] See para. 4.5.2, above.
[58] Pests Act 1954, s.1.
[59] *Ibid.*, s.1(2).
[60] See para. 4.2.10, above.
[61] Pests Act 1954, s.1(3)–(5).
[62] The legislation has been much amended to cope with the changes in local government structure since 1949. Functions can be transferred to housing action trusts in England and Wales (Housing Act 1988, s.68(1)).
[63] Prevention of Damage by Pests Act 1949, s.2.
[64] Other than agricultural land, unless otherwise prescribed (no agricultural land has yet been prescribed).
[65] Prevention of Damage by Pests Act 1949, s.4.

138   *Exploitation and Destruction of Wildlife*

offence.[66] There is a right of appeal against notices,[67] but in the event of non-compliance the council can arrange for the steps to be taken and recover the costs involved.[68]

4.5.7 In order to ensure the destruction of rats and mice escaping from hay stacks (Scotland) or ricks (England and Wales), regulations may impose special requirements on those involved in the threshing or dismantling of ricks and stacks.[69] The regulations which had been made under this provision for England and Wales have been revoked,[70] but those for Scotland remain in force,[71] affecting all stacks of grain, beans, peas, tares or mashlum and requiring such measures as the placing of fences round the stack before it is dismantled and the taking of all practicable steps to destroy any rats or mice escaping.

4.5.8 The provisions on the control of deer which are causing damage have already been discussed.[72] The measures to control non-indigenous pests such as mink and coypus are covered later.[73]

4.5.9 As far as birds are concerned, the general provisions on agricultural pest control apply to them as much as to earth-bound pests, and the protection given to wild birds is relaxed in order to allow action to be taken against the main pest species. Under the Wildlife and Countryside Act 1981, authorised persons[74] can be permitted to kill or take species listed in Part II of Schedule 2 to the Act, and to destroy, damage or take their eggs or nests,[75] but the authority for such action now rests in licences granted under the Act and no species are now listed in that Part of the Schedule.[76] Where action is required by

---

[66] *Ibid.*, s.4; the notice must require sufficiently specific steps for the occupier to know what is required of him, *Perry* v. *Garner* [1953] 1 Q.B. 335.
[67] *Ibid.*, s.4(5), (6).
[68] *Ibid.*, s.5.
[69] *Ibid.*, s.8.
[70] Prevention of Damage by Pests (Threshing and Dismantling of Ricks) (Revocation) Regulations 1978, S.I. 1978 No. 1614.
[71] Prevention of Damage by Pests (Threshing and Dismantling of Stacks) (Scotland) Regulations 1950, S.I. 1950 No. 980 (rendered metric by S.I. 1976 No. 1236).
[72] See paras. 4.2.20–4.2.21, 4.2.26, above.
[73] See para. 7.2.5, below.
[74] See para. 3.2.6, above.
[75] WCA, s.2(2).
[76] See paras. 3.3.7–3.3.8, above.

ministers in the exercise of their powers of agricultural pest control,[77] the death or injury of birds or damage to their eggs is not an offence except in relation to those species given enhanced protection under Schedule 1 to the 1981 Act.[78] In England and Wales, there is a further power for local authorities to take steps for abating or mitigating nuisance, annoyance or damage caused by the congregation in built-up areas of house doves, pigeons, starlings or sparrows.[79] Reasonable precautions must be taken to ensure that the seizure and destruction of birds is carried out humanely, and the provision does not authorise action contrary to the terms of the 1981 Act.[80]

4.5.10 The Secretary of State has the power to take steps to eliminate pests affecting shellfish from waters other than those covered by private fisheries.[81]

4.5.11 The legislation on animal health also provides for the destruction of wildlife. The agriculture ministers have the power to declare infected areas within which wide powers may be exercised.[82] If an area has been declared as being infected with rabies, provision can be made for the destruction of foxes and other wild animals in the area by persons authorised by the ministers.[83] In relation to other diseases, the destruction of any species of wild mammal or bird may be authorised if the ministers are satisfied that a disease existing among the wild members of a species is being transmitted to other animals,[84] and that the destruction of such wild creatures is necessary to eliminate or substantially reduce the incidence of the disease.[85] Orders made under this provision may authorise the use of methods for destroying animals which are otherwise unlawful, but only if such methods are the most appropriate in the light of

[77] See para. 4.5.2, above.
[78] WCA, s.4(1).
[79] Public Health Act 1961, s.74.
[80] The species in question are all covered by the licences granted under the 1981 Act.
[81] Sea Fisheries (Shellfish) Act 1967, s.15.
[82] Animal Health Act 1981, s.17 (amended by Animal Health and Welfare Act 1984, s.4).
[83] *Ibid.*, ss.19, 20.
[84] The animals which are protected by the Act are cattle, sheep, goats, other ruminating animals and swine, but the ministers can extend this definition to cover all other mammals (except man) and four-footed creatures (*ibid.*, s.87).
[85] *Ibid.*, s.21.

all relevant circumstances, including the need to avoid unnecessary suffering.[86] The conservancy councils must be consulted before such orders can be made.[87] In nature reserves managed by the councils seven days' notice must be given before any exercise of the powers of entry to enforce and carry out the required steps, and as far as possible action in such reserves is to be taken with regard to minimising the harm to the flora, fauna and other features of such reserves.[88] There are no provisions in the legislation relating to fish[89] and bees[90] authorising the destruction of animals in the wild.

[86] *Ibid.*, s.21(4).
[87] *Ibid.*, s.21(3).
[88] *Ibid.*, s.22(7).
[89] Diseases of Fish Acts 1937 and 1983.
[90] Bees Act 1980; Bee Diseases Control Order 1982, S.I. 1982 No. 107.

5. Conservation of Habitat

5.1.1 By itself, the law protecting individual creatures can never secure their survival. Without suitable habitat offering food and shelter, no animal can survive and it is the loss of habitat, rather than any form of direct attack, which poses the greatest threat to most species today. The protection of habitat is equally vital to any attempt to conserve wild plants. If the law is going to seek the conservation of wildlife, it must therefore take steps to ensure the continued existence of the range and expanse of habitat necessary for this. In some countries this can be achieved by setting aside large areas of land for the exclusive use of wildlife, but in heavily populated islands such as Great Britain this approach is not possible. Moreover abandoning the land to nature would in any event prove futile in many areas, since virtually all of Britain's "natural" countryside is in fact the product of centuries of man's involvement with the land and some degree of continuing management is required if it is to survive in its present diversity. The conservation of habitat has instead been addressed by the creation of a large number of different designations of land, each with its own objectives, procedures and legal consequences.

5.1.2 The piecemeal development of the law has resulted in there being about a dozen different legal regimes governing areas of land which have been identified as requiring protection in some form on account of their environmental quality. These regimes reflect different objectives: Areas of Outstanding Natural Beauty and National Scenic Areas are identified solely for their landscape, National Parks serve the twin purposes of protecting landscape and providing opportunities for recreation, National Nature Reserves aim solely at the conservation and study of nature, while Environmentally Sensitive Areas have their origins in moves to reduce agricultural overproduction. The effects of each designation vary in the extent to which the owner or occupier of land is restricted, the emphasis placed on voluntary agreements, the circumstances in which compensation

141

is available, and the restrictions placed on visitors to the land. The fragmented structure of the law, exacerbated by the number of different public authorities involved, inevitably leads to confusion and at times exaggerated fears on the part of residents and landowners as to the effects of designation.

5.1.3 The starting-point for all of these designations is that while some protection is offered to all land through the operation of the general law — planning controls, pollution controls, nuisance, etc. — particular areas can be identified which are so valuable or so sensitive that further measures are justified in order to preserve them. The first task therefore is to establish the criteria for identifying those sites which are to benefit from enhanced protection and procedures for their designation. Then an appropriate legal regime must be adopted to offer the desired level of protection. The following are the most commonly used legal devices.

Ownership
5.1.4 Taking the land into the ownership of a public body dedicated to nature conservation is probably the strongest way of securing that it will be managed in the interests of conservation. The owner is in the best position to ensure that damaging activities are avoided and to undertake any positive action required to maintain or enhance the value of the area as habitat for wildlife. Although there is provision for land being acquired, compulsorily in some circumstances, the acquisition of land has not been a major element in the approach to conservation. The cost of large-scale acquisitions, respect for property rights and a confidence in the ability of landowners to treat their land with respect have combined to limit the area of land taken over by the state.

Management Agreements
5.1.5 In place of acquiring land directly, the preference has been to allow existing owners and occupiers to retain their interest in the land, but to encourage them to use their land in ways which respect the needs of wildlife. In many situations reliance is placed on management agreements, whereby those with an interest in land agree with public authorities to deal with the land in a particular way in exchange for compensation which covers any expense incurred or profits foregone. Such agreements can include both negative and positive obligations on the part of the occupier, prohibiting certain forms of harmful

activity and requiring certain beneficial ones, and run with the land binding the successors to those who entered the agreements. It is hoped that since such agreements are voluntarily entered and offer compensation for the restrictions imposed on the land there should be more willing, and hence more effective, compliance with the agreed restrictions than if they were imposed by law, while a system of individual agreements allows all the particular needs and problems of each site to be taken into account in a way impossible if general legislation were employed. Critics, however, point out that this system of "buying off" landowners is not only unduly expensive, but also enables unscrupulous landowners, by threatening to develop their land, to blackmail the authorities into paying out large sums, regardless of how speculative the proposed development might be.

Bye-laws
5.1.6 Where legal restrictions are required, particularly to regulate the conduct of visitors to the land as opposed to that of those with a legal interest in it, recourse is frequently had to bye-laws. Again this allows the particular needs of each site to be taken into account and the restrictions to be shaped accordingly. Moreover, the consultation and confirmation procedures associated with the making of bye-laws allow there to be some check on what is being done in the name of nature conservation. However, there can be difficulties in ensuring that bye-laws are brought to the notice of the public, and visitors to a site often will not know that they have crossed into a special area, far less that they are now bound by an additional set of legal controls.

Planning controls
5.1.7 Throughout Great Britain, the town and country planning system offers a degree of control over many forms of development which could damage the value of an area as far as wildlife is concerned. One way of providing enhanced protection to those areas identified as being of particular value is to ensure that this value is properly respected in the operation of the planning system, which can be strengthened by the addition of further controls for particular areas.[1] Thus, development plans may have to reflect fully the status and objectives of the various designated areas, environmental assessments (or at the very

---

[1] See section 8.2, below.

least consultation with the conservation bodies) may be required when particular proposals are being considered, and express permission may be required for certain minor forms of development which are normally permitted without the need for individual application or consideration. However, two draw-backs of reliance on the planning system must be noted. In the first place, planning controls are operated by local authorities and central government departments which have responsibilities beyond nature conservation, in particular a concern for the economic well-being of their areas, and where conflicts arise, the interests of conservation may often be sacrificed in favour of other policy objectives. Secondly, planning controls do not extend to most activities in agriculture and forestry, so that many things which can be done on or to the land and which damage its value as a habitat for wildlife fall outwith the scope of planning controls.

Notifications
5.1.8 A further technique is used to avoid the imposition of too great a burden of legal restrictions. Where certain activities may be harmful, what the law provides is not that the activity is prohibited nor that it requires some form of official approval, but rather that the appropriate official body must simply be notified of the proposed activity before it takes place. Such notification enables the authority, where it considers it appropriate, to invoke any of the other control mechanisms which may be available in the circumstances. In this way it should be possible for steps to be taken where necessary to prevent damage occurring, whilst avoiding both the blanket im-position of restrictions which may often be inappropriate or unnecessary, and the formality, delay and bureaucracy of a system of licences, permissions or approvals. The efficacy of such an approach is, however, dependent on both adequate knowledge of and compliance with the notification requirement, and the availability of suitable tools to ensure that damage can in fact be avoided in those cases where it is considered necessary to intervene.

5.1.9 The techniques listed here appear in various forms throughout the legal regimes for the various designated areas, often in combination and with additional devices not mentioned here. More generally, the fact of designation should alert people to the value of a site and may influence their treatment of it, *e.g.* a public authority subject to a duty to have regard to the conservation of the countryside, etc.,[2] should consider the consequences of their action for nature conservation before doing anything which affects a designated site.[3] As with so much of the law affecting nature conservation, the fragmented form of the law means that any general comments are of limited practical value, and the detailed rules for each of the designations must now be considered. The various designations are not exclusive, and it is common for the same piece of land to be covered by a number of different legal regimes, in particular as a Site of Special Scientific Interest and as part of a broader conservation or landscape area.

5.1.10 The rest of this chapter deals with all of the designations given statutory recognition, but many others exist, with varying degrees of official recognition. In England and Wales stretches of Heritage Coast have been identified, and in Scotland there are Preferred Coastal Conservation Zones. The NCC compiled an inventory of Ancient and Semi-natural Woodlands which are worthy of particular care, while the Forestry Commission designates some of its land as Forest Parks. At the international level there are a number of Biosphere Reserves, designated under UNESCO's Man and the Biosphere Programme, and Biogenetic Reserves under a Council of Europe programme. There are also many other local or more specialised designations. In all cases, however, if these designations are to have any legal impact on the way in which the land is treated, the sites must also be included in one of the statutory designations described below. Table 5.1 indicates the extent of the main designations.

NATURE RESERVES

5.2.1 Nature reserves are defined in the National Parks and Access to the Countryside Act 1949 as:

"land managed for the purpose—
(a) of providing, under suitable conditions and control, special opportunities for the study of, and research into, matters relating to the fauna and flora of Great Britain and the physical conditions in which they live,

---

[2] See section 2.2, above.
[3] Land which has been designated may also be eligible for the exemption from Inheritance Tax available in the event of certain transfers to non-commerical organisations; Inheritance Tax Act (*née* Capital Transfer Tax Act) 1984, s.26.

and for the study of geological and physiographical
features of special interest in the area, or
(b)   of preserving flora, fauna or geological or physiographical features of special interest in the area,
or for both those purposes."[4]

Table 5.1   Protected areas in Great Britain 1991*

Status**	Number	Area (ha)	Notes
National Nature Reserves	242	168,100	
Local Nature Reserves	241	17,100	
Marine Nature Reserves	2	—	
Sites of Special Scientific Interest (covered by management agreement)	5,671	1,778,500 98,500	2,032 agreements
Special Protection Areas	40	134,400	
Ramsar Sites	44	133,700	
Environmentally Sensitive Areas	19	785,600	considerably extended since 1991
National Parks	10	1,400,000	not including the Broads
Areas of Outstanding Natural Beauty	39	2,000,000	England and Wales only
National Scenic Areas	40	1,000,000	Scotland only

* At the end of 1990 there were 29 Nature Conservation Orders in force
(source: W. Howarth & C.P. Rodgers (eds.), *Agriculture, Conservation and
Land Use* (1992), p. 95).
**Many areas will be included in more than one category.
Source: The UK Environment, Dept of Environment/Government Statistical
Service (1992, London, HMSO).

[4] NPACA, s.15.

The study and conservation of nature are thus the prime objectives in the management of the land, in marked contrast to the other designations where nature conservation is either accommodated within the landowner's own use of the land or is balanced with or subordinate to other aims such as the provision of recreation or the protection of landscape. The focus on nature conservation is perhaps most clearly shown by the fact that in order to protect a reserve bye-laws can be made excluding all visitors from the area.[5]

5.2.2 The establishment, maintenance and management of nature reserves is one of the general functions of the conservancy councils,[6] and is achieved by the use of management agreements or by the acquisition of land, supported by bye-laws. Areas of the foreshore and of tidal waters can be included in a reserve.[7] The powers relating to nature reserves can be exercised where it appears to a council expedient in the national interest that land should be managed as a nature reserve.[8] A declaration by a council that land is being managed as a nature reserve is conclusive; the council is under a duty to make a similar declaration if the land ceases to be managed in this way and all declarations must be publicised in the way best suited to informing those concerned.[9]

5.2.3 A management agreement may be made with any owner, lessee or occupier of the land. For the purpose of securing that the land is managed as a nature reserve, the agreement may impose restrictions on the exercise of any rights over the land by the parties, provide for the land to be managed in a particular manner and provide for work to be carried out on the land. The agreement may further provide for any management or other works to be carried out and/or paid for by the owner of the land, the council or other persons, and may contain terms relating to payments by the council, in particular sums in compensation for the restriction of the parties' rights.[10] Special

---

[5] See para. 5.2.5, below.
[6] EPA, s.132(1); NHSA, s.4(7).
[7] NPACA, s.114(1); *Burnet* v. *Barclay*, 1955 S.L.T. 282, *Evans* v. *Godber* [1974] 1 W.L.R. 1317.
[8] *Ibid.*, s.16.
[9] *Ibid.*, s.19.
[10] *Ibid.*, s.16(2), (3).

provision is made to allow agreements to be made with those with less than full ownership of the land, *e.g.* liferenters, tenants for life and trustees.[11] In Scotland agreements are to be registered in the Register of Sasines[12] and once registered can be enforced by the council against the parties and those deriving title from them.[13] In England and Wales the agreement operates essentially as a restrictive covenant with the council in the position of an absolute owner of adjacent land capable of benefiting from the covenant and for whose benefit the convenant is expressed.[14] These provisions mean that the agreement runs with the land and remains in force despite any change of occupation or ownership.

5.2.4 The conservancy councils may acquire any interest in the land forming a nature reserve by agreement,[15] or in some cases compulsorily. The power of compulsory purchase can be exercised, firstly, where a council considers it expedient in the national interest that land should be managed as a nature reserve and has been unable to obtain on what it considers to be reasonable terms an agreement relating to the interest in question securing that the land will be satisfactorily managed for this purpose.[16] The second situation in which compulsory purchase is possible is where a management agreement for a nature reserve has been breached.[17] This option is without prejudice to any of the council's other legal remedies, but where the breach is one capable of remedy, it can only be invoked if the defaulting party has not put things right within a reasonable

[11] *Ibid.*, ss.16(4), (5), 26; this is achieved by applying to management agreements the provisions for forestry dedication agreements in ss.1–4 of the Forestry Act 1947, saved for this purpose when repealed by the Forestry Act 1967, Sched. 7, Pt. II, para. 3.

[12] By virtue of the Land Registration (Scotland) Act 1979, s.29(2), all references to the Register of Sasines extend to the Land Register.

[13] NPACA, s.16(5), applying Forestry Act 1947 s.3(2) (see note 11 above); the agreement does not bind a person who bona fide onerously acquired his interest in the land prior to the registration of the agreement, nor those deriving title from such a person.

[14] NPACA, s.16(4), applying Forestry Act 1947 s.1(2), (3) (see note 11 above).

[15] There is no express provision on the agreed acquisition of land for nature reserves, but it is covered by the general powers of the councils; EPA, s.132(3), NHSA, s.2(1).

[16] NPACA, s.17.

[17] Any dispute over whether an agreement has been breached is to be determined by an arbiter appointed by the Lord President of the Court of Session or an arbitrator appointed by the Lord Chancellor.

time after being served with a notice from the council requiring remedial action.[18] The approval of the Secretary of State must be obtained before any compulsory acquisition, which proceeds under the provisions of the Acquisition of Land (Authorisation Procedure) (Scotland) Act 1947 and the Acquisition of Land Act 1981 or the Compulsory Purchase Act 1965.[19]

5.2.5 Bye-laws for the protection of a nature reserve can be made by a conservancy council where land is being managed as a reserve, whether directly by the council or under a management agreement, and has been declared to be a nature reserve.[20] Such bye-laws must be confirmed by the Secretary of State and are made under the procedures for local authority bye-laws, modified to refer to the conservancy councils and to require copies of proposed and confirmed bye-laws to be available for inspection at local authority offices in the relevant areas as well as at the council's own headquarters.[21] In particular, bye-laws can be made prohibiting or restricting the depositing of any rubbish or litter, the lighting of any fires or other acts likely to cause a fire, and the movement of any persons, vehicles, boats or animals into or within the reserve. Any killing, taking or disturbing of animals or plants, interference with the soil or damage to any objects in the reserve may be prohibited or restricted, as may the shooting of birds within the area surrounding or adjoining the reserve to the extent that this is required to protect the reserve itself. The bye-laws may also provide for permits to be granted permitting things otherwise prohibited.[22]

5.2.6 There are, however, limits to the scope of the bye-laws. The exercise of any right vested in a person as owner, lessee or occupier of the land cannot be interfered with — any restriction on such rights must be achieved directly by means of a

[18] NPACA, s.18.
[19] *Ibid.*, s.103 (amended by Nature Conservancy Council Act 1973, Sched. 1, para. 2; Acquisition of Land Act 1981, Sched. 4, para. 8).
[20] NPACA, s.20.
[21] *Ibid.*, s.106; Nature Conservancy Council (Byelaws) Regulations 1975, S.I. 1975 No. 1970, adapting Local Government Act 1972 ss.236–238; Nature Conservancy Council (Byelaws) (Scotland) Regulations 1984, S.I. 1984 No. 918, adapting Local Government (Scotland) Act 1973 ss.202–204 (amended by Civic Government (Scotland) Act 1982, s.110).
[22] NPACA, s.20(2).

management agreement, not through bye-laws.[23] Where the exercise of other vested rights (whether arising from an interest in the land, a licence or an agreement) is prevented or hindered by the bye-laws, compensation is payable by the council.[24] Also beyond the reach of bye-laws is any interference with the exercise of a public right of way,[25] with the functions of statutory undertakers, drainage authorities or salmon fishery district boards, or with the running of telecommunications systems.[26]

5.2.7 The special status of nature reserves is recognised in a number of other statutory schemes. Among other points, orders can be made restricting or prohibiting vehicles on roads in a reserve[27] and in England and Wales the conservancy councils must be consulted before a road building or improvement scheme in or near a reserve is initiated.[28] Land in a nature reserve cannot be accepted into the Farm Woodland Premium Scheme[29] and any exercise in a nature reserve of the powers under the Animal Health Act 1981 to destroy wildlife requires prior notice and efforts to minimise the harm done.[30]

National Nature Reserves

5.2.8 What has been described so far are nature reserves managed by or by agreement with the conservancy councils. There is, however, a potential for confusion as to their title and status. This arises because it is possible for reserves to be formally declared "National Nature Reserves" under the Wildlife and Countryside Act 1981.[31] This title can be conferred

---

[23] *Ibid.*, s.20(2).

[24] *Ibid.*, s.20(3).

[25] A right of navigation is not a public right of way for this purpose (*Evans* v. *Godber* [1974] 1 W.L.R. 1317; *cf. Attorney General (ex rel. Yorkshire Derwent Trust Ltd.)* v. *Brotherton* [1992] 1 A.C. 425); the exercise of rights on the foreshore may be restricted (*Burnet* v. *Barclay*, 1955 S.L.T. 282).

[26] Added by Telecommunications Act 1984, Sched. 4, para. 28.

[27] Road Traffic Regulation Act 1984, s.22.

[28] Highways Act 1980, s.105A (added by the Highways (Assessment of Environmental Effects) Regulations 1988, S.I. 1988 No. 1241, reg. 2); the equivalent Scottish provision does not include nature reserves among the designations invoking such consultation — Roads (Scotland) Act 1984, s.20A (added by the Environmental Assessment (Scotland) Regulations 1988, S.I. 1988 No. 1221, reg. 70).

[29] Farm Woodland Premium Scheme 1992, S.I. 1992 No. 905, para. 5(1).

[30] Animal Health Act 1981, s.22(7); see para. 4.5.11, above.

[31] WCA, s.35.

by a declaration[32] by a conservancy council where it considers that a nature reserve is of national importance. The risk of confusion lies in the fact that the title "National Nature Reserve" was in widespread but unofficial use for reserves managed by the NCC before being given statutory recognition in 1981. A problem may occur in relation to future legislation as it could be argued that any reference to National Nature Reserves applies only to reserves which have been formally declared as such under the 1981 Act, thereby excluding many older ones if they have not been subject to any such statutory declaration.

5.2.9 National Nature Reserves under the 1981 Act can be on land governed by a management agreement with a conservancy council, held and managed as a reserve directly by a council, or managed by another body approved by a council.[33] This last provision is particularly significant since it means that reserves managed by bodies such as the RSPB can be brought within the statutory scheme for nature reserves. A major consequence of this is that at the request of the body managing the reserve, the conservancy council can make bye-laws for such a reserve as if it were one managed through the council itself.[34] This allows further legal sanctions to supplement the restrictions imposed by the managing body by virtue of its interest in the land.

Local Nature Reserves
5.2.10 Nature reserves can also be established by local authorities. It is within the powers of general or district planning authorities in Scotland and county, county boroughs and districts in England and Wales to establish nature reserves where they consider it expedient that the land should be so managed.[35] The local authorities enjoy the same powers in this regard as the conservancy councils, including powers of compulsory purchase, with references to "the interests of the locality" being substituted for those to "the national interest."[36] The existence of the power to create local nature reserves allows the protection of small sites which are not of national significance, but which do offer valuable habitat, and enables authorities to provide opportunities for the study of nature as a

[32] Governed by NPACA, s.19.
[33] WCA, s.35(1).
[34] *Ibid.*, s.35(3).
[35] NPACA, s.21(1); Local Government Act 1972 Sched. 17, para. 34.
[36] NPACA, s.21(4).

recreational or educational facility. As always, though, there are competing demands on the resources of local authorities.[37]

MARINE NATURE RESERVES

5.3.1 Although nature reserves can extend to include areas covered by the sea,[38] the legal machinery of land ownership and management agreements is not apt to deal with the conservation of the marine environment. Special provision was made in 1981 for the creation of Marine Nature Reserves, but weaknesses in the legislation and an unwillingness to proceed in the absence of total consensus from all interested parties have meant that these reserves have had little impact in practice.[39]

5.3.2 Marine Nature Reserves can be created for areas of land covered by tidal waters, including the foreshore, or parts of the sea which lie within the baselines for measuring the territorial sea[40] or lie seaward of the baselines or coast to a distance of three nautical miles.[41] By Order in Council, other areas of the sea within British territorial waters (currently extending to 12 nautical miles from the shore-line or baselines) can become eligible for designation.[42] Reserves are designated by the Secretary of State on the basis of an application made by a conservancy council where it appears expedient that the land and covering waters should be managed for the purposes of conserving or studying the marine flora and fauna or the geological and physiographical features of special interest in the area. Once a reserve has been designated, it is managed by the council for either or both of these purposes.[43]

---

[37] *E.g.*, in *Giddens* v. *Harlow District Auditor* (1972) 70 L.G.R. 485 expenditure on the purchase of a wood as a local nature reserve was challenged, unsuccessfully, by a ratepayer on the grounds that it was providing facilities which would benefit only a privileged minority.

[38] See para. 5.2.2, above.

[39] See generally, J. Gibson, "Marine Nature Reserves" [1984] J.P.L. 699.

[40] Such baselines are drawn in accordance with international law and include lines drawn across the mouths of bays and firths and a line enclosing the Minch and all of the Inner and Outer Hebrides.

[41] WCA, s.36(1) (amended by Territorial Sea Act 1987, Sched. 1, para. 6); a nautical mile is defined in s.1(7) of the 1987 Act as an international nautical mile of 1852 metres.

[42] Territorial Sea Act 1987, s.3(2)(*b*).

[43] WCA, s.36(1).

5.3.3 The procedure for designation requires the council's application to be accompanied by a copy of the bye-laws which are proposed for the protection of the reserve[44] and provides for the Secretary of State to give wide publicity to the proposed designation and accompanying bye-laws. As well as notices in the local press and at prominent positions at local authority offices within the locality, notices must be served on all those with a vested interest in or right over the land affected and on a wide range of public authorities.[45] In the event of there being objections or representations which are not withdrawn, the Secretary of State must arrange for there to be a hearing or local inquiry before he decides whether to make an order giving effect to the designation.[46] Similar publicity is required for orders once they have been made[47] and there is a limited power to challenge the validity of an order within 42 days of its notification, after which the order is not to be questioned in any legal proceedings.[48]

5.3.4 The impact of an area being designated as a Marine Nature Reserve lies in the provisions of the bye-laws which are made for it, since other than through the bye-laws, the effect of designation is simply to empower the conservancy councils to manage a reserve and to install markers indicating its existence and extent.[49] Bye-laws are made by the conservancy councils for the protection of reserves[50] in accordance with the procedures for the making of local authority bye-laws, as modified by regulations.[51] As well as being the confirming authority for bye-laws,[52] the Secretary of State, after consulting a council, can direct it to revoke or amend any bye-laws which it has made.[53]

[44] *Ibid.*, s.36(2).
[45] *Ibid.*, Sched. 12, paras. 2–3; the public authorities concerned are the "relevant authorities" (see para. 5.3.6, below) and such other bodies as the Secretary of State considers appropriate.
[46] *Ibid.*, Sched. 12, para. 4; if he decides to make the order with modifications a similar procedure must be followed if additional land is affected (*ibid.*, para. 5).
[47] *Ibid.*, Sched. 12, para. 7.
[48] *Ibid.*, Sched. 12, para. 8.
[49] *Ibid.*, s.36(1), (5).
[50] *Ibid.*, s.37(1).
[51] *Ibid.*, s.37(5), applying the Local Government Act 1972, ss.236–238 (as modified by Wildlife and Countryside (Byelaws for Marine Nature Reserves) Regulations 1986, S.I. 1986 No. 143) and the Local Government (Scotland) Act 1973, ss.202–204 (amended by Civic Government (Scotland) Act 1982, s.110).
[52] *Ibid.*, s.37(6).
[53] *Ibid.*, s.37(7).

5.3.5 The bye-laws which are made may protect the reserve by prohibiting or restricting the entry or movement of individuals or vessels, the killing, destruction or disturbance of animals or plants, interference with the sea bed, damage to any object in the reserve, or the deposit of rubbish in the reserve.[54] The bye-laws can vary for different parts of the reserve and allow the granting of permits to do things otherwise prohibited. These apparently wide powers are, however, severely restricted in several ways. First, the bye-laws cannot prohibit or restrict the exercise of any right of passage by a vessel other than a pleasure boat, nor exclude even pleasure boats from all parts of the reserve at all times of the year.[55] There is no definition of a pleasure boat and many doubtful cases can be imagined. Secondly, the bye-laws cannot render unlawful the discharge of any substance from a vessel,[56] nor anything done more than 30 metres below the sea bed,[57] nor anything done for securing the safety of any vessel, preventing damage to a vessel or its cargo or saving life.[58]

5.3.6 The third restriction on the scope of the bye-laws also extends to anything else which a conservancy council might do in the exercise of its powers to manage a reserve. This is that nothing which is done can interfere with the exercise of any functions conferred by an Act of Parliament (before or after the creation of the reserve and the making of bye-laws), with the exercise of any right of any person or with the exercise of any function of a "relevant authority."[59] The "relevant authorities" for this purpose include all tiers of local authority, the National Rivers Authority, water and sewerage undertakers, river purification boards, navigation, harbour and pilotage authorities, lighthouse authorities, salmon district fishery boards and local fisheries committees.[60]

5.3.7 Marine conservation is always difficult because of the wide range of influences which can affect the different elements

[54] *Ibid.*, s.37(2).
[55] *Ibid.*, s.37(3).
[56] Such deposits are controlled by Part II of the Food and Environment Protection Act 1985 and other legislation on marine pollution.
[57] Detailed legal regimes exist to control the exploitation of minerals on the continental shelf.
[58] WCA, s.37(4).
[59] *Ibid.*, s.36(6).
[60] *Ibid.*, s.36(7) (amended by Water Act 1989, Sched. 25, para. 66).

of the marine environment from the surface to the sea-bed, and because of difficulties in enforcing any restrictions. However, the exclusion from the restrictions designed to protect the reserves of authorities whose activities can have a major impact on the seashore and inshore waters, together with the other exclusions, severely weakens the whole mechanism of Marine Nature Reserves. This has been further weakened by slow progress towards designating reserves, with the government reluctant to proceed without full consensus from all interested parties. By 1993, only two Marine Nature Reserves had been designated.

SITES OF SPECIAL SCIENTIFIC INTEREST

5.4.1 Whereas in nature reserves the land is primarily dedicated to the interests of nature conservation, much of the valuable habitat in Britain is provided by land which is used for other purposes, and can continue to be so used without damaging its value for wildlife. Those areas of particular value do, however, require some recognition and a degree of protection if they are not to be destroyed by their development for building, quarrying, etc., or damaged by other changes in their management. The objectives of the system of Sites of Special Scientific Interest (SSSIs) are to identify valuable sites, to notify those responsible for them of their value and to provide a mechanism whereby changes to the land which might harm that value are considered by the conservation authorities before they take place, offering the opportunity for a range of controls to be agreed or imposed at that stage. Under this system, operations on the land can be delayed for a few months, but unless other more stringent controls are invoked, it is not possible to prevent the occupier from carrying out his wishes, however damaging to the nature conservation value of the land.

5.4.2 SSSIs were first introduced in 1949,[61] but the original provisions were weak, merely requiring special consideration within the town and country planning system (the owners and occupiers of land were not even informed of the designation) and a new system was introduced by the Wildlife and

---

[61] NPACA, s.23; the legislation has always referred to "areas which are of special interest," but Sites of Special Scientific Interest is the universal usage.

Countryside Act 1981. This new regime applies only to SSSIs which have been notified in accordance with the procedures in the 1981 Act, and throughout the 1980s a major task for the NCC was the renotification of those SSSIs created under the previous legislation so that they could benefit from the new provisions. By 1991 this task had been virtually completed so that only the regime in the 1981 Act is considered here.[62]

5.4.3 The conservancy councils are under a duty to notify as SSSIs those areas of land which are, in their opinion, of special interest by reason of any of their flora, fauna, or geological or physiographical features.[63] All owners and occupiers of the land concerned, the relevant planning authority[64] and the Secretary of State must receive copies of the notification,[65] which must set out why the land is of special interest and specify those operations (known as "potentially damaging operations") which appear likely to damage the flora, fauna or other special features of the land and thus fall within the scope of the SSSI controls.[66] The notification takes effect at once,[67] but a period of at least three months must be allowed for representations or objections to be made.[68] The council must consider any representations which are made and within nine months of the original notification must notify the same people that the notification is being withdrawn, confirmed or confirmed with modifications (which cannot extend the area of the SSSI).[69] In England and Wales, notifications are local land charges to be

---

[62] See generally S. Ball, "Sites of Special Scientific Interest" [1985] J.P.L. 767.

[63] WCA, s.28(1).

[64] Regional, general and district planning authorities in Scotland, county and district planning authorities in England and Wales; *ibid.*, s.52(2).

[65] *Ibid.*, s.28(1); the service of notices is governed by WCA, s.70A (added by Wildlife and Countryside (Service of Notices) Act 1985, s.1, amended by Planning (Consequential Provisions) Act 1990, Sched. 2, para. 54) which applies the provisions of TCPSA, s.269 and TCPA, s.329.

[66] *Ibid.*, s.28(4); the word "operations" in the term "potentially damaging operations" does not bear the specialised meaning which it has been given in construing the planning legislation (*Sweet* v. *Secretary of State for the Environment* [1989] 2 P.L.R. 14, (1989) 1 J.E.L. 245).

[67] Prior to the Wildlife and Countryside (Amendment) Act 1985 the notice took effect only once confirmed by the NCC, but it was found that in the period between initial notification and confirmation some unscrupulous occupiers were taking steps which destroyed the features of the land which were of value, thereby defeating the whole system.

[68] WCA, s.28(2) (amended by Wildlife and Countryside (Amendment) Act 1985, s.2(2)).

[69] *Ibid.*, s.28 (4A)–(4C) (added *ibid.*, s.2(4)).

registered accordingly.[70] In Scotland, SNH has to compile and maintain a register of notifications for each planning authority, copies of which must be available for inspection at the authorities' offices.[71]

5.4.4 In Scotland, designations are also subject to consideration by the advisory committee on SSSIs established under the Natural Heritage (Scotland) Act 1991.[72] The task of this committee, whose members must be scientifically qualified and independent of Scottish Natural Heritage,[73] is to consider the grounds on which an area has been declared to be of special interest and to advise SNH on whether there is adequate scientific justification for designation — the committee cannot consider the range of activities notified as potentially damaging operations or any other aspect of the designation. Cases are referred to the committee if in response to the initial notification the owner or occupier makes representations to SNH about the grounds for designation.[74] The advice from the committee must be received and considered by SNH before the notification of an SSSI is confirmed, and a copy of its advice is sent to the owner or occupier concerned.[75] The committee has a purely advisory role, although if a designation is confirmed by SNH against the advice of the committee, a dissatisfied owner or occupier might be tempted to seek to challenge that decision in the courts by means of judicial review. Ultimately, though, the test for designating SSSIs is whether a conservancy council is *"of the opinion* that any area of land is of special interest,"[76] and the courts are likely to be reluctant to embark on any assessment of conflicting opinions from two expert scientific bodies.

5.4.5 The committee's role is not limited to new designations. Cases are also to be referred to it when the owner or occupier makes representations that any of the grounds for designation,

[70] *Ibid.*, s.28(11).
[71] *Ibid.*, s.28(12–12B) (amended *ibid.*, s.2(8)).
[72] NHSA, s.12.
[73] *Ibid.*, s.12(2).
[74] *Ibid.*, s.12(5).
[75] *Ibid.*, s.12(7); there are no provisions on the time within which the committee must provide its advice, but the notification lapses unless confirmed within nine months (WCA, s.28(4A) (added by Wildlife and Countryside (Amendment) Act 1985, s.2)).
[76] WCA, s.28(1), emphasis added.

as specified in the original notification,[77] have ceased to be valid.[78] In most cases, if the representations are not withdrawn within six months (this allows Scottish Natural Heritage time to assess the position itself and discuss the matter with the owner or occupier concerned), the case must then be referred to the committee, whose views must be considered before Scottish Natural Heritage decides whether to revoke or vary the designation.[79] This applies to designations made more than ten years ago or to more recent ones where relevant representations were made by the owner or occupier at the time of designation.[80] In all other circumstances, the procedure can be invoked no earlier than ten years after designation or ten years after the designation was last considered by the committee.[81]

5.4.6 This advisory procedure is much weaker than the full reconsideration of all aspects of designation which was originally proposed by the members of the House of Lords dissatisfied with the previous arrangements, but may lead to a number of designations being examined. In particular, difficulties may arise in those instances where large areas have been designated, since it may be argued that not all of the land concerned is in fact of special interest. However in a case involving Nature Conservation Orders,[82] an English court was prepared to hold that it was appropriate to consider a local environment as a whole, without distinguishing the particular places of greater and lesser importance.[83] A further potential problem is the extent to which "buffer zones" can be established around valuable sites; such zones may contain little of particular interest themselves, but without them important sites may be left vulnerable to damage or disturbance.

5.4.7 The notification of an SSSI will contain a list of potentially damaging operations (PDOs), operations which

---

[77] *Ibid.*, s.28(4)(*a*).
[78] NHSA, s.12(6).
[79] *Ibid.*, s.12(6), (7).
[80] *Ibid.*, s.12(6).
[81] *Ibid.*, s.12(8).
[82] See section 5.5, below.
[83] *Sweet* v. *Secretary of State for the Environment* [1989] 2 P.L.R. 14, (1989) 1 J.E.L. 245, *cf. R.* v. *Canterbury City Council, ex p. Halford* (1992) 64 P. & C.R. 513, where a similar approach was taken to conservation areas; see para. 5.5.2, below.

appear to the conservancy council likely to damage the flora, fauna or special features of the site.[84] These will obviously vary from site to site, but commonly listed operations include the cultivation of the land (ploughing, reseeding, etc.), changes to the grazing regime, the dumping of any materials, the application of fertilisers, pesticides or herbicides, the burning of vegetation, drainage works and the filling of ditches, pools or marshland, the planting or felling of trees, building, extraction of minerals and the killing or removal of any wild animal.[85] One of the weaknesses of the SSSI system is that in order to cover all activities which if carried to excess might damage a site, landowners are often presented with very daunting lists of PDOs, which give the impression that almost anything they could contemplate doing on their land, including things which they have been doing for years and which may very well have contributed to the conservation value of the site, are to come under some form of control. This impression of far-reaching control and interference with what a person can do on his own land means that the relationship between the conservancy councils and landowners can often start off on the wrong footing.

5.4.8 The PDOs are not prohibited. Indeed, the most that can happen without agreement is that they can be delayed for four months. The legal requirement is that the owner or occupier give written notice to the conservancy council of his intention to carry out any of the operations.[86] He is then not permitted to carry out or permit the operation until four months have passed, unless the council has given its consent to the particular operation, or the operation is carried out in accordance with a management agreement governing the land.[87] It is a criminal offence for the owner or occupier to proceed within the four months "without reasonable excuse"[88]; it is expressly provided that a reasonable excuse exists in the event of the operation

---

[84] WCA, s.28(4); on the meaning of "likely to damage" see *North Uist Fisheries Ltd.* v. *Secretary of State for Scotland*, 1992 S.L.T. 333, discussed at para. 5.5.6, below.

[85] Examples are given in Appendix 2 of L. Livingstone, *et al., Management Agreements for Nature Conservation in Scotland* (1990).

[86] WCA, s.28(5) (amended by Wildlife and Countryside (Amendment) Act 1985, s.2(5)).

[87] *Ibid.*, s.28(6) (amended by *ibid.*, s.2(6)).

[88] *Ibid.*, s.28(7); D. Withrington & W. Jones, "Enforcement of Conservation Legislation: Protecting Sites of Special Scientific Interest", in W. Howarth & C.P. Rodgers (eds.), *Agriculture, Conservation and Land Use* (1992).

being authorised by an express grant of planning permission[89] or being an emergency operation which has been notified to the council as soon as practicable.[90] For the purposes of these provisions an "occupier" is someone with a legal interest in the land in question, and does not include someone on the land merely to carry out particular works.[91]

5.4.9 The reason for imposing a four-month delay is to give the conservancy council the opportunity to consider the effect of the proposed operations and to act accordingly. If the operation is acceptable, consent will be given; if not the time can be used to find an appropriate means of preventing the operation, either by negotiating a management agreement for the site or by applying for further legal controls to be imposed through a Nature Conservation Order.[92]

5.4.10 In accordance with the voluntary principle which applies throughout so much of the law on nature conservation, the main tool for protecting SSSIs is intended to be the management agreement, made between the conservancy council and the owner and occupier of the land. An agreement can provide for compensation to be paid to the owner or occupier of an SSSI in return for his acceptance of restrictions on the use of the land, and may also provide for payments to be made in return for positive steps taken by the owner or occupier to maintain or improve the nature conservation value of the site.[93] Agreements can also be made for land adjacent to an SSSI where expedient for conserving the features of the site itself.[94] By giving consent to the management of the site within agreed practices, the

---

[89] What is required is
   "Planning permission granted on an application under Part III of the Town and Country Planning Act 1990 or Part III of the Town and Country Planning (Scotland) Act 1972"
(*ibid.*, s.28(8)(*a*) (amended by the Planning (Consequential Provisions) Act 1990, Sched. 2, para. 54)); this formulation means that a reasonable excuse is not provided by the fact that the operation is "permitted development" under the terms of the General Permitted Development Orders or otherwise exempt from normal planning control.
[90] *Ibid.*, s.28(8).
[91] *Southern Water Authority* v. *Nature Conservancy Council* [1992] 1 W.L.R. 775.
[92] See section 5.5, below.
[93] Agreements can be made under NPACA, s.16 or CA, s.15, which contains essentially the same provisions specifically for SSSIs.
[94] CA, s.15 (amended by EPA, Sched. 9, para. 4).

agreement can also obviate the need for individual notification and consent every time something falling within the broad terms of the PDOs is proposed.[95] The aims of the agreement may often be to maintain the existing way in which the land is being used, *e.g.* grazing to prevent the growth of scrub, so that in the end, and despite the apparently daunting list of PDOs and fears of external controls which accompany designation as an SSSI, the landowner may be continuing exactly as before. One of the anomalies of the SSSI system is that management agreements, and hence compensation, tend to be offered only when an owner or occupier proposes[96] to carry out damaging operations, whereas those who voluntarily manage their land in a way which conserves its natural interest may receive no recognition or reward.[97]

5.4.11 The period available for negotiating an agreement was extended in 1985 to the present four months from the original three,[98] but in many cases this is still not long enough for the terms of an agreement to be settled and formalised.[99] However, it is possible for the period to be extended by agreement, terminable at one month's notice, and during the extended period the proposed PDO cannot be carried out without the consent of the council.[1] Once a management agreement has been made it will bind successors in title to the original parties, and provision is made for agreements to be made by those who have less than full ownership of the land.[2] In Scotland agreements are registered in the Register of Sasines; in England and Wales they operate as restrictive covenants.[3]

5.4.12 The level of compensation available under a management agreement is determined in accordance with ministerial guidance.[4] This guidance is issued in the document *Financial*

[95] WCA, s.28(6)(*b*).
[96] Some might say "threatens."
[97] L. Livingstone *et al., op. cit.,* sections 3.4–3.5.
[98] Wildlife and Countryside (Amendment) Act 1985, s.2(6), amending WCA, s.28(6).
[99] L. Livingstone *et al., op. cit.,* section 3.6.
[1] WCA, s.28(6A)–(6C) (added by Wildlife and Countryside (Amendment) Act 1985, s.2(7)).
[2] NPACA, s.16(4), (5); CA, s.15(4), (6), both applying Forestry Act 1947 ss.1–4, saved for this purpose when repealed by Forestry Act 1967, Sched. 7, Pt. II, para. 3.
[3] NPACA, s.16(4), (5); CA, s.15(4), (6); see note 2.
[4] WCA, s.50(2).

Guidelines for Management Agreements, which is published by HMSO but is not a statutory instrument and hence not subject to any direct parliamentary or other controls. The guidelines lay down the basis on which annual and lump sum payments are to be made to owners and occupiers who have entered agreements. If the level of compensation cannot be agreed between the conservancy council and the owner or occupier, there is provision for arbitration on this issue, after which the council must either amend its offer in terms of the arbiter's determination or withdraw the offer.[5] In the one case in Scotland where this procedure has been invoked, the parties agreed to refer the case to the Lands Tribunal for Scotland.[6] The decision of the Tribunal, applying the criteria in the guidelines, produced a figure much higher than had been offered by the council,[7] and raised the issue of how widely management agreements could and should be offered in view of the many other calls on the councils' finances.

5.4.13 The existence of an SSSI has effects in other legal regimes. As far as agricultural developments are concerned, special rules apply to the consideration of applications for farm capital grants for land designated as an SSSI.[8] The agriculture ministers must exercise their functions under the grant schemes so as to further the conservation of the special features of the site, so far as is consistent with the purposes of the grant provisions, and consideration must be given to any objection from a conservancy council that the activities in question are damaging to the flora, fauna or special geological or physiographical features of the site.[9] Where a grant has been refused as a result of objections from the council, the council must within three months offer to enter a management agreement for the site.[10]

---

[5] *Ibid.*, s.50(3).

[6] *Cameron v. Nature Conservancy Council*, 1991 S.L.T. (Lands Tr.) 85; the Tribunal has jurisdiction to accept the reference under s.1(5) of the Lands Tribunal Act 1949.

[7] The final sum was £555,000 for SSSIs covering ca. 3160 hectares.

[8] "Farm capital grants" are defined as those provided by schemes under s.29 of the Agriculture Act 1970 or regulations giving effect to European Community provisions; WCA, s.32(3) (substituted by Agriculture Act 1986, s.20(3)).

[9] WCA, s.32(1), (amended by Agriculture Act 1986, s.20); in England the agriculture minister must also consult with the Secretary of State for the Environment.

[10] *Ibid.*, s.32(2).

5.4.14 As regards forms of development falling within the scope of the town and country planning system, the express grant of planning permission authorises the carrying out of any PDO.[11] This enables the planning authority, for which nature conservation may not be a priority in the light of the economic and social needs of its area, to permit development on an SSSI which can totally destroy its conservation value. The conservancy council must be consulted on any application which may affect an SSSI, not only those for development on the site itself,[12] and its views will be taken into account, but other considerations material to the decision may outweigh its objections. The fact that the land in question is an SSSI may also trigger the requirement for an environmental assessment to be carried out,[13] and SSSIs cannot be included in a Simplified Planning Zone (an area where planning controls are considerably relaxed in order to stimulate development).[14]

5.4.15 In England and Wales there are provisions in the water legislation which are also likely to affect SSSIs. Where a conservancy council considers that land is of special interest because of its flora, fauna or geological or physiographical features, may be affected by the schemes, works, or other activities carried out or authorised by the National Rivers Authority, an internal drainage board or a water or sewerage undertaker, then the council must notify such bodies of the special interest of the land.[15] The basic test for identifying land of special interest is the same as for SSSIs, but the provision is not restricted to land formally notified as an SSSI, whilst SSSIs which are safe from disturbance by the activities of the relevant bodies may be excluded. Before a relevant body carries out any works, etc., which it considers likely to destroy or damage the special features of a site which has been notified, it must consult with the conservancy council[16]; in the case of emergency works,

---

[11] *Ibid.*, s.28(8).

[12] Town and Country Planning General Development Order 1988, S.I. 1988 No. 1813, art. 18(1) (amended by Town and Country Planning (General Development) (Amendment) (No. 3) Order 1991, S.I. 1991 No. 2805, art. 4); Town and Country Planning (General Development Procedure) (Scotland) Order 1992, S.I. 1992 No. 224, art. 15(1).

[13] See section 8.3, below.

[14] TCPSA, s.21E(1) (added by Housing and Planning Act 1986, s.26); TCPA, s.87(1).

[15] Water Industry Act 1991, s.4(1); Water Resources Act 1991, s.17(1); Land Drainage Act 1991, s.13(1).

[16] *Ibid.*, s.4(3); *ibid.*, s.17(3); *ibid.*, s.13(3).

no prior consultation is required, but the council must be notified as soon as practicable.[17] The Secretary of State may require that an appropriate management agreement is entered before certain land held by water undertakers is sold.[18] Proposals in 1991 for similar legal duties to be imposed in Scotland were dropped in favour of a Code of Practice, such as that which accompanies the English provisions.[19]

5.4.16 The system of SSSIs is the cornerstone of habitat protection in Britain, but on all sides there is some dissatisfaction with its operation. From the point of view of conservation interests, the system does not do enough to guarantee the protection of sites, since damaging operations can be delayed for only a short time, the protection can be overridden by a planning authority granting permission for a development and only the activities of owners and occupiers are restricted, leaving the conduct of those with lesser rights over the land, *e.g.* commoners, of statutory undertakers and of visitors uncontrolled.[20] Moreover the whole approach is based on preventing particular damage, not ensuring the positive management of the land, so that the value of a site can be lost by neglect, *e.g.* by scrub invading downland, without any PDO being involved and hence no trigger for the (limited) further measures to be taken. Landowners and occupiers are often unhappy at the designation of their land on purely scientific grounds with no right of appeal and limited consideration for their ability to make a return from the land, whilst the system of notifying all potentially damaging operations presents them with what seems to be a frightening array of restrictions, apparently removing totally their right to treat their land as their own. Criticism comes from both sides over the compensation scheme and the purely negative approach of the PDO system.

[17] *Ibid.*, s.4(4); *ibid.*, s.17(4); *ibid.*, s.13(4); when these provisions were first introduced by the Water Act 1989, s.9, bodies were advised to refer all proposed works to the council to ensure that nothing of significance was missed; Water Act 1989 — Code of Practice on Conservation Access and Recreation, July 1989 (Dept. of Environment, MAFF, Welsh Office).

[18] Water Industry Act 1991, s.156.

[19] Ministerial announcement by Lord James Douglas-Hamilton, June 13, 1991; see now the Code of Practice on Conservation, Access and Recreation issued in August 1993.

[20] In 1990–91, 233 SSSIs suffered short-term damage, 33 long-term damage and 10 were wholly or partially destroyed so far as their conservation value is concerned; the greatest single cause of damage is agricultural activities (Source: Dept. of the Environment/Government Statistical Service, *The U.K. Environment* (1992)).

5.4.17 Some of the difficulties, from the landowners' side at least, are caused not by the actual impact of the designation but by the initial impression of a much stronger set of restrictions than exists in practice. In Scotland many of these problems were considerably exacerbated by the poor handling of matters by the NCC during the 1980s when it was under great pressure to complete quickly the renotification of sites so that they could benefit from the 1981 Act. The strength of feeling on the issue is amply illustrated by the views expressed by several members of the House of Lords during the passage of the Natural Heritage (Scotland) Act 1991, when attempts were made to introduce a total reassessment of all SSSI designations. Without greater understanding on both sides of the concerns and problems faced by the other, it may be hard to identify exactly how the system could be improved to the satisfaction of both.

NATURE CONSERVATION ORDERS

5.5.1 Where more protection is required for a site than can be offered by its designation as an SSSI, a Nature Conservation Order can be made. The protection offered by such Orders is an enhanced version of that offered by SSSIs, the main differences being that damaging operations can be delayed for longer, it is not merely owners and occupiers who are affected and a wider range of sanctions and compensation is available to ensure the success of the law.

5.5.2 There are three grounds for making a Nature Conservation Order: to secure the survival in Great Britain of any kind of animal or plant; to comply with any international obligation; or to conserve the flora, fauna or geological or physiographical features of a site which is of national importance.[21] Orders are made by the Secretary of State, after consultation with the relevant conservancy council, and can be made for any land which is considered by the Secretary of State to be of special interest by reason of its flora, fauna and geological or physiographical features[22]; this is the same test as for SSSIs, and any relevant land should already have been designated as such by the conservancy council. Orders are thus made to supplement the SSSI system, protecting the most valuable, or most

[21] WCA, s.29(1).
[22] *Ibid.*, s.29(2).

threatened, sites. It has been held that in determining the boundaries of the land to be covered by an Order it is acceptable to treat a locality as a single environment and to designate it as such, without distinguishing between the different elements within it of greater and lesser importance.[23]

5.5.3 Orders take effect at once, but there is then a nine-month period during which the Order must be considered, at the end of which it expires unless a formal decision on its future has been notified.[24] Once an Order has been made, it must be advertised in the local press and notices stating its general effect, where copies are available and where and when objections can be made, must be sent to all owners and occupiers of the land in question and to the relevant general or district (Scotland), or county (England and Wales) planning authorities.[25] If any objections or representations are withdrawn, or none is made, the Secretary of State may consider the Order as soon as practicable; if there are objections or representations, he must hold a local inquiry or hearing before proceeding. Once he has considered the Order, and any response to it, the Secretary of State may decide to allow the Order to stand, or that it should be amended or revoked.[26] The Secretary of State's decision must be publicised and notified in the same way as the original Order,[27] and after six weeks during which there is a limited right to challenge its validity,[28] the Order cannot then be questioned in any legal proceedings.[29] In Scotland, Orders are registered in the Land Register for Scotland or the General Register of Sasines.[30]

5.5.4 Each Nature Conservation Order specifies a number of potentially damaging operations which appear likely to destroy

[23] *Sweet* v. *Secretary of State for the Environment* [1989] 2 P.L.R. 14, (1989) 1 J.E.L. 245; *cf. R.* v. *Canterbury City Council, ex p. Halford* (1992) 64 P. & C.R. 513, where a similar approach was taken to conservation areas.
[24] WCA, Sched. 11, para. 1.
[25] *Ibid.*, para. 2; at least 28 days must be allowed for objections.
[26] *Ibid.*, paras. 3–4; amendments cannot extend the area covered (*ibid.*, para. 5).
[27] *Ibid.*, para. 6.
[28] *Ibid.*, para. 7; the operation of this procedure is illustrated in *Sweet* v. *Secretary of State for the Environment* (note 23 above) and *North Uist Fisheries Ltd.* v. *Secretary of State for Scotland*, 1992 S.L.T. 333, (1992) 4 J.E.L. 241 where Orders were challenged in the courts.
[29] *R.* v. *Secretary of State for the Environment, ex p. Upton Brickworks Ltd.* [1992] J.P.L. 1044.
[30] WCA, s.29(10).

or damage the features which led to the Order being made.[31] It is an offence for any person to carry out any of these operations without reasonable excuse; this contrasts with the position for SSSIs where only the owner and occupier are subject to the restrictions imposed.[32] For owners and occupiers the same mechanism applies as for SSSIs, in that any proposal to carry out a PDO must be notified to the conservancy council and can proceed without risk of liability provided that the council has given its consent, the operation is in accordance with a management agreement or a certain time, initially three months,[33] has passed.[34] It is again provided expressly that a reasonable excuse for any action is provided by an express grant of planning permission or by emergency operations notified to the council as soon as practicable.[35]

5.5.5 The effect of these provisions was considered in *North Uist Fisheries Ltd.* v. *Secretary of State for Scotland*,[36] where occupiers whose fish-farming activities were covered by the potentially damaging operations listed in an Order successfully challenged the validity of its confirmation. The occupiers objected to the making of the Order, leading to a public inquiry being arranged prior to its confirmation or expiry, but they also continued their activities and gave notice of their intention to carry out the operations. The court said that they had been acting unlawfully in carrying out a specified operation within three months of giving notice (no prosecution was in fact started), but that after the three-month period those activities were legitimate. Accordingly the decision to confirm the Order after the subsequent inquiry was invalid because it had failed to take into account the fact that the fish-farming activities, which were the main target of the Order, had acquired legitimacy and could no longer be restricted by the procedure for notification, etc., created by the Order. This case shows the unsuitability of the system for controlling existing operations as opposed to proposed ones, and demonstrates the need for the conservancy councils to be alert to the way in which the operation of the three-month deadline can preempt the fuller consideration of an issue at an inquiry to be held within the nine-month deadline for an Order to be confirmed.

[31] *Ibid.*, s.29(3).
[32] *Ibid.*, s.29(8).
[33] *Ibid.*, s.29(4) (amended by EPA, Sched. 9, para. 11), (5).
[34] See para. 5.5.7, below.
[35] *Ibid.*, s.29(9).
[36] See note 28, above.

5.5.6 A further point of note in the case, although not necessary for the decision, was the view expressed on the scope of the potentially damaging operations notified when an Order is made. The legislation refers to operations "likely to destroy or damage" the valuable features of the site,[37] and the court favoured the view that this should be read as referring to operations which would *probably* cause damage, not just those which might possibly have that result. This conclusion follows the traditional approach of giving a strict interpretation to any provision giving rise to a risk of criminal conviction or interfering with property rights, but certainly goes against the precautionary principle which is one of the foundations of European Community environmental law. The difficulty of demonstrating exactly how a complex ecosystem will be affected by any given operation means that if this view were accepted it may be impossible for the potentially damaging operations to cover many activities where experts confidently predict, but cannot prove, that the activities carry a real risk of damaging the site.

5.5.7 The basic period for which an owner or occupier must wait after notifying his intention to carry out a PDO is three months.[38] However, where the conservancy council offers to enter either an agreement to purchase the interest in the land or a management agreement providing compensation, the period is extended to twelve months from the notification or three months from the rejection or withdrawal of the offer, whichever is the later.[39] Compulsory acquisition of the interest in the land is a further option open to the council and where such an order is made, the period of delay expires when the council enters the land or the Secretary of State decides not to confirm the order.[40] The period available for negotiating a suitable management agreement or the purchase of the land is thus extended by the law itself, as opposed to relying on agreement between the parties as is the case in SSSIs. As for SSSIs, if a farm capital grant is refused as a result of objections from the conservancy council, a management agreement must be offered by the council.[41]

---

[37] WCA, s.29(3); similar wording is used in relation to SSSIs in *ibid.*, s.28(4).
[38] *Ibid.*, s.29(5)(c).
[39] *Ibid.*, s.29(6).
[40] *Ibid.*, s.29(7).
[41] *Ibid.*, s.32.

5.5.8 Those whose land is affected by a Nature Conservation Order may be entitled to some compensation, regardless of whether a management agreement is entered. Where an Order is made for land comprised in an agricultural unit,[42] anyone with an interest in the land can claim compensation from the conservancy council if he can show that the value of his interest is less than it would have been had no Order been made. The compensation is the difference between the two values.[43] Compensation is also available to a person with an interest in the land who has notified the council of his intention to carry out a potentially damaging operation; the compensation is payable where the period during which he is prevented from carrying out the operation has been extended from the basic three months (as the result of an offer of a management agreement, etc.[44]) and it can be shown that as a result of this extended delay before he can proceed, he has suffered loss or damage or has incurred expenditure which has been rendered abortive. No compensation is available under this heading for any reduction in the value of an interest in the land.[45] Disputes over compensation are referred to the Lands Tribunal for Scotland and the Lands Tribunal,[46] and a number of associated issues are governed by the application of the rules in the Land Compensation Act 1961 and the Land Compensation (Scotland) Act 1963.[47]

5.5.9 If a person has been convicted of carrying out operations which have damaged or destroyed the special features of land covered by a Nature Conservation Order, in addition to imposing a higher penalty than is possible for damage in an SSSI, the court may order him to carry out within a certain period work to restore the land to its former condition.[48] It is an

---

[42] "Land which is occupied as a unit for agricultural purposes, including any dwelling-house or other building occupied by the same person for the purpose of farming the land"; *ibid.*, s.30(11).

[43] *Ibid.*, s.30(2); a claim must be made in writing within six months of the notification of the Secretary of State's decision after considering the Order (Wildlife and Countryside (Claims for Compensation under section 30) Regulations 1982, S.I. 1982 No. 1346, reg. 2).

[44] See para. 5.5.7, above.

[45] WCA, s.30(3); claims must be made in writing within six months of the end of the extended period (Wildlife and Countryside (Claims for Compensation under section 30) Regulations 1982, S.I. 1982 No. 1346, reg. 3).

[46] *Ibid.*, s.30(8).

[47] *Ibid.*, s.30(4)–(7), (9).

[48] *Ibid.*, s.31(1); there are rules on how such an order is to be treated for appeals against conviction or sentence (*ibid.*, s.31(2), (3), (7)).

offence to fail to comply with such an order within the
prescribed period, with a daily fine for continuing default.[49]
Where the restoration work has not been carried out, the
conservancy council itself may enter the land and carry out the
work, recovering expenses from the person in default.[50] If
circumstances change so that compliance with the order is
impracticable or unnecessary, the order may be discharged or
varied by the court on the application of the person against
whom it was made.[51]

5.5.10 Land covered by a Nature Conservation Order is given
further protection by other legislation. As such sites will almost
certainly already have been designated as SSSIs the various
measures discussed previously in relation to SSSIs will apply.[52]
Additionally, the basic conditions for the approval of the use of
a pesticide for aerial application require that any such
application within three-quarters of a nautical mile of land
covered by an Order must be notified to the conservancy
council at least 72 hours beforehand.[53]

LIMESTONE PAVEMENT ORDERS

5.6.1 Special provision is made for the protection of areas of
limestone pavement, *i.e.* areas of limestone wholly or partly
exposed on the surface of the ground and fissured by natural
erosion[54] — such areas are of considerable botanical and
geological value. The making of Limestone Pavement Orders is
a two-stage process. In the first place, any area of limestone
pavement of special interest by reason of its fauna, flora or
geological or physiographical features is to be identified by the
conservancy councils or the Countryside Commission and
notified to the planning authorities for that area.[55] The decision
to make an Order then rests with the Secretary of State or the

[49] *Ibid.*, s.31(5).
[50] *Ibid.*, s.31(6).
[51] *Ibid.*, s.31(4).
[52] See paras. 5.4.13–5.4.15, above.
[53] Control of Pesticides Regulations 1986, S.I. 1986 No. 1510, Sched. 4,
para. 2.
[54] WCA, s.34(6).
[55] *Ibid.*, s.34(1); regional and district authorities in Scotland, county and
district in England and Wales (*ibid.*, s.52(2)).

general or district (Scotland) or county (England and Wales) planning authority[56]; this power is to be exercised where it appears that the character or appearance of the land is likely to be adversely affected by the removal or disturbance of the limestone.[57] The procedure for making Orders is the same as for Nature Conservation Orders, with the Order taking effect at once but being reviewed by the Secretary of State after an opportunity for objections and representation to be made; the Secretary of State considers all Orders, whether made by himself or a planning authority.[58]

5.6.2 The effect of an Order is to designate the land affected and to prohibit the removal or disturbance of limestone on or in it.[59] It is an offence without reasonable excuse to remove or disturb limestone on or in any designated land.[60] A reasonable excuse is however provided if the action is authorised by a grant of planning permission in response to an application under the planning legislation; as with SSSIs, there must be an express grant of permission, thereby excluding operations having only deemed permission under the General Permitted Development Orders.[61] Since any significant extraction of limestone is likely to require planning permission in any case as a "mining operation,"[62] the protection offered is in relation to operations which are incidental to other activities or which fall outwith the scope of planning control. No compensation is available to those whose land is designated under a Limestone Pavement Order.

AREAS OF SPECIAL PROTECTION

5.7.1 Sites which are of particular importance for birds can be offered additional protection through the creation of Areas of

[56] The local planning authority exercises this function in the metropolitan counties; *ibid.*, s.34(6) (amended by Local Government Act 1985, Sched. 3, para. 7).
[57] *Ibid.*, s.34(2).
[58] *Ibid.*, Sched. 11; see para. 5.5.3, above.
[59] *Ibid.*, s.34(2).
[60] *Ibid.*, s.34(4).
[61] *Ibid.*, s.34(5) (amended by Planning (Consequential Amendments) Act 1990, Sched. 2, para. 54).
[62] TCPSA, s.19; TCPA, s.55.

Special Protection. This designation replaces the more clearly
named Bird Sanctuaries,[63] and should not be confused with
Special Protection Areas under the European Community's
Birds Directive.[64] The effect of such areas is primarily on
visitors, since there are wide exemptions preserving the rights of
those with any interest in the land. Orders creating Areas of
Special Protection are made by the Secretary of State, and the
legislation lays down no specific criteria for when an order can
be made.[65] Any proposed order must be notified to all owners
and occupiers of the land affected, individually in writing or
through the local press where individual notification is impracticable,[66] and three months is allowed for objections or
representations to be made.[67] The order can be made by the
Secretary of State only if all the owners and occupiers consent,
or at least if there are no objections or any objections are
withdrawn.[68] Orders are made by Statutory Instrument subject
to annulment by either House of Parliament.[69]

5.7.2 Orders can contain a variety of provisions, strengthening
the general law protecting wild birds. Within the designated
area it may become an offence intentionally to kill, injure or
take any wild bird, to take, damage or destroy the nest of a wild
bird while it is in use or being built, to take or destroy eggs, to
disturb wild birds while they are building or tending a nest or to
disturb the dependent young of a wild bird; these prohibitions
can apply to all wild birds or to specified species.[70] The effect of
the order may thus be to apply the enhanced protection
normally offered only to those species listed in Schedule 1 to the
1981 Act to all birds in the Area of Special Protection.[71] It can
also be made an offence for any person to enter the designated
area, or any part of it, at any time or during certain periods,
e.g. protecting ground-nesting birds during the nesting season.[72]

---

[63] Bird Sanctuaries were governed by the Protection of Birds Act 1954, s.3
and, although there is no express provision, it is thought that the sanctuaries
designated under that Act continue in effect as if created under the 1981 Act;
Halsbury's Statutory Instruments (Vol. 2) (1993 reissue), p. 225.
[64] Directive 79/409; see paras. 5.12.3–5.12.7, 7.4.3–7.4.11, below.
[65] WCA, s.3(1).
[66] *Ibid.*, s.3(4).
[67] *Ibid.*, s.3(5)(*b*).
[68] *Ibid.*, s.3(5).
[69] *Ibid.*, s.26(2).
[70] *Ibid.*, s.3(1)(*a*).
[71] See para. 3.3.5, above.
[72] *Ibid.*, s.3(1)(*b*).

The order can also apply the more severe special penalties to any offence against the general law protecting birds, animals and plants committed in the designated area.[73]

5.7.3 There are, however, many exceptions to the prohibitions which can apply within Areas of Special Protection. Those with rights over the land are protected from restrictions not only by the fact that designations cannot be made in the face of objections by owners or occupiers, but also by the rule that none of the prohibitions in an order can affect the exercise by any person of rights vested in him, as owner or occupier of the land or under any licence or agreement.[74] Further exceptions apply to "authorised persons"[75] in relation to birds which may be listed in Part II of Schedule 2 to the 1981 Act[76]; it is not an offence for authorised persons to kill or take such birds, to take or destroy their eggs or to destroy or disturb their nests or young.[77] The defences which apply to the general law protecting wild birds under the 1981 Act also apply to offences under the provisions of an order creating an Area of Special Protection.[78] The effect of Areas of Special Protection is thus not to offer complete protection to all birds, but rather to provide a limited sanctuary for some birds without interfering with existing rights in the land.

ENVIRONMENTALLY SENSITIVE AREAS

5.8.1 Much of the landscape and habitat in Great Britain has been shaped by agricultural practices, but is threatened by the pressure on farmers to change to more intensive and more efficient, but environmentally more harmful, methods if they are to make a living in the current agricultural markets. The aim of Environmentally Sensitive Areas (ESAs) is to support agricultural practices which are compatible with conserving natural

---

[73] *Ibid.*, s.3(1)(c); the offences in question are those under *ibid.*, Pt. I.

[74] *Ibid.*, s.3(3).

[75] "Authorised persons" include owners, occupiers and those authorised by local authorities, the conservancy councils and a range of statutory bodies; *ibid.*, s.27(1) (see para. 3.2.6, above).

[76] The control of pest species is now authorised by licences rather than this provision; see paras. 3.3.7–3.3.8, above.

[77] WCA, s.3(2).

[78] *Ibid.*, s.4; see paras. 3.3.3.–3.3.4, above.

habitats, whilst ensuring an adequate income for the farmers who do not resort to damaging intensification.[79] The origin of the designation lies in an EC Regulation seeking to improve the efficiency of agricultural structures, which also allowed Member States to introduce special schemes to encourage the use of environmentally beneficial agricultural practices in areas of ecological or landscape importance.[80] The scheme adopted in this country is contained in the Agriculture Act 1986.[81]

5.8.2 The designation of ESAs is in the hands of the agriculture ministers, acting with the consent of the Treasury and after consultations in Scotland with Scottish Natural Heritage, in Wales with the Countryside Council for Wales, and in England with the Secretary of State for the Environment, the Countryside Commission and the Nature Conservancy Council for England.[82] The areas to be designated are those where it appears particularly desirable to conserve or enhance the natural beauty of the area, to conserve the flora, fauna, geological or physiographical features of the area or to protect buildings or other objects of archaeological, architectural or historic interest, and where these aims are likely to be facilitated by the maintenance or adoption of particular agricultural methods.[83] Orders are made by Statutory Instrument subject to annulment in either House of Parliament.[84]

5.8.3 Once an ESA has been designated, the agriculture ministers are empowered to enter agreements with those having an interest in agricultural land whereby in exchange for prescribed payments that person agrees to manage the land in accordance with the agreement.[85] The designation order may lay down certain terms for all the agreements in that area, although

[79] D. Baldock, *et al.*, "Environmentally Sensitive Areas: Incrementalism or Reform?" (1990) 6 J.Rural Studies 143; P. Wathern, "Less Favoured and Environmentally Sensitive Areas: A European Dimension to the Rural Environment" in W. Howarth & C.P. Rodgers (eds.), *Agriculture, Conservation and Land Use* (1992), Chap. 9.
[80] Regulation 797/85, Art. 19; see now Reg. 2328/91, Arts. 21–24.
[81] Agriculture Act 1986, s.18 (amended by EPA, Sched. 9, para. 13; NHSA, Sched. 10, para. 12; Agricultural Holdings (Scotland) Act 1991, Sched. 11, para. 45).
[82] Agriculture Act 1986, s.18(1), (2) (amended by EPA, Sched. 9, para. 13; NHSA, Sched. 10, para. 12).
[83] *Ibid.*, s.18(1).
[84] *Ibid.*, s.18(12).
[85] *Ibid.*, s.18(3).

each agreement may differ.[86] Special provision is made to allow agreements to be made by those with less than full ownership of the land,[87] and by grazings committees on crofting land.[88] In Scotland, agreements may be registered in the Land Register of Scotland or the General Register of Sasines, and once registered can be enforced by the Secretary of State against those deriving title from the original party.[89] In England and Wales the agreement is binding on those deriving title from the original party unless the contrary is stated.[90] The effect of these provisions is that agreements may run with the land, but that this is an issue to be decided when each individual agreement is made.

5.8.4 The designation of the ESA does not have any automatic consequences; it merely enables the agriculture ministers to enter agreements with individual farmers in the area. It is hoped that farmers will be encouraged to continue with more traditional farming methods by the availability of payments under the scheme to take the place of the income they could otherwise earn by converting to more intensive methods. The ministers must keep under review the effects of the scheme on each area and publish information on this.[91] The scheme does appear to have been generally successful, and the area covered by designations (and by agreements within the designated areas) has increased substantially in recent years.

NATURAL HERITAGE AREAS
(Scotland only)

5.9.1 Natural Heritage Areas (NHAs) are the newest designation of land to be introduced, originating in the Natural Heritage (Scotland) Act 1991. The aim is to provide a framework which is apt for larger areas than can be properly dealt with by SSSIs and which takes account of all aspects of the natural heritage, in contrast to the more limited objectives of National Scenic Areas. After such consultations as it thinks fit,

---

[86] *Ibid.*, s.18(4).
[87] *Ibid.*, s.18(9).
[88] *Ibid.*, s.19(4)–(7).
[89] *Ibid.*, s.19(1)–(3).
[90] *Ibid.*, s.18(7).
[91] *Ibid.*, s.18(8).

Scottish Natural Heritage may recommend to the Secretary of State those areas which are of outstanding value to the natural heritage of Scotland[92] and where special protection measures are appropriate.[93] Following a recommendation, the Secretary of State may make a direction designating the area, but he must advertise any proposed designation and consider any representations made within the specified period of at least three months.[94] A direction creating an NHA must be advertised in the local press.[95] The same procedure is followed where Scottish Natural Heritage recommends that it is no longer appropriate for all or part of an NHA to be designated as such and that the designation should be varied or cancelled.[96]

5.9.2 The legal effect of the designation of an NHA is minimal. The planning authority is obliged to maintain a list available for public inspection of any NHA in its district and to ensure that where an NHA has been designated special attention is paid to the desirability of preserving or enhancing its character or appearance in the exercise, with respect to any land in that area, of any powers under the Town and Country Planning (Scotland) Act 1972.[97]

5.9.3 However, the consultation paper issued when the proposal to introduce NHAs was first produced suggests a much greater significance in practice.[98] The intention is that for such areas, an overall Management Statement should be prepared, to be submitted to and approved by the Secretary of State when the recommendation for designation is made. This Management Statement should be prepared by SNH in cooperation with relevant public and private interests, and set forth a basis for sustainable land use throughout the area that can be implemented through the "voluntary principle." SNH will then oversee the implementation of the Management Statement, possibly with the assistance of a management committee,

---

[92] The "natural heritage of Scotland" includes the flora and fauna of Scotland, its geological and physiographical features and its natural beauty and amenity; NHSA, s.1(3).

[93] *Ibid.*, s.6(1).

[94] *Ibid.*, s.6(3), (4).

[95] *Ibid.*, s.6(5).

[96] *Ibid.*, s.6(6), (7).

[97] *Ibid.*, s.6(8), applying TCPSA, s.262C(3), (4) (added by Housing and Planning Act 1986, Sched. 11, para. 38).

[98] Consultation Paper on Natural Heritage Areas, Scottish Office, March 6, 1991.

coordinating the activities and strategies of the various interested parties.[99]

5.9.4 SNH's role in achieving the aims of the NHA will include involvement in the preparation of alterations to the planning authorities' development plans for the area and as a consultee in the consideration of applications for forestry grants, felling licences and agricultural grants. No new powers would be involved, but use would be made of the existing provisions for management agreements,[1] financial assistance, consultation and advice in order to assist the implementation of the Statement, with the powers to designate SSSIs and make access orders available as a last resort. The Secretary of State might also be asked to make directions removing permitted development status from certain forms of development in such areas, as is presently the case in National Scenic Areas (*e.g.* in relation to vehicle tracks).[2] The aim throughout, though, would be to integrate the strategies of the many public bodies and private individuals whose activities can affect the natural heritage of an area, and to lead them to cooperate in preserving and enhancing the value of the area.

NATIONAL PARKS
(England and Wales only)

5.10.1 National Parks in England and Wales are very different from the internationally accepted concept of national parks. The International Union for the Conservation of Nature has recommended that the term "national park" be reserved for relatively large areas where ecosystems are not materially altered by human exploitation and occupation, where the highest competent authority of the country has taken steps to prevent or eliminate exploitation and occupation and where visitors are allowed to enter under special conditions for

---

[99] See the discussion of possible NHA status for the Cairngorms in *Common Sense and Sustainability: A Partnership for the Cairngorms,* Report of the Cairngorms Working Party (1992), section 4.4.1.

[1] The power to make management agreements extends to anything "necessary to secure the conservation and enhancement or to foster the understanding and enjoyment of the natural heritage of Scotland"; CSA s.49A (added by Countryside (Scotland) Act 1981 s.9, amended by NHSA, Sched. 10, para. 4).

[2] See para. 5.11.5, below.

"inspirational, educative, cultural and recreative purposes." It is further recommended that the term should not be used for inhabited and exploited areas where landscape planning and measures for the development of tourism have led to areas where industrialisation and urbanisation are controlled and public outdoor recreation takes priority over the conservation of ecosystems.[3] The system of National Parks in England and Wales contravene this recommendation in many ways.[4]

5.10.2 The National Parks are not areas unaffected by man (indeed none of this country is free from significant human interference), and they are places where many people continue to live and to make a living off the land or in industrial or tourist developments. Responsibility for the parks lies primarily with local authorities and recreation and the preservation of natural beauty have a greater impact on policy than pure nature conservation. National Parks may indeed be better regarded as part of the town and country planning system, as areas where slightly stricter controls apply, than as a major element of the law relating to nature conservation. This is not to say that the parks do not play a part in this latter objective, but their impact tends to be indirect and to depend on the way in which discretionary powers are exercised.[5]

5.10.3 The National Park system is designed to further two objectives, the preservation and enhancement of natural beauty and the promotion of the enjoyment of the countryside by the public.[6] The designation, management and legal rules for National Parks all seek to accomplish these objectives, and it is for these purposes that the powers given to the various authorities involved can be exercised. One of the difficulties faced by the National Parks is that these twin objectives which they are created to serve are not always compatible. Increasing recreational use can put too much pressure on a fragile environment, and even those seeking to appreciate the peace of the countryside can destroy habitats through disturbance and

---

[3] Resolution 1 of 10th General Assembly of IUCN, New Delhi, December 1, 1969.

[4] For many purposes the Norfolk and Suffolk Broads are treated as a National Park, although subject to the individual legal regime established by the Norfolk and Suffolk Broads Act 1988; see paras. 5.10.14–5.10.16, below.

[5] See generally, A. McEwan & M. McEwan, *National Parks: Conservation or Cosmetics?* (1982).

[6] NPACA, s.5(1).

erosion, to say nothing of the effect of the facilities required to transport and cater for large numbers of visitors. Although the preservation of the natural beauty of an area includes the preservation of its flora, fauna and geological and physiographical features,[7] the emphasis in National Parks is on protecting wildlife and natural features as part of the beauty of the countryside to be enjoyed and made available to the public. The dual objectives of the parks must always be borne in mind and the interests of conservation must always be tempered by those of recreation.

5.10.4 The areas which can be chosen as National Parks are extensive tracts of country where action for the twin purposes of preserving natural beauty and promoting enjoyment is particularly desirable in view of the natural beauty of the areas and the opportunities which they afford for open air recreation in view of their character and location in relation to centres of population.[8] Designation is in the hands of the Countryside Commission (in England) and the Countryside Council for Wales (in Wales),[9] subject to confirmation by the Secretary of State after the proposal has been advertised and notified to all local authorities affected. If objections or representations are made, a local inquiry or a hearing must be held,[10] and further consultations are required if the Secretary of State decides to confirm the proposed designation with modifications.[11] The order designating a park can be subsequently varied by the Secretary of State or by the Commission or Council, subject to the same procedural rules.[12]

5.10.5 The administrative arrangements for the National Parks are complex, but in essence powers are exercised by local

[7] *Ibid.*, s.114(2) (amended by CA, s.21(7)); note the older usage of "preservation" as opposed to the current "conservation," which is thought to be more apt for living ecosystems.

[8] *Ibid.*, s.5(2).

[9] All of the powers with respect to National Parks previously exercised by the Countryside Commission for the whole of England and Wales are now exercised in Wales by the Countryside Council for Wales whilst remaining in the hands of the Countryside Commission for land in England; *ibid.*, s.4A (added by EPA, Sched. 8, para. 2).

[10] An inquiry must be held if there are representations from a local authority; *ibid.*, Sched. 1, para. 2.

[11] *Ibid.*, s.7, Sched. 1; National Parks and Access to the Countryside Regulations 1950, S.I. 1950 No. 1066, Pt. IV.

[12] *Ibid.*, s.7(4); WCA, s.45.

authorities operating through special bodies which include a number of outside members appointed by the Secretary of State.[13] In two of the parks, the Lake District and the Peak District, power lies in the hands of Planning Boards,[14] which operate as planning authorities and enjoy a number of other powers as if they were local authorities themselves, including the power to acquire land.[15] In the other parks, it is the county council or councils (acting together) for the area which exercise all of the planning and related powers, but a National Park Committee, one third of whose members are appointed by the Secretary of State after consultation with the Countryside Commission or Countryside Council for Wales, must be set up to exercise these functions.[16] Arrangements can be made for district councils to exercise some functions.[17] A National Park Officer must be appointed for each park.[18]

5.10.6 Whilst executive power rests with the boards and committees, an important advisory role is played by the Countryside Commission and the Countryside Council for Wales.[19] These bodies must be consulted before many of the powers of the boards and committees are exercised, and must keep the general position in the National Parks under review. In particular, the Commission and Council are to make recommendations to ministers and local authorities on the accomplishment of the objectives for which National Parks were created, advise on arrangements for the administration of the parks, give advice when consulted by ministers or planning authorities on the preparation of development plans or the handling of individual applications for planning permission, and make representations when developments incompatible with the aims of a park are

[13] A short guide to the arrangements is to be found in M. Grant's annotations to ss.1–5 of the Town and Country Planning Act 1990 in *Current Law Statutes 1990* (1990), Vol. 1, c.8.

[14] The Boards constituted under Sched. 17 to the Local Government Act 1972 are the Lake District Special Planning Board (Lake District Special Planning Board Order 1973, S.I. 1973 No. 2001) and the Peak Park Joint Planning Board (Peak Park Joint Planning Board Order 1986, S.I. 1986 No. 561).

[15] Local Government Act 1972, s.184, Sched. 17; TCPA, s.2; Planning (Hazardous Substances) Act 1990, s.3.

[16] Local Government Act 1972, s.184, Sched. 17 (amended by EPA, Sched. 8, para. 3); TCPA, s.4; Planning (Hazardous Substances) Act 1990, s.3.

[17] Local Government Act 1972, Sched. 17, para. 13.

[18] *Ibid.*, Sched. 17, para. 15.

[19] The Commission was originally created as the National Parks Commission; NPACA, s.1.

proposed and when their own advice is not being followed.[20] The Commission and Council can also make recommendations on the payment of grants to local authorities to assist in the management of the parks.[21] Only in very limited circumstances, *e.g.* for experimental schemes,[22] can the Commission or Council take direct action themselves.[23]

5.10.7 The Board or Committee responsible for each park must prepare a National Park Plan formulating its policy for the management of the park, and must review and revise this plan at least every five years.[24] This plan, together with the development plan prepared as a normal part of the planning system,[25] must be drawn up in consultation with the Countryside Commission or Countryside Council for Wales[26] and these form the basis on which the park will be managed with an eye to achieving the objectives of preserving and enhancing the natural beauty of the park and promoting its use for recreation. As well as it being likely that different policies will be applied, the normal planning controls are made more strict by restrictions to the range of works which qualify as "permitted development" and are thus exempt from the requirement to obtain express planning permission.[27]

5.10.8 For each park a map must be drawn up by the relevant county planning authorities showing those areas of the park whose natural beauty it is especially important to conserve.[28] The areas in question are areas of mountain, moor, heath, woodland, down, cliff and foreshore,[29] and they are to be identified in accordance with guidelines issued by the Countryside Commission and Countryside Council for Wales.[30] Such maps, which must be revised annually,[31] are to be for sale to the public, and serve as a guide identifying those areas where the

[20] *Ibid.*, s.6(3), (4).
[21] CA, s.2(9).
[22] *Ibid.*, s.4 (amended by WCA, s.40).
[23] See paras. 2.5.16, 2.6.2, above.
[24] Local Government Act 1972, Sched. 17, para. 18.
[25] TCPA, Pt. II.
[26] NPACA, ss.6(4), 9; Local Government Act 1972, Sched. 17, para. 19.
[27] Town and Country Planning General Development Order 1988, S.I. 1988 No. 1813, Scheds. 1, 2.
[28] WCA, s.43(1) (amended by Wildlife and Countryside (Amendment) Act 1985, s.3).
[29] *Ibid.*, s.43(3) (added by *ibid.*).
[30] *Ibid.*, s.43(1A)–(1C) (added by *ibid.*).
[31] *Ibid.*, s.43(1) (amended by *ibid.*).

authorities are likely to seek to exercise their various powers to regulate land use, etc.

5.10.9 While the operation of the planning system can be used to protect National Parks from many forms of development, agricultural and forestry developments are largely outwith the scope of such controls. However special provisions (akin to those for SSSIs) have been introduced to protect areas of moor and heath within the parks. Where such an area has been designated by the Secretary of State,[32] it is an offence to plough the land, convert it into agricultural land or carry out on it other agricultural or forestry operations which have been specified as likely to affect its character or appearance.[33] These prohibitions do not apply if the land in question has been agricultural land within the last twenty years,[34] or if the owner or occupier has given written notice to the planning authority and one of a number of other conditions is satisfied. The authority must notify the agriculture minister and in England the Secretary of State for the Environment, Countryside Commission and Nature Conservancy Council for England, in Wales the Countryside Council for Wales.[35] Once notice has been given, the operation can go ahead as soon as consent has been given by the authority, after three months if no decision has been made by the authority by that time, or after twelve months if consent has been refused.[36] As with SSSIs, the period of delay is intended to allow time for negotiations for management agreements or other measures to be introduced to deal with the situation. Where there is an application for a farm capital grant for land in a National Park, the outcome should so far as possible be consistent with the twin objectives of the parks, and if a grant is refused following an objection from the planning authority, an offer must be made by it to enter a management agreement.[37]

5.10.10 The planning authorities in National Parks enjoy a range of powers to further the aims of the parks. They can

[32] *Ibid.*, s.42(1); designating orders are to be made by statutory instrument subject to annulment by either House of Parliament (WCA, s.42(8)).

[33] *Ibid.*, s.42(2).

[34] *Ibid.*, s.42(2); "agricultural land" does not include land used only for rough grazing (*ibid.*, s.52(1)) and any conversion in breach of this section or of its predecessor (CA, s.14) is to be disregarded (WCA, s.42(7)).

[35] *Ibid.*, s.42(6).

[36] *Ibid.*, s.42(3), (4).

[37] *Ibid.*, s.41(3)–(5) (amended by Agriculture Act 1986 s.20(4)); *cf.* para. 5.4.13, above.

arrange for the provision of facilities for visitors, including accommodation, refreshments, litter bins, camping sites and parking places[38] as well as study centres and other facilities for learning about the history and natural history of the area.[39] Where there is a shortage of such facilities, arrangements can be made to facilitate the use of waterways for boating, bathing, fishing and other forms of recreation.[40] Traffic on roads in National Parks can be restricted to conserve and enhance their natural beauty and to afford better opportunities for recreation, enjoyment of the amenities of the area and the study of nature.[41] More generally planning authorities are given a general competence to do all things which they consider expedient for accomplishing the twin objectives of the National Parks, although where specific statutory powers exist those must be exercised in accordance with the relevant conditions and this general power cannot be used to interfere with the legal rights of others.[42] In particular grants and loans can be made to other bodies and individuals to further these aims.[43]

5.10.11 A further important power to assist in preserving the character of the National Parks, is the power of the planning authority to make bye-laws. These can be made for the preservation of order, to ensure that people do not behave so as to cause undue interference with the enjoyment of others, and to protect from damage the land or anything thereon or therein.[44] In particular bye-laws can cover matters such as traffic controls, litter and the lighting of fires.[45] For lakes and other stretches of open water in the parks bye-laws can be made prohibiting or restricting traffic of any description on the water for the purposes of ensuring the safety of those using the lake, regulating all forms of sport or recreation which use vessels, conserving the natural beauty and amenity of the lake and surrounding area and preventing any nuisance or damage, particularly nuisance caused by excessive noise.[46] In all cases the Commission or Council must be consulted before the bye-laws

---

[38] NPACA, s.12; CA, s.12(2).
[39] CA, s.12(1).
[40] NPACA, s.13; CA, s.12(3).
[41] Road Traffic Regulation Act 1984, s.22.
[42] NPACA, s.11 (amended by CA, Sched. 5; WCA, s.72(5)).
[43] WCA, s.44.
[44] NPACA, s.90(1).
[45] *Ibid.*, s.90(3).
[46] CA, s.13.

are made,[47] and the bye-laws must be confirmed by the Secretary of State in accordance with the standard procedures for local authority bye-laws.[48] Wardens can be appointed, to secure compliance with the bye-laws, advise and assist the public, and perform other functions as directed by the authorities.[49]

5.10.12 Land in National Parks can be acquired by the Secretary of State where he considers this expedient,[50] and is to be passed into the hands of others to be managed for the twin purposes of preserving and enhancing natural beauty and promoting public enjoyment of the area.[51] The terms on which land is passed on may include a financial contribution from the government for the management of the land.[52] The way in which land is dealt with by other authorities is also affected, *e.g.* before disposing of land in a National Park, water and sewerage undertakers must consult the Commission or Council and may enter management agreements to impose other conditions before the land is transferred.[53] The water legislation also provides that, as with SSSIs, areas within the parks can be identified by the authorities as being of special value so that any body concerned with authorising or carrying out works must notify the Commission or Council in advance.[54]

5.10.13 What all of this means is that the relevant authorities in National Parks enjoy wide powers which can be used for the benefit of nature conservation as part of the general aim of preserving and enhancing the natural beauty of these areas. The potential is there for things to be done to assist conservation through stricter planning controls, the making of bye-laws and

[47] NPACA, s.90(4); CA, s.13(4).
[48] *Ibid.*, s.106; *ibid.*, s.13(8); the procedure is set out in the Local Government Act 1972, ss.236–238.
[49] *Ibid.*, s.92; *ibid.*, ss.13(9), 42; WCA, s.49.
[50] *Ibid.*, s.14(1); acquisition is by agreement and with the consent of the Treasury.
[51] *Ibid.*, s.14(2).
[52] *Ibid.*, s.14(3).
[53] Water Industry Act 1991, s.156; the disposal of houses in National Parks may also be restricted in the effort to avoid the spread of holiday homes at the expense of accommodation for those living in the parks (Housing Act 1985, s.37 (amended by Housing Act 1988, s.125); Housing Associations Act 1985, s.11 and Sched. 2, para. 3).
[54] Water Industry Act 1991, s.4; Water Resources Act 1991, s.17; Land Drainage Act 1991, s.13; see para. 5.4.15, above.

the funding or carrying out of particular projects, and to assist in educating the public through the provision of study centres. However the mere fact that an area has been designated a National Park has very little immediate and direct significance for nature conservation — the controls on converting moor and heath apply only once introduced to an area by ministerial order — and even where action is taken to conserve nature the authority must balance this against the need to promote the recreational use of the land.

Norfolk and Suffolk Broads

5.10.14 Special provisions have been made for the Norfolk and Suffolk Broads, similar to those for the National Parks, but taking account of the special requirements arising from the fact that it is the waterways which are the main features of interest both for recreation and conservation.[55] A Broads Authority has been established with membership drawn from the relevant local authorities, water and navigation bodies, the Countryside Commission and Nature Conservancy Council for England, boating, farming and landowning interests.[56] The general duty of this authority is to manage the Broads for the purposes of conserving and enhancing their natural beauty,[57] promoting the enjoyment of the Broads by the public and protecting the interests of navigation.[58] Thus as with the National Parks, nature conservation must be balanced with and may be subordinated to the interests of recreation, and also in this case of the preservation and development of rights of navigation.

5.10.15 Many of the provisions for the National Parks are repeated for the Broads. A map must be drawn up and regularly revised showing the areas whose natural beauty it is especially important to conserve,[59] and a Broads Plan must be

---

[55] Norfolk and Suffolk Broads Act 1988; see generally M. Shaw, "The Broads Act 1988: A Framework for Environmental Planning and Management" [1989] J.P.L. 241.

[56] *Ibid.*, s.1 (amended by EPA, Sched. 9, para. 15; Water (Local Statutory Provisions) (Consequential Amendments) Order 1989, S.I. 1989 No. 1380, art. 4).

[57] This includes conserving the flora, fauna, geological and physiographical features of the area (*ibid.*, s.25(2)); it is worth remarking that the "natural beauty" of the Broads is largely man-made, being the result of the flooding of early peat workings.

[58] *Ibid.*, s.2.

[59] *Ibid.*, s.4.

prepared to set out the policy for managing the area.[60] Particular areas can be designated within which specified operations which might affect their character or appearance can go ahead only after the Broads Authority has been notified and has given its consent or a period of time has passed. The areas which can be designated are areas of grazing marsh, fen marsh, reed-bed or broad-leaved woodland and the time periods are three months if no response is given and twelve months if consent is refused.[61] Bye-laws can be made for areas owned or occupied by the Authority or commonly used by the public.[62] The Broads Authority counts as a local authority and the Broads as a National Park for many other pieces of legislation.[63]

5.10.16 The importance of the waterways is reflected by the creation of a separate Navigation Committee with membership drawn from the Broads Authority, the owners and hirers of pleasure craft and other users of the area.[64] This Committee is responsible for maintaining, improving and developing for the purposes of navigation the area specified as the "navigation area."[65] There is a power for the Committee to make bye-laws for the good management of the area, the conservation of its natural beauty and amenities and the promotion of its use for recreational purposes.[66]

LANDSCAPE AND PLANNING DESIGNATIONS

Areas of Outstanding Natural Beauty
(England and Wales only)

5.11.1 Areas of Outstanding Natural Beauty (AONBs) are areas which are not in a National Park, but are of such

[60] *Ibid.*, s.3.
[61] *Ibid.*, s.5.
[62] *Ibid.*, s.6.
[63] See *ibid.*, Sched. 6.
[64] *Ibid.*, s.9.
[65] *Ibid.*, s.10(1); the "navigation area" is defined in s.8(1).
[66] *Ibid.*, s.10(3).

outstanding natural beauty that it is desirable that special provisions, in essence changes to the planning system, should apply to them.[67] The areas are selected and designated by the Countryside Commission and the Countryside Council for Wales,[68] who must consult all the local authorities in the area and advertise the proposal.[69] The designation must be confirmed by the Secretary of State, who must receive any representations or objections made in response to the proposal[70] and consult the Commission, Council and local authorities if he intends to refuse to confirm the order or to confirm it with modifications.[71] Designation orders can be varied by the Secretary of State and the Commission and Council.[72]

5.11.2 Once an AONB has been created, the Countryside Commission and Countryside Council for Wales must be consulted by the planning authority on the preparation of development plans and on the making of arrangements for public access to land for recreation.[73] The authority is also empowered to make bye-laws for its own land in an AONB[74] and to appoint wardens,[75] whilst orders can be made by the Secretary of State restricting traffic on roads in the area.[76] Certain permitted development rights are withdrawn,[77] and as for National Parks there are special rules on the disposal of certain land by water and sewerage undertakers and housing bodies.[78]

5.11.3 The effect of AONBs is thus minimal with respect to nature conservation, although any strengthening of the policy and rules on development control in the interests of preserving the natural beauty of such areas may help to preserve the quality of the general habitat. The designation of an AONB will, however, have no direct effect on agricultural or forestry

[67] NPACA, s.87(1).
[68] *Ibid.*, s.87(1), (1A) (amended by EPA, Sched. 8, para. 1).
[69] *Ibid.*, s.87(2).
[70] *Ibid.*, s.87(3).
[71] *Ibid.*, s.87(5).
[72] *Ibid.*, s.87(7).
[73] *Ibid.*, s.88(1), applying ss.6(4)(*e*), 9, 62(1), 64(5), 65(5).
[74] *Ibid.*, s.90.
[75] *Ibid.*, s.92.
[76] Road Traffic Regulation Act 1984, s.22.
[77] Town and Country Planning General Development Order 1988, S.I. 1988 No. 1813, Scheds.1, 2.
[78] See para. 5.10.12, above.

developments, and a planning authority in balancing its many responsibilities may favour other interests over the preservation of the area.

National Scenic Areas
(Scotland only)

5.11.4 As with Areas of Outstanding Natural Beauty, the aim of National Scenic Areas (NSAs) is to strengthen aspects of the town and country planning system in order to preserve areas of high landscape value. NSAs are areas of outstanding scenic value and beauty in a national context where special protection measures are considered appropriate, and which were designated by the Secretary of State after consultation with the Countryside Commission for Scotland and other bodies as he thought fit.[79] In practice the areas designated were those proposed in the Commission's report "Scotland's Scenic Heritage" in 1978. No new NSAs can be created, their place being taken, in part at least, by Natural Heritage Areas, but existing designations continue unless and until cancelled by the same procedure.[80] Planning authorities maintain a list of NSAs in their area.[81]

5.11.5 Once an area has been designated, special attention must be paid to the desirability of preserving or enhancing its character or appearance in the exercise of functions under the Town and Country Planning (Scotland) Act 1972.[82] In order to assist this, permitted development rights have been withdrawn from certain forms of development in NSAs, *e.g.* the construction of vehicle tracks.[83] Scottish Natural Heritage must be consulted on certain kinds of planning application and any decision contrary to its advice must be notified to the Secretary

---

[79] TCPSA, s.262C(1) (added by Housing and Planning Act 1986, Sched. 11, para. 38); see note 80 below.

[80] By virtue of NHSA, s.6(8), (9) and Sched. 11, s.262C of TCPSA is partly repealed and the remainder amended so as to apply to Natural Heritage Areas, but its provisions continue to have effect unaltered in so far as they apply to areas which have already been designated as NSAs.

[81] TCPSA, s.262C(3) (amended but saved for existing NSAs; see note 80 above).

[82] *Ibid.*, s.262C(4) (amended but saved for existing NSAs; see note 80 above).

[83] Town and Country Planning (Restriction of Permitted Development) (National Scenic Areas) (Scotland) Direction 1987; this Direction and the one referred to in note 84 are conveniently printed in Appendix I of E. Young, *Greens Planning Acts* (1993).

of State.[84] Traffic on roads can be restricted for the sake of the natural beauty of the area or to offer better opportunities for recreation or the study of nature.[85] Within NSAs therefore there is a slight stretghening of planning controls and the beauty of the landscape is to be given special attention, but there is nothing to assist directly the interests of nature conservation.

Conservation Areas

5.11.6 Planning controls and policies are also made more strict in conservation areas.[86] Local planning authorities are under an obligation to designate as conservation areas those parts of their areas which are of special architectural or historic interest, the character or appearance of which it is desirable to preserve or enhance.[87] Once a conservation area has been designated, greater publicity has to be given to certain planning applications,[88] stricter controls on demolition apply,[89] whilst further restrictions can be imposed through directions made by the planning authority.[90] Certain permitted development rights are withdrawn, as is the case for National Parks and Areas of Outstanding Natural Beauty.[91] Throughout the country, any plan to cut down, lop or prune trees in a conservation area must be notified to the planning authority six weeks in advance, so as to allow time to consider whether a tree preservation order should be made protecting the trees.[92] Generally, the authority

---

[84] Town and Country Planning (Notification of Applications) (National Scenic Areas) (Scotland) Direction 1987.

[85] Road Traffic Regulation Act 1984, s.22 (amended by NHSA, Sched. 10, para. 10).

[86] TCPSA, ss.262–262B (substituted by Town and Country Amenities Act 1974, s.2(1); amended by Local Government and Planning (Scotland) Act 1982, Sched. 2, paras. 38–39, Sched. 4 Pt. I and by Housing and Planning Act 1986, s.50, Sched. 9, para. 21); Planning (Listed Buildings and Conservation Areas) Act 1990, Pt. II.

[87] *Ibid.*, s.262(1); Planning (Listed Buildings and Conservation Areas) Act 1990, s.69(1).

[88] *Ibid.*, s.25 (amended by Town and Country Amenities Act 1974, s.4, Sched. 29; Local Government (Scotland) Act 1973, Sched. 29; Local Government and Planning (Scotland) Act 1982, Sched. 2); *ibid.*, s.73.

[89] *Ibid.*, s.262A; *ibid.*, s.74.

[90] Town and Country Planning (General Permitted Development) (Scotland) Order 1992, S.I. 1992 No. 223, art. 4; Town and Country Planning General Development Order 1988, S.I. 1988 No. 1813, art. 4.

[91] *Ibid.*, Sched. 1; *ibid.* Scheds. 1, 2.

[92] TCPSA, s.59A (added by Town and Country Amenities Act 1974, s.9); TCPA, s.211.

should develop proposals to preserve and enhance its conservation areas, acting positively as well as simply preventing
degradation.[93] These provisions may serve to protect areas from
intensive development and to protect small areas of trees,
village greens, ponds, large gardens and other habitats of value.

EUROPEAN AND INTERNATIONAL DESIGNATIONS

5.12.1 Legislation from the European Community and international agreements may also call for the protection of sites of
particular importance. The legal impact of designations under
Community law may be considerable in view of the status of
European Community law as part of the legal systems of the
UK.[94] Whilst designations under international treaties may have
no direct impact on the law within this country, they may be
significant in terms of policy-making and the management of
particular sites.[95]

5.12.2 In both cases the main protection offered to sites
designated in accordance with external measures has come
through the application of the domestic provisions discussed
above, but the additional designation emphasises the importance
of, and commitment to, nature conservation measures for the
sites. In particular, such measures have helped to shape the
domestic law.[96] The presence of legal obligations at the
European or international level can also be a major factor in
ensuring that the policy affecting the management and
protection of a site does in fact give adequate protection to the
natural features in question, especially in relation to the exercise
of discretionary powers. Even where there is little likelihood of
meaningful action at the international level if such sites are
damaged, the bad publicity generated by allowing damage to
habitats which the government itself has stated to be of
international importance can play a real part in securing
continued protection. The three most important current designations are discussed here: Special Protection Areas under the EC
Birds Directive, Ramsar sites and World Heritage sites. The

---

[93] *Ibid.*, s.262B; Planning (Listed Buildings and Conservation Areas) Act
1990, s.71.
[94] See section 2.8, above.
[95] See section 7.5, below.
[96] *E.g.*, WCA; see para. 1.1.15, above.

Special Areas of Conservation which will be required under the EC Habitats and Species Directive are discussed in Chapter 7.[97] There are also many other designations under a host of international schemes, with varying degrees of official recognition and support but usually lacking any legal significance.

Special protection areas for birds

5.12.3 Under the Directive on the Conservation of Wild Birds,[98] the Member States of the European Communities are obliged to take measures for the conservation of wild birds in their territories. In particular, states must designate the most suitable territories in number and size as special protection areas for the conservation of the many rarer species listed in Annex I to the Directive,[99] and take "similar measures" for migratory birds not so listed.[1] Once such an area has been established, Member States must take "appropriate steps to avoid pollution or deterioration of habitats or any disturbances affecting the birds."[2] Once the Habitats and Species Directive comes into force these provisions will be replaced so as to apply the more general regime of Special Areas of Conservation to areas designated under the Birds Directive.[3]

5.12.4 In the UK this Directive has been implemented by the designation of a number of sites which already enjoy legal protection under domestic law as nature reserves, SSSIs or under Nature Conservation Orders. The designation of special protection areas is carried out by the government in consultation with the conservancy councils and must be notified to the Commission of the European Communities.[4]

5.12.5 Designation of sites already protected in such ways does not completely meet the requirements of the Directive. The existing regimes may not impose any obligation for the positive management which may be required to prevent a site deteriorating, and marine areas fall generally outwith the scope

[97] Directive 92/43; see paras. 7.4.17–7.4.24, below.
[98] Directive 79/409 (amended by Directives 81/854, 85/411, 86/122, 91/244); see paras. 7.4.3–7.4.11, below.
[99] *Ibid.*, Art. 4.1; *Commission* v. *Italy* (C–334/89) [1991] E.C.R. I–93.
[1] *Ibid.*, Art. 4.2.
[2] *Ibid.*, Art. 4.4.
[3] See paras. 7.4.17–7.4.24, below.
[4] Directive 79/409 (amended by Directives 81/854, 85/411, 86/122, 91/244) Art. 4.3.

of these domestic measures.[5] In particular, where a special
protection area is an SSSI, it is still lawful for damaging
operations to take place if there has been an express grant of
planning permission to authorise the works.[6] The government's
guidance to planning authorities had asked them to pay
particular attention to the interests of conservation in such
areas, but had suggested that development could be permitted
in some circumstances: where there were economic or recreational requirements which outweighed the conservation interests
or where the development would not produce significant effects
which threatened the survival or reproduction of birds in the
area.[7]

5.12.6 A decision of the European Court of Justice has,
however, emphasised that the Directive requires a greater level
of protection for the designated areas. In *Commission* v.
Germany (the "Leybucht Dykes" case),[8] the Court held that it
is only in exceptional circumstances that any action which
reduces the size (and by clear implication, the quality) of a
special protection area can be permitted, and held that the
balancing of conservation interests with economic and recreational requirements has no place in the treatment of special
protection areas once they have been declared.[9] Although not
expressly referred to in the judgment, it is clear that the court
also supported the Advocate General's rejection of the British
claim that it is only activities producing significant effects on
bird populations which are to be avoided, so that any
deterioration of the site should be prohibited.

5.12.7 The effect of the "Leybucht Dykes" decision is that
once a special protection area has been designated, it must be
protected from all deterioration or disturbance. Only activities
justified by important national needs can overcome this
protection — in the case in question works to prevent the
flooding of a large coastal area were permissible. Some other

[5] The Directive repeatedly refers to the "geographical sea and land area" to
which it applies, *e.g.* Art. 4.
[6] See para. 5.4.8, above.
[7] DoE Circular 27/87, SDD Circular 1/1988.
[8] Case C–57/89, [1991] E.C.R. I–883; the British Government intervened in
proceedings to support its interpretation of the Directive. See also *Commission*
v. *Spain* (C-355/90) ECJ August 2, 1993.
[9] Such balancing is provided for in Art. 2 of the Directive, but in the light of
this decision appears to be limited to initial assessment of the populations of
birds which it is appropriate to conserve.

works may also be tolerated, but only if they produce an environmental benefit for the area — in this case the creation of a new navigation channel would not in itself have justified the interference with the protected area, but was acceptable because, and only because, of the direct conservation benefit arising from the closure of the older channels which meant that there would no longer be disturbance and dredging operations within the special protection area. The wide discretion for planning authorities to permit damaging operations on designated sites is therefore clearly not compatible with the requirements of the Directive.

Ramsar sites

5.12.8 The Convention of Wetlands of International Importance, especially as Waterfowl Habitat, known as the Ramsar Convention,[10] makes various provisions for the protection of wetlands, which throughout the world are disappearing as a result of drainage, land reclamation and pollution.[11] Among the measures is the establishment of a List of Wetlands of International Importance, which states undertake to protect.[12] The selection of sites for the list is the responsibility of states themselves, taking account of each site's significance in terms of ecology, botany, zoology, limnology or hydrology. More precise guidance was issued at a conference of the parties in 1980, suggesting, for example, that sites regularly supporting 10,000 ducks or geese or 1 per cent. of the breeding pairs of a species should be designated.[13] The List is maintained by the IUCN,[14] which must also be informed of changes to the ecological character of the wetlands as a result of technological developments, pollution or human interference.[15]

5.12.9 Once a wetland has been added to the List, the state is obliged to formulate and implement its planning so as to promote the conservation of the site,[16] and for all wetlands must

---

[10] After the town in northern Iran where it was signed in 1971.

[11] Lyster, *International Wildlife Law* (1985), chap. 10; see paras. 7.5.11–7.5.14, below.

[12] Ramsar Convention, Art. 2.

[13] The recommendations are most easily found in Lyster, *op. cit.*, pp. 188–189.

[14] International Union for the Conservation of Nature; see P.W. Birnie & A.E. Boyle, *International Law and the Environment* (1992), pp. 77–78.

[15] Ramsar Convention, Arts. 3, 8.

[16] *Ibid.*, Art. 3.

promote the establishment of nature reserves with adequate supervision by wardens.[17] Sites which have been placed on the List can be reduced in size or deleted altogether if this is required by an "urgent national interest," but so far as possible the state concerned should compensate for such loss by the creation of additional nature reserves for birds and the protection, in the same area or elsewhere, of an adequate portion of the same habitat.[18] These obligations are far from precise and leave plenty of room for discretion on the part of each state, to say nothing of the difficulties of enforcing any such obligations in international law.

5.12.10 In Great Britain, the Convention has been implemented by the government's designation, after consultation with the conservancy councils, of a number of sites already enjoying protection as nature reserves, SSSIs and under Nature Conservation Orders. As with special protection areas under the Birds' Directive, this does not guarantee their protection, or even their protection in all but cases of "urgent national interest," but planning authorities are advised to have regard to the need to promote the conservation of such sites and to avoid as far as possible the loss of wetland resources within them.[19]

World Heritage sites

5.12.11 The Convention Concerning the Protection of the World Cultural and Natural Heritage (World Heritage Convention) was signed in 1972 to provide international recognition and assistance for the protection of monuments, buildings and sites which are the natural and man-made treasures of the world.[20] As far as nature conservation is concerned, a state can nominate any site within its territory for inclusion in the World Heritage List. The basic criterion is that the area be of "outstanding universal value" from a scientific, aesthetic or nature conservation point of view,[21] but before being added to the List each site must be approved by the World Heritage Committee which is responsible for compiling the List.[22] This Committee uses strict

---

[17] *Ibid.*, Art. 4.1.
[18] *Ibid.*, Art. 4.2.
[19] DoE Circular 27/87, SDD Circular 1/1988.
[20] See Lyster, *op. cit*, chap. 11; the Convention is the product of UNESCO; see paras. 7.5.6–7.5.10, below.
[21] World Heritage Convention, Art. 2.
[22] *Ibid.*, Art. 11.

operational guidelines in making its decisions. Only sites which are of the utmost value and are adequately protected, both by the scale and integrity of the area and by domestic law will be accepted.[23]

5.12.12 Each state has a duty to ensure "the protection, conservation, preservation, presentation and transmission to future generations" of the natural heritage in its territory and "to do all it can to this end, to the utmost of its own resources" and where appropriate with international assistance.[24] Effective and active measures are required, including the adoption of relevant policies, the establishment of appropriately staffed and resourced services to protect and conserve the natural heritage, the development and promotion of scientific and technical research and the adoption of the necessary legal, financial and scientific measures.[25] As with most international agreements, these provisions are broadly drafted, but the Australian High Court was prepared to hold that they did impose a duty on the state to act, although recognising that discretion was left as to precisely how this duty would be fulfilled.[26]

5.12.13 Again in Great Britain implementation of the Convention is carried out through the nomination of sites already subject to protective measures in domestic law, *e.g.* St Kilda which is a National Nature Reserve. The nature of sites eligible for inclusion and the more specific criteria for listing combine to mean that only sites enjoying the fullest protection will be accepted, chiefly Nature Reserves. Where a site has been accepted for the List, it must be protected and conserved from all threats.

---

[23] Lyster, *op. cit.*, pp. 212–218.
[24] World Heritage Convention, Art. 4; the commitment to international cooperation and the provision of resources for poorer countries is of particular importance for the protection of the natural heritage in many parts of the world.
[25] *Ibid.*, Art. 5.
[26] *Commonwealth of Australia* v. *State of Tasmania* (1983) 46 A.L.R. 625, 68 I.L.R. 266.

6. Plants

THE GENERAL LAW

6.1.1 The legal position of plants is very different from that of wild animals. Every growing plant is the legal property of someone, and thus is subject to the ordinary laws of property, as well as to the special laws devised to deal with the conservation and regulation of plants. This might suggest that plants enjoy a greater degree of protection than other forms of wildlife, but in practice this tends not to be the case as people do not think of wild plants as being privately owned, and the owners themselves tend to value only those plants from which they gain some appreciable benefit, commercial or aesthetic. In considering the law affecting plants it is necessary to consider how plants are dealt with by the general law, examining the issues of ownership and the ways in which plants are treated by the ordinary criminal law, before turning to the specific legislation which has been enacted to deal directly with issues arising in relation to plants. The fuller provisions affecting trees in relation to forestry and town and country planning are then considered.

Ownership

6.1.2 The rule that plants belong to the owner of the soil in which they grow is of long standing[1] and is common to both Scots and English Law.[2] Indeed the proposition that plants growing in the soil belong to the owner of the soil appears to be such a basic idea that it is more or less taken for granted, and any discussion and dispute has centred on its application between those holding different interests in the land.

---

[1] See, for example, in Roman Law D.41.1.7.13, 41.1.9.pr.
[2] See generally D.L. Carey Miller, *Corporeal Moveables in Scots Law* (1991), paras. 3.04–3.08; W.M. Gordon, *Scottish Land Law* (1989), paras. 5.38–5.40; W.S. Holdworth, *A History of English Law* (2nd ed., 1937), Vol. 7, pp. 485–488.

6.1.3 If the rule were strictly applied, problems would arise where interests in land are held by different people, *e.g.* in relation to agricultural tenants, as crops which they had planted would not be theirs to harvest and sell, but would belong to the landlord. In both jurisdictions the position of tenants was protected by the development of a rule that annual crops were treated as the tenant's moveable or personal property as opposed to the landlord's heritable or real property. In Scotland this exception tends to be discussed as part of the law of property in general,[3] whereas in England and Wales discussion has tended to appear in the more specialised context of succession and emblements,[4] with many other points affecting the right to take growing plants being dealt with by the rules on commons, waste and *profits à prendre*.[5] In practice such matters are nowadays dealt with by the specific terms of individual leases, etc., or by statutory rules.[6]

6.1.4 The legal consequence of plants being property which is owned by someone is that any unauthorised interference with a plant will amount to a civil wrong at common law. Consequently the owner could sue anyone who damages or takes his plants or obtain an interdict or injunction to prevent any harm which is threatened. Although this is an area lacking in reported authority, any damage to plants being usually only an incidental part of a wider claim,[7] it would appear that any deliberate or negligent harm caused to wild plants certainly could give rise to liability, with the possibility of wider liability if the claim can be framed in trespass, whether to land or (in England) to property. It would follow that anyone picking wild flowers or even causing damage by walking on vegetation could face a civil action at the instance of the owner of the plants affected.

6.1.5 However, although wild plants may be part of their owner's property, they are not generally recognised as having

---

[3] Stair, II, i, 34; Carey Miller, *op cit.*; Gordon, *op cit.*

[4] Modern texts tend not to offer any detailed discussion of these "vegetable chattels", but they are discussed in older books on personal property, *e.g.* J. Williams, T.C. Williams & W.J. Byrne, *Principles of the Law of Personal Property* (18th ed., 1926), pp. 161–162.

[5] R.M. Megarry & H.W.R. Wade, *The Law of Real Property* (5th ed., 1984), pp. 98–102, 895–897, 909–911.

[6] Agricultural Holdings Act 1986; Agricultural Holdings (Scotland) Act 1991.

[7] An example of a reported action based solely on plants is *Mills* v. *Brooker* [1919] 1 K.B. 555, where a neighbour was successfully sued in conversion for taking apples from trees overhanging his boundary.

any monetary value, so that the pursuer may be unable to demonstrate that any loss has been suffered by the harm done. This will pose a major practical problem in assessing the value of damage done, and may even lead the courts to say that in fact no actionable wrong has occurred.[8] The aesthetic or spiritual value placed on the wild plants is unlikely to affect this position, although a trust established for the purposes of nature conservation may have a stronger case if the achievement of its aims are being affected by damage to its plants, especially if it is seeking an interdict rather than damages.

Criminal Law

6.1.6 Since plants are private property, they are protected by the general criminal law. This is very much the case in Scotland, although in England and Wales statutory exceptions have been created to limit considerably the application of the law to wild plants. In Scotland there is nothing to restrict the application to plants growing wild of the ordinary law of theft, malicious mischief, vandalism and fire-raising[9] so that anyone taking or damaging a plant without the permission of the owner or other lawful excuse is guilty of a crime. The few reported cases have dealt with plants that were being to some extent cultivated, *e.g.* in *Rigg* v. *Trotter*[10] the accused were convicted of malicious mischief after treading down plants in a nursery and destroying turf prepared for and partially laid for a bowling green, while *James Miln*[11] involved the shearing and taking of grass and the pulling up of growing pease, and *John Young*[12] the digging of potatoes. Likewise in *HM Advocate* v. *Alexander Robertson*[13] the plants concerned in a charge of theft were turnips, although here the court reserved its opinion on whether this was an appropriate charge where the alleged theft was achieved by pasturing sheep in a field.

---

[8] *E.g.* in *Winans* v. *Macrae* (1885) 12 R 1051 one of the grounds for refusing interdict to prevent a cottar's pet lamb straying onto a 200,000 acre shooting estate where it might indeed have taken "a blade of grass," was that no appreciable wrong had been suffered so as to justify the court's intervention (Lord Young at pp. 1063–64).

[9] For muirburn see para. 8.4.13, below.

[10] (1714) Hume, i, 123.

[11] (1758) Hume, i, 79.

[12] (1800) Hume, i, 79.

[13] (1867) 5 Irv. 480.

200 *Plants*

6.1.7 Exactly the same should apply to wild plants, which are as much the landowner's property as the most carefully nurtured crops or garden plants, although in such circumstances it may be more difficult to establish the necessary *mens rea*. In *Ward* v. *Robertson*[14] the court was not prepared to say that a person was guilty of malicious mischief simply by reason of damage done by walking across a field of cultivated grass where the accused had not deliberately sought to do harm and indeed had thought that no harm was being done. It was suggested, though, that a conviction might have been possible had there been evidence of a deliberate trampling down of grass, or if the field had contained other crops in which case knowledge that harm was being done might have been inferred. In the case of picking wild flowers, it may be obvious that damage is being done, but belief that the owner would not object might again raise difficulties in establishing *mens rea*.

6.1.8 In England and Wales the position is different, as wild plants are expressly excluded from the law of theft and criminal damage. For theft, it is provided that a person who picks flowers, fruit or foliage from a plant growing wild, or who picks any fungus growing wild, does not steal them, unless he does so for reward or for sale or for some other commercial purpose.[15] A theft charge is therefore possible only if there is a commercial motive or if an entire plant is uprooted and taken, as opposed to merely parts of the plant being removed.[16] For criminal damage, no offence is committed if the only property affected is any fungus growing wild or the flowers, fruit or foliage of a plant growing wild. Again, therefore the uprooting of a plant or its total destruction may give rise to prosecution, but lesser damage cannot.[17]

STATUTORY PROVISIONS

6.2.1 Statutory measures relating to wild plants largely mirror those for wild animals, with the establishment of a general level of protection which is enhanced for certain species, while

[14] 1938 J.C. 32.
[15] Theft Act 1968, s.4(3).
[16] A news report in *The Times* of October 4th, 1992 records the conviction for theft of two men for digging up thousands of snowdrop bulbs in Norfolk.
[17] Criminal Damage Act 1971, s.10(1).

legislation also allows for pest control and measures against the spread of disease. Aside from the enforcement difficulties resulting from the fact that few people can identify the rare species entitled to special protection (especially as there are often similar cultivated or more common species) two particular problems afflict legislation relating to plants.

6.2.2 Firstly, the naming of plants in legislation can be problematic, as common names frequently apply to more than one species, or vary throughout the country, while plant taxonomists are continually reassessing the classification of plants, so that the scientific names,[18] and indeed the recognition of plants as distinct species, may be liable to change. Secondly, plants hybridise much more easily than animals, so that particularly in relation to weed species, one can be faced in the field with hybrids which do not fall exactly within the terms of the legislation but which may be as vigorous as the named species. Both of these issues affect the Japanese knotweed, an invasive alien the spreading of which is illegal.[19] In the legislation it is referred to as *Polygonum cuspidatum*, but it is also known as *Reynoutria japonica* and *Fallopia japonica*, while in the wild hybrids have been found between it and *Fallopia sachalinensis*.[20] The first problem is one of untidiness rather than substance, as the alternative names are well recorded and the relevant plant can be identified, but the second is potentially more serious, as the legal provisions will apply only to the named, pure-bred, species, not to hybrids.[21]

Protection

6.2.3 Wild plants are given legal protection under s.13 of the Wildlife and Countryside Act 1981. It is an offence for anyone other than an authorised person[22] intentionally to uproot any wild plant, unless he or she can show that the uprooting was the

---

[18] In any event the legislation rarely gives the full scientific name, almost invariably omitting the reference to the author who described the plant, a reference which forms an integral part of the proper scientific name.

[19] See para. 6.2.10, below.

[20] Full names, *Polygonum cuspidatum* Siebold & Zucc., *Reynoutria japonica* Houtt., *Fallopia japonica* (Houtt.) Ronse Decraene, *Fallopia sachalinensis* (F. Schmidt ex Maxim.) Ronse Decraene.

[21] *Cf.* the Scottish deer legislation where express reference has been added to hybrids between red and sika deer; para. 4.2.17, above.

[22] "Authorised persons" include the owner and occupier of the land and those authorised by the local authority (WCA, s.26(1)); see para. 3.2.6, above.

incidental result of a lawful act and could not reasonably have been avoided. A "wild plant" is one which is growing wild and is of a kind which ordinarily grows in Great Britain in a wild state,[23] a definition which may leave uncertain the status of certain plants which have escaped from gardens and which are not part of the indigenous British flora but are now widespread in a wild state, *e.g.* giant hogweed.[24] Licences may be granted by the appropriate bodies to authorise conduct otherwise unlawful under the provisions discussed here in and in the next paragraph.[25]

6.2.4 Further protection is offered to the many plants (including mosses and lichens) listed in Schedule 8 to the 1981 Act. It is an offence for anyone (even an authorised person) intentionally to pick, uproot or destroy any wild plant listed in that Schedule,[26] although again there is a defence where the harm is shown to be the incidental result of lawful operations which could not reasonably have been avoided.[27] It is also an offence to sell or offer for sale any live or dead plant listed in Schedule 8 (or any part or derivative of such a plant), or to possess or transport such items for the purpose of sale[28]; for the purpose of this provision any plant is presumed to be wild unless the contrary is shown.[29] An offence is also committed if a person publishes or causes to be published an advertisement indicating that he does or intends to buy or sell such plants or their derivatives.[30]

6.2.5 These provisions offer plants some protection from intentional direct harm, but obviously the conservation of plants will rely heavily on the various mechanisms to safeguard habitats as a whole.[31] It is only by ensuring broader protection under such measures that the non-listed plants can be safeguarded against the actions of the owner or occupier of the land, and that the conditions necessary for plants to survive and propagate can be ensured. A further practical problem faced by

[23] *Ibid.*, s.27(1).
[24] See para. 6.2.10, below.
[25] WCA, s.16; see Appendix C.
[26] *Ibid.*, s.13(1)(a); see Appendix A.
[27] *Ibid.*, s.13(2).
[28] *Ibid.*, s.13(2)(a).
[29] *Ibid.*, s.13(4).
[30] *Ibid.*, s.13(2)(b).
[31] See C. de Klemm, *Wild Plant Conservation and the Law* (1990).

those concerned with botanical conservation (as by those concerned with invertebrates) is that although there is widespread public support for protecting birds and other high-profile animals, the public generally shows little regard for the native flora, apart from, perhaps, a few dramatic orchids.

6.2.6 A very different form of statutory protection is offered to certain plants through the system of tree preservation orders, which is discussed in section 6.4, below.

Weeds

6.2.7 In the days before modern herbicides, the control of weeds was a major problem for agriculture. Nostalgic appreciation of the beauty of a wheatfield sprinkled with the bright flowers of poppies and cornflowers overlooks the fact that to the farmer these weeds posed a serious threat to the yield and value of his crop. The law did not ignore this threat, and in mediaeval Scotland legislation stated that not only did the tenant have to cleanse his land of *maneleta*, or *guld* (the corn marigold), but he was liable to a fine of one sheep for each plant found.[32]

6.2.8 The current legislation is to be found in the Weeds Act 1959, under which the Secretary of State can require the occupier of any land to take such action as may be necessary to prevent the spread of certain "injurious weeds."[33] The weeds affected are spear thistle, creeping or field thistle, curled dock, broad-leaved dock, and ragwort[34]; further weeds can be added to this list by the Secretary of State. If the occupier unreasonably fails to comply with a notice requiring him to take action against injurious weeds, an offence is committed, and a failure to take the required action within 14 days of conviction is a further offence.[35] If the occupier does not take the necessary steps, action can be taken by the Secretary of State himself,[36] the costs being recovered from the occupier.[37] The owner of the

[32] Frag.Coll. 11, 12 (A.P.S. I 750).
[33] Weeds Act 1959, s.1.
[34] *Cirsium vulgare* (Savi) Ten., *Cirsium arvense* L. Scop., *Rumex crispus* L., *Rumex obtusifolius* L., *Senecio jacobaea* L.; for once the statute includes the authors' names, but omits the conventional capital letter for the generic name.
[35] Weeds Act 1959, s.2.
[36] The standard legal phrasing conjures a lovely image of a team of Her Majesty's Ministers, in their best pinstripe suits of course, slowly digging weeds out of an unkempt field in some rural wilderness!
[37] Weeds Act 1959, s.3(1).

land is involved only where the Secretary of State has had to take direct action and it is not practicable to trace the occupier; in these circumstances the cost of the intervention can be recovered from the owner, but the owner has the right to recover from the missing occupier.[38]

6.2.9 More generally, it would appear that as weeds are not being deliberately cultivated, they fall within the definition of "wild plants" for the purpose of s.13 of the Wildlife and Countryside Act 1981, and therefore it is an offence for anyone other than an "authorised person" intentionally to uproot such a plant.[39] However, it may be expected that permission from the owner or occupier of the land will readily be given and may easily be inferred. The question of whether the spread of weeds could constitute an actionable nuisance at common law is discussed later.[40]

Introductions

6.2.10 In order to protect the native flora, and the country in general, from invasive aliens, the law prohibits the release into the wild of a number of plants which aggressively take over any habitat where they become established. It is an offence to plant or otherwise cause to grow in the wild any plant listed in Part II of Schedule 9 to the Wildlife and Countryside Act 1981.[41] The plants listed include giant hogweed, Japanese knotweed and several species of seaweed.[42] It is a defence that the accused took all reasonable steps and exercised all due diligence to avoid committing the offence, but where this defence involves an allegation that another person's act or default was responsible for the commission of the offence, prior notice identifying that person must be given to the prosecutor.[43] Those authorised by the Secretary of State enjoy a power of entry to land (other than a dwelling) to ascertain whether an offence has been committed, and obstruction of such an investigation is an offence.[44]

[38] *Ibid.*, s.3(2), (4).
[39] See para. 6.2.3, above.
[40] See section 8.8, below.
[41] WCA, s.14(2); as usual, licences may be granted to authorise such conduct (*ibid.*, s.16(4); see Appendix C).
[42] See Appendix A.
[43] WCA, s.14(3), (4).
[44] *Ibid.*, s.14(5), (6).

Plant health

6.2.11 Although designed to control pests and diseases injurious to trees and bushes and to agricultural and horticultural crops,[45] the legislation on plant health is broad enough in its scope to encompass all plants growing wild, necessarily so as wild plants may harbour threats to their cultivated relatives. The Plant Health Act 1967 and the Orders made under it confer on the "competent authorities" wide powers to take action to prevent or control pests, defined as including all forms of harmful insects, bacteria, fungi, plant and animal organisms, and all other agents causative of transmissible disease.[46] The "competent authorities" are the Secretary of State in Scotland and in Wales, the Minister of Agriculture in England, and the Forestry Commission throughout Great Britain for matters relating to forest trees and timber.[47] Orders made under the Act can require local authorities (regions, counties and metropolitan districts) to take the necessary steps to carry the measures into effect.[48]

6.2.12 The 1967 Act itself is an enabling provision, allowing for orders to be made to deal with specific problems and to comply with European Community requirements. The powers available include the removal, treatment or destruction of any crops, plant or seed found to be infected, the prohibition of the sale or keeping of any living specimens of a pest, the prohibition of the entry into this country of any pests or infected items, as well as powers of entry and inspection and powers to take direct action in default of compliance with official requirements. The detailed provisions are to be found in the orders made under the 1967 Act, of which the two most general are the Plant Health (Great Britain) Order 1993[49] and the Plant Health (Forestry) (Great Britain) Order 1993.[50] These specify a number of pests, and in relation to these impose import restrictions in relation to any plants, soil or other growing medium and machinery which might be infected, prohibit the keeping of living specimens of the pests and establish a regime of

[45] Plant Health Act 1967, s.1(1).
[46] *Ibid.*
[47] *Ibid.*, s.1(2).
[48] *Ibid.*, s.5 (amended for England and Wales by Local Government Act 1972, Sched. 29, Pt. II, para. 34; as applied in Scotland by Local Government (Scotland) Act 1973, s.144).
[49] S.I. 1993 No. 1320.
[50] S.I. 1993 No. 1283.

phytosanitary certificates to ensure the health of material being imported and exported. Further restrictions are imposed in relation to specific problems such as the Colorado beetle and progressive wilt disease of hops.

6.2.13 Only in a few cases are these provisions likely to have much effect on nature conservation, but the potential is there and has been demonstrated by the provisions made under the 1967 Act in relation to Dutch Elm Disease. In order to prevent the spread of the disease, the Dutch Elm Disease (Local Authorities) Order 1984[51] and its predecessors gave powers to local authorities in the specified areas to serve notices requiring particular elm trees to be cut down, destroyed by fire or subjected to specified treatments. The ravages of the disease itself and of such preventive action during the height of the recent outbreak wrought significant changes to the landscape and local habitats in many of the affected areas. An outbreak of some other pest or disease which affects both cultivated and wild plants could similarly lead to widespread action which could have major consequences for the flora of particular areas, and consequently for the habitat as a whole.

TREES: FORESTRY

6.3.1 Trees are the subject of a variety of special legal and administrative provisions. Almost all of the woodland in Great Britain has been managed or exploited at some time in the past, and even those which do not reveal signs of recent human intervention are referred to as "ancient" or "semi-natural" woodland, rather than as being truly natural, reflecting the likelihood of past human interference. Throughout the centuries trees have been planted to provide shelter, for their wood and other products, and as a decorative feature of the landscape.

6.3.2 The area of woodland in Britain had been constantly reduced for centuries as timber was harvested and land was cleared for other purposes, but during the twentieth century the conscious policy of reducing the country's dependence on imported timber, initially for strategic but now for commercial reasons, has led to considerable new planting and a significant increase in the area supporting trees. However it is only recently

[51] S.I. 1984 No. 687.

that environmental considerations have been taken into account in the preservation of ancient woodlands and the design of new plantations.

6.3.3 There are two areas of law which deal directly with trees, and although neither of them is primarily directed at nature conservation, the exercise of the relevant powers may lead to considerable benefits or harm to conservation interests. Firstly, there is forestry, where the planting, maintenance and felling of trees are regulated by some direct legal controls, but even more by the effects of the grant schemes operated by the Forestry Commission. Secondly, the town and country planning system makes a number of special provisions, recognising the value of trees to the character and amenity of particular localities. The first of these is dealt with in some detail here as there is a shortage of widely available information on this topic other than the very helpful material produced by the Forestry Commission itself.

6.3.4 The regulation of forestry lies primarily in the hand of the Forestry Commission,[52] which has in recent years shown a much greater awareness of environmental concerns. The imposition of a duty on the Commission to seek a balance between timber production and conservation[53] reflected a change of approach which was already becoming evident. The design of plantations nowadays takes account of the interests of landscape and nature conservation, and the grant schemes no longer limit their support to woodland grown exclusively for timber production.[54] The extent to which such policies really effect major changes in British forestry will become apparent in future years as the older plantations are felled and the recent ones grow to maturity.

6.3.5 The development of forestry has also been influenced by the tax system which contains a number of special provisions for commercial forestry.[55] Prior to 1988, the income tax system allowed a means of gaining considerable tax relief when a taxpayer was involved in the expensive stage of establishing a new plantation, but of escaping tax on the income when the

---

[52] See paras. 2.6.8–2.6.11, above.
[53] Forestry Act 1967, s.1(3A) (added by Wildlife and Countryside (Amendment) Act 1985, s.4); see para. 2.2.4, above.
[54] See para. 6.3.14, below.
[55] T.D. Lynch, *The Taxation of Woodlands in the U.K.* (1989).

timber came to be harvested. This led to claims that for short-term financial gain large plantations unsuitable and unsympathetic to local conditions were being established, and in the 1988 Budget the tax system was changed. The current position is that commercial forestry falls outwith the income tax system, so that the expenses of establishing a plantation cannot be set off against other income, but there is no tax to pay on the income when the trees are harvested.[56] For the purposes of capital gains tax, the value of growing timber is not included in any valuations,[57] and for inheritance tax, the payment of tax can be deferred until the woodland is harvested or disposed of, with no further tax due in the event of another death during the intervening period.[58]

Afforestation

6.3.6 The planting of trees is not subject to any direct legal control. No form of official permission is required to plant trees, however large an area is affected. Furthermore, it is expressly declared that the afforestation of land is not "development" for the purposes of the town and country planning system,[59] and consequently no permission is required for changing the use of land to forestry, while most forestry operations are likewise exempted from planning control.[60] However, planning authorities are encouraged to prepare indicative forestry strategies as part of the structure plans for their areas. These are intended to indicate the preferred, potential and sensitive areas for forestry, identifying areas where the physical and other conditions are suitable for commercial projects, where the ground is suitable but there are some constraining interests and other areas where there are serious or multiple constraints on forestry development.[61]

6.3.7 Instead of direct legal controls, the regulation of new planting is achieved through the grant schemes operated by the

[56] Finance Act 1988, s.65 and Sched. 6.
[57] Taxation of Chargeable Gains Act 1992, s.250.
[58] Inheritance Tax Act (*née* Capital Transfer Tax Act) 1984, ss.125–130.
[59] TCPSA, s.19(2)(e); TCPA, s.55(2)(e).
[60] Town and Country Planning (General Permitted Development) (Scotland) Order 1992, S.I. 1992 No. 223, art. 3, Sched. 1, Pt. 7 (class 22); Town and Country Planning General Development Order 1988, S.I. 1988 No. 1813, art. 3, Sched. 2, Pt. 7.
[61] SDD Circular 13/1990, DoE Circular 29/92; see A.S. Mather, "Indicative Forestry Strategies" (1990) 31 S.P.L.P. 77.

Forestry Commission and discussed below.[62] Before the changes in the tax regime in 1988, there were a few cases of planting taking place without grant support from the Forestry Commission, and accordingly outwith any form of regulation. The loss of the financial incentives in the pre-1988 tax system was balanced by increases in the sums available as grants, and it is accepted that currently all significant planting will in fact come to be considered under the grant schemes, as obtaining a grant is essential to the economic viability of projects at present. Small-scale planting and planting purely for amenity may receive finanical support from other public bodies, such as the Countryside Commission and the Scottish and Welsh conservancy councils in their countryside role, and accordingly come under some form of scrutiny. However if no financial support is sought, there is nothing to prevent a landowner planting as much of his land with whatever sort of trees in whatever form he chooses, regardless of environmental and amenity considerations.

6.3.8 Apart from the provision giving basic authority to pay grants,[63] the Forestry Commission's grant schemes and the procedural arrangements for them are not in statutory form, although it has been held that the Commission's decisions may be subject to judicial review.[64] The best sources of information on the schemes are the booklets produced by the Commission itself.

Procedures

6.3.9 Once an application for a grant is made, it is examined first by the Commission to consider whether the proposals are sensible in terms of silviculture, landscaping, nature conservation and other environmental concerns, then consultations will be held with a range of public bodies. The following bodies are involved when any application falls within the scope of the consultation arrangements agreed between them and the Commission:[65] the agriculture departments, local authorities, the conservancy councils, the Countryside Commission in England,

---

[62] See paras. 6.3.14–6.3.18, below.
[63] Forestry Act 1979, s.1.
[64] *Kincardine & Deeside District Council* v. *Forestry Commissioners*, 1992 S.L.T. 1180.
[65] See the Forestry Commission's *Woodland Grant Scheme Applicant's Pack* (1991), Grants and Procedures, section 3.

the Red Deer Commission and the Civil Aviation Authority.
This consultation procedure had been criticised for the lack of
any public involvement, but in 1992 the Commission established
a public register of grant applications, allowing the public access
to the full applications on request, and inviting comments. A
second public register records the outcome of all applications.[66]

6.3.10 If there are objections to the proposal, further
discussions are held to try to resolve these, the aim being to
produce a final proposal acceptable to all those concerned. If no
solution is possible, the case may be referred to the relevant
Regional Advisory Committee. There is one Committee for
each of the 20 conservancies of the Forestry Authority.[67] The
composition of these committees is governed partly by
convention and partly by statute. The relevant provisions were
amended recently, increasing the membership from nine to 12 to
allow for a greater representation of environmental interests
after criticism that there was an inherent bias in favour of
forestry developments in the Committees.[68] By law, at least four
of the members must be appointed after consultations with
organisations representing the interests of owners of woodlands
and timber merchants and with organisations concerned with the
study and promotion of forestry.[69] In practice these were joined
by an independent chairman and one person representing each
of agricultural, planning, trade union and environmental
interests. Although there is no legal prescription, the government has undertaken that the three additional members will be
chosen to reflect environmental interests, one of them concerned with public access and recreation.[70] There are thus four
members with environmental interests to balance the four with
forestry ones.

6.3.11 Although the Regional Advisory Committees meet in
private, the proposals which are referred to them are advertised
in the press and written representations from the public are
welcomed; if it is thought that it would be helpful, a person who

---

[66] Forestry Authority leaflet, *Register of New Planting* (1993).

[67] In practice each Committee in fact serves a few conservancies as the
structure of the Committees still reflects the larger conservancies existing before
the reorganisation of the Forestry Commission in 1992.

[68] Forestry Act 1967, s.38 (amended by Forestry Act 1991, s.1).

[69] *Ibid.*, s.38(3).

[70] Statements by the Earl of Lindsay during debate in the House of Lords,
June 11, 1991 House of Lords Official Report, Vol. 529, cols.1073–1078.

has submitted observations may be invited to attend a meeting. Again the aim of the proceedings is one of conciliation, to resolve the problem and to find a solution acceptable to all parties. In the event of failure, a report (which is published) is prepared for the Forestry Commission to make the final decision. Although there is no formal appeal, a dissatisfied applicant can make representations to the appropriate Forestry Minister[71] who may ask the Commission to reconsider its decision. Only a few cases are referred to the Committees,[72] but by the very nature of the procedure, they are the most controversial ones. The recent changes to membership of the Committee and the greater openness in their proceedings go some way to meeting the justified criticism that the grants procedure was biased towards forestry and secretive.

6.3.12 The only occasion when the law intervenes in the regulation of afforestation is when an environmental assessment is required. "Initial afforestation which may lead to adverse ecological changes" is one of the activities required by the European Community Directive to be the subject of a formal environmental assessment when a project is likely to have significant effects on the environment.[73] This has been implemented in Great Britain by the Environmental Assessment (Afforestation) Regulations 1988,[74] although the implementation has not been perfect. Not only did the Regulations come into force some days after the deadline for implementation,[75] but the assessment procedure is linked not to approval of the project itself, but rather to the award of a grant, so that it remains possible for a project to go ahead without any consideration of its environmental effects if the proposer is willing to forego grant aid.

6.3.13 The tests for when a formal assessment is necessary are very vague. In the first place one has to determine whether the afforestation is likely to produce "adverse ecological effects," a

[71] See para. 2.3.4, above.
[72] For the period 1984–1990, only 113 cases were referred to the Committees from 28,598 grant applications and 11,712 applications for felling licences (*Woodland Grant Scheme Applicant's Pack* (1991), Grants and Procedures, p. 12).
[73] Directive 85/337; see section 8.3, below.
[74] S.I. 1988 No. 1207.
[75] A point of crucial importance in *Kincardine & Deeside District Council* v. *Forestry Commission*, 1992 S.L.T. 1180.

rather odd concept as any ecological change such as afforestation will be adverse to some species (*e.g.* moorland birds) but
will benefit others (*e.g.* the pine beauty moth which can feast
itself on plantations of lodgepole pine). Secondly, it is only
those projects which are "likely to have significant effects on the
environment by virtue *inter alia* of their nature, size or
location"[76] which must be subject to an assessment. It is the
Forestry Commission which determines whether these criteria
have been met,[77] and its opinion on the point can be obtained
before a formal application is made.[78] If an applicant is
aggrieved that an assessment is required, he can apply to the
Minister for a direction on the issue,[79] while the Minister can
himself require an assessment to be carried out where the
Commission has not considered one necessary.[80] Of the projects
where an assessment has been required (about a dozen a year in
Scotland), the main factor prompting the requirement has been
that the proposal affects a site of particular environmental
sensitivity (SSSI, National Scenic Area, etc.), although the sheer
scale of some major projects has also been influential. Where an
environmental assessment is necessary, the applicant must
prepare an environmental statement detailing the likely effects
of the project.[81] This statement is made available for public
comment[82] and must be fully taken into account by the
Commission in deciding whether or not to award a grant to the
applicant.

Grant schemes

6.3.14 The main grant scheme at present is the Woodland
Grant Scheme, introduced in 1990. The purposes of the scheme
reflect the Commission's shift of emphasis away from simply
maximising timber production to take account of environmental,
amenity and other considerations. Whereas earlier schemes
stressed that "timber production must be the primary objective,"[83] the present scheme has multiple purposes:

[76] Directive 85/337, Art. 2(1); Environmental Assessement (Afforestation)
Regulations 1988, S.I. 1988 No. 1207, reg. 3.
[77] Environmental Assessment (Afforestation) Regulations 1988, S.I. 1988 No.
1207, reg. 5.
[78] *Ibid.*, reg. 4.
[79] *Ibid.*, reg. 6.
[80] *Ibid.*, reg. 7.
[81] *Ibid.*, reg. 5.
[82] *Ibid.*, reg. 8.
[83] Forestry Commission leaflet, *Forestry Grant Scheme* (1987), p. 1.

"(a) to encourage the creation of new forests and wood-
        lands which increase the production of wood, enhance
        the landscape, provide new habitats for wildlife and
        offer opportunities for sport and recreation;
  (b) to encourage the appropriate management, including
        timely regeneration, of existing forests and woodlands,
        with particular attention to the needs of ancient and
        semi-natural woodlands;
  (c) to provide jobs and increase the economic potential of
        rural and other areas with few alternative sources of
        economic activity;
  (d) to provide a use of land as an alternative to
        agriculture."[84]

6.3.15 This range of objectives is reflected in the conditions
which must be met before an application for a grant is likely to
be successful. In contrast to past practice, new proposals will
have to include some species diversity and show that due regard
is being given to landscape and conservation considerations in
the overall design of the planting, the choice of species and the
detailed features of the proposal, *e.g.* protecting watercourses
and leaving open ground for the benefit of wildlife. Detailed
plans of the planting and management plans must be submitted,
and the main grants are paid in instalments, or in arrears, to
ensure that good practice is maintained.

6.3.16 Under the Woodland Grant Scheme,[85] the main grants
are available for the establishment of woodlands, by planting or
by promoting natural regeneration. Higher sums are paid for
broadleaves than for conifers, reflecting the higher establishment costs, the longer period before any income can be made
from the trees, and the greater environmental value of
broadleaved woodland in terms of the diversity of other species
it supports and of landscape and amenity. The higher grants are
also available for establishing native Scots pines in Scotland.
Supplements are available for woodlands established on better
quality agricultural land,[86] and for new woodlands close to

---

[84] *Woodland Grant Scheme Applicant's Pack* (1991), Grants and Procedures,
p. 1.
[85] The details of the grant schemes are all contained in the Forestry
Commission's *Woodland Grant Scheme Applicant's Pack* (1991).
[86] Arable land or reseeded grassland; this is part of the broader policy of
combatting agricultural overproduction by encouraging farmers to turn to other
uses for their land.

towns and cities where public access will be permitted and where the wood will be of value for informal public recreation.

6.3.17 Management grants are available to assist during the years between the establishment of the woodland and the time when it can be expected to start producing a reasonable income. For conifers this covers woodland aged from 11–20 years, for broadleaves from 11–40 years. Special grants are payable for woodlands of special environmental value by virtue of their value for nature conservation, landscape or public recreation. There is a presumption that woodlands identified as both ancient and semi-natural in the inventory carried out by the Nature Conservancy Council will qualify for such grants whilst those in areas designated for their landscape (National Scenic Areas, National Parks, Areas of Outstanding Natural Beauty) will usually qualify, although the presence of such an official designation is not a prerequisite.

6.3.18 A separate scheme, the Farm Woodland Premium Scheme, exists to encourage farmers to take their land out of agricultural production.[87] This scheme is administered by the agriculture departments and under it farmers who are receiving establishment grants under the Woodland Grant Scheme can receive additional annual payments while the trees are growing to the stage when they can produce income, the sums varying according the quality of the land which has been planted and the agricultural classification of the area. The annual payments are available for 10 or 15 years after planting, depending on the species involved, and are to make up for the fact that the farmer who has been operating on the basis of receiving an annual income from all of his land cannot make any return on the land planted with trees until they reach a certain stage of maturity. As with all the forestry schemes, planting for Christmas trees does not qualify as that is a short-term crop.

Felling

6.3.19 Whereas the regulation of afforestation is carried out indirectly through the grant schemes, the felling of trees is

---

[87] Farm Woodland Premium Scheme 1992, S.I. 1992 No. 905; Leaflet *The Farm Woodland Premium Scheme: Rules and Procedures* (1992, from Ministry of Agriculture Fisheries and Food); set-aside schemes may also offer incentives to convert arable land to forestry, see paras. 8.4.7–8.4.10, below; see also EC Regulation 2080/92.

controlled by a legal licensing regime. Subject to many exceptions, it is a criminal offence to fell any growing trees without first having obtained a licence from the Forestry Commission.[88] The maximum penalty is a fine of level 4 on the standard scale, or twice the value of the trees which were felled, whichever is the higher.[89] The relationship between felling licences and tree preservation orders is discussed below.[90]

6.3.20 Topping and lopping of trees fall outwith this provision, as do the trimming and laying of hedges, the felling of trees in a garden, orchard, churchyard or public open space, and the felling of trees no more than 8 centimetres in diameter[91] (or 15 centimetres in the case of underwood or coppice).[92] The occupier of land is allowed to fell up to 5 cubic metres in any calendar quarter without a licence, provided that no more than 2 cubic metres are sold, and to fell trees of no more than 10 centimetres in diameter as thinnings.[93] Also exempt from the licensing requirement is felling in the following circumstances: in order to prevent danger or to prevent or abate a nuisance,[94] in compliance with a statutory obligation,[95] at the request of an electricity operator where the trees are close to electric lines or plant,[96] when immediately required for development authorised under the town and country planning system.[97] Further exemptions apply to felling by statutory undertakers, felling required by water and drainage authorities, the felling of elms badly affected by Dutch Elm disease,[98] and most significantly,

---

[88] Forestry Act 1967, ss.9, 17 (the provisions on tree felling do not apply in Inner London (*ibid.*, s.36)); *Forestry Commission* v. *Grace* (1992) 4 L.M.E.L.R. 127.

[89] *Ibid.*, s.17 (amended by Criminal Procedure (Scotland) Act 1975, ss.289F, 289G (added by Criminal Justice Act 1982, s.54); Criminal Justice Act 1982, s.46); *Campbell* v. *Webster*, 1992 S.C.C.R. 167.

[90] See paras. 6.4.20–6.4.23, below.

[91] Measured over the bark at 1.3 metres above ground level (Forestry Act 1967, s.9(6)); all of the measurements in these provisions were rendered metric by the Forestry Act 1979, s.2 and Sched. 1.

[92] Forestry Act 1967, s.9(2).

[93] *Ibid.*, s.9(3) (amended by the Forestry (Modification of Felling Restrictions) Regulations 1985, S.I. 1985 No. 1958).

[94] *Ibid.*, s.9(4).

[95] *Ibid.*

[96] *Ibid.*, (amended by Electricity Act 1989, Sched. 16, para. 13).

[97] *Ibid.*, (amended by TCPSA, Sched. 21, Pt. II; Planning (Consequential Provisions) Act 1990, Sched. 2, para. 14).

[98] Forestry (Exceptions from Restriction of Felling) Regulations 1979, S.I. 1979 No. 792, reg. 4.

felling in accordance with a plan of operations agreed with the Forestry Commission as part of one of its grant or dedication schemes.[99]

6.3.21 It is the landowner, or a tenant who is entitled to fell the trees, who must apply to the Forestry Commission for a licence.[1] The trees will usually be inspected, and consultations similar to those for grant applications will be held. Where it appears to the Commission expedient in the interests of good forestry, agriculture, the amenities of the district or the maintenance of an adequate supply of growing timber, conditions may be imposed on the grant of a licence,[2] requiring that after the felling has taken place the land (or other land agreed by the applicant and the Commission) be restocked with trees.[3] Such restocking conditions are usually imposed.

6.3.22 If a licence is refused, the applicant is entitled to compensation.[4] The sum available is the depreciation in the value of the trees which is attributable to the deterioration in the quality of their timber as a result of felling being refused. However, as the Commission is unlikely to refuse permission to fell trees which are so far past their prime that their value is diminishing, this appears to be a redundant provision in practice.

6.3.23 An applicant aggrieved by the conditions imposed on a licence may request the Minister to refer the case to a special reference committee, and the Minister must do so unless he considers the grounds for the request to be frivolous.[5] The reference committee will give the applicant a hearing and consider the matter before reporting to the Minister who may confirm, overturn or modify the Commission's decision. The committee is appointed by the Minister and comprises a chairman, and two members drawn from panels selected after

[99] *Ibid.*, (amended by Forestry (Exceptions from Restriction of Felling) (Amendment) Regulations 1988, S.I. 1988 No. 970).
[1] Forestry Act 1967, s.10; the time-limits and other procedural aspects of the licensing scheme and related matters are largely governed by the Forestry (Felling of Trees) Regulations 1979, S.I. 1979 No. 791 (amended by the Forestry (Felling of Trees) (Amendment) Regulations 1987, S.I. 1987 No. 632).
[2] *Ibid.*, s.10(2).
[3] *Ibid.*, s.12.
[4] *Ibid.*, s.11.
[5] *Ibid.*, s.16.

consultations with the relevant Regional Advisory Committee and organisations representing the interests of the owners of woodland and timber merchants, and organisations involved in the study and promotion of forestry.[6] A similar procedure is followed where an applicant is aggrieved by the refusal of a licence, but only if a licence for the same land has been refused more than three years previously.[7]

6.3.24 If a restocking condition is not complied with, the owner of the land can be served with a notice requiring him to make good the default within a set time.[8] If the recipient considers that the specified steps have already been taken or that they are not required in order to fulfil the condition, he can request the Minister to refer the matter to a special reference committee as described above, and the notice is suspended pending its review.[9] In the absence of a reasonable excuse, failure to carry out the steps required is a criminal offence,[10] and the Forestry Commission has the power to enter the land and carry out the necessary work itself,[11] recovering expenses from the landowner.[12]

6.3.25 If a person has been convicted of felling trees without a licence, the Commission can serve a notice requiring that the land concerned, or other land as agreed, be restocked with trees. Such a notice can be enforced in the same way as a restocking condition in a licence.[13]

6.3.26 The Forestry Commission also has the power to direct the felling of trees in order to prevent the deterioration in the quality of the timber in the trees or to improve the growth of other trees.[14] The recipient of a felling direction can ask for it to be reviewed in the same way as a condition in a felling licence,[15] and can require the Commission to buy the trees for immediate

---

[6] *Ibid.*, s.27.
[7] *Ibid.*, s.16(4).
[8] *Ibid.*, s.24(2).
[9] *Ibid.*, s.25.
[10] *Ibid.*, s.24(4).
[11] *Ibid.*, s.24(3).
[12] *Ibid.*, s.26.
[13] *Ibid.*, ss.17A–17C (added by Forestry Act 1986, s.1).
[14] *Ibid.*, s.18; this section includes a number of exceptions and factors which must be taken into account before the power is exercised — in practice the power is not used.
[15] *Ibid.*, s.20.

felling or the Minister to acquire his interest in the land where that interest does not entitle the recipient to sell the trees in this way.[16] A felling direction is enforced in the same way as a restocking condition in a licence.[17]

TREES: PLANNING

6.4.1 The importance of trees for the appearance and amenity of an area is recognised by the town and country planning system in several ways. Most important is the scheme for tree preservation orders (TPOs), but other provisions are also worthy of note. The most general is the requirement that planning authorities ensure where appropriate that conditions in a grant of planning permission should be used to ensure the preservation or planting of trees.[18] There is also in England and Wales a general power for local authorities to plant trees on land in their area for the purposes of preserving or enhancing natural beauty.[19]

6.4.2 Special rules exist for trees within conservation areas. Although the aim of such areas is to protect and enhance areas of special architectural and historical interest,[20] natural features will often play a major part in the overall appearance of the area. It is an offence in most circumstances to cut down, top, lop, uproot, or wilfully damage or destroy a tree in a conservation area unless notice has been given in advance to the planning authority, and either the authority has given its consent or six weeks have elapsed.[21] The aim of this provision is to allow time for the authority to decide whether a TPO should be made to protect the trees in question, and for this reason the provision does not apply to trees which are already subject to such an order.[22] The planning authority is not, however,

[16] *Ibid.*, s.21.
[17] *Ibid.*, s.24.
[18] TCPSA, s.57; TCPA, s.197.
[19] NPACA, s.89(1).
[20] TCPSA, s.262 (substituted by Town and Country Amenities Act 1974, s.2); Planning (Listed Buildings and Conservation Areas) Act 1990, s.69; see para. 5.11.6, above.
[21] *Ibid.*, s.59A (added by Town and Country Amenities Act 1974, s.9); TCPA, s.211.
[22] *Ibid.*, s.59A(2); *ibid.*, s.211(2).

prevented from making an order after the six weeks have elapsed.[23] If the operations have not been carried out within two years of the notice, a new notice must be served before the operations are lawful.[24] The planning authority must keep a register of the notices which it receives under these provisions.[25]

6.4.3 The criminal offence, which is subject to the same penalties as a breach of a TPO,[26] is committed by the person who carries out the unlawful felling, etc., but the owner of the land also becomes liable to plant another tree of appropriate size and species at the same place as the one unlawfully felled, uprooted or destroyed.[27] Replanting may also be required where the removal of the tree was not unlawful, but only because it fell within certain of the exceptions discussed below. It is made clear that this obligation is owed by the owner of the land from time to time, regardless of his involvement in the offence, although the owner can apply to the planning authority to dispense with this requirement. The obligation can be enforced in the same way as the replacement provisions relating to TPOs.[28]

6.4.4 Where a tree is already covered by a TPO, this more general offence does not apply, and several further categories of trees and operations are excluded from the provisions, in line with the exceptions which apply in relation to TPOs themselves.[29] Trees which are no bigger than 75 millimetres in diameter are exempt (100 mm. if the tree is in woodland and is uprooted or felled to improve the growth of others).[30] Felling in

[23] *R.* v. *North Hertfordshire District Council, ex p. Hyde* (1990) 88 L.G.R. 426.

[24] TCPSA, s.59A(3); TCPA, s.211(3).

[25] *Ibid.*, s.59A(7); *ibid.*, s.214.

[26] *Ibid.*, s.98(4) (added by Town and Country Amenities Act 1974, s.11); *ibid.* s.211(4); see para. 6.4.13, below.

[27] *Ibid.*, s.59A(8), (9); *ibid.*, s.213.

[28] See para. 6.4.18, below.

[29] Town and Country Planning (Tree Preservation Order and Trees in Conservation Areas) (Scotland) Regulations 1975, S.I. 1975 No. 1204, reg. 11; Town and Country Planning (Tree Preservation Order) (Amendment) and (Trees in Conservation Areas) (Exempted Cases) Regulations 1975, S.I. 1975 No. 148, reg. 3. The wording of the English legislation differs slightly from the Scottish, and the differences may be significant in some cases; this is discussed more fully at paras. 6.4.14–6.4.16, below.

[30] The measurement is to be taken 1.5m above the ground as opposed to at 1.3m for felling licences; does this mean that planning officers are taller than foresters?

accordance with a plan of operations agreed with or a felling licence granted by the Forestry Commission is exempt, as are actions by a planning authority and a range of statutory undertakers on land which they occupy. More generally no offence is committed if the uprooting, felling or lopping is in the interests of safety, or necessary for the prevention or abatement of nuisance.[31] Steps taken in compliance with an obligation imposed by an Act of Parliament are exempt, together with ministerially approved action taken to avoid danger or hindrance to air navigation.

6.4.5 Tree Preservation Orders offer the strongest protection to trees under the planning legislation, but also the most complex.[32] The issue is often a controversial one, not only because mature trees are a very conspicuous feature of the landscape, but also because the protection of even a single tree may thwart any plans for developing a particular site. In any event, the whole idea of tree "preservation" is somewhat odd, as trees are living organisms which grow old and die, and perhaps only fossilisation can truly "preserve" a tree effectively. Many of the most striking trees in the landscape are already mature, if not past their prime, and rather than trying to protect a tree in its declining years it may often be better in the long-term for efforts to be made to secure the planting and tending of young trees to ensure the regeneration and sustainability of attractive features. This is particularly the case in parks and avenues where all the trees may well have been planted together at the same time; unless thought is given to their replacement decades before the trees reach the end of their natural life, the

[31] The precise exceptions here are the same as relate to TPOs; see paras. 6.4.14–6.4.16, below.
[32] The legislation in Scotland is TCPSA, ss.57–60, 98–99C (significantly amended by the Town and Country Amenities Act 1974, s.11 and the Planning and Compensation Act 1991, s.54) and the Town and Country Planning (Tree Preservation Order and Trees in Conservation Areas) (Scotland) Regulations 1975, S.I. 1975 No. 1204 (significantly amended by the Town and Country Planning (Tree Preservation Order and Trees in Conservation Areas) (Scotland) Amendment Regulations 1981 and 1984, S.I.s 1981 No. 1385, 1984 No. 329) — hereafter the 1975 Regulations; in England and Wales, TCPA, ss.198–214D (significantly amended by the Planning and Compensation Act 1991 s.23) and the Town and Country Planning (Tree Preservation Order) Regulations 1969, S.I. 1969 No. 17 (significantly amended by the Town and Country Planning (Tree Preservation Order) (Amendment) and (Trees in Conservation Areas) (Exempted Cases) Regulations 1975, S.I. 1975 No. 148, Town and Country Planning (Tree Preservation Order) (Amendment) Regulations 1981 and 1988, S.I.s 1981 No. 14, 1988 No. 963) — hereafter the 1969 Regulations.

result will be many years of barren landscape as the trees die and young replacements grow slowly.

6.4.6 The legislation offers no definition of "tree," and this basic issue can cause difficulties, particularly in relation to hedgerows, where there may well be plants of differing sizes and species, some normally viewed as trees, others as shrubs. In one case Lord Denning expressed the view that, in woodland at least, only something over seven or eight inches in diameter should count as a tree,[33] but there seems to be no basis for such a requirement[34] and his view has been rejected by later courts.[35] The test appears to be left to common sense, and in *Bullock* v. *Secretary of State for the Environment*[36] Phillips J. said that an order could refer to anything which one would ordinarily call a tree, as opposed to bushes, shrub and scrub; accordingly coppice fell within the meaning of "trees" and could be made the subject of a TPO. The protection of hedgerows remains an issue of concern to conservation groups and specific legislation on this point was promised in the Conservative Party manifesto for the 1992 election.

6.4.7 Subject to the default powers of the Secretary of State,[37] it is the planning authority which has the power to make a TPO, the test being that it is "expedient in the interest of amenity" to make provision for the preservation of trees or woodland.[38] The trees may be specified individually, as trees in a specified area, or as a woodland.[39] The way in which the trees are described may be significant, as there are minor differences in the legislation for each form of order. The description may also affect the extent to which the order applies to trees established on the site after the order has been made. In *Brown* v. *Michael B. Cooper Ltd.*[40] it was held that an order referring to trees in a

---

[33] *Kent County Council* v. *Batchelor* (1976) 33 P. & C.R. 185 at p. 189.

[34] *E.g.*, the express exemption for trees below certain sizes in conservation areas clearly suggests that the legislation contemplates smaller plants counting as trees.

[35] *Bullock* v. *Secretary of State for the Environment* (1980) 40 P. & C.R. 246 at p. 251; see also *Brown* v. *Michael B. Cooper Ltd.*, 1990 S.C.C.R. 675 at p. 678. For a somewhat whimsical discussion of the issue see [1977] J.P.L. 5.

[36] (1980) 40 P. & C.R. 246.

[37] TCPSA, s.260; TCPA, s.202.

[38] *Ibid.*, s.58(1); *ibid.*, s.198(1).

[39] 1975 Regulations, First Schedule to Model Order; 1969 Regulations, First Schedule to Model Order.

[40] 1990 S.C.C.R. 675.

specified area applied only to trees in existence at the time
when the order was made, so that young trees in the area,
which could not be proven to have been in existence at that
date, were not protected. Had the order referred to an area of
woodland, it is likely that no such qualification would have
applied.[41]

6.4.8 Before an order can come into effect it must be made
available for inspection, advertised, and notified to the owners,
lessees and occupiers of the land, and to the Forestry
Commission[42] and in Scotland to the Keeper of the Registers of
Scotland, in England and Wales to the District Valuer.[43]
Objections and representations may be made within 28 days and
a local inquiry may be held. The planning authority must then
decide whether or not to confirm the order (with or without
modifications), and if confirmed, the same parties must be
notified, and the confirmed order advertised and deposited for
public inspection.[44] In Scotland the order must be recorded in
the Register of Sasines (or Land Register of Scotland)[45]; in
England and Wales the order is registrable as a local land
charge.[46] It is only when an order has been confirmed that it
takes effect, unless the authority directs that it should take
effect immediately without confirmation.[47] Such provisional
orders lapse after the passage of six months unless they are
confirmed. All orders may subsequently be revoked or
modified.

6.4.9 The precise extent and effect of the order will depend on
its terms, but essentially a TPO renders it a criminal offence for
any person to cut down, uproot, fell, lop, or wilfully damage or
destroy the protected trees without the consent of the planning
authority. Such consent is applied for in the same way as an

[41] It should be remembered that in any case a TPO will only protect trees, not
any of the other vegetation which is vital to the ecological and amenity value of
woodland.

[42] This requirement can be waived in Scotland; 1975 Regulations, reg. 5 (as
amended).

[43] 1975 Regulations, regs. 5–10; 1969 Regulations, regs. 5–9.

[44] If no copy is available for inspection the order is invalid; *Vale of
Glamorgan Borough Council* v. *Palmer and Bowles* (1983) 81 L.G.R. 678.

[45] 1975 Regulations, reg. 10 (read in the light of the Land Registration
(Scotland) Act 1979, s.29(2)).

[46] Local Land Charges Act 1975, s.1.

[47] TCPSA, s.59; TCPA, s.201; such directions are usual in order to avoid the
trees being removed or damaged during the interval between notification and
confirmation.

application for planning permission, and consent may be given subject to conditions.[48] If the applicant is aggrieved by a refusal of consent or the conditions imposed, there is a right of appeal to the Secretary of State.[49] There is, however, no right of appeal against the making of the order itself. In relation to woodland, it is stated that consent *shall* be given so far as it accords with the principles of good forestry, except where in the planning authority's opinion refusal is necessary in the interest of amenity in order to maintain the special character of the woodland or the woodland character of the area.[50]

6.4.10 If consent is refused, or granted subject to conditions, there is generally a right to compensation for any loss or damage suffered in consequence of such refusal.[51] The most significant form of loss may be a diminution in the value of the land since its potential uses are restricted, as in *Bell* v. *Canterbury City Council*,[52] where the refusal of consent to fell trees meant that the landowner was not able to convert his land from woodland to agricultural use. The court there held that this was a form of loss for which compensation was due, and that it was properly attributable to the refusal of consent, not to the initial making of the order as the council had argued. Other forms of loss may include the unrealisable timber value of the trees, the cost of an expert's report on the possible threat being caused to nearby buildings[53] and the additional costs of felling a tree in accordance with conditions attached to a consent.[54]

6.4.11 However, no compensation will be paid if the planning authority has certified that the refusal of consent or the conditions attached to it is in the interests of good forestry, or, in the case of trees other than those in woodlands, that the trees have an outstanding or special amenity value.[55] In England and Wales, this provision is extended to include groups of trees or

[48] TCPSA, s.58(1) and 1975 Regulations, Model Order paras. 3–7; TCPA, s.198(1) and 1969 Regulations, Model Order, paras. 3–7.
[49] 1975 Regulations, Third Schedule to Model Order paras. 33–34; 1969 Regulations, Third Schedule to Model Order, paras. 22–24.
[50] 1975 Regulations, Model Order para. 5; 1969 Regulations, Model Order, para. 4.
[51] TCPSA, ss.163–164 and 1975 Regulations, Model Order, paras. 9–12; TCPA, ss.203–204 and 1969 Regulations, Model Order, paras. 9–12.
[52] (1988) 56 P. & C.R. 211.
[53] *Fletcher* v. *Chelmsford Borough Council* [1992] J.P.L. 279.
[54] *Deane* v. *Bromley Borough Council* [1992] J.P.L. 279.
[55] 1975 Regulations, Model Order, paras. 6, 9.

woodland where the group or the woodland has an outstanding or special amenity value.[56] There is a right of appeal to the Secretary of State against the making of such a certificate.

6.4.12 It is a criminal offence for any person in contravention of a TPO to cut down, top, lop, uproot, wilfully damage or wilfully destroy[57] a tree, or to cause or permit such action.[58] The offence is committed by the person who actually carries out the act, and is an offence of strict liability, committed regardless of whether the offender knows of the order and its terms.[59] Employers may be vicariously liable for the acts of their employees,[60] but the occupier will not be liable if a contractor acts in defiance of instructions not to damage a tree.[61] A contractor hired to cut down trees should always check the legal position first as he will still be liable for breaching the TPO even though he has been assured by the occupier that the felling is lawful, although the penalty imposed in such circumstances should reflect the lack of culpability.[62] It has been suggested that there may be problems in ensuring that the person truly at fault in such circumstances can be prosecuted,[63] although there seems to be no reason why recourse should not be had to the general rules of art and part guilt and of incitement, aiding and abetting.

6.4.13 The penalties for breaching a TPO can be substantial, with no limit to the fines following conviction on indictment and

[56] 1969 Regulations, Model Order, paras. 5 (as amended by S.I. 1988/963), 9.

[57] For a tree to be "destroyed" it is sufficient that so radical an injury is inflicted on it that any reasonably competent forester would decide that it ought to be felled, taking into account all the circumstances, *e.g.* a tree by a highway requires greater vigour and stability than one in a field; *Barnet London Borough Council* v. *Eastern Electricity Board* [1973] 1 W.L.R. 430 (where the severing of between a half and one third of the root systems of trees was held to have destroyed them, even though the trees might have survived for some years).

[58] TCPSA, s.98 (substituted by Town and Country Amenities Act 1974, s.11), 1975 Regulations, Model Order, para. 2; TCPA, s.210, 1969 Regulations, Model Order, para. 2.

[59] *Maidstone Borough Council* v. *Mortimer* [1980] 3 All E.R. 552, where it was said that the preservation of trees was "of the utmost importance" (Park J. at p. 554).

[60] *Bath City Council* v. *Pratt (t/a Crescent Investments)* (unreported, see [1988] C.L.Y. 3422).

[61] *Groveside Homes Ltd.* v. *Elmbridge Borough Council* (1987) 55 P. & C.R. 214.

[62] *Maidstone Borough Council* v. *Mortimer*, note 59, above.

[63] C. Crawford & P. Schofield, "A Weak Branch in the Law of Trees?" [1981] J.P.L. 316.

in summary proceedings fines of up to £20,000 or twice the value of the trees.[64] In assessing the fine the courts are expressly instructed to take into account any financial benefit which appears likely to accrue to the offender as a result of the offence.[65] Deliberate flouting of a TPO is likely to incur a fairly large penalty,[66] and in *R.* v. *Razzell*[67] a developer who stood to gain £50,000 if he had been able to develop land free of trees was fined £10,000 on each of two charges of breaching a TPO, together with £12,000 costs. The planning authority can seek to support a TPO with an interdict or injunction,[68] although this is likely to be apt only where there is some aggravating feature such as a deliberate and flagrant flouting of the law.[69]

6.4.14 A number of exceptions are provided where the felling, etc., of a tree will not be unlawful, despite the existence of a TPO. The wording of some of the main exceptions differs in the two sets of legislation. In Scotland an order cannot prohibit the uprooting, felling or lopping of any tree if such action is urgently necessary in the interests of safety, or is necessary for the prevention or abatement of a nuisance, provided that notice is given to the planning authority as soon as may be after the necessity has arisen.[70]

6.4.15 In England and Wales the equivalent provision exempts actions affecting trees which are dying, dead or have become dangerous, or so far as may be necessary for the prevention or abatement of nuisance.[71] It has been held that the wording used means that once a tree has "become dangerous," any felling or lopping is exempt, even though it does nothing to remove or

[64] TCPSA, s.98(1) (substituted by Town & Country Amenities Act 1974, s.11, amended by Planning and Compensation Act 1991, s.54); TCPA, s.210(2) (amended by Planning and Compensation Act 1991, s.23). A lesser penalty is set for topping and lopping which is not likely to destroy the tree; TCPSA, s.98(2), TCPA, s.210(3).
[65] *Ibid.*, s.98(1); *ibid.*, s.210(3).
[66] E.g. a £1,000 fine in *White* v. *Hamilton*, 1987 S.C.C.R. 12.
[67] (1990) 12 Cr.App.R. (S) 142.
[68] TCPSA, s.260A (added by Planning and Compensation Act 1991, s.35); TCPA, s.214A (added by Planning and Compensation Act 1991, s.23).
[69] *Newport Borough Council* v. *Khan (Sabz Ali)* [1990] 1 W.L.R. 1185 (although this was decided before express provision for the use of injunctions was made in the Planning and Compensation Act 1991).
[70] TCPSA, s.58(6) (amended by Town and Country Amenities Act 1974, s.11).
[71] TCPA, s.198(6).

reduce the danger.[72] Whether a tree is dangerous is a matter of fact, the onus of proving which lies on the person claiming the exception,[73] and a tree may be dangerous as a result of its size and location (*e.g.* by damaging a building's foundations) even though it is perfectly healthy and safe in itself.[74] In one case it has been said that a developer cannot argue that a tree is a nuisance when he owns and occupies the land on which the nuisance is said to occur, nor that he can lawfully fell the tree as one which has become dangerous when it was his own actions as part of the continuing development which made it dangerous.[75]

6.4.16 Other exceptions apply in both jurisdictions. Felling required by any Act of Parliament is exempt,[76] as is felling in accordance with a plan of operations approved by the Forestry Commission, and felling immediately required for a development which has been authorised by a grant of planning permission. Also exempt is felling which is necessary in order to carry out works on or for the safety of operational land held by a range of statutory undertakers and equivalents, or necessary for the safety of air navigation.[77] In England and Wales, further exceptions apply to fruit trees cultivated for fruit production or in an orchard or garden and in some circumstances where the trees are interfering with the functions of water and drainage authorities in relation to the maintenance, improvement or construction of water courses or drainage works.[78] Express consent under the TPO may not be required for felling authorised by a felling licence from the Forestry Commission[79] or authorised for opencast coal works.[80]

6.4.17 In addition to the penalty, steps can be taken to ensure the replacement of the trees. The replacement provisions apply if a tree is unlawfully removed, uprooted or destroyed in

[72] *Smith* v. *Oliver* [1989] 2 P.L.R. 1.
[73] *R.* v. *Alath Construction Ltd.* [1990] 1 W.L.R. 1255.
[74] *Smith* v. *Oliver*, note 72, above.
[75] *Bath City Council* v. *Pratt (t/a Crescent Investments)* (unreported, see [1988] C.L.Y. 3422).
[76] TCPSA, s.58(6); TCPA, s.198(6).
[77] 1975 Regulations, Second Schedule to Model Order; 1969 Regulations, Second Schedule to Model Order (both as amended by the Electricity Act 1990 (Consequential Modifications of Subordinate Legislation) Order 1990, S.I. 1990 No. 526).
[78] 1969 Regulations, *ibid.*
[79] See paras. 6.4.20–6.4.23, below.
[80] TCPSA, s.58(10); TCPA, s.198(7).

contravention of a TPO, or except in relation to woodland is removed, uprooted or destroyed or dies at a time when its removal, etc., is lawful only in the interest of safety.[81] In such circumstances there is a duty on the owner of the land to plant another tree of appropriate size and species at the same place as soon as he reasonably can, or in the case of trees in woodland, to replace the trees by planting the same number of trees on or near the affected land, or on other land as agreed with the planning authority.[82] It is made clear that this obligation rests with the owner of the land for the time being,[83] but the planning authority can waive the replanting requirement.[84] The relevant TPO applies to any replacement trees as it applied to the original ones.[85] A replanting or replacement condition can also be imposed when the authority gives consent for trees to be felled,[86] and must be imposed in relation to any felling of woodland (other than silvicultural thinning) unless the consent was for development which has been granted planning permission or the Secretary of State approves the planning authority's waiver of this requirement.[87]

6.4.18 A replanting requirement (whether following a breach of an order or imposed as a condition to felling consent) can be enforced by the planning authority, in Scotland within two years of becoming aware of the failure to comply,[88] in England and Wales within four years of the date of the alleged failure.[89] A notice requiring compliance and specifying the necessary steps is served on the landowner, who has a right of appeal to the Secretary of State on the grounds that he has complied with the requirement, that the requirement is not applicable or should be dispensed with, that the specified timescale or species for the replacement are unreasonable, that the planting is not required in the interest of amenity or would be contrary to good forestry practice, or that the place specified is unsuitable for the

---

[81] TCPSA, s.60(1) (amended by Town and Country Amenities Act 1974, s.11; Town and Country Planning (Amendment) Act 1985, s.2); TCPA, s.206(1).
[82] *Ibid.*, s.60(1), (1A) (added by Town and Country Planning (Amendment) Act 1985, s.2); *ibid.*, s.206(1), (3).
[83] *Ibid.*, s.60(3); *ibid.*, s.206(5).
[84] *Ibid.*, s.60(1); *ibid.*, s.206(2).
[85] *Ibid.*, s.60(2); *ibid.*, s.206(4).
[86] 1975 Regulations, Model Order, para. 5; 1969 Regulations, Model Order, para. 4.
[87] *Ibid.*, Model Order, para. 7; *ibid.*, Model Order, para. 6.
[88] TCPSA, s.99 (amended by Planning and Compensation Act 1991, s.54).
[89] TCPA, s.207 (amended by Planning and Compensation Act 1991, s.23).

purpose.[90] If the notice is not complied with, the authority has the power to enter the land and carry out the required steps itself, the costs being recoverable from the landowner who has in turn a right to recover from the person responsible for the removal of the original trees.[91]

6.4.19 In order to assist in the operation of all of the provisions relating to TPOs, the planning authority enjoys a power of entry to land in order to ascertain whether its powers should be exercised, whether any order is being complied with and in order to take any necessary enforcement action. In the absence of cooperation, warrants can be obtained to ensure that the powers can be exercised, and wilful obstruction of anyone exercising the powers is a criminal offence.[92]

6.4.20 There is obviously an overlap between the provisions in the planning and in the forestry legislation relating to the felling of trees. This point is dealt with in the legislation, but the two schemes are so different in their aims and procedures, that the outcome is not wholly satisfactory. On land where the Forestry Commission has given a grant for forestry[93] or which is covered by a forestry dedication covenant,[94] a TPO can only be made if there is no agreed plan of operations for the land and the Forestry Commission agrees to the making of the order,[95] and the order cannot affect felling in accordance with any plan of operations approved by the Commission.[96]

6.4.21 Where both a felling licence[97] and consent under a TPO are necessary for the felling of trees, the starting point is that the matter should be dealt with under the forestry legislation

[90] TCPSA, s.99(3) (as amended); TCPA, s.208 (amended by Planning and Compensation Act 1991, s.23).
[91] *Ibid.*, s.99(5), applying s.88; *ibid.*, s.209 (as amended by Planning and Compensation Act 1991, s.23).
[92] *Ibid.*, ss.99A–99C (added by Planning and Compensation Act 1991, s.54); *ibid.*, ss.214B–214D (added by Planning and Compensation Act 1991, s.23).
[93] The English legislation refers to grants under s.1 of the Forestry Act 1979 and, by express reference, its predecessors; the Scottish legislation which predates the 1979 Act has not been amended and still refers to grants under s.4 of the Forestry Act 1967, a provision repealed by the 1979 Act.
[94] Under s.5 of the Forestry Act 1967; as far as new planting is concerned, the revised grant schemes have now in practice replaced this method of securing the long-term use of land for forestry.
[95] TCPSA, s.58(7); TCPA, s.200.
[96] *Ibid.*, s.58(8); *ibid.*, s.200(3).
[97] See paras. 6.3.19–6.3.25, above.

and no application for consent from the planning authority should be made.[98] If the Forestry Commission refuses a licence, that is the end of the matter. However, the Commission may decide to refer the matter to the planning authority for decision under the planning Acts, and in any event, if it proposes to grant a licence, then the planning authority must be notified.[99] If the authority objects to the proposed grant of a felling licence and the objections cannot be resolved, the Commission must refer the case to the Secretary of State for final determination and the matter is dealt with under the planning legislation.[1] Only if the matter has been referred in either of these ways will it be determined under the planning legislation; in all other cases the grant or refusal of the felling licence decides the issue.

6.4.22 The legal basis on which permission to fell is refused may have a major practical significance because of the differing schemes for compensation as a result of refusal. If the case is dealt with under the forestry legislation, the obligation to pay compensation rests with the Forestry Commission, but the sum is limited to the loss (if any) in the value of the trees as timber.[2] On the other hand, if the matter is dealt with by the refusal of consent under the tree preservation provisions, it is the planning authority which is responsible, and the measure of compensation is all of the loss suffered in consequence of the refusal.[3]

6.4.23 The general practice used to be for the Forestry Commission to refer applications for determination by the planning authority, but following *Bell* v. *Canterbury City Council*[4] it was realised that this might result in planning authorities being liable to pay very large sums in compensation, or being influenced to grant consent reluctantly in order to avoid such payments. It was therefore announced[5] that the Forestry Commission will itself give full consideration, taking into account amenity considerations, to all applications which do not involve a commitment to retaining the land as woodland. Only where the application for a felling licence includes a commitment to replanting will the matter be referred to the

[98] Forestry Act 1967, s.15(5).
[99] *Ibid.* s.15(1).
[1] *Ibid.*, s.15(2).
[2] See para. 6.3.22, above.
[3] See paras. 6.4.10–6.4.11, above.
[4] (1988) 56 P. & C.R. 211; see para. 6.4.10, above.
[5] See [1988] J.P.L. 531.

planning authority to determine under the planning legislation; in such cases any compensation will be insignificant — large sums are only likely where the refusal of consent hinders a protifable change in the use of the land. As discussed above, if the Commission proposes to grant a licence, the authority must be notified and if it objects the case will be dealt with under the planning legislation, by means of a reference to the Secretary of State. Responsibility for the majority of decisions, and for any compensation, has thus been effectively transferred from the planning authority to the Forestry Commission.

Miscellaneous

6.4.24 Trees also feature in other legislation which contains provisions to ensure that trees do not interfere with other activities. Thus trees or shrubs which cause a danger or obstruction to road-users or obstruct their view, a public lamp or a traffic sign (or additionally in Scotland increase the likelihood of a road being obstructed by drifting snow) may be removed by the roads or highways authority, initially by requiring action from the occupier, but with the possibility of direct action.[6] On the other hand, the roads legislation also grants express powers to plant trees.[7] Similarly action can be taken against trees which are overhanging a street in such a way as to obstruct telecommunications apparatus.[8]

---

[6] Roads (Scotland) Act 1984, s.91 (see also s.92); Highways Act 1980, ss.79, 154.

[7] *Ibid.*, ss.50, 51; *ibid.*, ss.141–142, 282.

[8] Telecommunications Act 1984, Sched. 2 para. 19.

7. European and International Aspects

7.1.1 Nature conservation law must obviously be tailored to meet the needs of each particular country — there is little point in a law protecting wild giraffes in Britain — but it should also take account of the fact that no ecosystem is wholly isolated. As far as natural connections are concerned, many birds, marine creatures and, in the case of continental states, land creatures are merely visitors to any particular country, living in or passing through several national jurisdictions as their annual or life cycles progress. Species in one country may depend on water or other resources flowing from the territory of another, and the viability of many populations may depend on contacts with individuals on the other side of international frontiers.

7.1.2 When man's activities are also considered, the potential for international repercussions becomes even greater. Alien species introduced, deliberately or accidentally, by man may threaten the native flora and fauna, as predators or as competitors for the same limited resources. Pests and diseases can be spread across the world and wreak havoc with populations never previously exposed to such threats. Man's exploitation of animals can reach across the globe so that plants and animals in one country are destroyed in order to meet a demand in another country thousands of miles away. For all of these reasons, it is essential that nature conservation law should not only look to what is happening in the national environment, but also consider the issue on an international scale.

7.1.3 In Britain, the law addresses these issues in several ways. Firstly, there are national laws regulating the introduction of alien species to the natural environment. Secondly, commerce in wild plants and animals is controlled by measures at the national, European and international levels. Thirdly, the European Community has taken steps to protect natural habitats and wildlife throughout the Community. Fourthly, there is a growing series of international agreements under which states throughout the world have agreed to take steps to further the interests of nature conservation. Each of these must be considered.

INTRODUCTIONS

7.2.1 Throughout history, as man has travelled from one land to another, he has taken with him plants and animals to establish in his new home, in order to provide food or other resources, either as a commercial enterprise or merely for pleasure. In countries such as New Zealand the capacity of introductions to devastate the indigenous wildlife can be clearly seen as the introductions and their effects have been recorded over a comparatively short period. In a country such as Britain, with a long history of settlers from beyond these shores, it can be almost impossible to determine whether some species which are firmly established here are truly indigenous or are rather introductions of long standing, and many species generally regarded as part of the natural scene are in fact introductions within historical times, *e.g.* the rabbit. Other species such as the coypu, mink and Japanese knotweed have made an impact in much more recent times.

7.2.2 Some introductions into the wild have been deliberate, but in other cases plants and animals have escaped from the gardens, parks or farms where they were being tended and have been able to establish themselves away from human care. Many introductions have been beneficial to man and caused little interference to the indigenous flora and fauna, but others have had serious and undesirable consequences.

7.2.3 The introduction of new species is controlled directly by s.14 of the Wildlife and Countryside Act 1981, and indirectly as some of the import restrictions extend to cover the keeping and release of the affected species.[1] It is an offence to release or to allow to escape into the wild any animal which is not ordinarily resident in or is not a regular visitor to Great Britain in a wild state.[2] In order to prevent the reinforcement of alien species

---

[1] See below.
[2] WCA, s.14(1)(a).

which have managed to establish a foothold here as a result of past releases and escapes (and may thus qualify as being "ordinarily resident in a wild state") the prohibition is extended to cover the specific species listed in Schedule 9, which are not native but may already be found in the wild somewhere in Great Britain.[3] This list ranges from well-known species which are now widespread (such as the grey squirrel) to the more exotic (such as the ring-necked parakeet and the red-necked wallaby). The EC Birds Directive also requires that any introductions of non-native birds should not be prejudicial to the native flora and fauna.[4] As far as plants are concerned, it is an offence to plant or otherwise cause to grow in the wild any of the species of plant listed in Part II of Schedule 9 to the 1981 Act.[5]

7.2.4 In relation to these charges it is a defence for the accused to prove that all reasonable steps were taken and that all due diligence was used in order to avoid committing the offence.[6] Prior notice must be given to the prosecution if this defence involves an allegation that the release or escape was due to the act or omission of another person.[7] Licences to authorise releases may be granted by the Secretary of State.[8] Those investigating whether an offence has been committed and authorised by the Secretary of State enjoy a power of entry to land,[9] and obstruction of those involved in the exercise of this power is itself a criminal offence.[10]

7.2.5 The restrictions on the import of animals and plants provide a further means of preventing damaging releases. In addition to the general measures, the import of some animals is further restricted by measures specifically designed to prevent the introduction of harmful pests. The Destructive Imported Animals Act 1932[11] and the orders made under it impose

[3] *Ibid.*, s.14(1)(b), Sched. 9, Pt. I; see Appendix A.
[4] Directive 79/409, Art. 11; see para. 7.4.4, below.
[5] WCA s.14(2), Sched. 9, Pt. II; see para. 6.2.10, above and Appendix A.
[6] *Ibid.*, s.14(3).
[7] *Ibid.*, s.14(4).
[8] *Ibid.*, s.16(4), (9); the agriculture minister exercises this power in relation to shellfish (*ibid.*, s.16(9)(d)).
[9] *Ibid.*, s.14(5).
[10] *Ibid.*, s.14(6).
[11] As amended to exclude imports from within the European Community (as part of the achievement of the Single Market) by the Destructive Imported Animals Act 1932 (Amendment) Regulations 1992, S.I. 1992 No. 3302.

controls on the importation and keeping of a number of species: musk rats,[12] grey squirrels,[13] non-indigenous rabbits,[14] mink[15] and coypus.[16] The legislation on zoos[17] and on keeping dangerous wild animals[18] also serves to ensure that alien species are unlikely to escape to the wild.

TRADE

7.3.1 The import and export of animals and plants is heavily regulated, primarily in order to ensure that no pests or diseases are allowed to enter the country. British law in this area has been strict, in order to continue the natural advantage enjoyed by an island nation, as most publicly shown by the anti-rabies measures preventing the landing of dogs without a long quarantine period. The law has become more complex following Britain's membership of the European Community, as the need to ensure the free movement of goods and to establish the Single Market[19] has required both common standards and the establishment of schemes for mutual recognition of licences, certificates, etc. Most of the law is primarily directed at domesticated animals and cultivated plants, and will not be discussed in detail here, although wild species will also be covered by its terms. However, there are important measures

[12] Musk Rats (Prohibition of Importation and Keeping) Order 1933, S.R. & O. 1933 No. 106.
[13] Grey Squirrels (Prohibition of Importation and Keeping) Order 1937, S.R. & O. 1937 No. 478.
[14] Non-indigenous Rabbits (Prohibition of Importation and Keeping) Order 1954, S.I. 1954 No. 927; strictly speaking, it is unlikely that any rabbits in this country are truly indigenous, and the order refers to rabbits "other than those of the species *Oryctolagus Cuniculus* [*sic.*] (commonly known as the European rabbit)."
[15] Mink (Importation) General Licence 1967, S.I. 1967 No. 1874; Mink (Keeping) Regulations 1975, S.I. 1975 No. 2233 (amended by Mink (Keeping) (Amendment) Regulations 1982 and 1987, S.I.s 1982 No. 1883 and 1987 No. 2225); Mink (Keeping) Order 1992, S.I. 1992 No. 3324.
[16] Coypus (Prohibition on Keeping) Order 1987, S.I. 1987 No. 2195.
[17] Zoo Licensing Act 1981; see, *e.g.*, s.5(3) which expressly authorises conditions in a licence requiring precautions against escapes.
[18] Dangerous Wild Animals Act 1976; see, *e.g.*, s.1(3) which states that a licence will only be granted if the animal is held in accommodation which secures that it will not escape.
[19] See, *e.g.*, the Animals and Animal Products (Import and Export) Regulations 1992, S.I. No. 3295, implementing Directives 90/425 and 91/496.

designed specifically to protect wild species from over-exploitation, and these will be looked at more thoroughly.

7.3.2 As far as animals are concerned, the main provisions affecting their import and export rest on the Animal Health Act 1981 and its predecessors. Under s.10 of the 1981 Act, the agriculture ministers may make orders as they think fit to prevent the introduction to or spread within Britain of disease through the import of animals, carcases, eggs, or any other animate or inanimate thing by which disease can be transmitted.[20] For the purpose of this provision, "animal" and "disease" are not restricted in their definition as they are for many other aspects of the Act, so that although directed at domesticated species, any import of wild animals is likely also to be affected.[21] Under this power, and equivalent powers under earlier legislation, a large volume of delegated legislation has been made, the most important (although now amended) orders being perhaps the Importation of Animals Order 1977[22] and the Rabies (Importation of Dogs, Cats and Other Mammals) Order 1974.[23] The orders detail the various licences, certificates, quarantine and other arrangements required for the lawful import of animals from abroad.

7.3.3 Exports are also subject to restrictions in order to prevent the spread of diseases to other members of the European Community. The relevant enabling provision is s.11 of the Animal Health Act 1981, and again there is delegated legislation making provision for licences, certificates, etc.[24]

7.3.4 Whilst fish and shellfish can be dealt with under the Animal Health Act 1981,[25] more specific provision has also been made. Under the Import of Live Fish (Scotland) Act 1978 and the Import of Live Fish (England and Wales) Act 1980,[26] the Secretary of State can make orders prohibiting or requiring a

[20] Animal Health Act 1981, s.10(1).
[21] *Ibid.*, s.10(4).
[22] S.I. 1977 No. 944.
[23] S.I. 1974 No. 2211.
[24] A brief guide is offered in *Halsbury's Laws of England* (4th ed. reissue, 1991), Vol. 2, paras. 492, 493, 502–506.
[25] See, *e.g.* the Shellfish and Specified Fish (Third Country Imports) Order 1992, S.I. 1992 No. 3301.
[26] A rare but most welcome example of a non-Scottish Act whose title properly indicates its limited application.

licence for the import, keeping or release of live fish or live eggs of fish of species which are not native and which it is thought might compete with, displace, prey on or harm the habitat of any freshwater fish, shellfish or salmon.[27] There are the usual provisions creating offences, granting powers of search, etc., to give effect to the basic provision. The Diseases of Fish Act 1937 likewise confers powers to restrict imports.[28]

7.3.5 Plant health within Great Britain is similarly protected by restrictions on imports. Again the main statute is an enabling Act, the Plant Health Act 1967, under which some general and other more specific measures have been introduced, with the usual requirements for licences, etc.[29]

Endangered species

7.3.6 Of greater significance for nature conservation are the measures designed to restrict trade in endangered species. Since ancient times the ownership of wild animals, their skins, plumage or other products, has frequently been strongly desired in some quarters, primarily as a luxury item or at times as a component in perfumes or medicinal products. Inevitably considerable efforts have been made to meet this demand, and since at least Roman times, it has been apparent that the efforts of hunters supplying this market can devastate and ultimately destroy populations of certain animals. Ironically, the value of the animal may increase as it becomes rarer, encouraging even greater efforts on the part of hunters and collectors, and increasing the risk that such exploitation will eventually lead to extinction. The present battles against elephant and rhinoceros poachers in parts of Africa and the threat which they pose to the survival of the species demonstrate both the effects of such exploitation and the strength of the incentive to continue the hunting even once a species becomes rare.

7.3.7 A similar fate can befall species of plant. At present orchids, cacti and Mediterranean bulbs are probably most at

---

[27] The only Orders under either provision are the Import of Live Fish (Coho Salmon) (Prohibition) (Scotland) Order 1980, S.I. 1980 No. 376 and the Prohibition of the Keeping or the Release of Live Fish (Pikeperch) (Scotland) Order 1993, S.I. 1993 No. 1288.

[28] *E.g.*, Importation of Live Fish of the Salmon Family Order 1986, S.I. 1986 No. 283.

[29] See para. 6.2.11, above.

risk, but in the past the fashion was for other species, particularly ferns, and great damage was done to many populations and whole species. In the case of both plants and animals the effect of the trade is exacerbated by the fact that the demand is usually in a part of the world distant from the supply (that, after all, is part of the attraction) and the difficulties of transporting live specimens mean that in order to supply a particular number of individual specimens in good condition, many, many more are collected from the wild and perish en route.

7.3.8 It should be recognised, however, that if properly regulated, trade in a species can actually be beneficial to its survival. The fact that a plant or animal has a commercial value can encourage measures to ensure its survival at a level permitting its long-term and sustainable exploitation. Thus its habitat may be preserved and those with an interest in its lawful trade may endeavour to protect it from accidental harm or destructive poaching. The strength of this argument and its validity in individual circumstances is, however, a point of heated debate among conservationists.

7.3.9 If destructive trade is to be controlled, the law can obviously try to control the hunters and collectors in the countries where the specimens are to be found, but it has also been realised that it may be at least as effective to approach the problem from the other end, regulating the market for such goods so as to stifle the demand which fuels the trade. In Great Britain, this approach was first taken at a time when the fashion for colourful feathers in ladies' hats was threatening a number of tropical bird species. With the exceptions of ostrich feathers and eider down, the Importation of Plumage (Prohibition) Act 1921 prohibited the import of any plumage from wild birds unless a special licence had been obtained.[30] More recently, the problem has been tackled on a global scale.

7.3.10 The basis for the current law at a British and European level is the Convention on International Trade in Endangered Species of Wild Fauna and Flora (CITES), concluded in

---

[30] This Act contains many of the features of the modern legislation, most notably the use of a variable Schedule to list the species covered by or excepted from the main rules and the appointment of a specialist body to advise on what should be included in the Schedule.

Washington in 1973.[31] Many states around the world have
become parties to this treaty which endeavours to regulate
international trade by requiring licences to be granted before
specimens of plants and animals, or items derived from them,
can be imported or exported. In some cases commercial trade is
essentially prohibited, in others controlled exploitation remains
possible, and the needs of individual countries are taken into
account both by the separate treatment of distinct populations
of certain species and the potential for a state to use the CITES
machinery to further its own conservation plans.

7.3.11 The animals and plants covered by the Convention are
divided into three categories.[32] Those listed in Appendix I, *e.g.*
tigers, are those "threatened with extinction which are or may
be affected by trade," and trade in these must be permitted only
in exceptional circumstances. Appendix II is for species which
"may become [threatened with extinction] unless trade in
specimens of such species is subject to strict regulation in order
to avoid utilization incompatible with their survival," *e.g.* all
species of southern fur seals. Also covered by Appendix II are
species whose listing is necessary to ensure the effectiveness of
the controls on the other Appendix II species — this allows for
"look-alike" species to be listed, preventing the enforcement of
the treaty being undermined by the difficulties of distinguishing
between similar species, only some of which are listed.
Appendix III is an optional one which allows individual states to
invoke the provisions of CITES for particular species which they
wish to protect but which have not been listed in the main
Appendices; these are protected only in relation to trade with
the states which added the species to the list. The listing applies
to living and dead specimens and to "any readily recognizable
part or derivative thereof."[33]

7.3.12 The contents of the Appendices can be amended at the
regular Conferences of the Parties which are a feature of
CITES,[34] and many changes have been made since the
Convention was first agreed. This issue reached the public's
attention during 1991 in relation to the heated debate over the

---

[31] For a detailed examination of the Convention see D.S. Favre, *International
Trade in Endangered Species* (1989); a shorter account is in S. Lyster,
International Wildlife Law (1985), Chap. 12.
[32] CITES, Art. 2.
[33] *Ibid.*, Art. 1(b).
[34] *Ibid.*, Art. 15.

status of the African elephant, concerning whether its long-term conservation is best served by a ban on the trade in ivory or the continuation of limited and controlled trade. Geographically separate populations of a species can be treated independently when it comes to listing,[35] so that it is possible for a plant or animal which is severely threatened in one part of its range to be fully protected there whilst allowing limited commercial trade from other parts where there is no risk of extinction.

7.3.13 The basic structure of the CITES provisions is that for species in Appendix I, any trade requires both an export permit from the supplying state and an import permit from the destination state. Export permits should be granted only where the trade will not be detrimental to the survival of the species, where the specimen has been lawfully obtained and an import permit has been granted by the receiving state, and where there are appropriate facilities to ensure that any living specimen is protected during transit. An import permit should only be granted if the import is for purposes not detrimental to the survival of the species, if there are appropriate facilities to house the specimen once it arrives, and the trade is not for primarily commercial purposes.[36] In essence therefore, there can be no lawful commercial trade in such species and only in exceptional cases can specimens be transferred from one country to another.

7.3.14 For species in Appendix II, it is merely an export permit which is required, the granting of such permits being subject to the same restrictions as for Appendix I, apart from the requirement for an import permit to have been issued. Imports do not require specific approval, but are subject to the prior presentation of an export permit.[37] For Appendix III, again it is merely an export permit which is required, to be issued if the specimen was lawfully taken and appropriate transit requirements are made.[38]

7.3.15 These essentials of CITES are supported by a number of other provisions dealing with exemptions,[39] the confiscation

[35] *Ibid.*, Art. 1(a).
[36] *Ibid.*, Art. 3.
[37] *Ibid.*, Art. 4.
[38] *Ibid.*, Art. 5.
[39] *Ibid.*, Art. 7.

and subsequent dealing with specimens unlawfully traded,[40] formalities for permits and certificates,[41] re-exports and the handling of goods in transit through a state,[42] the restriction of the ports, etc., through which such trade can be carried out,[43] and the landing of listed species taken on the high seas.[44] More significantly the treaty requires each party to identify a scientific authority and a management authority within the state which are to have responsibility for advising on and overseeing the operation of the treaty.[45] The treaty also requires that detailed records (open for public inspection) are kept of all trade authorised under CITES and that regular reports are made to the Secretariat.[46] This recording system ensures that the treaty does not become a dead-letter, although the experience has been that even where apparently full returns have been made, the records of imports and exports between countries rarely tally exactly. The reports also serve to demonstrate the scale and complexity of international trade in wild plants and animals.[47]

7.3.16 The vitality of CITES is also maintained by the biennial Conferences of the Parties, at which amendments to the treaty, and in particular the Appendices, are discussed.[48] These meetings are open to international agencies and approved non-governmental bodies, which can participate in discussions but not vote. In this way publicity is guaranteed and states may have to contend with open criticism from conservation bodies which are not affected by the broader considerations of international relations which can mute inter-governmental criticism.

7.3.17 As a result of these measures, CITES has proved to be a comparatively successful treaty, and because it allows both strict conservation and regulated trade it has attracted a large number of parties, both suppliers and recipients of animals,

---

[40] *Ibid.*, Art. 8(1)–(4).

[41] *Ibid.*, Art. 6.

[42] *Ibid.*, Arts. 3(4), 4(5), 5(4).

[43] *Ibid.*, Art. 8(3).

[44] *Ibid.*, Arts. 3(5), 4(6).

[45] *Ibid.*, Art. 9.

[46] *Ibid.*, Art. 8(6)–(8); the Secretariat was established through the United Nations Environment Programme (*ibid.*, Art. 12).

[47] The latest EC report, *Convention on International Trade in Endangered Species of Wild Fauna and Flora: EC Annual Report 1989* (1992) runs to 346 pages for imports and 244 pages for exports and re-exports.

[48] CITES, Art. 11.

plants and their products. Its provisions apply directly only to trade between parties, but the parties must impose some similar requirements on trade with other states, and the treaty expressly allows the parties to maintain stricter domestic rules on any international or internal trade.[49]

7.3.18 Both the United Kingdom and the European Community are parties to CITES and have taken steps to implement its provisions. At the European level, the main provision is Regulation 3626/82 which requires Member States to comply with the provisions of the treaty. The Regulation goes beyond the Convention's provisions by requiring both import and export permits for all of the listed species, not only those in Appendix I. It also provides for a number of additional species to be treated as if contained in Appendix I of CITES, and for import permits to be required in relation to others. The protected species are listed in the Annexes to the Regulation which are regularly updated in accordance with amendments to the CITES Appendices.[50] This measure is supported by a Regulation laying down standard requirements for the forms, certificates and labels necessary for the operation of the controls.[51]

7.3.19 Information on the scientific and management authorities within each of the Member States responsible for the operation of CITES and on the ports through which trade is permitted is collected and published at a European level,[52] and the Commission produces an annual report recording all the trade carried out by Member States under the CITES arrangements.[53]

7.3.20 The European Community has also introduced a handful of other measures specifically directed at the trade in wildlife products (in addition to the general laws on plant and animal health), although these have largely been overtaken by the implementation of CITES. The commerical importation of whale products is banned by the requirement for a licence for any import of any meat, oil or other products derived from cetaceans, or of goods treated with such products, coupled with

---

[49] *Ibid.*, Arts. 10, 14(1).
[50] See most recently Regulation 1970/92.
[51] Regulation 3418/83.
[52] Commission Information, OJ 89/C 327/01 and 327/02.
[53] *Convention on International Trade in Endangered Species of Wild Fauna and Flora: EC Annual Report 1989* (1992).

a provision that no such licence is to be granted for commercial purposes.[54] The commerical importation of the skins of whitecoat pups of harp seals and of the pups of hooded seals (blue-backs) is also prohibited.[55] There is also a specific requirement for an import permit for the importation of raw or worked ivory from the African elephant, subject to a number of exceptions which expressly deny any exception to modern tourist souvenirs.[56]

7.3.21 In the United Kingdom, the implementation of CITES and the relevant European legislation is somewhat complex as regulations to give effect to the European Community's adoption of CITES exist alongside the more general Endangered Species (Import and Export) Act 1976. The Control of Trade in Endangered Species (Enforcement) Regulations 1985[57] provide for offences in relation to breaches of the Community Regulation implementing CITES[58] and contain provisions on powers of search and entry to assist in its enforcement. The Control of Trade in Endangered Species (Designation of Ports of Entry) Regulations 1985[59] further assist the enforcement of CITES by designating particular groups of ports and airports as the only ones through which live animals of different categories may be imported.

7.3.22 The Endangered Species (Import and Export) Act 1976, initially enacted to give effect to the United Kingdom's individual accession to CITES, has to some extent been overtaken by developments at the Community level, but is still important for trade with non-parties to CITES and because its provisions and lists of species are in some cases broader than those required for CITES. Without a licence from the Secretary of State, it is an offence to import or export the animals, plants or their derivatives listed in the Schedules,[60] and a number of other controls are imposed in relation to endangered species. In

[54] Regulation 348/81.

[55] Directive 83/129.

[56] Regulation 2496/89.

[57] S.I. 1985 No. 1155; these and the Regulations at note 59 were made under the European Communities Act 1972, not the slightly more restricted delegated powers under the Endangered Species (Import and Export) Act 1976.

[58] Regulation 3626/82; see para. 7.3.18, above.

[59] S.I. 1985 No. 1154.

[60] Endangered Species (Import and Export) Act 1976, s.1 (amended by WCA, Sched. 10 paras. 1–3).

the operation of the Act, the Department of the Environment
has been designated as the "Management Authority" required
by CITES, with the conservancy councils serving as the
"Scientific Authority" for animals and the Royal Botanic
Gardens, Kew for plants.[61]

7.3.23 The import and export restrictions apply to the animals
(alive or dead) listed in Schedule 1 to the Act, the plants (alive
or dead) listed in Schedule 2 and the products listed in Schedule
3 (which are derived from such species). The Schedules are
broad in their scope, covering the species listed in CITES and
the European measures, and as far as mammals, birds, reptiles
and amphibians are concerned, they operate on the basis that all
species are covered by the licensing requirement apart from
those expressly exempted in Schedule 1. As with the EC's rules,
these provisions are broader than those in CITES, requiring
licences for both imports and exports of all listed species. The
Schedules can be amended by the Secretary of State after
consultation with the Scientific Authorities for a number of
reasons: to give effect to amendments to CITES, including
changes by any party to Appendix III, to promote the
conservation in any area of animals or plants which are or are
likely to become endangered there, to remove restrictions which
do not in the Secretary of State's opinion promote such
conservation, and to facilitate the effective administration of the
restrictions (*e.g.* by adding "look-alike" species).[62] This power
has been exercised on several occasions, most notably when
wholly new Schedules were substituted in 1982.[63]

7.3.24 Licences are only to be granted after consultation with
the Scientific Authority,[64] or in accordance with general advice
which it has provided,[65] and may be general or specific, may be
for the benefit of individuals, classes of person or everyone,
may contain conditions, but in all cases may be modified or
revoked by the Secretary of State.[66] The knowing or reckless

[61] See para. 7.3.15, above.
[62] Endangered Species (Import and Export) Act 1976, s.3 (amended by WCA, Sched. 10, Pt. I).
[63] Endangered Species (Import and Export) Act 1976 (Modification) Order 1982, S.I. 1982 No. 1230 (amended by Endangered Species (Import and Export) Act 1976 (Modification) Orders 1983 and 1985, S.I.s 1983 No. 1609, 1985 No. 1502).
[64] Endangered Species (Import and Export) Act 1976, s.1(3).
[65] *Ibid.*, s.1(3A) (added by WCA, Sched. 10, Pt. I).
[66] *Ibid.*, s.1(4) (amended *ibid.*).

presentation of false statements or documents in order to gain a
licence is a criminal offence,[67] and any licence granted in such
circumstances is void.[68] The onus is on the person having
control of the specimen to show that its import or export is or
was not unlawful, failing which the specimen is liable to
forfeiture.[69] Where a live specimen is involved, the expenses of
returning it to the wild or transferring it to an appropriate home
in the United Kingdom can be recovered from the person in
possession or control at the time of seizure.[70] A power of entry
and search is available in relation to plants and animals (but not
derivatives) which may have been unlawfully imported.[71]

7.3.25 In addition to these direct controls on imports and
exports, it is an offence for anyone to sell, offer or expose for
sale, or possess or transport with a view to sale[72] or to display in
public any plant or animal unlawfully imported, or anything
made from them as listed in Schedule 3.[73] Similar offences apply
in relation to the further species of animal listed in Schedule 4
or plant in Schedule 5, or anything made of these species, unless
the import was prior to the end of October 1981.[74] The offences
do not apply to imports authorised by a licence,[75] and it is a
defence for the person charged to show that at the time of the
offence he had no reason to believe that the item was restricted
under these provisions, and that when it first came into his
possession he made reasonable enquiries to ascertain whether it
was restricted.[76] The requirement for reasonable enquiries will
be satisfied if the item was acquired with a signed certificate
from the supplier stating that enquiries have been made and
that there is no reason to believe that the item was restricted at
the time the supplier passed it on.[77]

7.3.26 Further provisions in the 1976 Act allow the Secretary
of State to make orders restricting the airports and ports

[67] *Ibid.*, s.1(6).
[68] *Ibid.*, s.1(7).
[69] *Ibid.*, s.1(8).
[70] *Ibid.*, s.1(9) (added by WCA, Sched. 10, Pt. I).
[71] *Ibid.*, s.1(10) (added *ibid.*).
[72] For this purpose, "sale" includes hire, barter or exchange; *ibid.*, s.4(6)
(amended *ibid.*).
[73] *Ibid.*, s.4(1) (amended *ibid.*).
[74] *Ibid.*, s.4(2).
[75] *Ibid.*, s.4(1B) (added *ibid.*).
[76] *Ibid.*, s.4(2).
[77] *Ibid.*, s.4(3).

through which live animals can be imported to the United Kingdom,[78] and to make directions restricting where live animals covered by Schedule 1 to the Act can be kept after being imported.[79] Directions under the latter power can be made only after consultation with the Scientific Authority, and the premises specified must be suitable for keeping the animal in question. It is an offence for a person who knows or ought to know that a direction has been made to be involved in the movement of the animal except as directed.

7.3.27 As well as the specific offences created by the relevant provisions, any attempt to evade the restrictions on the import and export of wild animals and plants will constitute an offence under the general law relating to customs and excise.[80] This may allow for more severe penalties, including custodial sentences, than are prescribed in the more specific legislation.[81]

EUROPEAN COMMUNITY INITIATIVES

7.4.1 As well as the measures to implement CITES discussed in the preceding section and other restrictions on the trade in wildlife, the European Community has adopted two measures aimed to provide more direct protection for wild plants and animals within the Community. The first of these is the Directive on the Conservation of Wild Birds,[82] made in 1979[83] and taking full effect in 1981; the second is the Directive on the Conservation of Natural Habitats and of Wild Fauna and Flora,[84] made in May 1992[85] and due to take effect in May 1994. Both of these require the Member States to introduce laws to secure that the species and sites identified are given protection.

[78] *Ibid.*, s.5; in practice the designation has been carried out by regulations made to give effect to the European Community's accession to CITES; see para. 7.3.21, above.

[79] *Ibid.*, ss.6, 7.

[80] Customs and Excise Management Act 1979, s.170.

[81] *R.* v. *Sperr* (1992) 13 Cr.App.Rep.(S.) 8.

[82] Directive 79/409.

[83] Under the rather loose authority of Art. 235 of the EEC Treaty; see para. 2.8.2, above.

[84] Directive 92/43.

[85] Under the much clearer authority of Art. 130s of the Treaty; see para. 2.8.2, above.

7.4.2   As Directives, the main way in which their provisions take effect should be through the presence in the national law of each Member State of appropriate measures implementing their terms, and the Birds Directive has been important in shaping the British legislation on the issue. However, if the national law does not fully meet the requirements of the Directive, it should be remembered that under general Community law the courts (at national and Community level) should always interpret and apply any national provisions in the light of the Directive, and should give direct effect to any provision in the Directive which is clear, precise and unconditional. Where necessary, the terms of a Directive which are capable of having direct effect override any national law.[86] The terms of these two Directives should therefore be borne in mind whenever the British legislation on these matters is being considered.

The Birds Directive

7.4.3   The Directive on the Conservation of Wild Birds[87] begins by imposing a very general obligation on the Member States to take the requisite measures to maintain the population of all species of bird naturally occurring in their territory[88] at a level which corresponds to ecological, scientific and cultural require- ments, while taking account of economic and recreational requirements, or to adapt the populations to that level.[89] Not surprisingly, it has been held that this provision is too vague to have direct effect,[90] and it may in fact operate against the interests of nature conservation by acknowledging the validity of economic and recreational factors which might conflict with conservation requirements. To achieve the stated objective, Member States are to take the requisite measures to preserve, maintain or re-establish a sufficient diversity and area of habitats for all the naturally occurring species, primarily by the creation of protected areas, the management of habitats in

---

[86] See paras. 2.8.4–2.8.5, above.
[87] Directive 79/409; subsequent footnotes refer to this Directive unless and until otherwise stated.
[88] This Directive (by Art. 1(1)) and the Habitats and Species one (by Art. 2(1)) are limited to the European territory of the Member States, thereby excluding the French overseas territories, but including the Azores and Canary Islands.
[89] Art. 2.
[90] *Kincardine and Deeside District Council* v. *Forestry Commission*, 1992 S.L.T. 1180; it was suggested that some other provisions, *e.g.* those requiring controls on the sale and hunting of birds, may be sufficiently precise to have direct effect.

accordance with ecological needs, and the re-establishment or creation of habitats.[91] Again, this provision is too vague to have direct effect and remains essentially an exhortatory measure.

7.4.4 For all species, subject to certain exceptions, a general system of protection is to be established. In particular there is a prohibition on any deliberate killing or taking of birds, deliberate destruction of nests and eggs, deliberate disturbance of birds during the breeding season where this will be significant for the general aims of the Directive, and the taking and keeping of eggs; the keeping of birds apart from those whose hunting and capture is permitted should also be prohibited.[92] Even where hunting is permitted,[93] any methods used for the large-scale or non-selective capture or killing of birds is to be prohibited, especially those expressly listed in Annex IV(a), which includes limes, explosives, nets, artificial lights, mirrors, and semi-automatic and automatic weapons; also prohibited is hunting by the means described in Annex IV(b), namely from aircraft, motor vehicles and boats moving at above five kilometres per hour.[94] If any species of bird which does not naturally occur in the European territory of the Community is introduced, Member States must see to it that this does not prejudice the local flora and fauna.[95]

7.4.5 As usual with such legislation, particular categories of birds are picked out for special treatment, in some cases by additional protection, in others less.[96] Special conservation measures are to be taken for the species (over 170 in number[97]) listed in Annex I of the Directive, the listing taking account of species in danger of extinction, vulnerable to specific changes in their habitat, with small populations or restricted local distribution or requiring specific habitat.[98] For these species the most suitable areas are to be classified as Special Protection

[91] Art. 3.
[92] Art. 5.
[93] See para. 7.4.7, below.
[94] Art. 8, Annex IV.
[95] Art. 11.
[96] The various Annexes have been replaced and amended at various times; see *European Community Environment Legislation* (1992), Vol. 4 "Nature", p. 2.
[97] As they list the birds by their names in all of the Community's official languages, as well as by their scientific names, the Annexes provide a useful phrase book for any bird-watcher travelling in Europe.
[98] Art. 4(1).

Areas,[99] where appropriate steps are to be taken to avoid pollution or deterioration of habitats or disturbance of the birds. In other areas states are to strive to avoid pollution or deterioration of habitats.[1] Similar steps are to be taken for regularly occurring migratory species not listed in Annex I, paying particular attention to wetlands.[2] The Commission is to be kept informed of the steps taken with a view to coordinating such action to secure that the protective measures form a coherent whole.[3] The provisions for Special Protection Areas are to be replaced by those for Special Areas of Conservation under the Habitats and Species Directive.[4]

7.4.6 Whereas for most species there is a prohibition on the sale of birds, alive or dead, and of readily recognisable parts or derivatives, as well as on the transport and keeping for sale,[5] this ban is relaxed in some cases. For the species listed in Annex III/1 the ban is lifted throughout the Community provided that the birds have been lawfully killed or captured or otherwise acquired.[6] For those listed in Annex III/2, Member States have a discretion whether to make exceptions to the general rule, again provided that the birds have been lawfully taken, but subject to restrictions and an examination to ensure that the marketing will not lead to the species being endangered; this examination is to be carried out jointly by the State and the Commission.[7]

7.4.7 The hunting of birds may be allowed by national legislation, but only for those species in Annex II and always subject to a requirement that the hunting does not jeopardise conservation efforts in the hunting area.[8] The species listed in Annex II/1 may be hunted throughout the Community,[9] whereas those in Annex II/2 may be hunted only in the Member States specified.[10] The Commission must be informed of the relevant hunting laws, which should ensure the wise use and

[99] Art. 4(1); see paras. 5.12.3–5.12.7, above.
[1] Art. 4(4).
[2] Art. 4(2).
[3] Art. 4(3).
[4] See paras. 7.4.22–7.4.23, below.
[5] Art. 6(1).
[6] Art. 6(2).
[7] Art. 6(3).
[8] Art. 7(1).
[9] See note 88 above.
[10] Art. 7(2), (3).

ecologically balanced control of the species and protect them during the rearing season.[11]

7.4.8 Member States are allowed to derogate from the specific prohibitions and restrictions on the killing, taking, hunting and sale of birds, but only on a limited number of grounds and where there is no other satisfactory solution. Such derogations may be justified in the interests of public health and safety or of air safety, to prevent serious damage to crops, livestock, forests, fisheries and water, and for the protection of flora and fauna. Also permitted are action for teaching and education, action taken to allow for repopulation or reintroduction (including captive breeding) and other strictly supervised and selective keeping or other "judicious use" of small numbers of birds.[12] The derogations must be detailed and specific and must be notified to the Commission together with information on the authority which is empowered to declare that the criteria for the derogation have been met. By granting a legislative exemption of indefinite duration to all "authorised persons" in relation to a number of pest species, the Wildlife and Countryside Act 1981 was considered to fall foul of this requirement for specific derogations, and the control of pests is now authorised under a scheme of more precise annual licences granted by government departments.[13]

7.4.9 As well as these specific measures to protect birds, the Directive requires Member States to report to the Commission every three years on its implementation and to encourage research on the protection, management and use of birds.[14] It is expressly stated that Member States may introduce stricter measures than those provided for by the Directive.[15]

7.4.10 As in many other cases within the environmental field, the Member States have not been perfect in their implementation of the Directive. The Commission has taken enforcement action against several states which have failed to comply properly with its terms, and a number of cases have reached the

[11] Art. 7(4).
[12] Art. 9.
[13] Under WCA, s.16; see paras. 3.3.7–3.3.8, above.
[14] Art. 12.
[15] Art. 14.

European Court of Justice.[16] Even where appropriate national
laws are in place, there may be problems in enforcing the law at
the local level.

7.4.11   As far as Great Britain is concerned, the provisions in
the Wildlife and Countryside Act 1981, introduced partly to
secure such implementation, do achieve broad compliance with
the Directive, but even after the changes relating to pest
species, some problems remain. The number of Special
Protection Areas so far designated in the United Kingdom has
not yet lived up to expectations. Moreover, as many of them are
protected merely as SSSIs, the position here does not fully live
up to the high standards set by the European Court in the
"Leybucht Dykes" case,[17] nor does it ensure the positive
"upkeep and maintenance" of habitats,[18] unless management
agreements exist to prevent such natural changes as scrub
invading marsh land, etc. Within the existing legislative
structure, the provisions and general aims of the Directive may
be invoked in particular cases to bolster the argument that
where United Kingdom law allows an element of discretion to
an authority, *e.g.* a planning authority considering proposals for
development on a Special Protection Area, then that discretion
should be exercised in favour of conservation.

Habitats and Species Directive

7.4.12   The recent Directive on the Conservation of Natural
Habitats and of Wild Fauna and Flora[19] is more far-reaching
and will in some respects take over from the Birds Directive. It
is based on the Bern Convention[20] and aims to establish a
network of protection for habitats which are of ecological value

---

[16] *E.g.*, *Commission* v. *Belgium* (247/85) [1987] E.C.R. 3029; *Commission* v.
Italy (262/85) [1987] E.C.R. 3073; *Commission* v. *Germany* (412/85) [1987]
E.C.R. 3503 (see further *Commission* v. *Germany* (C–345/92) ECJ March 23,
1993); *Commission* v. *Netherlands* (236/85) [1987] E.C.R. 3989; *Commission* v.
France (252/85) [1988] E.C.R. 2243; *Commission* v. *Netherlands* (C–339/87)
[1990] E.C.R. I–851; *Commission* v. *Germany* (C–288/88) [1990] E.C.R. I–2721;
Commission v. *Italy* (C–157/89) [1991] E.C.R. I–57; *Commission* v. *Italy*
(C–334/89) [1991] E.C.R. I–93; *Commission* v. *Germany* (C–57/89) [1991]
E.C.R. I–883.
[17] *Commission* v. *Germany* (C–57/89) [1991] E.C.R. I–883; see
paras. 5.12.6–5.12.7, above.
[18] Art. 3.
[19] Directive 92/43; subsequent footnotes refer to this Directive unless and until
otherwise stated.
[20] Convention on the Conservation of European Wildlife and Natural
Habitats; see paras. 7.5.15–7.5.21, below.

(in themselves or as the host to threatened species) and to protect rare or vulnerable species of plants and animals from harm. Two novel features of the Directive are the potential for the Community to propose for special protection sites which have not been suggested by the Member State concerned, and the availability of Community funds to support conservation measures.

7.4.13 The overall objective is to "contribute towards ensuring bio-diversity through the conservation of natural habitats and wild flora and fauna."[21] However, in the preamble it is stated that the aim is to "promote the maintenance of biodiversity, taking account of economic, social, cultural and regional requirements, [making] a contribution to the general objective of sustainable development." This formulation, and similar provisions in the text of the Directive itself,[22] will allow Member States considerable room for manoeuvre when it comes to assessing what is required in order to give effect to the general objective. As with the Birds Directive, the scope of this new measure is limited to the European territory of the Member States.[23] Member States should have the appropriate legislative and administrative machinery in place by May 1994, although separate timetables are provided for the designation of special areas.[24]

7.4.14 The targets of the Directive are species and habitats "of Community interest," a concept defined in Art. 1. As far as species are concerned, this term covers those within the Community which are endangered, vulnerable, rare, or endemic and in need of particular attention.[25] Species which are endangered within the Community may be excluded if their presence in the Community is marginal to their natural range and they are not endangered or vulnerable in the broader western palaearctic region. For the United Kingdom this qualification may be of significance, as there are a number of species whose only presence in the Community is in small numbers within Britain, suggesting that they should qualify as endangered, but which are in fact plentiful in other northern lands. Vulnerable species are those believed likely to move into

[21] Art. 2(1).
[22] Art. 2(3).
[23] Art. 2(1).
[24] Art. 23(1); see below for details.
[25] Art. 1(g).

the endangered category in the near future "if the causal factors continue operating," presumably a reference to whatever causal factors are producing a decline in the species. Rare species are ones which are not at present endangered or vulnerable, but are at risk through being found in restricted geographical areas or being thinly scattered over a more extensive range. Species in all four of these categories can be listed for direct protection and to ensure protection for their habitat.

7.4.15 The habitat provisions are directed both at particular habitat types and at the habitat necessary for species of Community interest. Habitat types of Community interest which can qualify for listing are those which are in danger of disappearance in their natural state, have a small natural range by reason of their intrinsically restricted area or as a result of their regression, or present outstanding examples of one or more of the five listed biogeographical regions: Alpine, Atlantic, Continental, Macaronesian (*i.e.* the Azores) and Mediterranean.[26] The other category of habitats which can be listed is that which stipulates the homes of the listed species of Community interest.[27]

7.4.16 The Annexes of the Directive contain lists of the habitats and species which meet these criteria.[28] Annex I lists almost 200 habitat types of Community interest, varying from fairly general descriptions such as estuaries and large shallow inlets or bays, through more specific instances, *e.g.* Caledonian forest, to very detailed examples, *e.g. Tetraclinis articulata* forests in Andalusia. Under a quarter of these are probably present in the United Kingdom. Annex II lists the many species of animals and plants whose habitats are to be protected, with a separate list of plants for the Azores. Annex IV lists the animals and plants which are to be given direct protection. The lists of animals and plants contain only a few species found in the United Kingdom, the emphasis being more on Mediterranean species. Generally the animal lists cover a broad range of animals, including not only mammals which have in the past tended to dominate such lists, but many reptiles, amphibians, fish, insects, molluscs and other invertebrates. All of the lists are, however, somewhat difficult to use, requiring considerable

---

[26] Art. 1(c).
[27] Art. 4(1).
[28] There are some errors in the lists as published in the *Official Journal*.

knowledge of the ecological classification of habitats,[29] and giving only the Latin names of individual species.[30] As usual, there is provision for the lists to be amended.[31]

7.4.17 For the habitat provisions, there are marked in Annexes I and II the "priority natural habitat types" and the "priority species" identified in accordance with the definitions in Art.1. In both cases the crucial points are that either the habitat or species is in danger of disappearing and that there is a particular responsibility on the Community for their conservation in view of the proportion of their natural range which falls within its territory.[32]

7.4.18 The aim of the habitat provisions is to establish a coherent network of Special Areas of Conservation under the title "Natura 2000," enabling the conservation and restoration of the natural habitat types listed in Annex I and of the habitats necessary for the species listed in Annex II.[33] Each Member State is required to contribute to the creation of this network in proportion to the representation within its territory of the habitats concerned, primarily through the recognition of Special Areas of Conservation.

7.4.19 The designation of such areas is a two-stage process. In the first place, each Member State has to propose to the Commission a list of sites identified by the application of the criteria set out in Annex III (Stage I);[34] these criteria cover such factors as the degree of conservation and potential for restoration of the habitat, the extent to which the habitat is representative of the habitat type, the proportion of the habitat or of the local population of the particular species present in relation to their presence in the state as a whole, and a global assessment of the value of the site for conserving the habitat type or species. The grounds for proposing each site must be fully stated, and any priority habitat types or habitats for

---

[29] The classification used is that produced through the Community's Corine programme, established under Council Decision 85/338.

[30] From frustrating experience immediately after the Directive was made, it takes several days of consulting a wide range of books and experts to discover what some of the listed species are, far less whether they are likely to occur in the U.K., although a list was being prepared by the J.N.C.C.

[31] Art. 19.

[32] Art. 1(d), (h).

[33] Art. 3(1).

[34] Art. 4(1).

priority species must be identified in the proposal. This stage is to be initially completed by May 1995, although the process should be a continuing one.

7.4.20 The second stage involves the Commission preparing, from the individual lists and in agreement with each Member State, a draft list of sites of Community importance.[35] This selection is to be carried out in accordance with the criteria set out in Annex III (Stage II), which require the selection of all sites containing priority habitats or species, and consideration of the relative value of the site at national level, the situation of the site on migration routes or as part of a continuous ecosystem straddling national frontiers, the total area of the site, the number of habitat types or species present and its global ecological value. However, where the sites containing one or more priority habitat type or species amount to more than 5 per cent. of the national territory of a state, that state can request the flexible application of these criteria. The final list of sites selected as of Community importance is to be adopted by May 1998[36] by the Council of Ministers following consideration by a committee chaired by a member of the Commission and comprising representatives of the Member States.[37] The Committee and the Council can act on the basis of qualified majority votes.

7.4.21 This designation procedure obviously leaves the prime initiative in the hands of the Member State, and the interests of individual states are further protected by the potential for the rules to be relaxed if more than 5 per cent. of a state is likely to be designated. However, in a novel feature of this Directive, the Commission has "in exceptional cases" the power to initiate the designation of a site containing priority habitat or species and which the Member State has failed to mention.[38] Consultations are to take place (for up to six months), but ultimately (within three further months) the Council, acting unanimously, can take the final decision on including the site. The requirement for unanimity in effect preserves the Member State's veto over the designation of sites in its territory, but the potential for an outside body to intervene in the selection of such sites is a major innovation.

[35] Art. 4(2).
[36] Art. 4(3).
[37] Arts. 20, 21.
[38] Art. 5.

7.4.22 Once a site has been fully recognised at Community level, the Member State must designate it as a Special Area of Conservation as soon as possible and within six years at most,[39] giving priority according to the importance of the site for the listed habitat and species and for the coherence of Natura 2000 and to any threats to which the site is exposed.[40] The consequences of such designation are that the state shall establish the necessary conservation measures, inluding management plans and appropriate statutory, administrative or contractual measures to meet the ecological needs of the site. In particular steps are to be taken to avoid the deterioration of the habitat and the disturbance of the species for whose benefit the habitat has been designated.[41] These provisions for the protection of sites are to replace the provisions relating to Special Protection Areas under the Birds Directive.[42]

7.4.23 Where any plan or project other than one directly connected with the management of the site is likely to have a significant effect on the site,[43] it must be subject to a full assessment of its implications for the conservation objectives of the site. As a general rule only if it will not affect the integrity of the site can approval for the project be given.[44] However, despite a negative assessment, if there are no alternative solutions, a plan or project may be carried out for imperative reasons of overriding public interest, including social and economic ones. In such a case, appropriate compensatory measures are to be taken by the state to ensure that the overall coherence of Natura 2000 is not harmed. Where a site contains a priority habitat or species, the only overriding factors which are acceptable without seeking an opinion from the Commission are those relating to human health or public safety, or to environmental benefits of primary importance.[45] In this way the

---

[39] Action is likely long before then, but even without any failure to implement the Directive, it may still be 2004 before sites are fully designated at Community and national level.

[40] Art. 4(4).

[41] Art. 6(1), (2).

[42] Art. 7.

[43] Note that there is no requirement for the project to be on the site or even neighbouring it; what counts is that the site will be affected.

[44] Art. 6(3); it is further stated that the authorities should give approval "if appropriate, after having obtained the opinion of the general public," an unclear provision which may be satisfied by the degree of advertisement, etc., which applies to projects undergoing a standard environmental assessment (see section 8.3, below).

[45] Art. 6(4).

Special Areas of Conservation are to be given very considerable protection from development which might damage them.

7.4.24 Member States are to be assisted in fulfilling their obligations to conserve the Special Areas of Conservation by the availability of Community funds.[46] Each state is to submit to the Commission estimates of the co-financing considered necessary to allow it to meet its obligations, and after full discussions, a "prioritized action framework of measures" to be taken when the sites in question are designated. Final decisions in the light of the funds available rest with the Council acting after consideration of the issues by the Committee referred to above.[47]

7.4.25 Apart from their obligations with regard to Special Areas of Conservation, Member States are required generally to endeavour to improve the ecological coherence of Natura 2000 by maintaining and developing features of the landscape of major importance for wild fauna and flora.[48] Where they consider it necessary, land use planning and development policies should encourage the management of features of value to wildlife, as being essential for the migration, dispersal and genetic exchange of wild species.[49] The features identified are those whose linear or continuous structure offers corridors or pathways for wild species (*e.g.* rivers and their banks, traditional forms of field boundary) or which act as stepping stones (*e.g.* ponds or small woods). The obligation here is not strong and leaves ample discretion to the Member States, but if the United Kingdom is to implement this measure, the fate of such features should at least become a factor in the development of planning and related policies.

7.4.26 The Commission, in conjunction with the Committee established under the Directive, is to review periodically the contribution of Natura 2000 towards the achievements of the general objectives of the Directives.[50] Such reviews may consider the declassification of Special Areas of Conservation where warranted by natural developments. To inform such reviews and other decision-making, *e.g.* in relation to the

---

[46] Art. 8.
[47] See para. 7.4.20, above.
[48] Art. 3(3).
[49] Art. 10.
[50] Arts. 9, 21.

measures necessary for the species given direct protection as discussed below, Member States are required to undertake surveillance of the conservation status of the habitats and species covered by the Directive.[51]

7.4.27 The measures designed to protect particular species of plant follow a standard pattern. For the species listed in Annex IV(b), Member States are to take the requisite steps to prohibit their deliberate picking, collecting, cutting, uprooting or destruction in their natural range in the wild.[52] Also to be prohibited are the keeping, transport, sale, offer for sale or exchange of specimens taken in the wild, except those legally taken before the Directive is implemented.

7.4.28. The measures relating to animals are more complex. The main provision requires the protection of the species listed in Annex IV(a).[53] This requires the prohibition of all forms of deliberate capture or killing in the wild, or deliberate disturbance of these species especially during periods of breeding, rearing, hibernation or migration, and of deliberate destruction or taking of eggs in the wild,[54] as well as the banning of the keeping, transport, sale and offer for sale or exchange of specimens taken from the wild, except for those taken lawfully before the Directive is implemented.

7.4.29 These measures follow the standard pattern for such protective legislation, but there are two further requirements. First, Member States should prohibit the deterioration or destruction of breeding sites or resting places of these species.[55] Although some derogations may be allowed,[56] this is a potentially significant provision, especially as the prohibition is not restricted to *deliberate* deterioration or destruction, and reflects the general awareness throughout the Directive of the importance of directing the law at the conservation of habitat if nature conservation measures are to be effective. Secondly, states are required to establish a system to monitor the

[51] Art. 11.
[52] Art. 13.
[53] Art. 12.
[54] Birds are not included in the Annex, remaining subject to the separate Birds Directive, but virtually all of the non-mammalian species listed are oviparous.
[55] Art. 12(2).
[56] See below.

incidental capture and killing of the listed species, and to undertake research or conservation measures to ensure that the incidental capture and killing does not have a significant negative impact on the species.[57]

7.4.30 Annex V contains a list of animals and plants which are not automatically entitled to protection. However, if a Member State deems it necessary in the light of its general surveillance of conservation matters, it is to take measures to ensure that any taking in the wild or exploitation of a species is compatible with its being maintained at a favourable conservation status.[58] The protective measures may include regulations regarding access to property, temporary or local prohibitions of the taking of specimens in the wild or of exploiting particular populations, regulation of the periods and methods permitted for taking specimens, the establishment of licensing or quota systems, regulation of the purchase, sale, offering for sale and keeping of specimens, and the application of hunting and fishing rules which take account of conservation. The measures may also include strictly controlled captive breeding and artifical propagation schemes with a view to reducing the taking of specimens in the wild, and should include an assessment of the effect of the measures adopted.

7.4.31 Member States may claim exceptions from the provisions offering direct protection to the species in Annexes IV and V. Such derogations are admissible only where they are not detrimental to the maintenance of the affected population at a favourable conservation status, where no satisfactory alternative exists, and where they are claimed on one of the specified grounds.[59] These permit derogations: in the interests of protecting wild fauna and flora and in conserving natural habitats; to prevent serious damage, in particular to crops, livestock, forests, fisheries and water; in the interests of public health and public safety; for other imperative reasons of overriding public interest, including those of a social or economic nature and the achievement of beneficial consequences of primary importance to the environment. Also covered is action taken for research and education, and for repopulating an area or reintroducing species (including any breeding and artificial propagation which may be necessary).

---

[57] Art. 12(4).
[58] Art. 14; "favourable conservation status" is defined in Art. 1(e).
[59] Art. 16(1).

Apart from these specific grounds, Member States are permitted to allow under strictly supervised conditions, on a selective basis and to a limited extent, the taking of Annex IV species in the limited numbers determined by the appropriate national authorities.

7.4.32 Every two years the Member States must submit to the Commission a report on the derogations applied, giving details of the species affected, the reasons for the derogation, including where appropriate a reference to the alternatives considered and scientific data employed, the means of capturing or killing any animal which are permitted, the authority empowered to regulate and supervise the exceptions and the results of their supervision.[60] Within 12 months the Commission must give its opinion on the report and enforcement action may follow if the Commission considers that a state is in breach of its obligations under the Directive. The wide scope of some of the grounds for permitting exceptions, together with the general statement that social, economic, cultural and local factors are to be taken into account,[61] means that despite the apparently rigid rules laid down in the Directive, Member States will in fact enjoy a considerable discretion when it comes to carrying these provisions into practice.

7.4.33 In any case where the killing or capture of an animal listed in Annexes IV or V is permitted, Member States are to prohibit the use of all indiscriminate means capable of causing the local disappearance of, or serious disturbance to, populations of the animals.[62] In particular Annex VI lists a number of methods to be banned, including explosives, electric devices, tape recorders, blind or maimed decoys, artificial lights and mirrors, night sights, non-selective nets and traps, poisons, gases and automatic and semi-automatic weapons, as well as any killing from aircraft or moving motor vehicles. Derogations are possible in relation to the specific methods listed, but not from the general obligation to prohibit the use of destructively indiscriminate methods.[63]

7.4.34 The Directive contains further provisions relating to information and research. Member States are required to

[60] Art. 16(2), (3).
[61] Art. 2(3).
[62] Art. 15.
[63] Art. 16(1).

prepare a report on the implementation of the Directive every six years, containing information on the impact of the measures and the results of their surveillance[64] of the species and habitats affected.[65] On the basis of these reports, which are to be accessible to the public, the Commission is to prepare a composite report for presentation to the Member States, the European Parliament, the Council and the Economic and Social Committee.[66] More generally, the Member States and Commission should encourage research and scientific work related to the objectives of the Directive, ensuring the exchange of information and coordination of work.[67] Particular attention should be paid to transboundary cooperation and scientific work relating to the conservation of Special Areas of Conservation and other features of landscape valuable to wildlife.

7.4.35 The Habitats and Species Directive establishes another layer of protected areas, but will perhaps have as much impact in its broader obligations to take nature conservation into account and in its emphasis on the need to conserve habitats in themselves and as the breeding and resting places of protected animals. Although there are various provisions which ensure a degree of discretion for the Member States and allow for economic and social interests to be taken into account in competition with the claims of nature conservation, some response in domestic law can be expected. The broad framework of the Wildlife and Countryside Act 1981 and related provisions means that to a considerable extent British law already meets the Directive, especially in relation to the direct protection of the comparatively few British species which are listed.

7.4.36 However, if the provisions on the protection of habitat are to be properly implemented some legislative changes may be necessary, especially to ensure the positive management of protected habitat, *e.g.* to prevent its natural deterioration, and the conservation of marine areas. The existing SSSI regime will not always offer a sufficient degree of protection for sites designated as Special Areas of Conservation, but that for National Nature Reserves probably will suffice. Significant policy changes might also be required to ensure that the

[64] See para. 7.4.26, above and Art. 11.
[65] Art. 17(1).
[66] Art. 17(2).
[67] Art. 18.

discretion of planning authorities, etc., is exercised in accordance with the obligations under the Directive, particularly within designated areas. Consultation papers on this issue were issued in October 1993, proposing a number of minor legislative changes.

INTERNATIONAL OBLIGATIONS

7.5.1 As a party to a number of treaties, the United Kingdom has accepted obligations in international law with respect to nature conservation. Unlike the provisions of European Community law, the terms of these treaties are not part of the law which can be relied on in the British courts. It is only if an Act of Parliament has been passed to incorporate such terms into domestic law, as has happened with the Antarctic Treaty Act 1967, that the treaties have any legal effect within the United Kingdom. Nevertheless, the fact that the government is bound by these obligations at the international level should have a significant impact in the policy and legislation which are adopted here.

7.5.2 At the international level, there is no strict monitoring or enforcement mechanism to ensure that states are fully complying with their treaty obligations.[68] Moreover, many of the provisions in treaties in the environmental field are what is described as "soft law," *i.e.* they take the form of provisions which are very general in their phrasing and exhortatory in their tone, setting out broad aims and intentions rather than creating precise rules and obligations which it is intended should be enforced. Critics can therefore argue that these treaties are not "law" at all and essentially worthless.

7.5.3 Although the weaknesses of the international law must be acknowledged, the treaties which exist do play an important role. They provide the framework for international cooperation in the field of nature conservation, cooperation which is essential if long-term conservation measures are to be taken on a regional or global scale.[69] This cooperation can take many

---

[68] See generally S. Lyster, *International Wildlife Law* (1985), chaps. 1 and 14.
[69] See generally P.W. Birnie & A.E. Boyle, *International Law and the Environment* (1992).

forms, from providing protection to migratory species throughout their range, to ensuring practical support for developing countries to ensure that the demands of economic development do not always override conservation interests. At the very least treaties serve as public declarations of intent on the part of the states concerned, setting a standard against which their conduct can be judged. Some treaties, such as CITES, themselves provide some continuing mechanism, such as a central Secretariat or regular meetings of the parties, to ensure that states cannot simply forget about their terms, and in the modern world pressure groups can be relied on to draw attention to governmental failings. All governments are sensitive to criticism that they are in breach of their international obligations.

7.5.4 Perhaps more in the political than in the legal world, treaties do play a significant role in shaping the conduct of states, and provide strong bargaining counters when one state is trying to influence or seek cooperation from others. In a similar way, although the United Kingdom's treaty obligations lack legal force within this country, they have helped to shape domestic law and the need to comply with international obligations can be a strong argument in persuading the government to act in a particular way, even though there may be no realistic fear of any sanction being imposed if the obligation is broken.

7.5.5 The following conventions are discussed as examples of the main conservation treaties to which the United Kingdom is a party. There are many more agreements. Some are of largely historical interest, *e.g.* the late nineteenth-century agreements on sealing in the northern Pacific,[70] whereas others are very much the subject of heated current debate, *e.g.* the International Convention for the Regulation of Whaling.[71] The impact during the past ten years of the resolutions of the International Whaling Commission established by that treaty illustrate the power which such international agreements and organisations can have, as well as the ultimate weakness arising from the absence of direct, formal sanctions to ensure that decisions are observed. A number of other treaties deal directly with nature

---

[70] See, *e.g.* the Behring Sea Award Act 1894 and the Seal Fisheries (North Pacific) Acts 1895 and 1912.
[71] Agreed in 1949; see Lyster, *op. cit.*, chap. 2.

conservation, *e.g.* the Bonn Convention,[72] whilst many more, *e.g.* those relating to pollution of the seas and greenhouse gases, will also have an effect on the conservation of wild flora and fauna.

World Heritage Convention

7.5.6 The Convention Concerning the Protection of the World Cultural and Natural Heritage was agreed in 1972 under the auspices of UNESCO.[73] The Convention is based on the idea that certain great treasures of the world, such as the Taj Mahal and the Grand Canyon, constitute parat of the heritage not merely of one state but of mankind as a whole. Accordingly, such treasures should be given international recognition and protection, and the international community should provide positive and practical assistance to ensure their conservation. The aim is to ensure the long-term conservation of the outstanding natural and man-made features of the world.

7.5.7 The Convention imposes a general obligation on parties to ensure the identification, protection, conservation and transmission to future generations of the cultural and natural heritage situated in their territory.[74] The natural heritage is defined as: natural features consisting of physical or biological formations of outstanding universal value from the aesthetic or scientific point of view; geological and physiographical formations and precise areas which constitute the habitat of threatened species of animals and plants of outstanding value from the point of view of science or conservation; natural sites or precise areas which are of outstanding universal value from the point of view of science, conservation or natural beauty.[75] The definition thus covers aesthetic merits as well as scientific ones.

7.5.8 In relation to this heritage, the parties are to ensure that effective and active measures are taken for the protection, conservation and presentation of the heritage in their territory.[76] As far as possible, each party should adopt a general policy

[72] Convention on the Conservation of Migratory Species of Wild Animals; see Lyster, *op. cit.*, chap. 13.
[73] See Lyster, *op. cit.*, chap. 11.
[74] World Heritage Convention, Art. 4; the words used require states to "do all [they] can to this end, to the utmost of [their] resources;" subsequent footnotes refer to this convention unless and until otherwise stated.
[75] Art. 2.
[76] Art. 5.

integrating the protection of the heritage into its comprehensive planning programmes, establish services for the protection, etc., of the heritage, undertake research and develop operating methods to counteract dangers to the heritage, take legal, administrative, financial and scientific measures to ensure the identification, protection and rehabilitation of the heritage and foster the establishment of training for the protection, etc., of the heritage. Parties should also endeavour, particularly through education and information, to strengthen appreciation and respect by their peoples of the cultural and natural heritage and to keep the public broadly informed of the dangers threatening the heritage and the activities carried out under the Convention.[77]

7.5.9 In practice these obligations are focused on the sites which have been accepted for the World Heritage List, as discussed earlier,[78] but they do apply more generally and do require measures to identify the outstanding features within each state and to conserve them pending consideration for the List. With regard to other states, the parties are required to offer assistance when requested in the identification, protection, etc., of the heritage of other states, and to refrain from any deliberate measures which might damage that heritage directly or indirectly.[79] The obligation to offer assistance is given more tangible form through the World Heritage Fund,[80] to be used for financial or other assistance to states undertaking appropriate measures for the benefit of their heritage.[81] Parties may also take an active role in furthering the aims of the Convention by participating in the World Heritage Committee which is responsible for deciding on which sites are to be listed and on the use of the Fund and other forms of international assistance.[82]

7.5.10 Through the World Heritage Convention, the fate of the natural and man-made treasures of the world legitimately become the concern of the international community as a whole, not merely an internal matter for the state where each lies. For developing countries this concern can take the tangible form of

---

[77] Art. 27.
[78] See paras. 5.12.11–5.12.13, above.
[79] Art. 6.
[80] Arts. 15–18.
[81] Arts. 19–26.
[82] Arts. 8–14.

financial and technical support to ensure the conservation of those treasures. For the developed world, the international attention should ensure that states live up to their declared intentions of ensuring proper protection for the sites identified. Any detailed conservation measures will remain a matter for the particular state, but the obligations in the Convention present a standard against which they can be judged by the public and by other states.

Ramsar

7.5.11 The Convention on Wetlands of International Importance Especially as Waterfowl Habitat was signed in 1971 in the town of Ramsar in northern Iran, whence it takes its common name. The loss of wetlands through drainage, development and pollution was identified as being a major and widespread occurrence, threatening many species of plants and animals. The impact of such loss of habitat may be felt far distant from the wetlands themselves, as such habitat may provide breeding, feeding and resting grounds for animals, fish and birds which travel far from a particular site in their life cycles or annual migrations. The Convention imposes fairly general obligations, centred on the identification of particular sites to be designated by the parties as Wetlands of International Importance.[83]

7.5.12 For the purposes of Ramsar, "wetlands" is given a broad definition covering areas of marsh, fen, peatland or water, natural or artificial, permanent or temporary, with water that is static or flowing. The water may be fresh, salt or brackish and the definition includes marine areas where the depth of water at low tide does not exceed six metres.[84] In relation to all wetlands in their territory, parties should formulate and implement their planning to promote as far as possible the wise use of wetlands,[85] and should promote the conservation of wetlands and waterfowl[86] by establishing nature reserves and providing for their wardening.[87] Parties must also encourage research and the exchange of data and publications relating to wetlands and their flora and fauna,[88] promote the

[83] See generally, Lyster, *op. cit.*, chap. 10.
[84] Ramsar Convention, Art. 1(1); subsequent footnotes refer to this convention unless and until otherwise stated.
[85] Art. 3(1).
[86] Defined as "birds ecologically dependent on wetlands"; Art. 1(2).
[87] Art. 4(1).
[88] Art. 4(3).

training of personnel competent in relevant research, management and wardening,[89] and should endeavour through management to increase the waterfowl populations on appropriate wetlands.[90] International consultation and cooperation are required, especially where parties share a water system.[91]

7.5.13 Each party is also bound to designate suitable wetlands for inclusion in the List of Wetlands of International Importance, as discussed in Chapter 5.[92] The conservation of these wetlands should be promoted and their condition monitored,[93] and compensatory measures taken if a party in its "urgent national interest" deletes any wetland from the List or restricts it.[94] The List is to be maintained by a bureau operated by the IUCN,[95] and conferences of the parties can be called to discuss the implementation of and amendments to the Convention, and other related matters.[96]

7.5.14 The obligations imposed by Ramsar are not particularly strong, requiring the promotion and encouragement of and endeavour towards the stated aims, rather than demanding more specific action. Although its terms may not provide any strict legal protection, nevertheless, by focusing attention on the plight of wetlands and establishing the List conferring international status on particular sites, the Convention should ensure that the parties cannot ignore the fate of wetlands and should pay some heed to their conservation in their policy and legislation. The extent to which this will be reflected in practice will obviously depend on the importance of nature conservation in the political battles within each state.

Bern Convention

7.5.15 The Convention on the Conservation of European Wildlife and Natural Habitats was agreed in Bern in 1979,[97]

---

[89] Art. 4(5).
[90] Art. 4(4).
[91] Art. 5.
[92] Art. 2; see paras. 5.12.8–5.12.10, above.
[93] Art. 3.
[94] Art. 4(2).
[95] Arts. 2(1), 8.
[96] Art. 6; it is expressly provided that the parties' representatives should include experts on wetlands and waterfowl (Art. 7(1)).
[97] See Lyster, *op. cit.*, chap. 8.

under the auspices of the Council of Europe.[98] It aims to conserve wild flora and fauna and their habitats, especially where this will require the cooperation of several states and particularly with regard to endangered and vulnerable species.[99] The Convention has played a major role in inspiring and providing the formulation for the European Community Directives on Wild Birds and on Habitats and Species.[1]

7.5.16 The Convention begins by imposing very general obligations on the parties to maintain the population of wild flora and fauna at, or to adapt it to, a level which corresponds to ecological, scientific and cultural requirements, taking account of economic and recreational requirements.[2] Steps are to be taken to promote national policies for the conservation of wild flora, wild fauna and natural habitats, while regard is to be paid to the requirements of such conservation in each party's planning and development policies and in measures to control pollution. Each party should also promote education and disseminate general information on the need to conserve species of wild flora and fauna and their habitats.[3] The parties undertake to coordinate their efforts under the Convention in relation to migratory species,[4] and to encourage and coordinate research related to the purposes of the Convention.[5] Also to be encouraged is the reintroduction of native species where this would contribute to the conservation of endangered species, while the introduction of non-native species is to be strictly controlled.[6]

7.5.17 As far as habitat is concerned, the parties are obliged to take appropriate and necessary legislative and administrative measures to ensure the conservation of the habitats of wild flora and fauna, especially those listed in Appendices I and II. As far as possible the deterioration of such habitat should be minimised by conservation requirements being taken into account in planning and development policies. Special attention

[98] The Convention is open to signature by non-members of the Council and indeed by non-European states, as its provisions affect species which travel beyond Europe; Bern Convention, Art. 20; subsequent footnotes refer to this convention unless and until otherwise stated.
[99] Art. 1.
[1] See section 7.4, above.
[2] Art. 2; *cf.* Birds Directive, Art. 2 (para. 7.4.3, above).
[3] Art. 3.
[4] Art. 10.
[5] Art. 11(1).
[6] Art. 11(2).

should be paid to sites used by migratory species, and states should coordinate their efforts in relation to habitats in frontier areas.[7] Such provisions, whilst ensuring that regard should be had to the needs of conservation, do allow very considerable discretion to each party and avoid any identification of particular sites at an international level.

7.5.18 The particular species of plants in Appendix I and animals in Appendix II are to be given special protection by appropriate legislative and administrative measures. For the plants listed in Appendix I, the deliberate picking, collecting, cutting or uprooting is to be prohibited, as is their possession and sale.[8] For the animals in Appendix II, the measures should include the prohibition of all forms of deliberate capture, keeping and killing, deliberate damage to or destruction of breeding or resting sites, deliberate disturbance which is significant in relation to the aims of the Convention, deliberate destruction, taking or keeping of eggs, and the possession and trading in the animals, alive or dead.[9]

7.5.19 For a further category of animals, listed in Appendix III, measures are to be taken to ensure their protection.[10] The exploitation of such animals is permitted, but must be controlled by measures such as close seasons, temporary or local prohibitions on exploitation to allow populations to recover, and regulation of their sale and related activities.[11] Where capture and killing is permitted, either of Appendix III animals or those of Appendix II under special exceptions, all indiscriminate methods are to be prohibited, as are those capable of causing serious disturbance to the local population and those methods specified in Appendix IV.[12]

7.5.20 Exceptions to the protective measures discussed above are permitted where there is no other satisfactory solution, the exception will not be detrimental to the survival of the population concerned, and is required on one of the following grounds:

(a)   the protection of flora and fauna;

---

[7] Art. 4.
[8] Art. 5.
[9] Art. 6.
[10] As opposed to the "special protection" for Appendix II animals.
[11] Art. 7.
[12] Art. 8.

(b) the prevention of serious damage to crops, livestock, forests, fisheries, water and other forms of property;
(c) in the interests of public health and safety, air safety or other overriding public interests;
(d) research, education, repopulation and reintroduction;
(e) judicious and selective exploitation of certain species under strictly supervised conditions.[13]

These exceptions must be notified in reports made every two years to the Standing Committee established under the Convention.

7.5.21 As mentioned earlier, these provisions are similar to some of the more general obligations now imposed under the European Community's Birds and Habitats Directives. As these Directives have legal force within the United Kingdom and impose more specific obligations, especially in relation to particular sites and the scrutiny of any exceptions to the protection provided, the practical impact of the Convention is likely to be further diminished. However, in extending beyond the twelve Member States the commitment to and cooperation on nature conservation, and in providing a further layer of legal recognition for the needs of certain endangered species, the Convention does still play a role in the conservation of Europe's natural heritage.

Convention on Biological Diversity

7.5.22 The Convention on Biological Diversity was signed at the Earth Summit in Rio de Janeiro in June 1992. The aims of the Convention are the conservation of biological diversity, the sustainable use of its components ("genetic resources, organisms ... or any other biotic component of ecosystems with actual or potential use or value for humanity"), and the fair and equitable sharing of the benefits of such use, including access to biological resources and the transfer of technology.[14] Much of the Convention, and most of the controversy surrounding it, concerns the provisions on access to biological resources, the exploitation of which is clearly stated to be a sovereign right of the state where they are found.[15] Other states should have

[13] Art. 9; *cf.* Habitats and Species Directive, Art. 16 (see para. 7.4.31, above).
[14] Convention on Biological Diversity, Art. 1; subsequent footnotes refer to this convention unless and until otherwise stated.
[15] Art. 3.

access to a nation's resources on an agreed basis, which should include arrangements for sharing the benefits of their use and the transfer of the technology to exploit them.[16] In particular the developed countries should provide technical and financial assistance to the developing countries to further the aims of the Convention.[17]

7.5.23 As far as conservation is concerned, there are broadly phrased obligations on all of the signatories, obligations qualified by phrases such as "as far as possible and appropriate." National strategies for the conservation and sustainable use of biological resources should be developed and integrated into the other policies of the state.[18] Protected areas should be established, and in the areas surrounding these environmentally sound and sustainable development should be promoted to further their protection. Degraded ecosystems should be rehabilitated, threatened species should be protected and the introduction of damaging aliens should be prohibited or controlled.[19] Away from the habitats in question, but preferably within the state of origin, steps should be taken to further such *in situ* measures,[20] and to promote research and training and public education and awareness.[21] Economically and socially sound measures that act as incentives for the conservation and sustainable use of biological resources should be adopted.[22] Environmental impact assessment should be employed where proposed projects are likely to have significant adverse effects on biological diversity, such effects should be minimised, and responses prepared to emergencies, natural or man-made, presenting grave and imminent danger to biological diversity.[23]

7.5.24 All of these measures, and the general exhortation to international cooperation,[24] are too vague to have any direct legal significance here. The Convention is primarily a political

[16] Arts. 15–19.
[17] Art. 20; it is expressly stated that the extent to which the developing world will effectively implement its obligations will depend on the extent to which the developed world effectively implements its commitments in relation to finance and the transfer of technology (Art. 20(4)).
[18] Arts. 6, 10.
[19] Art. 8.
[20] Art. 9.
[21] Arts. 12, 13.
[22] Art. 11.
[23] Art. 14.
[24] Art. 5.

statement, and it remains to be seen whether states are in fact willing to take the measures required of them. It may be that the Convention sets the agenda for further more detailed arrangements, but it is clear that the main focus will continue to be the relationship between the developed and developing countries, and the extent to which the former are prepared to pay, directly or through technology transfer, for the rights to exploit the biological riches of the latter or to insist on the latter foregoing projects for economic development in order to conserve nature. The immediate results of the Convention may be very limited, but it serves to place issues of conservation and sustainable use firmly on the international negotiating table.

Antarctic Treaties

7.5.25 Although unlikely to be of practical relevance to many readers of this book, the various treaties designed to protect the Antarctic environment merit a brief mention as certain key provisions have been incorporated into domestic law. In 1961 the parties to the Antarctic Treaty adopted Agreed Measures for the Conservation of Antarctic Fauna and Flora.[25] These prohibit the killing, taking or disturbance of native mammals and birds in Antarctica and surrounding waters, prohibit the introduction of non-indigenous species, establish specially protected areas, identify specially protected species, and provide for permits to authorise conduct otherwise prohibited. Further international measures have been adopted to take wider conservation measures for the natural environment of the Antarctic, in the form of the Convention for the Conservation of Antarctic Seals, agreed in 1972, and the Convention on the Conservation of Antarctic Marine Living Resources, agreed in 1980.[26]

7.5.26 The Antarctic Treaty Act 1967 has incorporated certain of these provisions into the law of the United Kingdom and

[25] See Sched. 2 to the Antarctic Treaty Act 1967; Antarctic Treaty (Specially Protected Species) Order 1968, S.I. 1968 No. 889; Antarctic Treaty (Agreed Measures) Order 1988, S.I. 1988 No. 586; Antarctic Treaty (Agreed Measures) (No. 2) Order 1988, S.I. 1988 No. 1296.

[26] See Lyster *op. cit.*, Chap. 9; *Handbook of the Antarctic Treaty System (7th ed.)* (1990); G.F. Triggs (ed.), *The Antarctic Treaty Regime—Law, Environment and Resources* (1987); J.A. Gulland, "The Management Regime for Living Resources" and J.N. Barnes, "Legal Aspects of Environmental Protection in Antarctica" in C.C. Joyner & S.K. Chopra (eds.), *The Antarctic Legal Regime* (1988).

gives the power for Orders in Council to implement further measures. Under the 1967 Act[27] it is an offence for any British citizen[28] wilfully to kill, injure, molest or take any native mammal or bird in Antarctica, to bring into Antarctica any non-indigenous plant or animal, or to gather any native plant or drive a vehicle in any of the specially protected areas designated under the Act and the treaty arrangements.[29] No offence is committed if the conduct is authorised by a permit granted by the Secretary of State or his delegates,[30] or in cases of extreme emergency involving the possible loss of human life or the safety of a ship or aircraft.[31] It has subsequently been made an offence for any British citizen to enter any of the specially protected areas without a permit.[32] For the purposes of this legislation, Antarctica was originally defined as the area south of the sixtieth parallel of south latitude, excluding the high seas (where not covered in an ice shelf),[33] but the application of the provisions has been extended to include the high seas south of that parallel as well.[34]

---

[27] Antarctic Treaty Act 1967, s.1.

[28] A detailed definition of those covered by the Act is given in s.1(3) (amended by the British Nationality Act 1981, Sched. 7 and the Schedule to the Hong Kong (British Nationality) Order 1986, S.I. 1986 No. 948).

[29] Antarctic Treaty (Special Protection Areas) Orders 1968, 1971, 1977, 1988 and 1991, S.I.s 1968 No. 888, 1971 No. 1236, 1977 No. 1235, 1988 No. 587, 1991 No. 756.

[30] The permitted delegates are defined in s.3(2).

[31] Antarctic Treaty Act, 1967, s.2.

[32] Antarctic Treaty (Agreed Measures) (No. 2) Order 1988, S.I. 1988 No. 1296, art. 3; no defence based on emergencies is provided.

[33] Antarctic Treaty Act 1967, s.10(5).

[34] Conservation of Antarctic Mammals and Birds (High Seas) Order 1973, S.I. 1973 No. 1755.

8. Miscellaneous

8.1.1 The previous chapters have covered the law which is most directly concerned with nature conservation, but many other areas of the law can also have a considerable impact on conservation and on the fate of wild plants and animals and their habitat. This chapter aims to draw attention to some of these further areas of law. As almost all human activities do or could have some effect on the environment many more areas of legal regulation could be included. Indeed one of the challenges for environmentalists today is to ensure that the political rhetoric on sustainability and environmental concern is matched by an awareness of the ways in which so many areas of policy and law have environmental consequences, albeit unintentionally and indirectly.

8.1.2 Town and country planning is an obvious candidate for a brief treatment here, followed by a more detailed discussion of the linked topic of environmental assessment. As its effect on the countryside is so great, agriculture must be considered, and pollution control is important both for the general health of the environment and to protect sites from particular threats. The control of water resources is crucial to many habitats, while the development of genetic modification has added a new dimension to concerns about contamination of the natural world. Finally the extent to which wildlife can be a legal liability to a landowner is considered.

TOWN AND COUNTRY PLANNING

8.2.1 The system of town and country planning is the most important means by which land use is regulated in this country and is therefore of great importance to nature conservation. We have already seen in Chapter 5 how in many cases provisions designed to conserve habitats operate in conjunction with the planning legislation. This is not the place for a detailed account of the planning system, especially as the subject is so thoroughly covered by other books and journals.[1] Instead, after the briefest of outlines of the system, an indication will be given of the opportunities at various stages in the planning process for nature conservation to be taken into account.

8.2.2 The planning system is operated by a partnership (not always harmonious) of central and local government. General policy is set by the Secretary of State, expressed primarily through the many circulars which are of major importance in determining how the system operates in practice. He also decides appeals against the individual decisions taken by local planning authorities and can "call in" particular cases for his own initial determination. At local level, planning functions are generally divided between the tiers of local government.

8.2.3 In Scotland, most matters, including development control (*i.e.* the determination of individual applications for planning permission) are in the hands of district councils. However, strategic planning, in particular the preparation of structure plans, rests with the regional council, while in Highland, Borders, and Dumfries and Galloway Regions the regional council has sole responsibility for all planning, as do the islands area councils for their areas. In England and Wales, there is a similar divide between the district and county councils except in the metropolitan areas where the London and metropolitan borough councils have sole responsibility. Special rules do or may apply for many specially designated areas, *e.g.* National Parks, urban development areas.

---

[1] In Scotland, E. Young & J. Rowan-Robinson, *Scottish Planning Law and Procedure* (1985); M.E. Deans, *et al.,* in *Stair Memorial Encyclopaedia of the Laws of Scotland* (1991), Vol. 23, "Town and Country Planning" and the journal *Scottish Planning and Environmental Law* (formerly *Scottish Planning Law and Practice*). In England there is a very wide choice of books — the most recent general texts include M. Purdue, *et al., Planning Law and Procedure* (1989); A.E. Telling, *Planning Law and Procedure* (8th ed., 1990); D. Heap, *Outline of Planning Law* (10th ed., 1991); V. Moore, *A Practical Approach to Planning Law* (3rd ed., 1992); there are a number of loose-leaf works and the leading periodical is the *Journal of Environmental and Planning Law*.

8.2.4 The system of town and country planning requires authorities to establish broad plans for their areas, setting out general policies for development.[2] It has recently been expressly provided that "unless material considerations indicate otherwise," individual planning decisions are to be made in accordance with these development plans.[3] As these plans will obviously be of great significance for individual decisions, those with an interest in land use issues must ensure that they take the opportunity to become involved in the making of the plans, as by the time that a specific application comes to be considered it may be too late to raise questions of general policy.

8.2.5 In London and the metropolitan areas of England and Wales there are unitary development plans, but elsewhere the development plans are the combination of structure plans, prepared at the regional or county level, and local plans, prepared at the district level. The structure plan is designed "to provide a strategic policy framework ... for the development and control of the physical environment in the interests of the community",[4] setting out major policies and proposals and providing strategic development control policies, which will also guide the preparation of local plans. The public must have an opportunity to be involved in the making of these plans, and certain issues may form the subject of an "examination in public," a form of public inquiry. Before it can take effect the final plan must be approved by the Secretary of State, who can make modifications to it.

8.2.6 Local plans are more specific, including a map of the area affected, and should provide clear guidance to potential developers and a clear statement of the planning authority's development control policies. Again public participation is required in the formulation of the plan, which must be in conformity with the structure plan for the area (if such a plan exists). Only exceptionally will the Secretary of State's approval be required for the adoption of a local plan. Although the current system of development plans has been in existence since the mid-1970s, several areas are not yet covered by plans, and where plans do exist there is a problem of keeping them up to

[2] TCPSA, Pt. II; TCPA, Pt. II.
[3] *Ibid.*, s.18A (added by Planning and Compensation Act 1991, s.58); *ibid.*, s.54A (added by Planning and Compensation Act 1991, s.26).
[4] SDD Planning Advice Note no. 27, 1981 (Structure Planning), para. 1.

date. There is likely to be considerable pressure for the preparation of the remaining plans and the constant revision of all plans if the recent legislative changes do in practice confer greater weight to development plans in the determination of particular applications.

8.2.7 The most obvious aspect of the planning system is development control, the grant or refusal of planning permission for particular proposals.[5] The most important concept here is "development," as whether or not permission is required for a proposal depends on whether or not it qualifies as "development." In this context "development" is defined as "the carrying out of building, engineering, mining or other operations in, on, over or under land or the making of any material change in the use of any buildings or other land."[6] This definition has given rise to a wealth of case-law, individual cases being complicated by the problems of multiple and ancillary uses and the difficulty of ascertaining the correct area of ground ("planning unit") in relation to which the activity in question should be considered. Only through a study of the case-law can the full meaning of this evolving term be understood.[7]

8.2.8 The scope of "development" is qualified by a number of other provisions. Some things are expressly declared not to amount to development, *e.g.* the use of land for agriculture or forestry, while others are expressly declared to be development, *e.g.* the deposit of waste material (however authorised) to a height above that of the surrounding land.[8] Further qualifications exist through the Use Classes Orders,[9] which provide that a change of use within a particular class, *e.g.* various kinds of shop, or particular categories of industrial uses, is to be taken as not involving development, whilst the General Permitted

---

[5] TCPSA, Pt. III; TCPA Pt. III.

[6] *Ibid.*, s.19(1); *ibid.*, s.55(1).

[7] " 'Development' is a key word in the planners' vocabulary but it is one whose meaning has evolved and is still evolving. It is impossible to ascribe to it any certain dictionary meaning, and difficult to analyse it accurately from the statutory definition."
Lord Wilberforce in *Coleshill and District Investment Co.* v. *Minister of Housing and Local Government* [1969] 1 W.L.R. 746 at p. 763.

[8] TCPSA, s.19(2), (3); TCPA, s.55(2), (3).

[9] Town and Country Planning (Use Classes) (Scotland) Order 1989, S.I. 1989 No. 147; Town and Country Planning (Use Classes) Order 1987, S.I. 1987 No. 764 (amended by Town and Country Planning (Use Classes) (Amendment) Orders 1991 and 1992, S.I.s 1991 No. 1567, 1992 No. 610, 1992 No. 657).

Development Orders[10] grant deemed permission to certain
operations and uses, *e.g.* minor alterations to houses, agricultural and forestry operations, land drainage works. There are
thus several sources to be considered before it can be said with
certainty whether a particular proposal does involve development and thus requires planning permission.

8.2.9 From the point of view of nature conservation, several of
the activities falling outwith the meaning of development, and
hence outwith the planning system, are of considerable
significance, particularly in relation to agriculture and forestry.
It does not amount to a material change of use, and hence is
not development, if what is involved is "the use of land for the
purposes of agriculture or forestry (including afforestation)[11]
and the use for any of those purposes of any building occupied
together with land so used."[12] This means that no permission is
required for converting land to such uses, a change which can
radically transform the nature of the land and the habitats
provided. Equally, the General Permitted Development Orders
grant deemed permission, subject to some limitations, to
agricultural buildings and operations (including mineral workings reasonably necessary for agricultural purposes on that
unit)[13] and to forestry operations and buildings.[14] Thus there is
no need to seek planning permission before carrying out such
operations, even though they fundamentally alter the land
affected, *e.g.* ploughing moorland, clear felling mature woodland. Also of potentially major significance are deemed
permissions (again subject to various limitations) for land

[10] Town and Country Planning (General Permitted Development) (Scotland)
Order 1992, S.I. 1992 No. 223 (amended by Town and Country Planning
(General Permitted Development) (Scotland) Amendment Orders 1992 and
1993, S.I.s 1992 No. 1078, 1992 No. 2084, 1993 No. 1036); Town and Country
Planning General Development Order 1988, S.I. 1988 No. 1813 (amended by
Town and Country Planning General Development (Amendment) Orders 1989,
1990, 1991 and 1992, S.I.s 1989 No. 603, 1989 No. 1590, 1990 No. 457, 1990
No. 2037, 1991 No. 1536, 1991 No. 2268, 1991 No. 2805, 1992 No. 609, 1992
No. 658, 1992 No. 1280, 1992 No. 1493, 1992 No. 1563, 1992 No. 2450).
[11] This definition is not restricted to the land where the trees, crops, etc., are
being grown, and can even include land some distance from the primary site;
Farleyer Estate v. *Secretary of State for Scotland*, 1992 S.L.T. 476.
[12] TCPSA, s.19(2)(*e*); TCPA, s.55(2)(*e*).
[13] Town and Country Planning (General Permitted Development) (Scotland)
Order 1992, S.I. 1992 No. 223 (as amended — see note 10 above), Sched. 1,
Pt. 1; Town and Country Planning General Development Order 1988, S.I. 1988
No. 1813 (as amended — see note 10 above), Sched. 2, Pt. 6.
[14] *Ibid.*, Sched. 1, Part 7; *ibid.*, Sched. 2, Pt. 7.

drainage works,[15] operations carried out by statutory undertakers,[16] operations relating to mineral exploration and ancillary
to mineral workings,[17] and in Scotland the taking of peat for
individual domestic requirements.[18]

8.2.10 If planning permission is required, an application must
be made to the relevant planning authority. Full permission may
be sought, or outline permission, which approves the general
principle of a particular development but leaves detailed aspects
for approval at a later stage, allowing developers to test the
acceptability of a proposal without the effort (and cost) of
preparing fully detailed plans and enabling the final development to be shaped in accordance with the planning authority's
concerns as expressed in the grant of outline permission.
Applications are available for inspection and must generally be
notified to neighbours and in some cases advertised in the press.
Members of the public have the opportunity to make
representations to the planning authority before it decides
whether or not to grant permission. In some instances an
environmental assessment may be necessary.[19]

8.2.11 The authority may grant or refuse permission, or grant
permission subject to conditions. It may also seek to enter an
agreement with the developer to cover related matters which
cannot be dealt with by means of conditions.[20] If a development
goes ahead without planning permission or in breach of
conditions, the authority can take enforcement action, leading
ultimately to criminal prosecution if the developer fails to
comply with the various forms of enforcement notice which can
be served.

8.2.12 If permission is refused, or if the developer is unhappy
with any conditions imposed, the developer can appeal to the
Secretary of State. Although the minister may become
personally involved in major cases, appeals are usually decided
by the reporters (inspectors in England and Wales) appointed to

[15] *Ibid.*, Sched. 1, class 20; *ibid.*, Sched. 2, Pt. 14.
[16] *Ibid.*, Sched. 1, Pt. 13; *ibid.*, Sched. 2, Pt. 17.
[17] *Ibid.*, Sched. 1, Parts 15–19; *ibid.*, Sched. 2, Pts. 19–23.
[18] *Ibid.*, Sched. 1, class 21.
[19] See section 8.3, below.
[20] TCPSA, s.50; TCPA, s.106.

hear them, most commonly on the basis of written representations but sometimes after a public inquiry at which the
developer, the authority and any objectors or others who have
become involved in the process have the opportunity to present
evidence and arguments before the reporter. If permission is
granted, there is no right of appeal to objectors, although they
may seek to challenge the decision by means of judicial review,
a course also open to developers who consider that appeal
proceedings in which they were unsuccessful were flawed.[21]

8.2.13 In addition to the general pattern of development
control described above, special rules apply to regulate
particular aspects of development.[22] As already noted in
Chapter 5, there are special rules for conservation areas and
other areas designated for landscape or similar purposes.
Buildings of special architectural or historical interest can be
listed by the Secretary of State, becoming subject to special
rules designed to conserve them, while trees can become subject
to Tree Preservation Orders.[23] Advertisements and mineral
workings are also governed by special rules. New controls have
also been introduced on the storage and use of hazardous
substances.[24] These require that a special hazardous substances
consent be obtained if any of the prescribed substances is to be
kept or used on land in more than the prescribed quantities.
Transitional arrangements allow existing uses to continue with
the benefit of a deemed consent provided that the authority is
notified within a set time-limit, although the authority has a
discretion to refuse or revoke consent where it considers this
expedient.

8.2.14 The basic planning procedures described above offer
several opportunities for nature conservation to be taken into
account. As planning is undoubtedly a statutory function
relating to land, planning authorities in the exercise of their
powers are under a duty to have regard to conserving the
natural heritage of Scotland (Scotland) or to the desirability of

---

[21] Several statutory procedures are provided for referring matters to the
courts, rather than the general judicial review procedures being used; TCPSA,
Pt. XII, TCPA, Pt. XII.

[22] TCPSA, Pt. IV; TCPA, Pt. VIII, Planning (Listed Buildings and Conservation Areas) Act 1990.

[23] See section 6.4, above.

[24] TCPSA, ss.56A–56O, 97B (added by Housing and Planning Act 1986,
ss.35, 36); Planning (Hazardous Substances) Act 1990.

conserving the natural beauty and amenity of the countryside (England and Wales).[25] Moreover, the EC Habitats and Species Directive[26] requires that land use planning and development policies should encourage the management of features of value to wildlife.[27] Arguments based on nature conservation are thus very relevant to the planning process.

8.2.15 If attention is going to be paid to nature conservation, it is important that it should be considered at an early stage in proceedings. Conservation should not be seen as something to be added on at the last minute once all the important points of a plan or a proposal have been finalised. That is a recipe for conflict. Instead, nature conservation should be one of the fundamental factors considered right from the start, just as is the basic infrastructure provision. If conservation is thought about at this stage, it will often be possible to choose an option which satisfies all sides and achieves real benefits at essentially no cost. Nature conservation should help to shape the final decision, and not be seen as something fighting against it. The following aspects of the planning system offer particular opportunities to take nature conservation into account.

Development Plans
8.2.16 Some heed should be paid to nature conservation in the making and review of development plans.[28] Plans can include policies to protect the most valuable sites, to discourage development likely to be harmful and to preserve the variety of habitats in the relevant area. Such points can be seen as making a worthwhile contribution to the amenity of an area, not as a negative factor. In development plans it is also possible to give positive assistance to nature conservation by ideas such as the preservation of "green corridors," *i.e.* corridors of undeveloped land which link areas of park and countryside. Such corridors are very valuable in providing pathways for wildlife between different areas, enabling plants and animals to colonise new

---

[25] CSA, s.66 (amended by NHSA, Sched. 10); CA, s.11; the references to the natural heritage and the natural beauty of the countryside are expressly stated to include the flora and fauna and geological and physiographical features of the land — see para. 2.2.2, above.

[26] Directive 92/43; see paras. 7.4.12–7.4.36, above.

[27] *Ibid.*, Art. 10.

[28] The regulations for England and Wales expressly require that regard should be had to "environmental considerations" in making plans; Town and Country Planning (Development Plan) Regulations 1991, S.I. 1991 No. 2794, reg. 9(1).

habitats and to recover from any local setbacks, thereby
preserving the value of parks, etc., and are also likely to be of
amenity value as walks, cycle tracks or simply breaks in
otherwise built-up areas.

Planning Applications
8.2.17 Nature conservation is a material consideration in the
determination of individual applications for planning permission.
Conservation arguments may help to bolster the case for or
against a particular development, and may be particularly
relevant where the possibility of alternative sites is considered.
If a proposal will cause serious damage to the natural
environment, permission could be refused. Frequently, though,
a concern for nature can be accommodated by fairly minor
changes to the proposed development or by the imposition of
conditions, *e.g.* ensuring that watercourses are protected, that
areas of a site are left undisturbed, that appropriate restoration
work is carried out after construction is completed. Indeed the
planning legislation includes an express provision that where
appropriate, conditions should be used to ensure the preservation or planting of trees.[29] More generally, it may be possible to
take account of the needs of flora and fauna, not merely
aesthetics, in considering the landscaping, etc., of the final
development, *e.g.* providing for the creation of wildlife ponds
and an appropriate mix of vegetation. Again, such requirements
can be seen as a positive factor for a developer and future
occupiers; they offer good publicity, and should be no more
onerous than the sort of landscaping more commonly carried
out.

Planning Agreements
8.2.18 Planning agreements under s.50 of the Town and
Country Planning (Scotland) Act 1972 and s.106 of the Town
and Country Planning Act 1990 may be made "for the purpose
of restricting or regulating the development or use of the land"
affected. Clearly it is possible to use this device for the purposes
of nature conservation, *e.g.* to ensure appropriate protection or
enhancement of a local habitat, or to secure the long-term
management of a site or cooperation and assistance in the
conservation work being carried out by others. There is a
further possibility in the power of a planning authority at any
time to enter an agreement with a landowner to do whatever is

[29] TCPSA, s.57; TCPA, s.197.

thought necessary to preserve and enhance the natural beauty of the countryside.[30]

Conservation Areas[31]

8.2.19 Although the aim of conservation areas is to protect and enhance areas of special architectural and historic interest, not the natural heritage,[32] the natural environment will often be a significant element in their special features. Large gardens, open spaces and mature trees, may all contribute to the character and appearance of the areas which are to be preserved and enhanced, and all can make a contribution to nature conservation. Action taken to achieve the objectives of a conservation area can also be useful for nature conservation, and this aspect should be taken into account when considering how to deal with such areas.

Tree Preservation Orders

8.2.20 Tree preservation orders are also part of the town and country planning system and, as discussed in Chapter 6,[33] can be used for the benefit of nature conservation, to protect individual trees or, more usefully, groups of trees or small areas of woodland.

ENVIRONMENTAL ASSESSMENT

8.3.1. The modern planning system has always offered an opportunity for the environmental impact of proposed development to be considered, but special emphasis is placed on assessing the environmental consequences of proposals as a result of a European Community initiative on this topic. Under a Directive made in 1985[34] there is a requirement that before certain types of major project are given official approval there should be carried out a thorough assessment of the impact of the project on the environment. This Directive has been

---

[30] CSA, s.49A(2) (added by Countryside (Scotland) Act 1981, s.9 and amended by NHSA, Sched. 10); WCA, s.39.

[31] See para. 5.11.6, above.

[32] TCPSA, s.262(1) (substituted by Town and Country Amenities Act 1974, s.2); Planning (Listed Buildings and Conservation Areas) Act 1990, s.69.

[33] See section 6.4, above.

[34] Directive 85/337; N. Haigh, "Environmental Assessment — The EC Directive" [1987] J.P.L. 4.

implemented in Britain by adding the requirement for an environmental assessment to existing procedures for approval. In most cases the mechanism involved is the planning system, as the projects in question already required planning permission before they could proceed, but for some projects the environmental assessment has had to be grafted on to other procedures.

8.3.2 Directive 85/337 requires that before consent is given, projects likely to have a significant effect on the environment by virtue *inter alia* of their nature, size or location are subjected to an assessment of their effects.[35] The assessment must deal with the direct and indirect effects of the project on human beings, flora and fauna, soil, water, air, climate, the landscape, material assets and cultural heritage.[36] The proposer of the project must supply information on the project and its environmental effects, with any public authorities holding relevant information making that available to him,[37] and the resulting statement should be the subject of consultation with environmental bodies and the public.[38] All of the information gathered through this process must be taken into consideration in the development consent procedure.[39]

8.3.3 This measure therefore does not attempt to state that certain environmental consequences should be avoided. Rather it aims to ensure that those taking the decision on whether or not to approve a project are fully aware of its likely environmental effects so that these can be put in the balance with the other factors — economic, social, perhaps aesthetic — to be considered before the final determination is made. The requirement for public consultation is a significant feature of the process and offers an opportunity for pressure groups and concerned individuals to ensure that environmental considertions are truly taken into account. In order to ensure that this consultation is meaningful, it is expressly stated that the information provided must include a non-technical summary[40] thereby preventing the developer from stifling public comment

[35] Directive 85/337, Art. 2(1).
[36] *Ibid.*, Art. 3.
[37] *Ibid.*, Art. 5.
[38] *Ibid.*, Art. 6; if significant effects are likely to be felt in another Member State, then cross-boundary consultation should also take place (Art. 7).
[39] *Ibid.*, Art. 8.
[40] *Ibid.*, Annex III, para. 6.

by providing a statement which may be technically excellent but is incomprehensible to all but experts in the various scientific fields involved.

8.3.4 The Directive identifies when an environmental assessment is required. It specifies the projects affected, dividing them into two categories. For projects listed in Annex I, an environmental assessment will always be necessary; for those in Annex II, it is only when a particular project in its individual circumstances is likely to have significant effects on the environment that the assessment must be carried out. The requirement does not, however, apply to projects approved by a specific act of national legislation,[41] and there is a power for Member States in exceptional cases to exempt specific projects.[42]

8.3.5 Annex I includes major projects with obvious environmental effects such as oil refineries, power stations, radioactive waste sites, integrated chemical works, motorways, airports, trading ports, and waste disposal installations for the incineration, treatment or landfill of toxic and dangerous wastes. The list of projects in Annex II is longer and much more varied, and only some of the projects in each category will actually require an environmental assessment as being "likely to have significant effects on the environment by virtue *inter alia* of their nature, size or location."[43] More than 80 kinds of project are listed under 12 headings: Agriculture (*e.g.* pig or poultry-rearing installations), Extractive Industry (*e.g.* mining and quarrying), Energy Industry (*e.g.* generating stations and overhead electricity transmission lines), Processing of Metals (*e.g.* iron and steelworks, manufacture and assembly of motor vehicles), Manufacture of Glass, Chemical Industry, Food Industry (*e.g.* packing and canning, slaughter of animals), Textile, Leather, Wood and Paper Industries, Rubber Industry, Infrastructure Projects (*e.g.* industrial estates, urban developments, transport works), Other Projects (*e.g.* holiday complexes, waste disposal installations, waste water treatment plants, storage of scrap iron), Short-term Modifications to Annex I projects.

8.3.6 The requirements of the Directive have been implemented in Great Britain by means of a number of regulations

[41] *Ibid.*, Art 1(5).
[42] *Ibid.*, Art. 2(3).
[43] *Ibid.*, Art. 4(2).

made under the authority of the European Communities Act 1972.[44] This power is limited to the making of legislation necessary to implement Community law, so that the regulations can do no more than is necessary for this purpose. Accordingly the environmental assessment requirements under the British regulations have been limited to the categories of project listed in the Directive, despite the somewhat artificial limits which these impose, *e.g.* salmon farming is included but other fish farming is not. However, in order to make it possible for the requirement to be extended to additional projects, the Planning and Compensation Act 1991 authorises further regulations requiring an environmental assessment in additional cases.[45]

8.3.7 In most cases the projects listed in the Annexes of the Directive were already subject to formal approval through the planning system, so that the environmental assessment procedure has been added to the existing planning process.[46] Special provision has however been necessary for a number of projects which are subject to approval under different statutory procedures or for which there was no formal approval mechanism in place. Thus a requirement for environmental assessment has been added to the special rules for electricity projects,[47] land drainage works,[48] roads,[49] and some harbour

---

[44] European Communities Act 1972, s.2(2).

[45] Planning and Compensation Act 1991, ss.15 (adding s.71A to TCPA), 48 (adding s.26B to TCPSA).

[46] Environmental Assessment (Scotland) Regulations 1988, S.I. 1988 No. 1221, Pt. II (Pt. IV deals with the special position of some new town developments in Scotland); Town and Country Planning (Assessment of Environmental Effects) Regulations 1988, S.I. 1988 No. 1199, (amended by Town and Country Planning (Assessment of Environmental Effects) (Amendment) Regulations 1990 and 1992, S.I.s 1990 No. 367, 1992 No. 1494); S. Mertz, "The European Economic Community Directive on Environmental Assessments: How Will It Affect UK Developers?" [1989] J.P.L. 483.

[47] Environmental Assessment (Scotland) Regulations 1988, S.I. 1988 No. 1221, Pt. III (amended by Electricity Act 1989 (Consequential Modifications of Subordinate Legislation) Order 1990, S.I. 1990 No. 526); Electricity and Pipeline Works (Assessment of Environmental Effects) Regulations 1990 No. 442.

[48] Environmental Assessment (Scotland) Regulations 1988, S.I. 1988 No. 1221, Pt. V; Land Drainage Improvement Works (Assessment of Environmental Effects) Regulations 1988, S.I. No. 1217.

[49] Roads (Scotland) Act 1984, ss.20A, 55A (added by Environmental Assessment (Scotland) Regulations 1988, S.I. 1988 No. 1221, Pt. VI); Highways Act 1980, s.105A (added by Highways (Assessment of Environmental Effects) Regulations 1988, S.I. 1988 No. 1241).

and coastal protection works.[50] For salmon farming in the sea, where there was no existing statutory procedure, the environmental assessment (where necessary) has been made a prerequisite of consent from the Crown Estate Commissioners.[51] For initial afforestation, the assessment has been added to the procedure for the award of a grant by the Forestry Commission, a solution which does not meet the requirements of the Directive as it is possible (although commercially unrealistic) for planting to take place without a grant and therefore to escape the environmental assessment procedure.[52]

8.3.8 The exemption in the Directive for projects specifically authorised by the legislature creates a potential gap in the system in view of the actual and potential use of private legislation procedure to approve major and controversial projects. This gap has been filled by changes to the detailed rules of procedure so that an environmental assessment can now be held as part of the legislative process,[53] and by the Transport and Works Act 1992 which establishes a wholly new procedure for authorising many projects in England and Wales which would previously have been the subject of private legislation. The procedural rules made under the 1992 Act make provision for environmental assessments.[54]

8.3.9 The various sets of regulations all follow the same pattern, giving effect to the main provisions of the Directive as described above. Thus the regulations state the test to be applied in deciding whether an assessment is necessary (namely, is the project one for which an assessment is mandatory in accordance with Annex I of the Directive or if it falls within Annex II, is it likely to have significant effects on the environment?). They then specify in varying degrees of detail the information and issues to be contained in the environmental statement provided by the proposer, the obligations on the

[50] Harbours Act 1964, Sched. 3, Pt. I (amended by Harbour Works (Assessment of Environmental Effects) Regulations 1988 and 1992, S.I.s 1988 No. 1336, 1992 No. 1421); Harbour Works (Assessment of Environmental Effects) (No. 2) Regulations 1989, S.I. 1989 No. 424.
[51] Environmental Assessment (Salmon Farming in Marine Waters) Regulations 1988, S.I. 1988 No. 1218.
[52] Environmental Assessment (Afforestation) Regulations 1988, S.I. 1988 No. 1207; see paras. 6.3.12–6.3.13, above.
[53] See B. Winetrobe, "Environmental Assessment and Private Legislation" (1992) 35 S.P.L.P. 7; J. Rowan-Robinson & B. Winetrobe, "Environmental Assessment and Private Legislation Procedures" (1992) 36 S.P.L.P. 51.
[54] Transport and Works (Applications and Objection Procedure) Rules 1992, S.I. 1992 No. 2902, rules 5, 6.

conservancy councils and other bodies to supply information useful in preparing the statement, the requirements for publicity and consultation and the obligation on the determining authority to take the results of the statement and consultation into account.

8.3.10 A difficulty in many instances is in deciding whether a particular project which falls within Annex II of the Directive meets the test of being "likely to have significant effects on the environment by virtue *inter alia* of its nature, size or location." This is a very vague test, and although various guidance notes have been issued, there remains considerable scope for argument. Large-scale projects and those on sites where there is an SSSI or other conservation or landscape designation are the most likely to meet the test. In the planning system it is possible for a developer to seek an opinion from the planning authority on whether an environmental assessment will be required for a particular application, subject to an application to the Secretary of State for a final direction on the matter.[55] A criticism of some of the other procedures is that the same authority is responsible for deciding whether an assessment is necessary and for considering its results, with no real check on whether it has acted properly, and little opportunity for third parties to become involved.[56] In practice, however, many developers prepare and submit environmental statements even where they may not be required under the legislation.[57]

8.3.11 Whether the United Kingdom has in fact adequately implemented the Directive has given rise to some controversy. It is clear that some of the British legislation took effect only after the date by which the Directive should have been fully implemented,[58] but the source of the most public arguments

[55] Environmental Assessment (Scotland) Regulations 1988, S.I. 1988 No. 1221, regs. 7, 9; Town and Country Planning (Assessment of Environmental Effects) Regulations 1988, S.I. 1988 No. 1199, regs. 5, 6; most of the other regulations contain similar provisions.

[56] But see *Kincardine and Deeside District Council* v. *Forestry Commission*, 1992 S.L.T. 1180.

[57] Details of the cases where environmental assessments have been required or carried out are published intermittently in the *Journal of Planning and Environmental Law, e.g.* [1991] J.P.L. 445.

[58] This was a crucial issue in *Kincardine and Deeside District Council* v. *Forestry Commissioners* (note 56 above) where the disputed application was made during the twelve days between the Directive's deadline for implementation and the British regulations taking effect.

between the government and the European Commission has been the application of the Directive to projects already under consideration before the date for implementation but actually begun only after that date.[59] Such disputes on transitional matters should be resolved or become of no practical relevance in the near future, but there are still points where the British system may not fully meet the Directive's requirements. It has been suggested that in relation to Annex I projects the Directive may have direct effect in the United Kingdom, overriding any inconsistent legislation,[60] but that in relation to Annex II projects there is too much scope for discretion at the national level for direct effect to be granted.[61] It remains to be seen whether any of the disputes will actually lead to authoritative legal pronouncements on aspects of the environmental assessment.

AGRICULTURE

8.4.1 As so much of Britain is actively farmed, changes in agricultural practices have a great impact on nature conservation. Agriculture in turn is greatly affected by the range of subsidies and other aids by means of which governments give effect to their agricultural policies, and by the laws which regulate the rights of agricultural tenants and others involved in the industry. Indeed, changing agricultural practices during the second half of the twentieth century have almost certainly had a greater effect on nature conservation than any other factor. Therefore, any thorough examination of the law affecting nature conservation must at least mention the law relating to agriculture.[62]

8.4.2 The agricultural policy adopted by the British government and by the European Community through the Common

---

[59] See generally J.R. Salter "Environmental Assessment: The Challenge from Brussels" [1992] J.P.L. 14, "Environmental Assessment — the Question of Implementation" [1992] J.P.L. 214, "Environmental Assessment — The Need for Transparency" [1992] J.P.L. 313.

[60] *Twyford Parish Council* v. *Secretary of State for the Environment* [1992] 1 C.M.L.R. 276, (1992) 4 J.E.L. 273 and 298.

[61] *Kincardine and Deeside District Council* v. *Forestry Commissioners* (note 56 above); see (1992) 4 J.E.L. 289 and 298.

[62] See generally, W. Howarth & C.P. Rodgers (eds.), *Agriculture, Conservation and Land Use* (1992).

Agricultural Policy used to be the simple one of maximising production. This has led in Britain to highly mechanised and highly specialised agricultural units which produce high yields but require large fields for intensive crop growing or industrial buildings for intensive livestock rearing, in all cases calling for the substantial use of fertilisers, pesticides and herbicides. Such developments have been encouraged by a range of grants and other aids available to farmers wishing to "improve" their land through the construction of new buildings, drainage, or the cultivation of rough grassland or heath. These changes have been harmful to the "traditional" countryside and to the flora and fauna which it supports.

8.4.3 Now, however, it has been realised that this policy has been too successful. The Community is faced with an overproduction of many agricultural products, which cannot be sold on the open market but which are still paid for in order to prevent agricultural collapse leading to the depopulation of large areas of Europe. It has also been recognised that the incentives to greater intensity and further production are putting the environment at increasing risk. Accordingly, agricultural policies are changing, and one aspect of this is the view that the farmers' role in protecting the rural environment and managing the landscape should be recognised more fully and remunerated accordingly.[63]

8.4.4 This change of attitude is reflected in several specific schemes and in broader measures, such as the obligation on the agriculture ministers to seek a balance between the promotion of agriculture and the conservation and enjoyment of the countryside.[64] Some of the specific schemes are discussed below. In the long term, though, of greater significance will be whether the totality of agricultural reforms affecting policy, subsidies and markets will lead to general changes in practice as thorough as those produced in past decades by the drive for maximum production.

8.4.5 At the Community level an "agri-environment" pro-gramme has been started, with provision for a scheme to

---

[63] EC Commission, *The Development and Future of the CAP — Reflections Paper* (COM (91) 100 Final) and *Follow-up* (COM (91) 258 Final/3).
[64] See para. 2.2.4, above.

encourage agricultural methods compatible with the requirements for the protection of the environment and the maintenance of the countryside.[65] This allows for support to be given to farmers to reduce their use of fertilisers, herbicides and pesticides, to introduce organic methods, to change to less intensive forms of farming, to use farming practices compatible with the maintenance of the countryside, to set aside land for at least 20 years to establish nature reserves and to manage the land for public access and enjoyment.[66] This has produced proposals here for *inter alia* a habitat creation scheme to encourage the long-term withdrawal of land from agriculture to create valuable wildlife habitats.[67]

8.4.6 The most obvious current scheme recognising the relationship between agriculture and nature conservation is that for Environmentally Sensitive Areas.[68] Under a European Community Regulation,[69] Member States were permitted to develop their own schemes to assist farmers who undertake to farm environmentally important areas so as to preserve or improve the environment there. This was given effect here through the system of Environmentally Sensitive Areas introduced by s.18 of the Agriculture Act 1986. This scheme recognises the importance of traditional farming methods in preserving the habitat and landscape in many areas, and within the designated areas offers payments to farmers willing to continue such methods, in order to discourage them from changing to more intensive methods which might offer them a greater yield. The scheme has proved to be popular and has been considerably extended since the first group of designations was made.

8.4.7 Agricultural set-aside schemes have proved to be more controversial.[70] These aim to reduce the overproduction of food in the European Community by giving farmers grants for taking arable land out of production for a number of years. The benefits of such a scheme for nature conservation, and indeed

---

[65] Regulation 2078/92.

[66] *Ibid.*, Art. 2.

[67] Consultation Papers on *Agri-Environment Programme* (1992), from the Scottish Office Agriculture and Fisheries Department.

[68] See section 5.8, above.

[69] Regulation 797/85, Art. 19; replaced by Regulation 2328/91, Title VII.

[70] A.A. Lennon, "Set-aside of Agricultural Land: Policy Practice and Problems" in W. Howarth & C.P. Rodgers (eds.), *Agriculture, Conservation and Land Use* (1992).

for achieving the primary goal of reducing agricultural production, have been subject to considerable debate, but the schemes are a major part of Community policy. The legal basis of the initiative lies in European legislation dealing with a number of aspects of agricultural structures,[71] which now provides for set-aside[72] and includes among its objectives "to contribute to the safeguarding of the environment and the preservation of the countryside."[73] This European initiative has been implemented by the creation of a set-aside scheme in the United Kingdom. Short-term schemes have also been approved.[74]

8.4.8 Under the British scheme,[75] farmers can receive grant aid for setting aside for five years arable land amounting to at least 20 per cent of the arable area of their farms. To set land aside means that it is not to be used for growing crops, but must be used as permanent or rotational fallow, as grazing fallow, as woodland, or for non-agricultural purposes. The detailed rules for fallow land require that plant cover be established on the land and cut at least once a year, that no inorganic fertilisers are used and organic ones only in limited circumstances, that there is no dumping of organic or inorganic material on the land, and that pesticides are not used and only herbicides which operate through the leaves and stems of plants leaving no residue in the soil. These rules are intended to ensure that the soil is not polluted nor suffers excess erosion or leaching, whilst preventing the land being taken over by scrub.

8.4.9 More specific rules are included in the set-aside scheme for the benefit of nature conservation. At the initial stage, land in an SSSI, National Park or the Broads can only be accepted into the scheme if the relevant conservancy council or park authority has been notified, presumably to allow them an opportunity to make representations to the minister if they consider that set-aside is not appropriate.[76] Where land is to be

---

[71] Regulation 2328/91, replacing Regulation 797/85 (as amended); detailed rules for the set-aside schemes are provided in Regulations 1272/88, 1273/88, 3981/89, 3481/90, 466/92.

[72] Title I of Regulation 2328/91, replacing Title 01 of Regulation 797/85, as added by Regulation 1094/88 (see note 71 above).

[73] Regulation 2328/91, Art. 1(1)(iv).

[74] See, *e.g.* Temporary Set-Aside Regulations 1991, S.I. 1991 No. 1847.

[75] Set-Aside Regulations 1988, S.I. 1988 No. 1352 (amended by the Set-Aside (Amendment) Regulations 1989, 1990 and 1991, S.I.s 1989 No. 1042, 1990 No. 1716, 1991 No. 1993).

[76] Set-Aside Regulations 1988, S.I. 1988 No. 1352, reg. 6(3).

used as permanent or rotational fallow, exemptions from the requirement to cut the plant cover at least once a year can be obtained on the basis of a written proposal to create or maintain wildlife habitat on the land.[77] Inorganic fertilisers may be permitted on land which is used as, and managed so as to provide, a feeding ground for over-wintering migratory geese.[78] It can, however, be argued that some of the detailed rules of general application act against the interests of nature conservation as they do not fit the needs of the wildlife likely to benefit from the absence of intensive agriculture, *e.g.* the prescribed dates by which fields must be mown may not give time for ground-nesting birds to rear their broods successfully.

8.4.10 Within the scheme, on and adjacent to land to be left fallow there is an obligation to maintain all existing hedges and rows of trees (including hedgerow trees), all existing lochs, lakes, watercourses, pools and ponds, all existing unimproved grassland, moorland and heath, and all existing vernacular buildings and stone walls.[79] Similar rules apply to land being used as grazing fallow, where there are further prohibitions on irrigation and on the installation of new or the modification of existing drainage systems.[80]

8.4.11 More generally, other agricultural support schemes now include at least some consideration for environmental factors. The Farm and Conservation Grant Scheme in Britain[81] does not extend to offer grants for some agricultural "improvements" which in the past have damaged increasingly rare habitats, *e.g.* moorland and heath are excluded from the grants for the improvement of grassland, while features of the scheme favour traditional and "environmentally-friendly" techniques, *e.g.* considerably higher levels of grant are available for building walls made with traditional materials and for hedges compared to those available for other fencing.[82] Likewise, the Farm

---

[77] *Ibid.*, Sched. 2, para. 5.

[78] *Ibid.*, Sched. 2, para. 7A (added by Set-Aside (Amendment) Regulations 1989, S.I. 1989 No. 1042, reg. 9).

[79] *Ibid.*, Sched. 2, para. 13 (amended by Set-Aside (Amendment) Regulations 1990, S.I. 1990 No. 1716).

[80] *Ibid.*, Sched. 3 (added by Set-Aside (Amendment) Regulations 1990, S.I. 1990 No. 1716).

[81] Farm and Conservation Grant Regulations 1991, S.I. 1991 No. 1630.

[82] *Ibid.*, Sched. 1; as the costs of such work are also higher it may be fairer to say that the increased grants do not strongly discourage, rather than that they positively favour, the use of traditional methods.

Woodland Premium Scheme takes into account the environmental benefits of woodland, not merely its commercial potential.[83]

8.4.12 Particular aspects of agricultural activity which might have implications for nature conservation are also regulated. Some regulatory schemes allow action to be taken which might be prejudicial to the wild flora and fauna, but often limitations are imposed which should reduce the harm resulting. There are detailed legal schemes on animal and plant health which include powers to destroy diseased or suspect animals and plants, including those in the wild.[84] A range of pest control measures allows action to be taken against particular species, primarily rodents, but at the same time places restrictions on the use of indiscriminate measures.[85] The use of pesticides is controlled by Part III of the Food and Environment Protection Act 1985 and associated regulations. Under these provisions pesticides must gain ministerial approval before they can be advertised, sold or used, and the conditions in any approval will include a duty to take all reasonable precautions to safeguard the environment.[86]

8.4.13 Fire has long been used as an agricultural tool, but can be particularly destructive to natural habitats. Legal controls affect both muirburn and the burning of crop residues. As far as muirburn is concerned in Scotland, the basic rule is that it is an offence to make muirburn except before April 16 or after September 30 in any year, although for the proprietor of land (or tenant with the proprietor's approval) the permitted period is extended to April 30, or May 15 for land over 450 metres. A direction from the Secretary of State can extend the generally permitted period until a specified date not later than May 1, or May 16 in the case of land over 450 metres.[87] It is an offence to make muirburn between one hour after sunset and one hour before sunrise, and in all cases the person responsible must notify neighbours and provide sufficient staff and equipment to control the burning operations so as to prevent damage to woodlands and all neighbouring land and property.[88] Making

[83] See para. 6.3.18, above.
[84] Animal Health Act, 1981, see para. 4.5.11, above; Plant Health Act 1967, see paras. 6.2.11–6.2.13, above.
[85] See section 4.5, above.
[86] See para. 4.4.2, above; see also the rules on Nitrate Sensitive Areas (see paras. 8.4.18–8.4.20, below).
[87] Hill Farming Act 1946, s.23 (amended by Agriculture (Adaptation of Enactments) (Scotland) Regulations 1977, S.I. 1977 No. 2007); WCA, s.72).
[88] *Ibid.*, s.25.

muirburn without due care so as to cause damage to adjoining lands is a criminal offence[89] as well as giving rise to civil liability.[90]

8.4.14 In England and Wales the burning of heather, bracken, grass and vaccinium is controlled by regulations made by the Secretary of State.[91] These prohibit burning between March 31 and November 1, or between April 15 and October 1 in upland areas,[92] although a special licence from the Secretary of State can authorise burning at other times.[93] No burning is allowed between sunrise and sunset, neighbours must be notified, sufficient staff and equipment must be provided to control the fires and all reasonable precautions must be taken to prevent injury or damage to adjoining property.[94] The prohibitions do not apply to pleasure grounds, private gardens and allotments,[95] and special rules apply for railway land.

8.4.15 The burning of crop residues is now also subject to strict legal control, as much to prevent nuisance, air pollution and the dangers from smoke obstructing visibility on roads, as to avoid the dangers of fires getting out of control. The Secretary of State has the power to make regulations to prohibit or restrict the burning of crop residues on agricultural land by persons engaged in agriculture,[96] but so far this power has only been exercised in relation to England and Wales.

8.4.16 Under the Crop Residues (Burning) Regulations 1993[97] it is an offence to burn on agricultural land any of the specified crop residues[98] except for the purposes of education or research, or for disease control under statutory notices.[99] Where burning

---

[89] *Ibid.*, ss.25, 27.

[90] *Mackintosh* v. *Mackintosh* (1864) 2 M. 1357; *Lord Advocate* v. *Rodger*, 1978 S.L.T. (Sh.Ct.) 31.

[91] Heather and Grass, Etc. (Burning) Regulations 1986, S.I. 1986 No. 428 (amended by Heather and Grass, Etc. (Burning) (Amendment) Regulations 1987, S.I. 1987 No. 1208), made under the Hill Farming Act 1946, s.20 (amended by Hill Farming (Amendment) Act 1985, s.1).

[92] As defined on maps kept for this purpose; *ibid.*, reg. 2(1).

[93] *Ibid.*, reg. 6; the provisions governing licences are in reg. 7.

[94] *Ibid.*, reg. 5.

[95] *Ibid.*, reg. 3.

[96] EPA, s.152.

[97] S.I. 1993 No. 1366.

[98] Cereal straw or stubble, and residues of oil-seed rape or of field beans or peas harvested dry; *ibid.*, Sched. 1.

[99] Plant Health (Great Britain) Order 1993, S.I. 1993 No. 1320, art. 22.

of these residues is permitted, or where linseed residues are burnt, very detailed requirements must be complied with. These extend to such matters as the times and dates of burning (not at weekends or on bank holidays), the precautions to prevent fire or smoke affecting buildings, trees, hedges, nature reserves, ancient monuments, roads and railway lines, the notice to be given to various authorities, and the fire-fighting equipment and personnel to be available, as well as imposing an obligation to incorporate the ash into the soil within 24 hours.[1] Burning is permitted for the disposal of straw stack remains or broken bales.

8.4.17 Special measures have also been taken to prevent water pollution arising from agricultural activities, particularly in an attempt to control the build-up of nitrates in lochs, rivers and groundwater. As well as its potential to harm human health, the presence of nitrates in water can radically affect the fauna and especially the flora which it supports. The eutrophication of water previously low in nutrients destroys the habitat of many species which have evolved to take advantage of poor conditions and can lead to huge "blooms" of algae, which can stifle all other life in the water and can in themselves be poisonous to animals and man. This phenomenon is largely attributable to years of intensive cultivation, as both inorganic fertilisers and natural processes, working on the much increased volumes of vegetable matter, have led to nitrates entering and accumulating in the water system. Any measures taken now can at most prevent the accelerated deterioration of the situation; there are decades of accumulated damage to be dealt with, and the slow leaching of nitrates currently in the soil will continue to affect the water system for years to come.

8.4.18 There is now provision for the Secretary of State[2] to designate areas as Nitrate Sensitive Areas in order to prevent the entry of nitrate into waters as a result of or in connection with the use of land for agricultural purposes.[3] Within such areas agreements may be made with landowners whereby in return for payments they accept obligations with respect to the

[1] Crop Residues (Burning) Regulations 1993, Sched. 2.
[2] Minister of Agriculture in England.
[3] Control of Pollution Act 1974, ss.31B–31D (added by Water Act 1989, Sched. 23); Water Resources Act 1991, ss.94–96 (and see the Nitrate Sensitive Areas (Designation) Order 1990, S.I. 1990 No. 1013).

management of their land, whilst the Secretary of State retains a power to make orders prohibiting or restricting particular activities, or imposing positive obligations on the landowner.

8.4.19 In the areas which have been designated so far, the operation of the scheme rests on the use of agreements rather than the imposition of prohibitions and obligations.[4] Farmers entering the scheme receive payments in return for accepting a number of conditions on how they manage their land. These cover such matters as the volume of organic or inorganic nitrogen fertiliser which can be used, the periods during which it may be applied, the maintenance of crop cover on the soil, restrictions on the use of irrigation, the maintenance of trees and woodland, the keeping of records of when, where and what fertilisers have been applied, and the storage of slurry and liquid sewage in a manner to prevent it entering the water system.[5] Enhanced payments are available where arable land is converted to grassland, or grassland with woodland, and again a number of conditions are imposed, relating to such matters as the sorts of grass mixtures which can be used, the removal of cuttings if the grass is cut, the stocking levels if the land is grazed, and the species to be planted if woodland is to be established.[6] The schemes therefore regulate in considerable detail the way in which the farmland is managed.

8.4.20 The introduction of such measures in Great Britain has been influenced by developments within the European Community, where legislation has also been made.[7] After a number of more far-reaching drafts, the final provisions require Member States to identify waters which contain more than 50 mg/l nitrates, fall foul of the limits set in Community legislation on drinking water,[8] are found to be subject to eutrophication, or may fall into any of these categories if steps are not taken. The areas draining into such waters are to be designated as vulnerable zones, and within these action programmes are to be implemented in the endeavour to reduce water pollution caused or induced by nitrates from agricultural sources and to prevent

---

[4] Nitrate Sensitive Areas (Designation) Order 1990, S.I. 1990 No. 1013 (amended by Nitrate Sensitive Areas (Designation) (Amendement) Order 1990, S.I. 1990 No. 1187).

[5] *Ibid.*, Sched. 1.

[6] *Ibid.*, Sched. 2.

[7] Directive 91/676.

[8] Established under Directive 75/440 (as amended).

further such pollution.[9] These programmes, and voluntary codes of practice to be introduced more rapidly[10] throughout the Member States, will deal with issues such as the periods during which the application of fertilisers[11] is inappropriate, the methods of application, the ground conditions in which application is inappropriate (*e.g.* saturated or frozen ground, steeply sloping ground), and the storage of livestock manure to prevent run-off. Other matters such as crop rotation, the maintenance of vegetation cover on the soil, the prevention of run-off and individual fertiliser limits for farms may also be included.

8.4.21 Further measures include the Control of Pollution (Silage, Slurry and Agricultural Fuel Oil) (Scotland) Regulations 1991[12] and their equivalent for England and Wales.[13] These contain requirements on the construction and siting of tanks for the making of silage and the storage of silage, slurry and oil in order to prevent water pollution, including the leaching of nitrates into the soil. The requirements apply to facilities built or significantly modified after March 1991, but the river purification authority (National Rivers Authority in England and Wales) can serve a notice requiring work to be carried out on older structures where there is a significant risk of pollution. There is also provision for Codes of Practice to be issued giving practical advice and promoting good practice with a view to preventing or minimising water pollution arising from agricultural activities.[14] A breach of such codes does not give rise to any civil or criminal liability but is a factor to be taken into account when the river purification authorities or National Rivers Authority consider whether to exercise their other powers.

[9] Areas are to be designated by December 1993, action programmes established within two years of designation and implemented within a further four years.

[10] By December 1993.

[11] All forms of fertiliser containing nitrogen compounds are included, including animal manure and sewage sludge.

[12] S.I. 1991 No. 346.

[13] Control of Pollution (Silage, Slurry and Agricultural Fuel Oil) Regulations 1991, S.I. 1991 No. 324.

[14] Control of Pollution Act 1974, s.51 (substituted by Water Act 1989, Sched. 23, para. 5); Water Resources Act 1991, s.97. Codes have been approved by the Water (Prevention of Pollution) (Code of Practice) (Scotland) Order 1992, S.I. 1992 No. 395, and the Water (Prevention of Pollution) (Code of Practice) Order 1991, S.I. 1991 No. 2285.

8.4.22 A final point to note in relation to agriculture is the potential significance of the law on land tenure in restricting the extent to which the occupier of agricultural land can give priority to nature conservation. Much of the countryside is held under the terms of agricultural tenancies, which impose obligations on the tenant to farm the land in an efficient manner. The rights of the landowner to trees,[15] minerals, game and other aspects of the land may also affect the ability or willingness of tenants to manage their land in particular ways. Notice to quit can be served on tenants who are failing to farm the land in accordance with the rules of good husbandry.[16] A landlord can apply to the Land Court (Scotland) or the Agricultural Land Tribunal (England and Wales) for a certificate to this effect,[17] and once this has been granted a notice to quit on that basis is not subject to further scrutiny.[18] Similarly one of the statutory conditions applied to crofts is that the crofter shall cultivate the croft.[19]

8.4.23 The rules of good husbandry require that the tenant maintains a reasonable standard of efficient production, and in Scotland specify such matters as the proper stocking of livestock units, regular muirburn on hill farms, and systematic control of vermin, bracken, whins, broom and injurious weeds.[20] However, practices adopted as the result of obligations arising from the designation of a Nitrate Sensitive Area may be disregarded.[21] The English rules are similar,[22] but it is stated that any practice adopted in pursuance of any term of the tenancy or other agreement between tenant and landlord which has as its objective the conservation of flora, fauna or geological or physiographical features, or the protection of buildings or sites of archaeological, architectural or historic interest, or the conservation and enhancement of the natural beauty and

---

[15] For example, special legislation was necessary to enable crofters to use common grazings for forestry purposes; Crofter Forestry (Scotland) Act 1991.

[16] See below.

[17] Agricultural Holdings (Scotland) Act 1991, s.26; Agricultural Holdings Act 1986, Sched. 3, Pt. I Case C, Pt. II, para. 9.

[18] *Ibid.*, s.22; *ibid.*, s.26.

[19] Crofters (Scotland) Act 1955, s.3, Sched. 2, paras. 3, 12.

[20] Agriculture (Scotland) Act 1948, Sched. 6 (applied by Agricultural Holdings (Scotland) Act 1991, s.85(2)).

[21] Agricultural Holdings (Scotland) Act 1991, s.26(2).

[22] Agriculture Act 1947, s.11 (applied by Agricultural Holdings Act 1986, s.96(3)).

amenity of the countryside, should be disregarded.[23] However, such qualifications give no protection to an agricultural tenant who at his own initiative takes measures which may benefit nature conservation but which do not result in efficient agricultural production. Moreover it has been held that the Land Court has no discretion to refuse a certificate of bad husbandry once it has concluded that the rules are being broken, regardless of mitigating circumstances.[24] The extent to which occupiers may dedicate their land to nature conservation may thus be restricted by their status as agricultural tenants.[25]

CONTROL OF POLLUTION

8.5.1 The environment is now protected by a large number of measures designed to prevent or restrict pollution. Most of these have been introduced with a view to human health and comfort, but obviously they will also serve to benefit the wild flora and fauna of the countryside. Such measures are found in European legislation, Acts of Parliament and detailed statutory regulations and operate in a number of ways, imposing emission controls, setting quality standards for air and water, and providing product standards so that only goods meeting certain anti-pollution requirements can enter the market. The volume of legislation involved is daunting.[26]

8.5.2 The position is made even more complicated by the number of recent changes. The restructuring of the water industry in England and Wales resulted in many changes to the law on water pollution, some of which have been reflected in

[23] Agricultural Holdings Act 1986, Sched. 3, Pt. II, para. 9(2) (amended by Water Consolidation (Consequential Provisions) Act 1991, Sched. 1, para. 43).
[24] *Cambusmore Estate Trustees* v. *Little,* 1991 S.L.T. (Land Ct.) 33.
[25] See M. Cardwell, "Set-aside Schemes and Alternative Land Uses: Some Problems for the Tenant Farmer" [1992] Conv. 180. See also *Williams* v. *Schellenberg,* 1988 G.W.D. 29–1254 where one *pro indiviso* owner of land argued that her interest had been damaged by the proprietor in occupation encouraging the designation of the land as an SSSI, thereby restricting its management and reducing its value.
[26] For general surveys see: S. Ball and S. Bell, *Environmental Law* (2nd ed., 1994); D. Hughes, *Environmental Law* (2nd ed., 1992); C.T. Reid (ed.), *Green's Guide to Environmental Law in Scotland* (1992); most of the domestic legislation is collected and annotated in J.F. Garner, *et al.*, *Garner's Environmental Law* (formerly *The Control of Pollution Encyclopaedia*) (1992–).

Scotland where equally fundamental changes to the whole structure of the industry are being discussed. The Environmental Protection Act 1990 transformed much of the law, *e.g.* introducing Integrated Pollution Control as opposed to controls based solely on individual environmental media, but its provisions are only gradually coming into effect, and will be further affected by proposals to create single Environmental Protection Agencies for Scotland and for England and Wales. Any attempt here even to sketch the outline of the law on pollution would not only be hopelessly inadequate, but is likely to be either out of date or premature.

8.5.3 What is worthy of note, is the extent to which the broader environment, including the health of flora and fauna, is now included in the aims of the anti-pollution measures. The Environmental Protection Act 1990 is designed to prevent pollution and harm, and such terms are defined in a way which protects other species in addition to man. For example in relation to Integrated Pollution Control,[27] "pollution of the environment" is defined as "pollution of the environment due to the release (into any environmental medium) from any process of substances which are capable of causing harm to man or any other living organisms supported by the environment," and "harm" includes "harm to the health of living organisms or other interference with the ecological systems of which they form part."[28] Similar broad definitions apply to other Parts of the Act.[29] The powers to control pollution are therefore to be exercised for the benefit of plants and animals as well as man.

8.5.4 This recognition of the importance of protecting the broader environment is present throughout much of the recent legislation. The provisions on waste in the Environmental Protection Act 1990[30] create a general offence of treating, keeping or disposing of waste in a manner likely to cause pollution of the environment (which is given a broad definition similar to that above[31]),[32] while pollution of the environment is one of the grounds on which a waste management licence can

---

[27] EPA, Pt. I.
[28] *Ibid.*, s.1(3), (4).
[29] *E.g.*, *ibid.*, ss.29, 107.
[30] *Ibid.*, Pt.II (ss.29–78); this Part of the Act was due to come fully into force on April 1, 1993, then in June 1993, but has been delayed.
[31] *Ibid.*, s.29(3), (5).
[32] *Ibid.*, s.33(1).

be refused.[33] The interests of flora and fauna are even expressly mentioned in places, *e.g.* one of the grounds on which the Secretary of State can direct the revocation or modification of a consent to discharge into waters is for "the protection of ... flora and fauna dependent on an aquatic environment".[34]

8.5.5 The protection of designated sites is also given some recognition by means of consultation requirements with the conservancy councils when an SSSI or the like is to be directly involved in waste disposal proposals, etc.[35] However, such requirements are somewhat inconsistent and tend to be limited to proposals for the sites themselves, not to all proposals which are likely to have a significant effect on them. It therefore behoves the conservancy councils and local conservation groups to make use of the increased publicity under the new legislation to keep an eye on applications and proposals which may affect valuable sites, and to check that any permitted discharges are in fact being kept within the permitted limits.

WATER RESOURCES

8.6.1 Many communities and species of plants and animals depend directly on an aquatic environment, from otters and kingfishers to the less appreciated midges whose larval stages are aquatic. Moreover the maintenance of the underlying water table at particular levels is crucial to the existence of many kinds of habitat, including water meadows, marshes and fens. The conservation of water resources is thus of great significance. Threats to a healthy aquatic environment come from drainage, pollution and the overuse of water taken from rivers, lochs and underground strata. All of these are to some extent regulated by law.

8.6.2 The law in this field is a complex mixture of common law and statute, as the rights of landowners to do as they wish on their land is balanced with the protection of the rights of

[33] *Ibid.*, s.36(3); compare the current provision in s.5 of the Control of Pollution Act 1974, where the only grounds of refusal are preventing pollution of water and damage to public health.
[34] Control of Pollution Act 1974, s.37(2) (substituted by the Water Act 1989, Sched. 23); Water Resources Act 1991, Sched. 10, para. 6(4).
[35] *E.g.*, EPA, s.36(7) in relation to applications for waste management licences.

neighbours and of downstream owners and with the public interest, both in preventing abuses of water resources and in ensuring that individual landowners cannot prevent or hinder schemes which offer a wider benefit.[36] Statutory controls exist over discharges into water[37] (including dumping at sea[38]), land drainage,[39] and the abstraction of water,[40] with further powers in relation to flood control[41] and drought.[42] A range of public authorities is involved in the administration of these controls.[43]

8.6.3 In England and Wales, one aspect of the reform and consolidation of the relevant statutory provisions has been the inclusion of express duties on the various authorities to have regard to and to further the interests of nature conservation. Thus the National Rivers Authority, so far as consistent with its other obligations, is under a duty to exercise its powers so as to further the conservation of flora, fauna and geological and physiographical features of special interest,[44] as well as having a general duty to promote the conservation of flora and fauna which are dependent on an aquatic environment.[45] There is also provision for the preparation of Codes and Practice giving practical guidance and promoting good practice on such matters.[46] Similar obligations are present in the other legislation.[47]

8.6.4 In Scotland, following a consultation exercise on this issue, it was decided that for the time being it was adequate to

[36] See generally, F. Lyall in *Stair Memorial Encyclopaedia of the Laws of Scotland* (1989), Vol. 25, "Water and Water Rights"; J. Bates, *Water and Drainage Law* (1990); W. Howarth, *Wisdom's Law of Watercourses* (5th ed., 1992).
[37] Control of Pollution Act 1974, Pt. II (much amended by Water Act 1989, Sched. 23); Water Resources Act 1991, Pt. III.
[38] Food and Environment Protection Act 1985, Pt. II.
[39] Land Drainage (Scotland) Acts 1930, 1941 and 1958; Land Drainage Acts 1976 and 1991.
[40] Water (Scotland) Act 1980, NHSA, Pt. II; Water Resources Act 1991, Pt. II, Chap. II.
[41] Flood Prevention (Scotland) Act 1961; Water Resources Act 1991, Pt. IV.
[42] NHSA, Part III; Water Resources Act 1991, Pt. II, Chap. III.
[43] See paras. 2.6.4–2.6.7, above.
[44] Water Resources Act 1991, s.16.
[45] *Ibid.*, s.2.
[46] *Ibid.*, s.18; Water and Sewerage (Conservation, Access and Recreation) (Code of Practice) Order 1989, S.I. 1989 No. 1152.
[47] *E.g.* Water Industry Act 1991, s.3; Land Drainage Act 1991, s.12; Food and Environment Protection Act 1985, s.8; see paras. 2.2.6, 2.6.5, above.

rely on the general duty on all public bodies to have regard to the desirability of conserving the natural heritage,[48] but that a voluntary code of practice should be prepared to offer guidance.[49] If the administration of water resources is changed in the near future, as seems likely, more specific obligations may well be introduced.

GENETICALLY MODIFIED ORGANISMS

8.7.1 A new threat to the conservation of flora and fauna is posed by the creation of genetically modified organisms. For thousands of years man has been involved in genetic manipulation through the selective breeding of crops and domesticated animals, but now much more rapid and much more far-reaching changes to organisms are possible. The effects of such modified organisms being released or escaping and coming into contact with wild plants and animals, as predators, competitors or through interbreeding, are largely unknown — the experience of releases of natural but geographically alien species such as coypus and mink has shown the damage which can be caused. The production and release of genetically modified organisms is thus subject to regulation.

8.7.2 The issue is governed by Part VI of the Environmental Protection Act 1990 and by two main sets of regulations,[50] implementing Community measures on the topic.[51] The Act gives a broad definition of "genetically modified organisms," allowing the term to cover all forms of genetic manipulation other than those involving merely assistance to naturally occurring reproductive processes, *e.g.* selective breeding,[52] and

---

[48] CSA, s.66 (amended by NHSA, Sched. 10, para. 4(7)).

[49] Ministerial announcement by Lord James Douglas-Hamilton, June 13, 1991; see now the Code of Practice on Conservation, Access and Recreation issued in August 1993.

[50] Genetically Modified Organisms (Contained Use) Regulations 1992 and 1993, S.I.s 1992 No. 3217, 1993 No. 15; Genetically Modified Organisms (Deliberate Release) Regulations 1992 and 1993, S.I.s 1992 No. 3280, 1993 No. 152; see R. Burnett-Hall, "Genetically Modified Organisms—Origin and Effect of the UK Regulations" (1993) 5 E.L.M. 107.

[51] Directives 90/219 and 90/220.

[52] EPA, s.106 (4), (5).

more precise and technical definitions are provided in the regulations.[53] Broad definitions are also given to phrases such as "damage to the environment" and "harm," which ensure that effects on flora and fauna are to be fully considered. Organisms are said to be "released" or to have "escaped" when they are no longer subject to physical, chemical or biological barriers for ensuring that either the organisms do not enter the environment, do not produce descendants which are not contained, or that they or their descendants are harmless.[54]

8.7.3 Under the Act, risk assessments are required from anyone intending to import, acquire, release or market genetically modified organisms, and notification to the Secretary of State may be required.[55] If there is a risk of damage to the environment despite precautions which are to be taken, the organism should not be imported, kept, etc., and at all times the best available techniques not entailing excessive costs shall be used to prevent damage to the environment.[56] The Secretary of State can prohibit any dealings with organisms[57] or require that consents be obtained before organisms are imported, kept, released, etc., the conditions of such consents including continuing obligations on the person authorised to keep informed of any risks involved and to inform the Secretary of State if the risks appear more serious than at the time the consent was given.[58] As usual, there are a number of powers granted to assist the enforcement of these controls, and the Secretary of State has the power to act immediately in the case of imminent danger to the environment in order to render any genetically modified organism harmless.[59]

8.7.4 For the contained use of such organisms advance notice, including a risk assessment, must be given to the Health and Safety Executive for both the use of premises for this purpose and for each particular operation, and in some cases consent from the Executive is required. Emergency plans for dealing with any escape are also required.[60] Any deliberate release of

[53] S.I. 1992 No. 3217, Sched. 1.
[54] EPA, s.107.
[55] *Ibid.*, s.108.
[56] *Ibid.*, s.109.
[57] *Ibid.*, s.110.
[58] *Ibid.*, s.112.
[59] *Ibid.*, s.117.
[60] S.I.s 1992 No. 3217 and 1993 No. 15.

genetically modified organisms requires consent from the Secretary of State; applications must be advertised, the conservancy councils (and many other bodies) must be consulted and information on the proposed release and its effects provided under almost 90 headings.[61] In both cases there are registers of notifications, applications and consents.

8.7.5 The legislation should ensure that genetically modified organisms are used only after a very thorough assessment of the known risks involved, and it is significant that there is an obligation to reveal any information which subsequently comes to light suggesting that there are addtional risks.[62] The precautionary principle suggests that in this area which is very much at the frontier of scientific knowledge and technology the law should ensure that there are adequate safeguards against the potential dangers arising from genetic modifications, even at the cost of hindering beneficial advances.

LIABILITY FOR WILDLIFE

8.8.1 The encouragement of wild plants and animals on a piece of land may cause problems if the result is an increase in what others regard as weeds and pests which then spread to neighbouring land. There are a number of statutory measures under which a landowner can be forced to take action to control "injurious weeds"[63] or pests[64] on his land, but there is also the question of whether the neighbour who claims that his property is being damaged is entitled to compensation? This issue is currently one of some difficulty as it is not wholly clear how far the law has moved from its once definite position that no compensation was available in such circumstances. In practice, anyone seeking compensation may also face difficulties in establishing that the defender's land is indeed the source of the problem, that the problem has been worsened by his action, and that the level of damage caused by the weeds or pests is greater than could normally be expected.

[61] S.I.s 1992 No. 3280 and 1993 No. 152.
[62] EPA, s.111(6A) (added by Genetically Modified Organisms (Deliberate Release) Regulations 1992, S.I. 1992 No. 3280, reg. 13); Genetically Modified Organisms (Contained Use) Regulations 1992, S.I. 1992 No. 3217, reg. 10(4).
[63] See paras. 6.2.7–6.2.9, above.
[64] See section 4.5, above.

8.8.2 A convenient starting point for both Scots and English law is *Giles* v. *Walker*,[65] where a farmer sought to sue his neighbour for the damage caused by thistles spreading from the latter's land after it had been cleared of trees and brought into cultivation. This claim was rejected by the court which asserted that there could be "no duty as between adjoining occupiers to cut the thistles, which are the natural growth of the soil."[66] This approach was followed in both jurisdictions in relation to rats in *Stearn* v. *Prentice Bros. Ltd.*,[67] pheasants in *Seligman* v. *Docker*,[68] and rabbits in *Marshall* v. *Moncrieffe*,[69] *Gordon* v. *Huntly Lodge Estates Co. Ltd.*[70] and *Forrest* v. *Irvine*.[71] In these cases though, the courts noted that the defender had not been taking any active or unusual steps to encourage the offending wildlife and left open the possibility of the position being different if such steps had been taken. Unless the measures taken were specifically designed for the multiplication of the damaging species, it seems unlikely that nature conservation measures would fall into that category.

8.8.3 More recent developments in England and related jurisdictions have overturned this general rule that a landowner cannot be liable for the spread of naturally occurring items from his land. In an Australian case, *Goldman* v. *Hargrave*,[72] the Privy Council imposed liability for the spread of a naturally occurring fire, while the New Zealand courts have allowed compensation for the harm caused by the spread of thistles to grazing land.[73] Finally, *Giles* v. *Walker* was formally overruled by the English courts in *Leakey* v. *National Trust for Places of Historic Interest and Scenic Beauty*,[74] where it was held that a landowner was liable for the fall of earth due to natural causes from a steep bank overlooking another's house.

8.8.4 It follows that in these jurisdictions the law may allow compensation for harm caused by the spread of naturally

[65] (1890) 24 Q.B.D. 656.
[66] *Ibid.* at p. 657, Lord Coleridge C.J.
[67] [1919] 1 K.B. 394.
[68] [1949] Ch. 53.
[69] (1912) 28 Sh.Ct.Rep. 343.
[70] (1940) 56 Sh.Ct.Rep. 112.
[71] (1953) 69 Sh.Ct.Rep. 203.
[72] [1967] 1 A.C. 645.
[73] *French* v. *Auckland City Corporation* [1974] 1 N.Z.L.R. 340.
[74] [1980] Q.B. 485.

occurring things from one piece of land to another. However, liability does not rest on the fact of harm alone. Strict liability exists under the rule in *Rylands* v. *Fletcher*[75] only in cases of non-natural use of the land (which appears to rule out liability arising as a result of all but the most eccentric nature conservation measures), so that in the absence of deliberate harm, one is left with a claim based directly on negligence or on the arguments in *Leakey*.[76] There, although the claim was held to be appropriately framed in nuisance,[77] liability rested on a failure of the landowner to take such steps as were reasonable to prevent or minimise the risk of harm which the landowner knew or ought to have known would be caused to his neighbour. Therefore, whether the claim is framed in nuisance or negligence, there must be shown some failure to take reasonable care on the part of the landowner from whose land the danger has spread.

8.8.5 In *Goldman* v. *Hargrave*[78] and *Leakey*[79] the harm was caused by a one-off occurrence against which specific preventive action might have been taken, but assessing whether reasonable steps have been taken will be much harder where the injury is in the form of more diffuse harm, such as that caused by weeds or rabbits or other pests. In *French* v. *Auckland City Corporation*,[80] where liability was imposed for damage caused by thistles growing from seed blown from neighbouring land, the court emphasised that everything depended on the surrounding circumstances, such as the extent of the spread of weeds, the damage likely to ensue, the cost and practicality of preventing the spread and the location of the properties. It was suggested in *French* and in *Goldman* that the individual circumstances of the parties may be relevant in assessing this, *i.e.* a poor defendant may not be required to do what might be expected of a rich one, and the duty may in some circumstances be satisfied simply by the defendant enabling the plaintiff to enter the land to take remedial steps as he thinks fit. It may therefore be difficult to predict whether liability will exist in any particular case, but it is clear that the courts will be looking for

---

[75] (1868) L.R. 3 H.L. 330.
[76] [1980] Q.B. 485.
[77] Megaw L.J., *ibid.*, at p. 514; *cf.* McMullin J. in *French* v. *Auckland City Corporation* [1974] 1 N.Z.L.R. 340 at p.350.
[78] [1967] 1 A.C. 645.
[79] [1980] Q.B. 485.
[80] [1974] 1 N.Z.L.R. 340.

something much more than mere annoyance arising from generally acceptable land management practices employed by a neighbour.

8.8.6 As yet, the Scottish courts have not given any indication of whether they would be prepared to follow the English movement away from the position stated in *Giles* v. *Walker*, a position expressly approved in the Scottish cases noted above.[81] In any event, it has been made abundantly clear in *R.H.M. Bakeries (Scotland) Ltd.* v. *Strathclyde Regional Council*[82] that the basis of liability in nuisance is *culpa*, so that some fault on the part of the landowner would have to be established. As discussed in the previous paragraph, this raises issues as to the extent to which the management of land in a way which causes unintentional but foreseeable harm to others can be classed as culpable when the harm arises not from any specific danger but from an allegedly greater incidence of a sort of naturally occurring harm which everyone must accept as part of the everyday risks of owning land.

8.8.7 Although it cannot be wholly ruled out, it therefore seems unlikely that a landowner taking measures on his own land to further nature conservation will be liable to a neighbour who claims to have suffered damage as a result of wild plants or animals being encouraged.

---

[81] See W.M. Gordon, "Is Moving Land a Nuisance?" (1980) 25 J.L.S.S. 323.
[82] 1985 S.L.T. 214.

Appendix A
Schedules to the Wildlife and Countryside Act 1981

Each Schedule is accompanied by a note in the following terms:

> "The common name or names given in the first column of this Schedule are included by way of guidance only; in the event of any dispute or proceedings, the common name or names shall not be taken into account."

SCHEDULE 1
BIRDS WHICH ARE PROTECTED BY SPECIAL PENALTIES

Part I   At All Times

Common name	Scientific name
Avocet	Recurvirostra avosetta
Bee-eater	Merops apiatser
Bittern	Botaurus stellaris
Bittern, Little	Ixobrychus minutus
Bluethroat	Luscinia svecica
Brambling	Fringilla montifringilla
Bunting, Cirl	Emberiza cirlus
Bunting, Lapland	Calcarius lapponicus
Bunting, Snow	Plectrophenax nivalis
Buzzard, Honey	Pernis apivorus
Chough	Pyrrhocorax pyrrhocorax
Corncrake	Crex crex
Crake, Spotted	Porzana porzana
Crossbills (all species)	Loxia
Curlew, Stone	Burhinus oedicnemus
Divers (all species)	Gavia
Dotterel	Charadrius morinellus

Common name	*Scientific name*
Duck, Long-tailed	Clangula hyemalis
Eagle, Golden	Aquila chrysaetos
Eagle, White-tailed	Haliaetus albicilla
Falcon, Gyr	Falco rusticolus
Fieldfare	Turdus pilaris
Firecrest	Regulus ignicapillus
Garganey	Anas querquedula
Godwit, Black-tailed	Limosa limosa
Goshawk	Accipiter gentilis
Grebe, Black-necked	Podiceps nigricollis
Grebe, Slavonian	Podiceps auritus
Greenshank	Tringa nebularia
Gull, Little	Larus minutus
Gull, Mediterranean	Larus melanocephalus
Harriers (all species)	Circus
Heron, Purple	Ardea purpurea
Hobby	Falco subbuteo
Hoopoe	Upupa epops
Kingfisher	Alcedo atthis
Kite, Red	Milvus milvus
Merlin	Falco columbarius
Oriole, Golden	Oriolus oriolus
Osprey	Pandion haliaetus
Owl, Barn	Tyto alba
Owl, Snowy	Nyctea scandiaca
Peregrine	Falco peregrinus
Petrel, Leach's	Oceanodroma leucorrhoa
Phalarope, Red-necked	Phalaropus lobatus
Plover, Kentish	Charadrius alexandrinus
Plover, Little Ringed	Charadrius dubius
Quail, Common	Coturnix coturnix
Redstart, Black	Phoenicurus ochruros
Redwing	Turdus iliacus
Rosefinch, Scarlet	Carpodacus erythrinus
Ruff	Philomachus pugnax
Sandpiper, Green	Tringa ochropus
Sandpiper, Purple	Calidris maritima
Sandpiper, Wood	Tringa glareola
Scaup	Aythya marila
Scoter, Common	Melanitta nigra
Scoter, Velvet	Melanitta fusca
Serin	Serinus serinus

Common name	Scientific name
Shorelark	Eremophila alpestris
Shrike, Red-backed	Lanius collurio
Spoonbill	Platalea leucorodia
Stilt, Black-winged	Himantopus himantopus
Stint, Temmink's	Calidris temminckii
Swan, Bewick's	Cygnus bewickii
Swan, Whooper	Cygnus cygnus
Tern, Black	Chlidonias niger
Tern, Little	Sterna albifrons
Tern, Roseate	Sterna dougallii
Tit, Bearded	Panurus biarmicus
Tit, Crested	Parus cristatus
Treecreeper, Short-toed	Certhia brachydactyla
Warbler, Cetti's	Cettia cetti
Warbler, Dartford	Sylvia undata
Warbler, Marsh	Acrocephalus palustris
Warbler, Savi's	Locustella luscinioides
Whimbrel	Numenius phaeopus
Woodlark	Lullula arborea
Wryneck	Jynx torquilla

Part II   During the Close Season

Common name	Scientific name
Goldeneye	Bucephala clangula
Goose, Greylag (in Outer Hebrides, Caithness, Sutherland and Wester Ross only)	Anser anser
Pintail	Anas acuta

SCHEDULE 2
BIRDS WHICH MAY BE KILLED OR TAKEN

Part I   Outside the Close Season

Common name	Scientific name
Capercaillie	Tetrao urogallus
Coot	Fulica atra
Duck, Tufted	Aythya fuligula

Appendix A

Common name	Scientific name
Gadwall	Anas strepera
Goldeneye	Bucephala clangula
Goose, Canada	Branta canadensis
Goose, Greylag	Anser anser
Goose, Pink-footed	Anser brachyrhynchus
Goose, White-fronted (in England and Wales only)	Anser albifrons
Mallard	Anas platyrhynchos
Moorhen	Gallinula chloropus
Pintail	Anas acuta
Plover, Golden	Pluvialis apricaria
Pochard	Aythya ferina
Shoveler	Anas clypeata
Snipe, Common	Gallinago gallinago
Teal	Anas crecca
Wigeon	Anas penelope
Woodcock	Scolopax rusticola

Part II By Authorised Persons at all Times

[All the birds previously listed in this Part of the Schedule were removed by the Wildlife and Countryside Act 1981 (Variation of Schedules 2 and 3) Order 1992, S.I. 1992 No. 3010.]

SCHEDULE 3
BIRDS WHICH MAY BE SOLD

Part I Alive at all Times if Ringed and Bred in Captivity

Common name	Scientific name
Blackbird	Turdus merula
Brambling	Fringilla montifringilla
Bullfinch	Pyrrhula pyrrhula
Bunting, Reed	Emberiza schoeniclus
Chaffinch	Fringilla coelebs
Dunnock	Prunella modularis
Goldfinch	Carduelis carduelis
Greenfinch	Carduelis chloris
Jackdaw	Corvus monedula
Jay	Garrulus glandarius
Linnet	Carduelis cannabina
Magpie	Pica pica

Common name	Scientific name
Owl, Barn	Tyto alba
Redpoll	Carduelis flammea
Siskin	Carduelis spinus
Starling	Sturnus vulgaris
Thrush, Song	Turdus philomelos
Twite	Carduelis flavirostris
Yellowhammer	Emberiza citrinella

Part II   Dead at all Times

Common name	Scientific name
Woodpigeon	Columba palumbus

[As amended by the Wildlife and Countryside Act 1981 (Variation of Schedules 2 and 3) Order 1992, S.I. 1992 No. 3010.]

Part III   Dead from 1 September–28 February

Common name	Scientific name
Capercaillie	Tetrao urogallus
Coot	Fulica atra
Duck, Tufted	Aythya fuligula
Mallard	Anas platyrhynchos
Pintail	Anas acuta
Plover, Golden	Pluvialis apricaria
Pochard	Aythya ferina
Shoveler	Anas clypeata
Snipe, Common	Gallinago gallinago
Teal	Anas crecca
Wigeon	Anas penelope
Woodcock	Scolopax rusticola

SCHEDULE 4
BIRDS WHICH MUST BE REGISTERED AND RINGED IF KEPT IN CAPTIVITY

Common name	Scientific name
Avocet	Recurvirostra avosetta
Bee-eater	Merops apiaster

Common name	*Scientific name*
Bittern	Botaurus stellaris
Bittern, Little	Ixobrychus minutus
Bluethroat	Luscina svecica
Bunting, Cirl	Emberiza cirlus
Bunting, Lapland	Calcarius lapponicus
Bunting, Snow	Plectrophenax nivalis
Chough	Pyrrhocorax pyrrhocorax
Corncrake	Crex crex
Crake, Spotted	Porzana porzana
Crossbills (all species)	Loxia
Curlew, Stone	Burhinus oedicnemus
Divers (all species)	Gavia
Dotterel	Charadrius morinellus
Duck, Long-tailed	Clangula hyemalis
Falcons (all species)	Falconidae
Fieldfare	Turdus pilaris
Firecrest	Regulus ignicapillus
Godwit, Black-tailed	Limosa limosa
Grebe, Black-necked	Podiceps nigricollis
Grebe, Slavonian	Podiceps auritus
Greenshank	Tringa nebularia
Hawks, True (except Old World vultures) that is to say, Buzzards, Eagles, Harriers, Hawks and Kites (all species in each case)	Accipitridae (except the genera Aegypius, Gypaetus, Gypohierax, Gyps, Neophron, Sargogyps and Trigonoceps)
Hoopoe	Upupa epops
Kingfisher	Alcedo atthis
Oriole, Golden	Oriolus oriolus
Osprey	Pandion haliaetus
Petrel, Leach's	Oceanodroma leucorrhoa
Phalarope, Red-necked	Phalaropus lobatus
Plover, Kentish	Charadrius alexandrinus
Plover, Little ringed	Charadrius dubius
Quail, Common	Coturnix coturnix
Redstart, Black	Phoenicurus ochruros
Redwing	Turdus iliacus
Rosefinch, Scarlet	Carpodacus erythrinus
Ruff	Philomachus pugnax
Sandpiper, Green	Tringa ochropus
Sandpiper, Purple	Calidris maritima

Common name	Scientific name
Sandpiper, Wood	Tringa glareola
Scoter, Common	Melanitta nigra
Scoter, Velvet	Melanitta fusca
Serin	Serinus serinus
Shorelark	Eremophila alpestris
Shrike, Red-backed	Lanius collurio
Spoonbill	Platalea leucorodia
Stilt, Black-winged	Himantopus himantopus
Stint, Temminck's	Calidris temminckii
Tern, Black	Chlidonias niger
Tern, Little	Sterna albifrons
Tern, Roseate	Sterna dougallii
Tit, Bearded	Panurus biarmicus
Tit, Crested	Parus cristatus
Treecreeper, Short-toed	Certhia brachydactyla
Warbler, Cetti's	Cettia cetti
Warbler, Dartford	Sylvia undata
Warbler, Marsh	Acrocephalus palustris
Warbler, Savi's	Locustella luscinioides
Whimbrel	Numenius phaeopus
Woodlark	Lullula arborea
Wryneck	Jynx torquilla

SCHEDULE 5
ANIMALS WHICH ARE PROTECTED

Common name	Scientific name
Adder (in respect of s.9(1) (in part), (5) only)	Vipera berus
Allis shad (in respect of s.9(1) only)	Alosa alosa
Atlantic Stream Crayfish (in respect of s.9(1) (in part), (5) only)	Austropotamobius pallipes
Anemone, Ivell's Sea	Edwardsia ivelli
Anemone, Startlet Sea	Nematosella vectensis
Apus	Triops cancriformis
Bats, Horseshoe (all species)	Rhinolophidae

Common name	*Scientific name*
Bats, Typical (all species)	Vespertilionidae
Beetle	Graphoderus zonatus
Beetle	Hypebaeus flavipes
Beetle	Paracymus aeneus
Beetle, Lesser Silver Water	Hydrochara caraboides
Beetle, Mire Pill (in respect of s.9(4)(a) only)	Curimopsis nigrita
Beetle, Rainbow Leaf	Chrysolina cerealis
Beetle, Violet Click	Limoniscus violaceus
Butterfly, Heath Fritillary	Mellicta athalia (otherwise known as Melitaea athalia)
Butterfly, Large Blue	Maculinea arion
Butterfly, Swallowtail	Papilio machaon
Butterfly, Northern Brown Argus	Aricia artaxerxes
Butterfly, Adonis Blue	Lysandra bellargus
Butterfly, Chalkhill Blue	Lysandra coridon
Butterfly, Silver-studded Blue	Plebejus argus
Butterfly, Small Blue	Cupido minimus
Butterfly, Large Copper	Lycaena dispar
Butterfly, Purple Emperor	Apatura iris
Butterfly, Duke of Burgundy Fritillary	Hamearis lucina
Butterfly, Glanville Fritillary	Melitaea cinxia
Butterfly, High Brown Fritillary	Argynnis adippe
Butterfly, Marsh Fritillary	Eurodryas aurinia
Butterfly, Pearl-bordered Fritillary	Boloria euphrosyne
Butterfly, Black Hairstreak	Strymonidia pruni
Butterfly, Brown Hairstreak	Thecla betulae
Butterfly, White Letter Hairstreak	Strymonidia w-album
Butterfly, Large Heath	Coenonympha tullia
Butterfly, Mountain Ringlet	Erebia epiphron
Butterfly, Chequered Skipper	Carterocephalus palaemon
Butterfly, Lulworth Skipper	Thymelicus acteon
Butterfly, Silver Spotted Skipper	Hesperia comma
Butterfly, Large Tortoiseshell	Nymphalis polychloros
Butterfly, Wood White	Leptidea sinapis
Cat, Wild	Felis silvestris

Common name	Scientific name
Cicada, New Forest	Cicadetta montana
Cricket, Field	Gryllus campestris
Cricket, Mole	Gryllotalpa gryllotalpa
Dolphin, Bottle-nosed	Tursiops truncatus (otherwise known as Tursiops tursio)
Dolphin, Common	Delphinus delphis
Dolphins (all species)	Cetacea
Dormouse	Muscardinus avellanarius
Dragonfly, Norfolk Aeshna	Aeshna isosceles
Freshwater pearl mussel (in respect of s.9(1) (in part))	Margaritifera margaritifera
Frog, Common (in respect of s.9(5) only)	Rana temporaria
Grasshopper, Wart-biter	Decticus verrucivorus
Hatchet Shell, Northern	Thyasira gouldi
Lagoon Snail	Paludinella littorina
Lagoon Snail, De Folin's	Caecum armoricum
Lagoon Worm, Tentacled	Alkmaria romijni
Leech, Medicinal	Hirudo medicinalis
Lizard, Sand	Lacerta agilis
Lizard, Viviparous (in respect of s.9(1) (in part), (5) only)	Lacerta vivipara
Marten, Pine	Martes martes
Mat, Trembling Sea	Victorella pavida
Moth, Barberry Carpet	Pareulype berberata
Moth, Black-veined	Siona lineata (otherwise known as Idaea lineata)
Moth, Essex Emerald	Thetidia smaragdaria
Moth, New Forest Burnet	Zygaena viciae
Moth, Reddish Buff	Acosmetia caliginosa
Moth, Sussex Emerald	Thalera fimbrialis
Moth, Viper's Bugloss	Hadena irregularis
Newt, Great Crested (otherwise known as Warty Newt	Triturus cristatus
Newt, Palmate (in respect of s.9(5) only)	Triturus helveticus
Newt, Smooth (in respect of s.9(5) only)	Trituris vulgaris
Otter, Common	Lutra lutra
Porpoises (all species)	Cetacea
Sandworm, Lagoon	Armandia cirrhosa

Common name	Scientific name
Sea Fan, Pink (in respect of s.9(1), (2) and (5) only)	Eunicella verrucosa
Sea Slug, Lagoon	Tenellia adspersa
Shrimp, Fairy	Chirocephalus diaphanus
Shrimp, Lagoon Sand	Gammarus insensibilis
Slow-worm (in respect of s.9(1) (in part), (5) only)	Anguis fragilis
Snail, Glutinous	Myxas glutinosa
Snail, Sandbowl	Catinella arenaria
Snake, Grass (in respect of s.9(1) (in part), (5) only)	Natrix helvetica
Snake, Smooth	Coronella austriaca
Spider, Fen Raft	Dolomedes plantarius
Spider, Ladybird	Eresus niger
Squirrel, Red	Sciurus vulgaris
Sturgeon	Acipenser sturio
Toad, Common (in respect of s.9(5) only)	Bufo bufo
Toad, Natterjack	Bufo calamita
Turtles, Marine (all species)	Dermochelyidae and Cheloniidae
Vendace	Coregonus albula
Walrus	Odobenus rosmarus
Whale (all species)	Cetacea
Whitefish	Coregonus lavaretus

[As amended by the Wildlife and Countryside Act 1981 (Variation of Schedules) Orders 1988, 1989 and 1991 and the Wildlife and Countryside Act 1981 (Variation of Schedules 5 and 8) Order 1992, S.I.s 1988 No. 288, 1989 No. 906, 1991 No. 367, 1992 No. 2350].

SCHEDULE 6
ANIMALS WHICH MAY NOT BE KILLED OR TAKEN BY CERTAIN METHODS

Common name	Scientific name
Badger	Meles meles
Bats, Horseshoe (all species)	Rhinolophidae

Common name	Scientific name
Bats, Typical (all species)	Vespertilionidae
Cat, Wild	Felis silvestris
Dolphin, Bottle-nosed	Tursiops truncatus (otherwise known as Tursiops tursio)
Dolphin, Common	Delphinus delphis
Dormice (all species)	Gliridae
Hedgehog	Erinaceus europaeus
Marten, Pine	Martes martes
Otter, Common	Lutra lutra
Polecat	Mustela putorius
Porpoise, Harbour (otherwise known as Common porpoise)	Phocaena phocaena
Shrews (all species)	Soricidae
Squirrel, Red	Sciurus vulgaris

SCHEDULE 8
PLANTS WHICH ARE PROTECTED

Common name	Scientific name
Adder's-tongue, Least	Ophioglossum lusitanicum
Alison, Small	Alyssum alyssoides
Blackwort	Southbya nigrella
Broomrape, Bedstraw	Orobanche caryophyllacea
Broomrape, Oxtongue	Orobanche loricata
Broomrape, Thistle	Orobanche reticulata
Cabbage, Lundy	Rhynchosinapis wrightii
Calamint, Wood	Calamintha sylvatica
Caloplaca, Snow	Caloplaca nivalis
Catapyrenium, Tree	Catapyrenium psoromoides
Catchfly, Alpine	Lychnis alpina
Catillaria, Laurer's	Catellaria laureri
Centaury, Slender	Centaurium tenuiflorum
Cinquefoil, Rock	Potentilla rupestris
Cladonia, Upright Mountain	Cladonia stricta
Clary, Meadow	Salvia pratensis
Club-rush, Triangular	Scirpus triquetrus
Colt's-foot, Purple	Homogyne alpina
Cotoneaster, Wild	Cotoneaster integerrimus

Common name	*Scientific name*
Cottongrass, Slender	Eriophorum gracile
Cow-wheat, Field	Melampyrum arvense
Crocus, Sand	Romulea columnae
Crystalwort, Lizard	Riccia bifurca
Cudweed, Broad-leaved	Filago pyramidata
Cudweed, Jersey	Gnaphalium luteoalbum
Cudweed, Red-tipped	Filago lutescens
Diapensia	Diapensia lapponica
Dock, Shore	Rumex rupestris
Earwort, Marsh	Jamesoniella undulifolia
Eryngo, Field	Eryngium campestre
Fern, Dickie's Bladder	Cystopteris dickieana
Fern, Killarney	Trichomanes speciosum
Flapwort, Norfolk	Leiocolea rutheana
Fleabane, Alpine	Erigeron borealis
Fleabane, Small	Pulicaria vulgaris
Frostwort, Pointed	Gymnomitrion apiculatum
Galingale, Brown	Cyperus fuscus
Gentian, Alpine	Gentiana nivalis
Gentian, Dune	Gentianella uliginosa
Gentian, Early	Gentianella anglica
Gentian, Fringed	Gentianella ciliata
Gentian, Spring	Gentiana verna
Germander, Cut-leaved	Teucrium botrys
Germander, Water	Teucrium scordium
Gladiolus, Wild	Gladiolus illyricus
Goosefoot, Stinking	Chenopodium vulvaria
Grass-poly	Lythrum hyssopifolia
Grimmia, Blunt-leaved	Grimmia unicolor
Gyalecta, Elm	Gyalecta ulmi
Hare's-ear, Sickle-leaved	Bupleurum falcatum
Hare's-ear, Small	Bupleurum baldense
Hawk's-beard, Stinking	Crepis foetida
Hawkweed, Northroe	Hieracium northroense
Hawkweed, Shetland	Hieracium zetlandicum
Hawkweed, Weak-leaved	Hieracium attenuatifolium
Heath, Blue	Phyllodoce caerulea
Helleborine, Red	Cephalanthera rubra
Helleborine, Young's	Epipactis youngiana
Horsetail, Branched	Equisetum ramosissimum
Hound's-tongue, Green	Cynoglossum germanicum
Knawel, Perennial	Scleranthus perennis

Common name	*Scientific name*
Knotgrass, Sea	Polygonum maritimum
Lady's-slipper	Cypripedium calceolus
Lecanactis, Churchyard	Lecanactis hemisphaerica
Lecanora, Tarn	Lecanora archariana
Lecidea, Copper	Lecidea inops
Leek, Round-headed	Allium sphaerocephalon
Lettuce, Least	Lactuca saligna
Lichen, Arctic Kidney	Nephroma arcticum
Lichen, Ciliate Strap	Heterodermia leucomelos
Lichen, Coralloid Rosette	Heterodermia propagulifera
Lichen, Ear-lobed Dog	Peltigera lepidophora
Lichen, Forked Hair	Bryoria furcellata
Lichen, Golden Hair	Teloschistes flavicans
Lichen, Orange Fruited Elm	Caloplaca luteoalba
Lichen, River Jelly	Collema dichotomum
Lichen, Scaly Breck	Squamarina lentigera
Lichen, Stary Breck	Buellia asterella
Lily, Snowdon	Lloydia serotina
Liverwort	Petallophyllum ralfsi
Liverwort, Lindenberg's Leafy	Adelanthus lindenbergianus
Marsh-mallow, Rough	Althaea hirsuta
Marshwort, Creeping	Apium repens
Milk-parsley, Cambridge	Selinum carvifolia
Moss	Drepanocladius vernicosus
Moss, Alpine Copper	Mielichoferia mielichoferi
Moss, Baltic Bog	Sphagnum balticum
Moss, Blue Dew	Saelania glaucescens
Moss, Blunt-leaved Bristle	Orthotrichum obtusifolium
Moss, Bright Green Cave	Cyclodictyon laetevirens
Moss, Cordate Beard	Barbula cordata
Moss, Cornish Path	Ditrichum cornubicum
Moss, Derbyshire Feather	Thamnobryum angustifolium
Moss, Dune Thread	Bryum mamillatum
Moss, Glaucous Beard	Barbula glauca
Moss, Green Shield	Buxbaumia viridis
Moss, Hair Silk	Plagiothecium piliferum
Moss, Knothole	Zygodon forsteri
Moss, Large Yellow Feather	Scorpidium turgescens
Moss, Millimetre	Micromitrium tenerum
Moss, Multifruited River	Cryphaea lamyana
Moss, Nowell's Limestone	Zygodon gracilis
Moss, Rigid Apple	Bartramia stricta

Common name	*Scientific name*
Moss, Round-leaved Feather	Rhyncostegium rotundifolium
Moss, Schleicher's Thread	Bryum schleicheri
Moss, Triangular Pygmy	Acaulon triquetrum
Moss, Vaucher's Feather	Hypnum vaucheri
Mudwort, Welsh	Limosella australis
Naiad, Holly-leaved	Najas marina
Naiad, Slender	Najas flexilis
Orache, Stalked	Halimione pedunculata
Orchid, Early Spider	Ophrys sphegodes
Orchid, Fen	Liparis loeselii
Orchid, Ghost	Epipogium aphyllum
Orchid, Lapland Marsh	Dactylorhiza lapponica
Orchid, Late Spider	Ophrys fuciflora
Orchid, Lizard	Himantoglossum hircinum
Orchid, Military	Orchis militaris
Orchid, Monkey	Orchis simia
Pannaria, Caledonia	Pannaria ignobilis
Parmelia, New Forest	Parmelia minarum
Parmentaria, Oil Stain	Parmentaria chilensis
Pear, Plymouth	Pyrus cordata
Pennyroyal	Mentha pulegium
Penny-cress, Perfoliate	Thlaspi perfoliatum
Pertusaria, Alpine Moss	Pertusaria bryontha
Physcia, Southern Grey	Physcia tribacioides
Pigmyweed	Crassula aquatica
Pine, Ground	Ajuga chamaepitys
Pink, Cheddar	Dianthus gratianopolitanus
Pink, Childling	Petroraghia nanteuilii
Plantain, Floating Water	Luronium natans
Pseudocyphellaria, Ragged	Pseudocyphellaria lacerata
Psora, Rusty Alpine	Psora rubiformis
Ragwort, Fen	Senecio paludosus
Rampion, Spiked	Phyteuma spicatum
Ramping-fumitory, Martin's	Fumaria martinii
Restharrow, Small	Ononis reclinata
Rock-cress, Alpine	Arabis alpina
Rock-cress, Bristol	Arabis stricta
Rustworth, Western	Marsupella profunda
Sandwort, Norwegian	Arenaria norvegica
Sandwort, Teesdale	Minuartia stricta
Saxifrage, Drooping	Saxifraga cernua
Saxifrage, Marsh	Saxifraga hirculus

Common name	Scientific name
Saxifrage, Tufted	Saxifraga cespitosa
Solenopsora, Serpentine	Solenopsora lipinara
Solomon's-seal, Whorled	Polygonatum verticillatum
Sow-thistle, Alpine	Cicerbita alpina
Spearwort, Adder's-tongue	Ranunculus ophioglossifolius
Speedwell, Fingered	Veronica triphyllos
Speedwell, Spiked	Veronica spicata
Star-of-Bethlehem, Early	Gagea bohemica
Starfruit	Damasonium alisma
Stonewort, Bearded	Chara canescens
Stonewort, Foxtail	Lamprothamnium papulosum
Strapwort	Corrigiola litoralis
Turpswort	Geocalyx graveolens
Viper's-grass	Scorzonera humilis
Violet, Fen	Viola persicifolia
Water-plantain, Ribbon leaved	Alisma gramineum
Wood-sedge, Starved	Carex depauperata
Woodsia, Alpine	Woodsia alpina
Woodsia, Oblong	Woodsia ilvensis
Wormwood, Field	Artemisia campestris
Woundwort, Downy	Stachys germanica
Woundwort, Limestone	Stachys alpina
Yellow-rattle, Greater	Rhinanthus serotinus

[As amended by the Wildlife and Countryside Act 1981 (Variation of Schedules) Order 1988 and the Wildlife and Countryside Act 1981 (Variation of Schedules 5 and 8) Order 1992, S.I.s 1988 No. 288, 1992 No. 2350.]

SCHEDULE 9
ANIMALS AND PLANTS TO WHICH SECTION 14 APPLIES

[Alien species not to be released]

Part I Animals which are Established in the Wild

Common name	Scientific name
Bass, Large-mouthed Black	Micropterus salmoides
Bass, Rock	Ambloplites rupestris

Appendix A

Common name	*Scientific name*
Bitterling	Rhodeus sericeus
Budgerigar	Melopsittacus undulatus
Capercaillie	Tetrao urogallus
Coypu	Myocastor coypus
Crayfish, Noble	Astacus astacus
Crayfish, Signal	Pacifastacus leniusculus
Crayfish, Turkish	Astacus leptodactylus
Deer, Sika	Cervus nippon
Dormouse, Fat	Glis glis
Duck, Carolina Wood	Aix sponsa
Duck, Mandarin	Aix galericulata
Duck, Ruddy	Oxyura jamaicensis
Eagle, White-tailed	Haliaetus albicilla
Flatworm, New Zealand	Artiposthia triangulata
Frog, Edible	Rana esculenta
Frog, European Tree (otherwise known as Common tree frog)	Hyla arborea
Frog, Marsh	Rana ridibunda
Gerbil, Mongolian	Meriones unguiculatus
Goose, Canada	Branta canadensis
Goose, Egyptian	Alopochen aegyptiacus
Heron, Night	Nycticorax nycticorax
Lizard, Common Wall	Podarcis muralis
Marmot, Prairie (Otherwise known as Prairie Dog)	Cynomys
Mink, American	Mustela vison
Newt, Alpine	Triturus alpestris
Newt, Italian Crested	Triturus carnifex
Owl, Barn	Tyto alba
Parakeet, Ring-necked	Psittacula krameri
Partridge, Chukar	Alectoris chukar
Partridge, Rock	Alectoris graeca
Pheasant, Golden	Chrysolophus pictus
Pheasant, Lady Amherst's	Chrysolophus amherstiae
Pheasant, Reeves'	Syrmaticus reevesii
Pheasant, Silver	Lophura nycthemera
Porcupine, Crested	Hystrix cristata
Porcupine, Himalayan	Hystrix hodgsonii
Pumpkinseed (otherwise known as Sun-fish or Pond-perch)	Lepomis gibbosus

Common name	Scientific name
Quail, Bobwhite	Colinus virginianus
Rat, Black	Rattus rattus
Snake, Aesculapian	Elaphe longissima
Squirrel, Grey	Sciurus carolinensis
Terrapin, European Pond	Emys orbicularis
Toad, African Clawed	Xenopus laevis
Toad, Midwife	Alytes obstetricans
Toad, Yellow-bellied	Bombina variegata
Wallaby, Red-necked	Macropus rufogriseus
Wels (otherwise known as European catfish)	Silurus glanis
Zander	Stizostedion lucioperca

Part II Plants

Common name	Scientific name
Hogweed, Giant	Heracleum mantegazzianum
Kelp, Giant	Macrocystis pyrifera
Kelp, Giant	Macrocystis angustifolia
Kelp, Giant	Macrocystis integrifolia
Kelp, Giant	Macrocystis laevis
Kelp, Japanese	Laminaria japonica
Knotweed, Japanese	Polygonum cuspidatum
Seafingers, Green	Codium fragile tomentosoides
Seaweed, Californian Red	Pikea californica
Seaweed, Hooked Asparagus	Asparagopsis armata
Seaweed, Japanese	Sargassum muticum
Seaweeds, Laver (except native species)	Porphyra spp. except—
	P. amethystea
	P. leucosticta
	P. linearis
	P. miniata
	P. purpurea
	P. umbilicalis
Wakame	Undaria pinnatifida

[As amended by the Wildlife and Countryside (Variation of Schedule) Order 1992 and the Wildlife and Countryside Act 1981 (Variation of Schedule) (No. 2) Order 1992, S.I.s 1992 Nos. 320, 2674.]

Appendix B
Open Seasons

Birds

	Scotland	England & Wales	Authority
Red grouse	Aug. 12–Dec. 10	Aug. 12–Dec. 10	1772/1831[1]
Ptarmigan	Aug. 12–Dec. 10	—	1772/1831
Black grouse	Aug. 20–Dec. 10	Aug. 20–Dec. 10	1772/1831
Capercailzie	Oct. 1–Jan. 31	—	WCA[2]
Pheasant	Oct. 1–Feb. 1	Oct. 1–Feb. 1	1772/1831
Partridge	Sep. 1–Feb. 1	Sep. 1–Feb. 1	1772/1831
Common snipe	Aug. 12–Jan. 31	Aug. 12–Jan. 31	WCA
Woodcock	Sep. 1–Jan. 31	Oct. 1–Jan. 31	WCA
Wild duck and geese (below high-water mark)	Sep. 1–Feb. 20	Sep. 1–Feb. 20	WCA
All other cases	Sep. 1–Jan. 31	Sep. 1–Jan. 31	WCA

Notes
1. Game (Scotland) Act 1772, s.1; Game Act 1831, s.3.
2. Wildlife and Countryside Act 1981, s.2(4).

Deer

		Scotland[1]	England & Wales[2]
Red Deer[3]	stags	July 1–Oct. 20	Aug. 1–April 30
	hinds	Oct. 21–Feb. 15	Nov. 1–Feb. 28/29
Sika Deer[3]	stags	July 1–Oct. 20	Aug. 1–April 30
	hinds	Oct. 21–Feb. 15	Nov. 1–Feb. 28/29
Fallow Deer	bucks	Aug. 1–April 30	Aug. 1–April 30
	does	Oct. 21–Feb. 15	Nov. 1–Feb. 28/29

		Scotland[1]	England & Wales[2]
Roe Deer	bucks	April 1–Oct. 20	April 1–Oct. 31
	does	Oct. 21–March 31	Nov. 1–Feb. 28/29

Notes

1. Deer (Scotland) Act 1959, s.21; Deer (Close Seasons) (Scotland) Order 1984, S.I. 1984 No. 76.
2. Deer Act 1991, Sched. 1.
3. In Scotland, expressly including hybrids.

Permitted Firearms

Scotland[1]

All deer	Rifle	Bullet of expanding type not less than 100 grains; muzzle velocity not less than 2450 feet per second; muzzle energy not less than 1750 foot pounds.
	Shotgun[2]	Not less than 12 bore; rifled slug not less than 380 grains or cartridge of not less than 450 grains of shot not smaller than 0.268 inches in diameter (size SSG).
Roe Deer	Rifle	Bullet of expanding type of not less than 50 grains; muzzle velocity not less than 2450 feet per second; muzzle energy not less than 1000 foot pounds.
	Shotgun[2]	Not less than 12 bore; cartridge of not less than 450 grains of shot not smaller than 0.203 inches in diameter (size AAA).

England and Wales[3]

| All deer | Rifle | Calibre not less than 0.240 inches or muzzle energy of 1700 foot pounds; bullet soft or hollow-nosed. |

All deer	Shotgun[2]	Not less than 12 bore; slug not less than 350 grains or cartridge of shot not smaller than 0.203 inches in diameter (size AAA).

Notes

1. Deer (Firearms) (Scotland) Order 1985, S.I. 1985 No. 1168.
2. The use of shotguns is permitted only in preventing serious damage on cultivated or enclosed land.
3. Deer Act 1991, s.7(2), Sched. 2.

Appendix C
Licences

Under s.16 of the Wildlife and Countryside Act 1981, licences authorising conduct otherwise unlawful under the provision of Part I of the Act may be granted for the following purposes by the authorities shown.

In Relation to Birds

Purpose(s)	*Authority*
Scientific or educational	Secretary of State or Conservancy Council
Ringing, marking or examining any ring or mark on wild birds	
Conserving wild birds	
Protecting any collection of wild birds	Secretary of State
Falconry or aviculture	
Public exhibition or competition	
Taxidermy	
Human consumption[1]	
Sale or advertising for sale	
Photography	Conservancy Council
Preserving public health or public or air safety	Agriculture Minister
Preventing the spread of disease	
Preventing serious damage to livestock, foodstuffs for livestock, crops, vegetables, fruit, growing timber or fisheries	

Notes

1. Gannets on Sula Sgeir, gulls' eggs and lapwings' eggs
    (before April 15 only).

In Relation to Animals and Plants

Purpose(s)	*Authority*
Scientific or educational	Conservancy Council
Ringing, marking or examining any ring or mark on wild animals	
Conserving wild animals or wild plants or introducing them to particular areas	
Protecting any zoological or botanical collection	
Photography	
Preserving public health or public safety	Agriculture Minister
Preventing the spread of disease	
Preventing serious damage to livestock, foodstuffs for livestock, crops, vegetables, fruit, growing timber or any other form of property or to fisheries	
Sale or advertising for sale	Secretary of State
Introduction of foreign species	
(Fish or shellfish)	(Agriculture Minister)

INDEX

333